PERSPECTIVES ON AMERICA VOLUME 2:

READINGS IN UNITED STATES HISTORY SINCE 1877

Edited by
Kenneth G. Alfers
C. Larry Pool
Mountain View College
William Mugleston
Floyd College

CUSTOM PUBLISHING

60 FIFTH AVE · NEW YORK, NY · 10011

"Last Ghastly Moments at the Little Bighorn" by John Stands in Timber, Copyright © 1966 by publisher Yale University Press.

"Epitaph for the Steelmaster" by Robert L. Heilbroner, Copyright © 1960 Robert L. Heilbroner.

"The Haymarket: Strike and Violence in Chicago" by R. Jackson Wilson is from *Freedom & Crisis*.

"Populism and Modern American Politics" by Peter Frederick. Reprinted by permission.

"Hell on Saturday Afternoon" by John F. McCormack, Jr. published in *Mankind Magazine*, February 1976.

"'I was arrested, of course . . . 'An Interview with Miss Alice Paul" by Robert S. Gallagher. Copyright © 1974.

"Vietnam: The War That Won't Go Away" by George Herring. Dallas County Community College District.

"I Am Not a Crook! Corruption in Presidential Politics" by Kenneth G. Alfers. Owned by the Dallas County Community College District printed in America: *The Second Century Study Guide* 1980.

"Can We Still Afford To Be A Nation Of Immigrants?" by David Kennedy. Copyright © 1996 David M. Kennedy, as first published in *The Atlantic Monthly*. Reprinted by permission.

"Can We All Get Along?" by Dale Maharidge. Copyright © 1993. Watkins Loomis Agency.

Reprinted 1999.

CIP Data is available.
Printed in the United States of America
10 9 8 7 6 5 4 3

ISBN 0–8281–0997–4

CONTENTS

PART ONE

1877–1900

The great war between the states had been over for more than a decade. The nation was celebrating the centennial of the Declaration of Independence. It was 1876 and the United States was in a remarkable age of growth and transition. Over the next quarter of a century, the nation would change from an agrarian, rural society to an urbanized, industrialized one.

The late 19th century would see the final conquest of the trans Mississippi west with the census showing no discernable frontier line by 1890. That demographic change would come at the tragic expense of the Native Americans of the Plains and the Southwest. The westward movement would also see the rise of new political forces, like the Populists, when farmers discovered the folly of the Homestead Act as they tried to eke out an existence on a mere 160 acres on the Great Plains.

But the West was only one part of the story of change in America in the late 1800s. That was also the age of industrialization. These were to be the first real halcyon days for American capitalists as they amassed unbelievable fortunes. The great wealth of the robber barons and the captains of industry, like Carnegie and McCormick, would often come, however, at the expense of American workers and their families.

Workers and Native Americans were not the only ones who would not enjoy all of the great pleasures of the Gilded Age. African Americans, though freed from slavery and insured the full rights and privileges of citizenship, would see the creation of a world of segregation and discrimination. The world of Jim Crow would force them into a second class of citizenship. Although African Americans would protest against the loss of their rights, with the Supreme Court turning against them, their efforts would be to no avail. The great struggle and ultimate triumph for civil rights would have to wait until the last half of the 20th century.

The late 19th century would also see the United States enter an age of imperialism. A nation that celebrated a declaration against imperial power would ironically find itself becoming just such a power. By the end of the century the United States would possess colonies stretching from Puerto Rico in the Caribbean to the Philippines in Asia.

America, as it entered the 20th century, was a radically different nation than it had been only a quarter of a century before. The United States was an economic, imperial giant as it entered what could easily be called America's century. The articles in this section describe the people, events and movements of the late 19th century that helped to shape the world's most powerful nation.

LAST GHASTLY MOMENTS AT THE LITTLE BIGHORN

John Stands in Timber
Edited and with an Introduction by Margot Liberty

In 1876, as much of the nation was celebrating the centennial of the Declaration of Independence, in the West the U.S. Army was in the process of subduing the Plains Indians. In the summer of that fateful year, an ambitious officer, who as a brevet general in the Civil War had been labeled "the Murat of the American Army," sought glory, more fame and possible political reward. George Armstrong Custer was in command of the Seventh Cavalry as it went toward the Little Bighorn River in search for Indians. While some in the East talked of a possible presidential nomination for the golden maned colonel, the brash officer would be seeking another victory. Instead Custer would find defeat and death in a battle that would become one of the most famous in the long war of the U.S. government against Native Americans. But the fame of the Battle of the Little Bighorn would be built around the white man's view of the event. In this article the battle is seen through the eyes of the Native Americans. This fresh perspective strips the event of its Hollywood legend and presents it as it was.

So much has been written about the Battle of the Little Bighorn that it would seem that everything that can be said about it is already known. But interest in the slaughter of some 225 soldiers and civilians under Lieutenant Colonel George Custer by Sioux and Northern Cheyenne warriors in June of 1876 has remained high, and the search for new scraps of information about it continues unabated. At the heart of this interest is a mystery which has never been fully solved. It is this: How was it that Custer and all his men were killed?

Some students of Indian warfare have speculated that the warriors simply wore down the surrounded troopers of Custer's Seventh Calvary from a distance until casualties were so severe that they could ride in on the survivors. But, in direct contradiction to this, others point to many notable Indian fights of the Plains (Beecher Island, the Wagon Box, the Big Hole, and even another sector of the Little Bighorn battle itself—the attack on Custer's subordinates, Major Marcus Reno and Captain Frederick Benteen) to show that such tactics would have been contrary to Indian custom. In all of these cases the Indians encircled troops for long periods of time, riding around the besieged whites at a safe distance, potshotting at them, dashing at them from time to time, and finally breaking off the engagement and riding away.

Such tactics were traditional with the Plains tribes. Once the warriors were satisfied that they had acquitted themselves well and gained honors, had halted the enemy and rendered him powerless, or had secured their camps and enabled their women and children to get safely away, they saw no sense in risking further the lives of their brave men. This was especially true when the tribes began to suffer casualties; then the chiefs would usually counsel their men to end the fight quickly and withdraw.

The following document suggests a hitherto unsuspected factor in the battle: a group of warriors who formed a kind of suicide squad. Their example may provide an explanation of why Custer's detachment was slaughtered to the last man. Nothing resembling this story has appeared in any previous account of the fight. The question naturally arises, Why not? One answer is that only a comparatively few individuals in the two tribes knew enough about the event to talk about it, and white questioners never happened to talk to these individuals. Another and more likely answer is that those who did know about it considered it too revered a rite to discuss with the race that had conquered them.

It should be remembered that Indians were the only surviving witnesses to the Last Stand and that everything written about Custer's final moments stems from these Indian informants. The value of many of these accounts is questionable. Most were collected, under extreme pressure, soon after the battle. The Indians who did talk feared, on the one hand, punishment by the whites, and on the other, contempt from their own people for being informers. Under these circumstances, they often said what they thought their questioners wanted them to say, and concealed information which they thought might bring trouble upon the tribes. They also withheld information concerning tribal customs and beliefs which they felt they had no right to impart to white men, or which white men might have misunderstood. Thus it is not surprising that a number of events at the Little Bighorn went unrecorded except in the oral traditions of the tribes who fought there.

The story that follows is based entirely on the traditions of the Northern Cheyennes, who today live in Montana close to the field on which their forebears fought Custer. The battle accounts were gathered with care and devotion over many years by John Stands in Timber, a Northern Cheyenne who some fifty years ago dedicated himself to the task of being the historian of his people. He decided then that when the time was right he would tell the white man the history of his tribe as his own people knew it. Stands in Timber, a grandson of Lame White Man, who was killed at the Little Bighorn, was educated at the Haskell Institute, a school for Indians in Lawrence, Kansas, and part of his dedication to the history of his people is the result of hearing white men's versions of events that contradicted what the Indians knew. After returning to the reservation from Haskell, he began to collect tribal stories, gathering them, when possible, from eyewitnesses to and participants in important events. The fear of punishment by whites and the reluctance to reveal many aspects of Indian history persisted among his people for decades. But the old people of the tribe who might be hurt or who might resent the recording of their actions for the whites are now dead. Today, with John Stands in Timber in his eighties, his document can at last be made public.

It will be helped by a brief summation of what is already known of the battle. The command led by Colonel Custer had been an element in a three–pronged drive designed to trap a large group of Sioux and Northern Cheyennes who had refused to go onto their reservations. One prong, commanded by General George Crook, moving north into Montana from the North Platte River, had been mauled and turned back by Sioux and Northern Cheyennes at the Rosebud River on June 17, 1876. The second prong, troops from western Montana, and the third prong, a force moving west from the Missouri River, had met on the Yellowstone at the mouth of the Rosebud. In the third prong was Custer's Seventh Cavalry. Unaware of

Crook's withdrawal, the troops on the Yellowstone now planned to turn south and catch the hostile Indians between themselves and Crook's force.

One unit, under Colonel John Gibbon, was ordered to go up the Yellowstone to the Bighorn, then march south along that river to the Little Bighorn. Custer was directed to move south along the Rosebud, parallel to Gibbon; the idea was to trap the Indians between them. Custer, it is believed, was to make a leisurely march and not start across from the Rosebud to the Little Bighorn until the evening of June 25, when Gibbon would have had time to arrive opposite him for a joint attack on June 26. The units separated, and at noon on June 22, Custer started up the Rosebud with some six hundred soldiers, forty-four Arikara and Crow scouts, about twenty packers and guides, and a civilian newspaper correspondent named Mark Kellogg.

The Sioux and Northern Cheyenne warriors who had repulsed Crook on the Rosebud had meanwhile moved their camps to the Little Bighorn. Their villages, set up in five large circles of tepees and several smaller ones, stretched about three miles along the river's west bank. The northernmost circle was the village of the Northern Cheyennes, while at the south was that of Sitting Bull's Hunkpapa Sioux. Between them were Oglalas and other Sioux, together with a small number of Arapahoes. There were probably some ten thousand Indians present, of whom at least three thousand were fighting men.

Custer came up the Rosebud, but on learning from scouts that the hostiles were west of him on the Little Bighorn, turned in that direction, and on the morning of June 25 was ready to do battle alone, without waiting for Gibbon. After surveying the valley of the Little Bighorn, but failing to see the Indian camp and thus understand its exact size and population, he divided his men into four units. One was left in the rear to protect the slow—moving pack train. A second, under Captain Frederick Benteen, was sent to scout the hills to the southwest and to prevent the escape of the Indians in that direction. The third, under Major Marcus Reno, was ordered to attack the camp at its southern end, while Custer took the remaining unit of about 225 men to strike the northern end and catch the tribes between his troops and Reno's.

The forces, of course, were much bigger than Custer had suspected. Reno's men, accompanied by Arikara scouts, had a sharp battle in the valley, mainly with Sitting Bull's Hunkpapas; after heavy losses, they retreated to a high bluff across the Little Bighorn from the Indian camp, where they were soon joined by the pack train and Benteen. Heavy firing could be heard from Custer's direction and an attempt was made to reach him, but it failed. Reno and Benteen then stood off the Indians all night and the next day. The rest of the troops from the Yellowstone arrived the morning of the twenty-seventh. The Indian camp had disbanded the evening of the twenty-sixth. No further fighting had seemed necessary to the Indians, and they had all moved away, out of range of the troops.

Custer's command was discovered entirely destroyed.

With that background, one can now read John Stands in Timber's account.

—Margot Liberty

The attack of Colonel Custer on the Northern Cheyennes and Sioux did not surprise the Indians as much as many people think. They knew the soldiers were in the country looking for them, and they expected trouble, though they did not know just when it would come. My grandfather, Lame White Man, told my grandmother, Twin Woman, the morning before the fight that scouts had reported soldiers on the Rosebud, and when they went farther down [the Rosebud] they also saw the steamship that had brought them supplies, there in the Yellowstone River. White Man Bear's people were on their way to the Black Hills when they saw them. They did not turn back, but kept on their way, but they met other scouts coming this way and gave them the news. It was after that that the word spread.

The Sioux leaders in the villages sent word that they wanted all the chiefs to gather to discuss what to do if the soldiers approached. They had decided not to start anything, but to find out what the soldiers were going to do, and talk to them if they came in peacefully. "It may be something else they want us to do now, other than go back to the reservation," they said. "We will talk to them. But if they want to fight we will let them have it, so everybody be prepared."

They also decided that the camp should be guarded by the military bands, to keep individual warriors from riding out to meet the soldiers. It was a great thing for anyone to do that—to go out and meet the enemy ahead of the rest—and the chiefs did not want this to happen. So it was agreed that both the Sioux and Northern Cheyenne military bands would stand guard. Each band called its men, and toward evening they went on duty. Bunches of them rode to ten or fifteen stations on both sides of the Little Bighorn where they could keep good watch. About sundown, they could be seen all along the hills there.

There was good reason for them to watch well. The people usually obeyed the orders of the military bands. Punishment [ranging from a beating to destruction of horses, tepees, or other property] was too severe if they did not. But that night young men [who had not yet gained war honors, and in their eagerness to achieve them often put personal goals above tribal welfare] were determined to slip through. Soon after the bands had begun patrolling, my step–grandfather's friend, Bigfoot, came to him. "Wolftooth," he said, "we could get away and go on through. Maybe some others will too, and meet the enemy over on the Rosebud."

They began watching to see what the military bands were doing, and to make plans. They saw a bunch of them start across to the east side of the river and another bunch on the hill between what became the Reno and Custer battlefields. Many more were on the high hills at the mouth of Medicine Trail Creek. So they decided what to do. After sundown they took their horses way up on the west side of the river and hobbled them, pretending to be putting them there so they could get them easily in the morning. Then they returned to camp. But when it was dark, they walked back out there and got the horses, and went back down to the river. When they did, they heard horses crossing and were afraid to go ahead. But the noise died away, and they went on into the river slowly, so even the water would splash more quietly. They got safely to the other side and hid in the brush all night there so they would not be discovered.

In the meantime, there was some excitement in the camp. Some of the Sioux boys had just announced that they were taking the suicide vow, and others were putting on a dance for them at their end of the camp. This meant that they were throwing their lives away. In the next battle they would fight till they were killed. The Northern Cheyennes claimed that they had originated the suicide vow; then the Sioux learned it from them, and they called this dance they put on to announce it "Dying Dancing."

A few Northern Cheyenne boys had announced their decision to take the vow at the same time, so a lot of Northern Cheyennes were up there in the crowd watching. Spotted Elk and Crooked Nose are two that remembered that night and told me about it. They said the people were already gathering, early in the evening. By the time they got to the upper end there, a big place had been cleared and they were already dancing. When those boys came in, they could not hear themselves talk, there was so much noise, with the crowd packed around and both the men and women singing.

They did not remember how many took part, and never thought of counting them, but Spotted Elk said later there were not more than twenty. They remembered the Northern Cheyenne boys that were dancing: Little Whirlwind, Cut Belly, Closed Hand, and Noisy

Walking. They were all killed the next day. But none of them knew that night that the soldiers were coming next day for sure; they were just suspicious.

The next morning the Indians held a parade for the boys who had been in the suicide dance the night before. Different ones told me about it; one was my grandmother, Twin Woman, the wife of Lame White Man, the only Northern Cheyenne chief who was killed in the battle. It was customary to put on such a parade after a suicide dance. The boys went in front, with an old man on either side announcing to the public to look at these boys well; they would never come back after the next battle.

They paraded down through the Northern Cheyenne camp on the inside and back on the outside, and then returned to their own village.

While the parade was still going on, three boys went down to the river to swim: William Yellowrobe, Charles Headswift, and Wandering Medicine. They were down there in the water when they heard a lot of noise, and thought the parade had just broken up. Some riders in war clothes came along the bank yelling and shooting. Then somebody hollered at them, "The camp is attacked by soldiers!" So they never thought about swimming any more. They jumped out and ran back to their families' camps. Headswift's people had already run away toward the hills at the west, but his older brother came back after him. They had to run quite a distance to get his brother's horse. Then they rode double to join the women and children where they were watching the beginning of the fight.

Meanwhile, after the parade had ended, my grandmother said a man named Tall Sioux had put up a sweat lodge, and Lame White Man went over to take part in his sweat bath there. It was just a little way from the tepees. She said they had closed the cover down a couple of times—they usually did it four times in all, pouring water over the hot stones to make steam—and the second or third time, the excitement started in the valley above the village [where Reno was attacking the Hunkpapas]. She did not see which way the soldiers came, but there were some above the village. And some more [Custer's troops] came from straight across the river.

The men in the sweat tepee crawled out and ran to help their families get on horses and get away. Lame White Man did not have time to get war clothes on. He just wrapped a blanket around his waist and grabbed his moccasins and belt and a gun. He went with Grandmother a little way to the west of some small hills there. Then he turned down below and crossed after the rest of the warriors.

Of course, Wolftooth and Bigfoot had come out of the brush long before then. At daylight they could see the Indian military patrols still on the hills, so they waited for some time. They moved along, keeping under cover, until they ran into more warriors and then some more. Close to fifty men had succeeded in slipping through the military bands and crossing the river that way. They got together and were about halfway up a wooded hill [about four miles east of where the battle was to occur] when they heard someone hollering. Wolftooth looked back and saw a rider on a ridge a mile below them, calling and signalling them to come back.

They turned and galloped back, and when they drew near, the rider began talking in Sioux. Bigfoot could understand it. The soldiers had already ridden down toward the village. Then this party raced back up the creek again to where they could follow one of the ridges to the top, and when they got up there, then saw the last few soldiers going down out of sight toward the river—Custer's men. Reno's men had attacked the other end already, but they did not know it.

As the soldiers disappeared, Wolftooth's band split up. Some followed the soldiers, and the rest went on around a point to cut them off. They caught up there with some that were still going down, and came around them on both sides. The soldiers started shooting; it was the first skirmish of the Custer part of the battle, and it did not last very long. The Indians said they did not try to go in close. After some shooting, both bunches of Indians retreated back to the hills, and the soldiers crossed the south end of the ridge.

The soldiers followed the ridge down to the present cemetery site. Then this bunch of forty or fifty Indians came after them again and started shooting down at them a second time. But the soldiers were moving on down toward the river, across from the Northern Cheyenne camp. Some of the warriors there had come across, and they began firing at the soldiers from the brush in the river bottom. This made the soldiers turn north, but then they went back in the direction they had come from, and stopped when they got to where the cemetery is now. And they waited there—twenty minutes or more. [It may be noted that this Cheyenne version places Custer's farthest advance a mile or so beyond and west of the ridge where he died and has him retreat to that final position. The most generally accepted story up to now is that he was cut down along the ridge as he moved from the southeast toward the site of his final stand.] The Indians have a joke about his long wait. Beaver Heart said that when the scouts warned Custer about the village, he laughed and said, "When we get to that village, I'm going to find the Sioux girl with the most elk teeth on her dress and take her along with me." So that is what he was doing those twenty minutes. Looking.

Wolftooth and his band of warriors moved in meanwhile along the ridge above the soldiers. Custer went into the center of a big basin below where the monument is now, and the soldiers of the Gray Horse Company [Company E, under Lieutenant Algernon Smith] got off their horses and moved up on foot. If there had not been so many Indians on the ridge above, they might have retreated over that way, either then or later when the fighting got bad, and gone to join Reno. But there were too many up above, and the firing was getting heavy from the other side now.

Most of the Northern Cheyennes were down at the Custer end of the fight, but one or two were up at the Reno fight with the Sioux. Beaver Heart saw Reno's men come in close to the Sioux village and make a stand there in some trees after they had crossed the river. But they were almost wiped out. They got on their horses and galloped along the edge of the cottonwood trees on the bank and turned across the river, but it was a bad crossing. The bank on the other side was higher, and the horses had to jump to get on top. Some fell back when it got wet and slick from the first ones coming out, and many soldiers were killed trying to get away. Some finally made it up onto the hill where they took their stand.

It was about that time that Custer was going in at the lower end, toward the Cheyenne camp. It was hard to keep track of everything at the two battles. A number of Indians went back and forth between the two, but none of them saw everything. Most of them went toward the fight with Custer, once Reno was up on the hill. Wolftooth saw they were all shooting at the Custer men from the ridge, but they were careful all the time, taking cover.

Before long, some Sioux criers came along behind the line, and began calling in the Sioux language to get ready and watch for the suicide boys. They said they were getting ready down below to charge together from the river, and when they came in, all the Indians up above should jump up for hand-to-hand fighting. That way the soldiers would not have a chance to shoot, but would be crowded from both sides. The idea was that they had been firing both ways. When the suicide boys came up, they would turn to them and give those behind a chance to come in close. The criers called out those instructions twice. Most of the Cheyennes could not understand them, but the Sioux there told them what had been said.

So the suicide boys were the last Indians to enter the fight. Wolftooth said they were really watching for them, and at last they rode out down below. They galloped up to the level ground near where the museum is now; some turned and stampeded the gray horses of the soldiers. By then they were mostly loose, the ones that had not been shot. The rest of the boys charged right in at the place where the soldiers were making their stand, and the others followed them as soon as they got the horses away.

The suicide boys started the hand-to-hand fighting, and all of them were killed there or were wounded and died later. When the soldiers started shooting at them, the Indians above with Wolftooth came in from the other side. Then there was no time for the soldiers to take aim or anything. The Indians were right behind and among them. Some soldiers started to run along the edge under the top of the ridge, and for a distance they scattered, some going on one side and some the other. But they were all killed before they got far.

At the end it was quite a mess. They could not tell which was this man or that man, they were so mixed up. Horses were running over the soldiers and over each other. The fighting was really close, and they were shooting almost any way without taking aim. Some said it made it less dangerous than fighting at a distance; then the soldier would aim carefully and be more likely to hit you. After they emptied their pistols this way, there was no time to reload. Neither side did. But most of the Indians had clubs or hatchets, while the soldiers had guns; they were using those to hit with and knock the enemy down. A Sioux, Stinking Bear, saw one Indian charge a soldier who had his gun by the barrel., and he swung it so hard he knocked the Indian over and fell over himself.

Yellow Nose was in there close. He saw two Indian horses run right into each other—the horses both fell down and rolled, and he nearly ran into them himself., but managed to turn aside. The dust was so thick he could hardly see. He swung his horse out and turned to charge back in again, close to the end of the fight, and suddenly the dust lifted away. He saw a troop flag [guidon] not far in front of him. Over on the other side some soldiers were still fighting, so he galloped past and picked the flag up and rode into the fight, and he used it to count coup on a soldier.

After the suicide boys came in, it did not take long: haft an hour perhaps. Many had agreed with what Wolftooth said, that if it had not been for the suicide boys, it might have ended the way it did at the Reno fight. The Indians all stayed back and fought there; no suicide boys jumped in to begin the hand-to-hand fight. The Custer fight was different because these boys went in that way, and it was their rule to be killed.

Another thing many of the Cheyennes said was that if Custer had kept going—if he had not waited there on the ridge so long—he could have made it back to Reno. But he probably thought he could stand off the Indians and win.

Everyone always wanted to know who killed Custer. I have interpreted twice for people asking about this, and whether anyone ever saw a certain Indian take a shot and kill him. But all the Indians say too many people were shooting; nobody could tell whose bullet killed a certain man. There were rumors some knew but would not say anything for fear of trouble. But it was more like Spotted Blackbird said: "If we could have seen where each bullet landed, we might have known. But hundreds of bullets were flying that day."

After the Indians had killed every soldier, my grandmother's brother, Tall Bull, came across the river and said, "Get a travois fixed. One of the dead is my brother-in-law, and we will have to go over and get his body." It was my grandfather, Lame White Man. So they went across to where he was lying. he did not have his war clothes on; as I said, he had not had time. And some sioux had made a mistake on him. They thought he was an Indian Scout with Custer—they often fought undressed that way. And his scalp was gone from the top of his head. Nearby was the body of another Cheyenne, one of the suicide boys.

I heard the Sioux lost sixty-six men and the Northern Cheyennes just seven, but there might have been more. The Indian dead were all moved from the battlefield right away.

Many Indians were up on the battlefield after it was over, getting the dead or taking things from the soldiers. I asked Grandmother if she went. Women were up there as well as men. But she said the fight was still going on up above with Reno, and many women were afraid to go near the field. They thought the soldiers might break away and come in their direction.

White Wolf (also called Shot in the Head), who was in this fight, said that afterwards a lot of young men searched the soldiers' pockets. That square green paper money was in them, so they took some. Later when they were making mud horses, they used the money for saddle blankets. Silver money was found too. The Northern Cheyennes made buckles out of it.

The camp broke up the next day after the battle. Some people even left that evening to move up near Lodge Grass. Some of the warriors stayed behind to go on fighting with Reno, but they did not stay more than a day. They knew other soldiers were n the country., and they were out of meat and firewood. The split into many groups, some following the river, and others going up Reno Creek and to other places.

By the time the other solders [Terry's men] got to the battlefield, the Indians were gone. A Cheyenne named Lost Leg rode back a few days later looking for horses. A lot had strayed away and he thought he might be able to get some of them. he said he could smell the battle-field a long way off. He had planned to go in and look at it, but he could not even come close, it was so strong. So he gave up and returned. There was no more real fighting that summer.

EPITAPH FOR THE STEEL MASTER

Robert L. Heilbroner

An immigrant lad from Scotland comes to America and by hard work, intelligence and guile rises to the pinnacle of wealth. Although this is a tale worthy of an Horatio Alger novel, it is instead the true story of Andrew Carnegie, 19th century icon of fame and fortune. Carnegie's rise through the corporate world of the Gilded Age to become the master of a vast empire of steel and one of the world's richest men is a fascinating story. Just as remarkable as his rise to wealth is the enigmatic nature of his character. While ruthless and often brutal in his business dealings, Carnegie became the epitome of philanthropy and a believer in what he would call the gospel of wealth. Professor Robert Heilbroner, author of such works as The Worldly Philosophers *and* The Future as History, *tells the story of Carnegie's life in this article and shows his influence on American society and the Industrial Revolution.*

Toward the end of his days, at the close of World War I, Andrew Carnegie was already a kind of national legend. His meteoric rise, the scandals and successes of his industrial generalship—all this was bluffed into nostalgic memory. What was left was a small, rather feeble man with a white beard and pale, penetrating eyes, who could occasionally be seen puttering around his mansion on upper Fifth Avenue, a benevolent old gentleman who still rated an annual birthday interview but was even then a venerable relic of a fast-disappearing era. Carnegie himself looked back on his career with a certain savored incredulity. "How much did you say I had given away, Poynton?" he would inquire of his private secretary; "$324,657,399" was the answer. "Good Heaven!" Carnegie would exclaim. "Where did I ever get all that money?"

Where he *had* got all that money was indeed a legendary story, for even in an age known for its acquisitive triumphs, Carnegie's touch had been an extraordinary one. He had begun, in true Horatio Alger fashion, at the bottom; he had ended, in a manner that put the wildest of Alger's novels to shame, at the very pinnacle of success. At the close of his great deal with J. P. Morgan in 1901, when the Carnegie steel empire was sold to form the core of the new United States Steel Company, the banker had extended his hand and delivered the ultimate encomium of the times: "Mr. Carnegie," he said, "I want to congratulate you on being the richest man in the world."

It was certainly as "the richest man in the world" that Carnegie attracted the attention of his contemporaries. Yet this is hardly why we look back on him with interest today. As an enormous money-maker Carnegie was a flashy, but hardly a profound, hero of the times;

and the attitudes of Earnestness and Self-Assurance, so engaging in the young immigrant, become irritating when they are congealed in the millionaire. But what lifts Carnegie's life above the rut of a one-dimensional success story is an aspect of which his contemporaries were relatively unaware.

Going through his papers after his death, Carnegie's executors came across a memorandum that he had written to himself fifty years before, carefully preserved in a little yellow box of keepsakes and mementos. It brings us back to December, 1868, when Carnegie, a young man flushed with the first taste of great success, retired to his suite in the opulent Hotel St. Nicholas in New York, to tot up his profits for the year. It had been a tremendous year and the calculation must have been extremely pleasurable. Yet this is what he wrote as he reflected on the figures:

> Thirty-three and an income of $50,000 per annum! By this time two years I can so arrange all my business as to secure at least $50,000 per annum. Beyond this never earn—make no effort to increase fortune, but spend the surplus each year for benevolent purposes. Cast aside business forever, except for others.

> Settle in Oxford and get a thorough education, making the acquaintance of literary men—this will take three years of active work—pay especial attention to speaking in public. Settle then in London and purchase a controlling interest in some newspaper or live review and give the general management of it attention, taking part in public matters, especially those connected with education and improvement of the poorer classes.

> Man must have an idol—the amassing of wealth is one of the worst species of idolatry—no idol more debasing than the worship of money. Whatever I engage in I must push inordinately; therefore should I be careful to choose that life which will be the most elevating in its character. To continue much longer overwhelmed by business cares and with most of my thoughts wholly upon the way to make more money in the shortest time, must degrade me beyond hope of permanent recovery. I will resign business at thirty-five, but during the ensuing two years I with to spend the afternoons in receiving instruction and in reading systematically.

It is a document which in more ways than one is Carnegie to the very life: brash, incredibly self-confident, chockablock with self-conscious virtue—and more than a little hypocritical. For the program so nobly outlined went largely unrealized. Instead of retiring in two years, Carnegie went on for thirty-three more; even then it was with considerable difficulty that he was persuaded to quit. Far from shunning further money-making, he proceeded to roll up his fortune with an uninhibited drive that led one unfriendly biographer to characterize him as "the greediest little gentleman ever created." Certainly he was one of the most aggressive profit seekers of his time. Typically, when an associate jubilantly cabled: "No. 8 furnace broke all records today," Carnegie coldly replied, "What were the other furnaces doing?"

It is this contrast between his hopes and his performance that makes Carnegie interesting. For when we review his life, what we see is more than the career of another nineteenth-century acquisitor. We see the unequal struggle between a man who loved money—loved making it, having it, spending it—and a man who, at bottom, was ashamed of himself for his acquisitive desires. All during his lifetime, the money-maker seemed to win. But what lifts Carnegie's story out of the ordinary is that the other Carnegie ultimately triumphed. At his death public speculation placed the size of his estate at about five hundred million dollars. In fact it came to $22,881,575. Carnegie had become the richest man in the world—but something had also driven him to give away ninety percent of his wealth.

Actually, his contemporaries knew of Carnegie's inquietude about money. In 1889, before he was world-famous, he had written an article for the *North American Review* entitled "The Gospel of Wealth"—an article that contained the startling phrase: "The man who dies thus rich dies disgraced." It was hardly surprising, however, if the world took these sentiments at a liberal discount: homiletic millionaires who preached the virtues of austerity were no novelty; Carnegie himself, returning in 1879 from a trip to the miseries of India, had been able to write with perfect sincerity, "How very little the millionaire has beyond the peasant, and how very often his additions tend not to happiness but to misery."

What the world may well have underestimated, however, was a concern more deeply rooted than these pieties revealed. For, unlike so many of his self-made peers, who also rose from poverty, Carnegie was the product of a *radical* environment. The village of Dunfermline, Scotland, when he was born there in 1835, was renowned as a center of revolutionary ferment, and Carnegie's family was itself caught up in the radical movement of the times. His father was a regular speaker at the Chartist rallies, which were an almost daily occurrence in Dunfermline in the 1840s, and his uncle was an impassioned orator for the rights of the working class to vote and strike. All this made an indelible impression on Carnegie's childhood.

"I remember as if it were yesterday," he wrote seventy years later, "being awakened during the night by a tap at the back window by men who had come to inform my parents that my uncle, Bailie Morrison, had been thrown in jail because he dared to hold a meeting which had been forbidden . . . It is not to be wondered at that, nursed amid such surroundings, I developed into a violent young Republican whose motto was 'death to privilege.'"

From another uncle, George Lauder, Carnegie absorbed a second passion that was also to reveal itself in his later career. This was his love of poetry, first that of the poet Burns, with its overtones of romantic egalitarianism, and then later, of Shakespeare. Immense quantities of both were not only committed to memory, but made into an integral—indeed, sometimes an embarrassingly evident—part of his life: on first visiting the Doge's palace in Venice he thrust a companion in the ducal throne and held him pinioned there while he orated the appropriate speeches from *Othello*. Once, seeing Vanderbilt walking on Fifth Avenue, Carnegie smugly remarked, "I would not exchange his millions for my knowledge of Shakespeare."

But it was more than just a love of poetry that remained with Carnegie. Virtually alone among his fellow acquisitors, he was driven by a genuine respect for the power of thought to seek answers for questions that never even occurred to them. Later, when he "discovered" Herbert Spencer, the English sociologist, Carnegie wrote to him, addressing him as "Master," and it was as "Master" that Spencer remained, even after Carnegie's lavishness had left Spencer very much in his debt.

But Carnegie's early life was shaped by currents more material than intellectual. The grinding process of industrial change had begun slowly but ineluctably to undermine the cottage weaving that was the traditional means of employment in Dunfermline. The Industrial Revolution, in the shape of new steam mills, was forcing out the hand weavers, and one by one the looms which constituted the entire capital of the Carnegie family had to be sold. Carnegie never forgot the shock of his father returning home to tell him, in despair, "Andra, I can get nae mair work."

A family council of war was held, and it was declared that there was only one possible course—they must try their luck in America, to which two sisters of Carnegie's mother, Margaret, had already emigrated. With the aid of a few friends the money for the crossing was scraped together, and at thirteen Andrew found himself transported to the only country in which his career would have been possible.

It hardly got off to an auspicious start, however. The family made their way to Allegheny, Pennsylvania, a raw and bustling town where Carnegie's father again sought work as an independent weaver. But it was as hopeless to compete against the great mills in America as in Scotland, and soon father and son were forced to seek work in the local cotton mills. There Andrew worked from six in the morning until six at night, making $1.20 as a bobbin boy.

After a while his father quit—factory work was impossible for the traditional small enterpriser—and Andrew got a "better" job with a new firm, tending an engine deep in a dungeon cellar and dipping newly made cotton spools in a vat of oil. Even the raise to $3 a week—and desperately conjured visions of Wallace and the Bruce—could not overcome the horrors of that lonely and foul-smelling basement. It was perhaps the only time in Carnegie's life when his self-assurance deserted him: to the end of his days the merest whiff of oil could make him deathly sick.

Yet he was certain, as he wrote home at sixteen, that "anyone could get along in this Country," and the rags-to-riches sap shortly began. The telegraph had just come to Pittsburgh, and one evening over a game of checkers, the manager of the local office informed Andrew's uncle that he was looking for a messenger. Andy got the job and, in true Alger fashion, set out to excel in it. Within a few weeks he had carefully memorized the names and the locations, not only of the main streets in Pittsburgh, but of the main firms, so that he was the quickest of all the messenger boys.

He came early and stayed late, watched the telegraphers at work, and at home at night learned the Morse code. As a result he was soon the head of the growing messenger service, and a skilled telegrapher himself. One day he dazzled the office by taking a message "by ear" instead of by the commonly used tape printer, and since he was then only the third operator in the country able to turn the trick, citizens used to drop into the office to watch Andy take down the words "hot from the wire."

One such citizen who was especially impressed with young Carnegie's determination was Thomas A. Scott, in time to become one of the colorful railway magnates of the West, but then the local superintendent of the Pennsylvania Railroad. Soon thereafter Carnegie became "Scott's Andy"—telegrapher, secretary, and general factotum—at thirty-five dollars a month. In his *Autobiography* Carnegie recalls an instance which enabled him to begin the next stage of his career.

> One morning I reached the office and found that a serious accident on the Eastern Division had delayed the express passenger train westward, and that the passenger train eastward was proceeding with a flagman in advance at every curve. The freight trains in both directions were standing on the sidings. Mr. Scott was not to be found. Finally I could not resist the temptation to plunge in, take the responsibility, give "train orders" and set matters going. "Death or Westminster Abbey" flashed across my mind. I knew it was dismissal, disgrace, perhaps criminal punishment for me if I erred. On the other hand, I could bring in the wearied freight train men who had lain out all night. I knew I could. I knew just what to do, and so I began.

Signing Scott's name to the orders, Carnegie flashed out the necessary instructions to bring order out of the tangle. The trains moved; there were no mishaps. When Scott reached the office Carnegie told him what he had done. Scott said not a word but looked carefully over all that had taken place. After a little he moved away from Carnegie's desk to his own, and that was the end of it. "But I noticed," Carnegie concluded good-humoredly, "that he came in very regularly and in good time for some mornings after that."

It is hardly to be wondered at that Carnegie became Scott's favorite, his "white-haired Scotch devil." Impetuous but not rash, full of enthusiasm and good-natured charm, the small lad with his blunt, open features and his slight Scottish burr was every executive's dream of an assistant. Soon Scott repaid Andy for his services by introducing him to a new and very different kind of opportunity. He gave Carnegie the chance to subscribe to five hundred dollars' worth of Adams Express stock, a company which Scott assured Andy would prosper mightily.

Carnegie had not fifty dollars saved, much less five hundred, but it was a chance he could ill afford to miss. He reported the offer to his mother, and that pillar of the family unhesitatingly mortgaged their home to raise the necessary money. When the first dividend check came in, with its ornate Spencerian flourishes, Carnegie had something like a revelation. "I shall remember that check as long as I live," he subsequently wrote. "It gave me the first penny of revenue from capital—something that I had not worked for with the sweat of my brow. 'Eureka!' I cried, 'Here's the goose that lays the golden eggs.'" He was right; within a few years his investment in the Adams Express Company was paying annual dividends of $1,400.

It was not long thereafter that an even more propitious chance presented itself. Carnegie was riding on the Pennsylvania line one day when he was approached by a "farmer-looking" man carrying a small green bag in his hand. The other introduced himself as T. T. Woodruff and quite frankly said that he wanted a chance to talk with someone connected with the railroad. Whereupon he opened his bag and took out a small model of the first sleeping car.

Carnegie was immediately impressed with its possibilities, and he quickly arranged for Woodruff to meet Scott. When the latter agreed to give the cars a trial, Woodruff in appreciation offered Carnegie a chance to subscribe to a one-eighth interest in the new company. A local banker agreed to lend Andy the few hundred dollars needed for the initial payment—the rest being financed from dividends. Once again Andy had made a shrewd investment: within two years the Woodruff Palace Car Company was paying him a return of more than $5,000 a year.

Investments now began to play an increasingly important role in Carnegie's career. Through his railroad contacts he came to recognize the possibilities in manufacturing the heavy equipment needed by the rapidly expanding lines, and soon he was instrumental in organizing companies to meet these needs. One of them, the Keystone Bridge Company, was the first successful manufacturer of iron railway bridges. Another, the Pittsburgh Locomotive Works, made engines. And most important of all, an interest in a local iron works run by an irascible German named Andrew Kloman brought Carnegie into actual contact with the manufacture of iron itself.

None of these new ventures required any substantial outlay of cash. His interest in the Keystone Bridge Company, for instance, which was to earn him $15,000 in 1868, came to him "in return for services rendered in its promotion"—services which Carnegie, as a young railroad executive, was then in a highly strategic position to deliver. Similarly the interest in the Kloman works reflected no contribution on Carnegie's part except that of being the human catalyst and buffer between some highly excitable participants.

By 1865 his "side" activities had become so important that he decided to leave the Pennsylvania Railroad. He was by then superintendent, Scott having moved up to a vice presidency, but his salary of $2,400 was already vastly overshadowed by his income from various ventures. One purchase alone—the Storey farm in Pennsylvania oil country, which Carnegie and a few associates picked up for $40,000—was eventually to pay the group a million dollars in dividends in one year. About this time a friend dropped in on Carnegie and asked him how he was doing. "Oh, I'm rich, I'm rich!" he exclaimed.

He was indeed embarked on the road to riches, and determined, as he later wrote in his *Autobiography*, that "nothing could be allowed to interfere for a moment with my business career." Hence it comes as a surprise to note that it was at this very point that Carnegie retired to his suite to write his curiously introspective and troubled thoughts about the pursuit of wealth. But the momentum of events was to prove far too strong for these moralistic doubts. Moving his headquarters to New York to promote his various interests, he soon found himself swept along by a succession of irresistible opportunities for money-making.

One of these took place quite by chance. Carnegie was trying to sell the Woodruff sleeping car at the same time that a formidable rival named George Pullman was also seeking to land contracts for his sleeping car, and the railroads were naturally taking advantage of the competitive situation. One summer evening in 1869 Carnegie found himself mounting the resplendent marble stairway of the St. Nicholas Hotel side by side with his competitor.

"Good evening, Mr. Pullman," said Carnegie in his ebullient manner. Pullman was barely cordial.

"How strange we should meet here," Carnegie went on, to which the other replied nothing at all.

"Mr. Pullman," said Carnegie, after an embarrassing pause, "don't you think we are making nice fools of ourselves?" At this Pullman evinced a glimmer of interest: "What do you mean?" he inquired. Carnegie quickly pointed out that competition between the two companies was helping no one but the railroads. "Well," said Pullman, "what do you suggest we do?"

"Unite!" said Carnegie. "Let's make a joint proposition to the Union Pacific, your company and mine. Why not organize a new company to do it?" "What would you call it?" asked Pullman suspiciously. "The Pullman Palace Car Company," said Carnegie and with this shrewd psychological stroke won his point. A new company was formed, and in time Carnegie became its largest stockholder.

Meanwhile, events pushed Carnegie into yet another lucrative field. To finance the proliferating railway systems of America, British capital was badly needed, and with his Scottish ancestry, his verve, and his excellent railroad connections Carnegie was the natural choice for a go-between. His brief case stuffed with bonds and prospectuses, Carnegie became a transatlantic commuter, soon developing intimate relations both with great bankers like Junius Morgan (the father of J. P. Morgan), and with the heads of most of the great American roads. These trips earned him not only large commissions—exceeding on occasion $100,000 for a single turn—but even more important, established connections that were later to be of immense value. He himself later testified candidly on their benefits before a group of respectfully awed senators:

> For instance, I want a great contract for rails. Sidney Dillon of the Union Pacific was a personal friend of mine. Huntington was a friend. Dear Butler Duncan, that called on me the other day, was a friend. Those and other men were presidents of railroads . . . Take Huntington; you know C. P. Huntington. He was hard up very often. He was a great man, but he had a great deal of paper out. I knew his things were good. When he wanted credit I gave it to him. If you help a man that way, what chance has any paid agent going to these men? It was absurd.

But his trips to England brought Carnegie something still more valuable. They gave him steel. It is fair to say that as late as 1872 Carnegie did not see the future that awaited him as the Steel King of the world. The still modest conglomeration of foundries and mills he was gradually assembling in the Allegheny and Monongahela valleys was but one of many business interests, and not one for which he envisioned any extraordinary future. Indeed, to repeated pleas that he lead the way in developing a steel industry for America by substituting steel for iron rails, his reply was succinct: "Pioneering don't pay."

What made him change his mind? The story goes that he was awe-struck by the volcanic, spectacular eruption of a Bessemer converter, which he saw for the first time during a visit to a British mill. It was precisely the sort of display that would have appealed to Carnegie's mind—a wild, demonic, physical process miraculously contained and controlled by the dwarfed figures of the steel men themselves. At any rate, overnight Carnegie became the perfervid prophet of steel. Jumping on the first available steamer, he rushed home with the cry, "The day of iron has passed!" To the consternation of his colleagues, the hitherto reluctant pioneer became an advocate of the most daring technological and business expansion; he joined them enthusiastically in forming Carnegie, McCandless & Company, which was the nucleus of the empire that the next thirty years would bring forth.

The actual process of growth involved every aspect of successful business enterprise of the times: acquisition and merger, pools and commercial piracy, and even, on one occasion, an outright fraud in selling the United States government overpriced and underdone steel armor plate. But it would be as foolish to maintain that the Carnegie empire grew by trickery as to deny that sharp practice had its place. Essentially what lay behind the spectacular expansion were three facts.

The first of these was the sheer economic expansion of the industry in the first days of burgeoning steel use. Everywhere steel replaced iron or found new uses and not only in railroads but in ships, buildings, bridges, machinery of all sorts. As Henry Frick himself once remarked, if the Carnegie group had not filled the need for steel another would have. But it must be admitted that Carnegie's company did its job superlatively well. In 1885 Great Britain led the world in the production of steel. Fourteen years later her total output was 695,000 tons less than the output of the Carnegie Steel Company alone.

Second was the brilliant assemblage of personal talent with which Carnegie surrounded himself. Among them, three in particular stood out. One was Captain William Jones, a Homeric figure who lumbered through the glowing fires and changing machinery of the works like a kind of Paul Bunyan of steel, skilled at handling men, inventive in handling equipment, and enough of a natural artist to produce papers for the British Iron and Steel Institute that earned him a literary as well as a technical reputation. Then there was Henry Frick, himself a self-made millionaire, whose coke empire naturally complemented Carnegie's steelworks. When the two were amalgamated, Frick took over the active management of the whole, and under his forceful hand the annual output of the Carnegie works rose tenfold. Yet another was Charles Schwab, who came out of the tiny monastic town of Loretto, Pennsylvania, to take a job as a stake driver. Six months later he had been promoted by Jones into the assistant managership of the Braddock plant.

These men, and a score like them, constituted the vital energy of the Carnegie works. As Carnegie himself said, "Take away all our money, our great works, ore mines and coke ovens, but leave our organization, and in four years I shall have re-established myself."

But the third factor in the growth of the empire was Carnegie himself. A master salesman and a skilled diplomat of business at its highest levels, Carnegie was also a ruthless driver of his men. He pitted his associates and subordinates in competition with one another until a feverish atmosphere pervaded the whole organization. "You cannot imagine the abounding sense of freedom and relief I experience as soon as I get on board a steamer and sail past Sandy Hook," he once said to Captain Jones. "My God!" replied Jones. "Think of the relief to us!"

But Carnegie could win loyalties as well. All his promising young men were given gratis ownership participations—minuscule fractions of one per cent, which were enough, however, to make them millionaires in their own right. Deeply grateful to Jones, Carnegie once offered him a similar participation. Jones hemmed and hawed and finally refused; he would be unable to work effectively with the men, he said, once he was a partner. Carnegie insisted that his contribution be recognized and asked Jones what he wanted. "Well," said the latter, "you might pay me a hell of a big salary." "We'll do it!" said Carnegie. "From this time forth you shall receive the same salary as the President of the United States." "Ah, Andy, that's the kind of talk," said Captain Bill.

Within three decades, on the flood tide of economic expansion, propelled by brilliant executive work and relentless pressure from Carnegie, the company made immense strides. "Such a magnificent aggregation of industrial power has never before been under the domination of a single man," reported a biographer in 1902, describing the Gargantuan structure of steel and coke and ore and transport. Had the writer known of the profits earned by this aggregation he might have been even more impressed: three and a half million dollars in 1889, seven million in 1897, twenty-one million in 1899, and an immense forty million in 1900. "Where is there such a business!" Carnegie had exulted, and no wonder—the majority share of all these earnings, without hindrance of income tax, went directly into his pockets.

Nevertheless, with enormous success came problems. One of these was the restiveness of certain partners, under the "Iron-Clad" agreement, which prevented any of them from selling their shares to anyone but the company itself—an arrangement which meant, of course, that the far higher valuation of an outside purchaser could not be realized. Particularly chagrined was Frick, when, as the culmination of other disagreements between them, Carnegie sought to buy him out "at the value appearing on the books." Another problem was a looming competitive struggle in the steel industry itself that presaged a period of bitter industrial warfare ahead. And last was Carnegie's own growing desire to "get out."

Already he was spending half of each year abroad, first traveling, and then, after his late marriage, in residence in the great Skibo Castle he built for his wife on Dornoch Firth, Scotland. There he ran his business enterprises with one hand while he courted the literary and creative world with the other, entertaining Kipling and Matthew Arnold, Paderewski and Lloyd George, Woodrow Wilson and Theodore Roosevelt, Gladstone, and of course, Herbert Spencer, the Master. But even his career as "Laird" of Skibo could not remove him from the worries—and triumphs—of his business: a steady flow of cables and correspondence intruded on the "serious" side of life.

It was Schwab who cut the knot. Having risen to the very summit of the Carnegie concern he was invited in December, 1900, to give a speech on the future of the steel industry at the University Club in New York. There, before eighty of the nation's top business leaders he painted a glowing picture of what could be done if a super-company of steel were formed, integrated from top to bottom, self-sufficient with regard to its raw materials, balanced in its array of final products. One of the guests was the imperious J. P. Morgan, and as the speech progressed it was noticed that his concentration grew more and more intense. After dinner Morgan rose and took the young steel man by the elbow and engaged him in private conversation for half an hour while he plied him with rapid and penetrating questions; then a few weeks later he invited him to a private meeting in the great library of his home. They talked from nine o'clock in the evening until dawn. As the sun began to stream in through the library windows, the banker finally rose. "Well," he said to Schwab, "if Andy wants to sell, I'll buy. Go and find his price."

Carnegie at first did not wish to sell. Faced with the actual prospect of a withdrawal from the business he had built into the mightiest single industrial empire in the world, he was frightened and dismayed. He sat silent before Schwab's report, brooding, loath to inquire into details. But soon his enthusiasm returned. No such opportunity was likely to present itself again. In short order a figure of $492,000,000 was agreed on for the entire enterprise, of which Carnegie himself was to receive $300,000,000 in five per cent gold bonds and preferred stock. Carnegie jotted down the terms of the transaction on a slip of paper and told Schwab to bring it to Morgan. The banker glanced only briefly at the paper. "I accept," he said.

After the formalities were in due course completed, Carnegie was in a euphoric mood. "Now, Pierpont, I am the happiest man in the world," he said. Morgan was by no means unhappy himself: his own banking company had made a direct profit of $12,500,000 in the underwriting transaction, and this was but a prelude to a stream of lucrative financings under Morgan's aegis, by which the total capitalization was rapidly raised to $1,400,000,000. A few years later, Morgan and Carnegie found themselves aboard the same steamer en route to Europe. They fell into talk and Carnegie confessed, "I made one mistake, Pierpont, when I sold out to you."

"What was that?" asked the banker.

"I should have asked you for $1,000,000,000 more than I did."

Morgan grinned. "Well," he said, "you would have got it if you had."

Thus was written *finis* to one stage of Carnegie's career. Now it would be seen to what extent his "radical pronouncements" were serious. For in the *Gospel of Wealth*—the famous article combined with others in book form—Carnegie had proclaimed the duty of the millionaire to administer and distribute his wealth during his lifetime. Though he might have "proved" his worth by his fortune, his heirs had shown no such evidence of their fitness. Carnegie bluntly concluded: "By taxing estates heavily at his death, the State marks its condemnation of the selfish millionaire's unworthy life."

Coming from the leading millionaire of the day, these had been startling sentiments. So also were his views on the "labor question" which, if patronizing, were nonetheless humane and advanced for their day. The trouble was, of course, that the sentiments were somewhat difficult to credit. As one commentator of the day remarked, "His vision of what might be done with wealth had beauty and breadth and thus serenely overlooked the means by which wealth had been acquired."

For example, the novelist Hamlin Garland visited the steel towns from which the Carnegie millions came and bore away a description of work that was ugly, brutal, and exhausting: he contrasted the lavish care expended on the plants with the callous disregard of the pigsty homes: "the streets were horrible; the buildings poor; the sidewalks sunken and full of holes . . . Everywhere the yellow mud of the streets lay kneaded into sticky masses through which groups of pale, lean men slouched in faded garments . . . " When the famous Homestead strike erupted in 1892, with its private army of Pinkerton detectives virtually at war with the workers, the Carnegie benevolence seemed revealed as shabby fakery. At Skibo Carnegie stood firmly behind the company's iron determination to break the strike. As a result, public sentiment swung sharply and suddenly against him; the *St. Louis Post-Dispatch* wrote: "Three months ago Andrew Carnegie was a man to be envied. Today he is an object of mingled pity and contempt. In the estimation of nine-tenths of the thinking people on both sides of the ocean he has . . . confessed himself a moral coward."

In an important sense the newspaper was right. For though Carnegie continued to fight against "privilege," he saw privilege only in its fading aristocratic vestments and not in the new hierarchies of wealth and power to which he himself belonged. In Skibo Castle he now played the role of the benign autocrat, awakening to the skirling of his private bagpiper and proceeding to breakfast to the sonorous accompaniment of the castle organ.

Meanwhile there had also come fame and honors in which Carnegie wallowed unashamedly. He counted the "freedoms" bestowed on him by grateful or hopeful cities and crowed, "I have fifty-two and Gladstone has only seventeen." He entertained the King of England and told him that democracy was better than monarchy, and met the German Kaiser: "Oh, yes, yes," said the latter worthy on being introduced. "I have read your books. You do not like kings." But Mark Twain, on hearing of this, was not fooled. "He says he is a scorner of kings and emperors and dukes," he wrote, "whereas he is like the rest of the human race: a slight attention from one of these can make him drunk for a week . . . "

And yet it is not enough to conclude that Carnegie was in fact a smaller man than he conceived himself. For this judgment overlooks one immense and irrefutable fact. He did, in the end, abide by his self-imposed duty. He did give nearly all of his gigantic fortune away.

As one would suspect, the quality of the philanthropy reflected the man himself. There was, for example, a huge and sentimentally administered private pension fund to which access was to be had on the most trivial as well as the most worthy grounds: if it included a number of writers, statesmen, scientists, it also made room for two maiden ladies with whom Carnegie had once danced as a young man, a boyhood acquaintance who had once held Carnegie's books while he ran a race, a merchant to whom be had once delivered a telegram and who had subsequently fallen on hard times. And then, as one would expect, there was a benevolent autocracy in the administration of the larger philanthropies as well. "Now everybody vote Aye," was the way Carnegie typically determined the policies of the philanthropic "foundations" he established.

Yet if these flaws bore the stamp of one side of Carnegie's personality, there was also the other side—the side that, however crudely, asked important questions and however piously, concerned itself with great ideals. Of this the range and purpose of the main philanthropies gave unimpeachable testimony. There were the famous libraries—three thousand of them costing nearly sixty million dollars; there were the Carnegie institutes in Pittsburgh and Washington, Carnegie Hall in New York, the Hague Peace Palace, the Carnegie Endowment for International Peace, and the precedent-making Carnegie Corporation of New York, with its original enormous endowment of $125,000,000. In his instructions to the trustees of this first great modern foundation, couched in the simplified spelling of which he was an ardent advocate, we see Carnegie at his very best:

> Conditions on earth [sic] inevitably change; hence, no wise man will bind Trustees forever to certain paths, causes, or institutions. I disclaim any intention of doing so . . . My chief happiness, as I write these lines lies in the thot [sic] that, even after I pass away, the welth [sic] that came to me to administer as a sacred trust for the good of my fellow men is to continue to benefit humanity . . .

If these sentiments move us—if Carnegie himself in retrospect moves us at last to grudging respect—it is not because his was the triumph of a saint or a philosopher. It is because it was the much more difficult triumph of a very human and fallible man struggling to retain his convictions in an age, and in the face of a career, which subjected them to impossible temptations. Carnegie is something of America writ large; his is the story of the Horatio Alger hero *after* he has made his million dollars. In the failures of Andrew Carnegie we see many of the failures of America itself. In his curious triumph, we see what we hope is our own steadfast core of integrity.

III

THE HAYMARKET:
STRIKE AND VIOLENCE IN CHICAGO

R. Jackson Wilson

The late 19th century was a period of increasing trouble for America's industrial work-ers. Instead of laboring in small factories where they knew and were known by the busi-ness owners, workers were now employees of massive corporations. They were now only units of production. This transition was evident in the McCormick factory in Chicago. The manufacturer of farm equipment began to experience strife with its workers shortly after the Civil War. By the mid 1880s labor trouble at the family owned factory had reached a crisis level. In May, 1886 that trouble would become a part of one of the cen-tury's most infamous labor conflicts. The tragedy that occurred on the night of May 4, 1886 in Chicago's Haymarket Square would be a major blow to organized labor. It would also result in an even more tragic travesty of criminal justice in which men would be convicted of a violent crime solely on the basis of their political beliefs. This ar-ticle gives an excellent description of the labor problems of the late 19th century and ob-stacles faced by unions and leftist radicals in American society.

April 15, 1885

My Dear Virginia,

We have had a week of trial and anxiety on the great subject of disturbances in our main factory—the serious labor troubles we have encountered—a great "strike," and all the resulting derangement of our relations—old and pleasant as they were—with our workmen.

Trouble has come to hundreds of families in consequence; hatred and fierce passions have been aroused; and an injury has resulted to our good name.

It began with a few molders and went on, one force operating on another, until 1,200 men went out, part of them by intimidation and part of them led by ignorant and blind passion. It ended by our conceding the terms demanded.

What a sore heart I have carried these days!

Your Devoted Mother

This letter was written by a bewildered woman in her early seventies to her daughter. The writer, Nettie Fowler McCormick, was the widow of Cyrus Hall McCormick. An ambitious and ingenious Virginia farm boy, McCormick had made millions of dollars from the invention and manufacture of the reaper, a machine that harvested crops mechanically. He opened his Chicago factory, the McCormick Harvester Works, in the 1840s. It was the largest producer of harvesting machines in the world.

Nettie McCormick had always paid close attention to the family business. Now, just a year after her husband's death, a stable and profitable enterprise seemed to be falling to pieces before her eyes. At first, her husband had known all the original 23 workmen by name. He had worked alongside them in the little Chicago factory. Even when, after a few years, there were about 200 workers producing over 1,000 reapers a year, he could still name those who had been with the company for any length of time.

As the business grew, relations with the workers had become more difficult. During the Civil War, when labor had been scarce and prices had jumped every week, there had been many strikes or threats of strikes. McCormick had been forced to agree to one wage increase after another. But after the war ended, McCormick was able to cut wages in the plant five times in five years.

During the two decades after the Civil War, the McCormick company had grown rapidly. In 1884, when Cyrus McCormick died, the main factory covered dozens of acres. Its modern machinery, including two huge steam engines that supplied power for the whole factory, covered twelve acres of floor space. On these floors, about 1,300 men put in six 10-hour days a week. They turned 10 million feet of lumber and thousands of tons of iron into about 50,000 reapers a year. And these machines were making possible an agricultural miracle in the United States.

For the McCormicks, the result was money and status. In 1884 the company showed a profit of 71 percent. The family lived in a great mansion staffed with servants. They had invitations to the "best" Chicago homes, counted other wealthy people among their friends, sent their sons to Princeton, traveled luxuriously, and supported carefully selected philanthropies. Nettie Fowler McCormick had ample reason to be concerned about "our good name."

She had some reason to carry a "sore heart," too. The McCormick workers had always seemed content enough. Nine out of ten of them were Germans, Norwegians, or Swedes, and most lived in the neighborhoods just west of the factory—neighborhoods built by the McCormicks—with Swedish and German street names. All this made the strike of 1885 difficult for Nettie Fowler McCormick to understand. Perhaps her husband's death was part of the problem. But McCormick's was still a family business. Her son, Cyrus McCormick II, had taken over the presidency, and other members of the family had always held important positions in the company. What had happened, then, to the "old and pleasant" relations with the workmen?

The problem had to lie, the McCormicks believed, with some small, misguided minority within the plant. And the most likely candidates for this role were clearly the molders. Ethnically, the molders were a distinct group. Almost all of them were Irish—"fighting Irish," as one plant official called them. And they had a tight, successful craft union, Molders Local No. 233. This union had been making trouble for the McCormicks for twenty years. There were only about ninety molders, but their operation was crucial to the manufacture of reapers. They could bring production to a complete standstill, and they had successfully used the power of this threat several times. Every time old Cyrus McCormick had tried to cut wages, the molders had been the first to resist.

The strike of 1885 had its origins in a decision by the new young president of the company to cut wages again. In December 1884 he had announced a 10 percent pay cut throughout the work force—except for the molders, who were to be cut by 15 percent. At first, there was quiet. Even the molders appeared to accept the reduction. But they were only biding their time until production reached its annual peak in the spring. In March 1885, the molders demanded that the wage cut be restored to them. When McCormick refused, the molders went out on strike. And, to the McCormicks' alarm, some of the other workers followed them out.

McCormick was anxious to prove himself. To break the strike, he sent telegrams to Mc-Cormick salesmen all over the Midwest, asking them to send strikebreaking molders to Chicago. He even had these workers listed on the company payroll as "scabs"—the union term of insult for nonunion workmen who replaced striking members. The newcomers were housed inside the plant in a barracks listed in the company records as "scab house."

But McCormick's efforts to break the strike did not work. The "scabs" could not be trusted. Early in April, these two revealing telegrams were sent from company headquarters to salesmen in Iowa and Illinois:

> To Tom Braden, Agent, Des Moines, Iowa: Out of the lot of men you sent us yesterday, but two of them showed up in Chicago. We find it not safe to ship these critters at our expense unless nailed up in a box car or chained.

> To J. F. Utley, Agent, Sterling, Illinois: The gentleman you sent to us as a molder did not remain over an hour or two until he packed his valise and skipped. We took special pains to get him into the Works by his riding with Mr. McCormick in his buggy. If you are able to do so, try and collect back his Rail Road fare.

Just a week after Cyrus McCormick had sneaked this unreliable scab into the plant, hidden in the president's own buggy, the strike reached a climax. On April 14, with the police scattered all over the city to patrol a local election, strikers attacked McCormick workers outside the plant. McCormick, like many other companies of the period, had hired a small private army of the Pinkerton "detective" agency to maintain peace. A wagon loaded with Pinkerton men and a case of Winchester repeating rifles tried to enter the plant gate. The strikers attacked the wagon and burned it, and the rifles disappeared into the crowd. The captain in charge of the few Chicago police still in the area did nothing. His name, O'Donnell, was as obviously Irish as that of any molder.

The violence confirmed the McCormick family's opinion of the "fighting Irish" molders. If twenty years' experience were not enough, the Pinkerton agents' secret reports confirmed what the family had long suspected: They were the victims of an ethnic "conspiracy." Just after the violent episode of April 14, one Pinkerton man submitted this report:

> The assault on the Pinkerton police during the strike of last week was urged by Irishmen, who are employed at McCormick's as molders and helpers. These Irishmen are nearly all members of the Ancient Order of Hibernians [an Irish social fraternity] who have a bitter enmity against the agency.

To the Pinkertons, it seemed clear that the molders were actually supported by their fellow Irishmen on the police force:

> It looks somewhat strange that these men at McCormick's could have police protection. On each occasion, the police stood by during the assaults and made no effort to stop the outrage.

Once, during the strike, a group of molders had attacked a group of nonunion workers outside the plant gate. The police, according to Pinkerton reports, had this time not merely

stood by but had actually chased and arrested the Pinkerton men who were trying to restrain the molders:

> The police made the utmost speed in calling a patrol wagon, which followed the Pink-
> erton men and arrested them! The men who made the arrests were treated by the strik-
> ers in saloons, and from their talk and insinuations, the police urged the mob to more
> violence by saying the Pinkerton men were sons of bitches, no better than scabs, there
> to take the bread out of women and children's mouths.

After the molders' triumphant April 14 attack on the Pinkertons, Cyrus McCormick
went looking for help and advice. He appealed first to the mayor, Carter Harrison. But Harrison remembered full well that the McCormicks had consistently opposed him in local politics. He politely advised the young industrialist to give in to the molders' demands.
McCormick then turned to what he hoped would be a more sympathetic listener, old Philip
Armour, head of a large meat-packing company and a veteran of many labor troubles. But
even Armour told McCormick that the molders had won. There seemed to be no choice. Mc-
Cormick offered to give back to the molders 5 percent out of their original 15 percent pay
cut. But they refused this, and he ended by restoring the whole 15 percent.

To both Cyrus McCormick and his mother, their defeat at the hands of a few Irishmen
was a painful mystery. But it was a mystery that had to be solved. Cyrus wrote to his mother
as he mulled over the problem:

> The whole question of these labor troubles is vast and important and throws more
> new light on a department of our manufacturing interests which we have not hitherto
> studied with sufficient depth and understanding.

But to this twenty-five-year-old, who had only two years earlier been taken out of Princeton
to run the plant, "depth and understanding" were limited to one fact and one conclusion. The
fact was that a handful of disaffected molders could bring the entire McCormick enterprise to
a standstill. The conclusion was that such a situation must be avoided in the future by making
the skills of the molders unnecessary. He wrote his mother:

> I do not think we will have a similar trouble again because we will take measures to
> prevent it. I do not think we will be troubled if we take proper steps to weed out the
> bad element among the men.

McCormick went to work at once to "weed out" the offending Irish molders. He focused
his efforts on a daring technological gamble. During the summer of 1885, the summer following the strike, the McCormick company bought a dozen new "pneumatic molding machines." They were supposed to perform mechanically most of the foundry tasks that the
skilled molders had always done by hand. The machines were expensive, and they were experimental. No one knew whether they would work. McCormick hoped that they would enable
the company to rid itself once and for all of the troublesome molders.

In August the McCormick foundry closed for two months so that the machines could be
installed. The closing was not unusual, since reapers were manufactured seasonally—much as
automobiles are today, with a new model season every fall. August and September were always
light months at the harvester works. But when the foundry reopened for fall production, the
new machines were in place. Not one molder who had participated in the spring strike was
back on the payroll.

McCormick seemed to have won a complete victory. All he had done was spend a vast sum of money on the new machinery. A few months after the machines went into operation, he wrote his mother triumphantly that the machines,

> are working even beyond our expectations and everybody is very much pleased with the result. Two men with one of these machines can do an average of about three days work in one. Add to this fact that we have only nine molders in the whole foundry (the rest are all laborers), and you can see what a great gain this will be to us.

But McCormick was being more optimistic than he should have been—probably to reassure his anxious mother. Actually, there were troubles with the machines. In October the McCormick company complained to the manufacturer that the castings turned out by the pneumatic molding device were too brittle to use. And in November, Cyrus McCormick was called home from a trip to New York because of a crisis in the foundry. He wrote in his diary for November 11: "Telegram from mother urging come home at once about molding machines—probably failure. Critical situation."

The machines were fixed, but even when they worked they seemed to require an endless amount of labor to keep them functioning. Before the machines were installed, the total wage bill in the foundry was about $3,000 a week. After the machines had been in operation for about six months, foundry wages totaled $8,000 a week. Most of the labor was common, unskilled work. But gradually the company had to hire additional new molders to supervise the work. Economically, the machines were a complete failure.

Still, the new technology had broken the molders' union at McCormick. And the union was unhappy. The leader of the molders was a veteran union man named Myles McPadden. He devised a new scheme that was much more dangerous to the McCormicks than the old union, with only ninety members. If there was to be no molders' union, then McPadden would simply organize all the other workers in the plant into one union or another. The workers were discontented, so the time was ripe. By February 1886 he had succeeded in organizing every major group of workers in the plant. The skilled workers—blacksmiths, machinists, and so on—joined the Metalworkers Union. McPadden encouraged the others to join the Knights of Labor, a general, nationwide union. Only 300 of the 1,400 McCormick workers remained nonunion. The lines of a new strike battle were shaping up clearly.

During this time McCormick, too, was busy. After his frustrated attempt to enlist Mayor Harrison's help, McCormick had gone to some lengths to make peace with the powerful political leader of the city. In every election before 1885 the McCormicks had opposed Harrison. After that year they supported him. As a result, Captain O'Donnell, the Irish police official who had been sympathetic to the workers in the spring of 1885, was replaced. The new man in charge of the area where the works were located was Police Inspector John Bonfield.

Bonfield had a reputation as a tough antilabor cop. He had once literally beaten his way through a crowd of strikers, shouting a slogan for which he became famous: "Clubs today spare bullets tomorrow." If there was going to be trouble in 1886, McCormick could count on the police in a way impossible a year before.

In mid-February 1886 a union committee representing all three unions—the Knights of Labor, the Metalworkers, and the Molders—presented McCormick with a series of demands:

> First, that all wages of laboring men be advanced from $1.25 to $1.50 a day. Second, that all vise hands[1] be advanced to $2.00 a day, and that blacksmith helpers be advanced to $1.75. Third, that the time the men spend in the water closet [the toilet] not be limited as heretofore. Fourth, that, inasmuch as the molding machines are a failure, the preference should be given the old hands. The scabs in the

-foundry must be discharged, and a pledge given that no man would be discharged for taking part in a strike.

The company offered to meet some of the demands, but not the fourth, which was one that must have made Cyrus McCormick furious. The unions rejected the offer and called a strike.

Before the strike was scheduled to begin, however, the company announced a complete shutdown of the plant for an indefinite period of time. Union pickets started marching near the plant, but they were kept away by 400 city policemen, now under Bonfield's command. To show its gratitude, the company served free hot meals to the police, with Cyrus McCormick sometimes personally pouring the coffee.

After two weeks the works were reopened, but only to nonunion employees. There was a loyal holdover force of only 82 men. The company furnished them with pistols. McCormick hoped they would lead an enthusiastic rush for jobs, but only 161 men showed up the first day. The second day was not much better. Once again the company's agents scoured the region for workers. Gradually, the company's situation improved a little. McCormick was willing to sacrifice almost half a year's production in order to settle the union question once and for all.

For the men on strike the situation was just as important. If they lost, their future at McCormick (or any other manufacturing plant in the city) was dim. As March turned into April, families got hungrier and tempers hotter. The explosion McCormick had avoided the year before by giving in to union demands now looked inevitable.

The situation at McCormick was complicated by the fact that during the spring of 1886 strikes were taking place all over Chicago. On May 1 all the unions in the city began a general strike for the eight-hour day, one of the largest and most heated labor actions in American history. The strike at McCormick merged with the more general agitation, involving thousands of skilled and unskilled workers from plants all over the city.

Then, on May 3, two days into the general strike for an eight-hour day, a lumber workers' union held a mass meeting to hear an address by August Spies, a radical labor agitator. The meeting took place on Black Road, just a short distance from the McCormick factory. Some McCormick men were at the meeting, even though none was a lumber worker.

The McCormicks had been so desperate for workers that they had already granted the eight-hour day (with ten hours' pay) to their scab workers. So at 3:30, two hours before the former 5:30 closing, the bell at the plant rang, and the strikebreaking workers streamed out of the plant. The striking union men at the meeting watched the scabs leave the plant on their new short schedule.

Here were union men, on strike for an eight-hour day, watching scabs who were *working* an eight-hour day. The sight proved too much. Several hundred men, some of them McCormick strikers and some of them lumber workers, mobbed the scabs leaving the plant, driving them back inside the gate. The strikers began to smash windows, unleashing anger that had been building for months. About 200 policemen, under Inspector Bonfield, were there. Suddenly, they began firing their revolvers into the crowd, forgetting Bonfield's slogan about using clubs to spare bullets. When the noise died away, two workers lay dead and several others had been wounded.

August Spies, who had been addressing the meeting, followed the crowd and witnessed the violence that occurred. The next day, in the newspaper office where he worked, he heard

---

1. "Vise hands," were workers who used a vise, a tool for holding metal being worked. They had a skill and were, therefore, to receive higher wages than the "laboring men," who were unskilled workers.

that a mass meeting was scheduled at Haymarket Square to protest the shootings at McCormick. A circular announcing the meeting was being printed in both German and English when Spies arrived at the paper.

Spies agreed to address the meeting, but he insisted that the final line in the circular be omitted. About 200 of the circulars had already been printed, but the line was removed from the rest. Few of the 20,000 circulars that were finally distributed on the streets of Chicago contained the words "Workingmen Arm Yourselves."

Spies was not, strictly speaking, a workingman. He might best be described as a radical journalist. At the time of the Chicago troubles he was thirty years old and the editor of the *Arbeiter-Zeitung*, a German-language newspaper with a radical viewpoint. He was also the business manager of an organization called the Socialist Publishing Society, a propaganda organization of a small political party known as the Socialist Labor Party.

From time to time Spies had been in trouble with the police. Only a year before, during the McCormick strike of 1885, he had angered the police by intervening in the case of a poor German servant girl who had been arrested by the police and held in jail for several days. When Spies and the girl's mother went to the jail, they discovered that the girl had been sexually molested repeatedly. Rather than keep quiet, Spies swore out a warrant for the police sergeant in charge of the jail. He lost the case for lack of evidence, but he became well known to the Chicago police.

Spies was, in short, a politically active radical who did not hesitate to condemn people in positions of authority. He was also a committed socialist politician. He hoped that the rally at Haymarket would attract enough people to fill the square, which could hold about 20,000.

Spies reached Haymarket Square late, at about 8:30 on the night of May 4. He must have felt disappointed. No meeting was in progress, and there were only about a thousand people scattered around the square. The other main speaker, a socialist named Albert R. Parsons, was nowhere in sight. Spies climbed on a wagon, sent someone to look for Parsons, and began his talk. He was a good speaker, and soon the small crowd became enthusiastic:

> The fight is going on. Now is the chance to strike for the oppressed classes. The oppressors want us to be content. They will kill us. The day is not far distant when we will resort to hanging these men. [Applause, and shouts of "Hang them now came" from the crowd.] McCormick is the man who created the row on Monday, and he must be held responsible for the murder of our brothers! [More shouts of "Hang him!"]

Spies went on in the same vein for about an hour, trying to rouse his working-class audience to anger and a sense of solidarity against their "oppressors." Then someone announced that Albert R. Parsons had been found. Spies turned over his wagon rostrum to the second speaker.

The crowd had been waiting for Parsons, for he had a reputation as a spellbinder. Unlike Spies and many other Chicago socialists, he was a native American. Born in Alabama in 1848, Parsons came from a family whose ancestry went back to 1632 in New England. He was a self-trained printer in Texas before the Civil War. During the war he fought for the Confederacy in a Texas artillery company. After the war Parsons became converted to socialism and moved to Chicago, the center of working-class politics in the United States.

Like Spies, Parsons was not a worker at all but a political journalist. He edited a radical workingmen's paper called the *Alarm*. The Haymarket rally was just one more in a long series of political speeches for him. His speech was much like that of Spies but slightly stronger in tone:

> I am not here for the purpose of inciting anybody, but to speak out, to tell the facts as they exist, even though it shall cost me my life before morning. It behooves you, as

you love your wife and children—if you don't want to see them perish with hunger, killed or cut down like dogs in the street—Americans, in the interest of your liberty and independence, to *arm*, to *arm* yourselves!

Here again there was applause from the crowd and shouts of "We'll do it! We're ready!"

What Parsons and Spies did not know was that the crowd was full of police detectives. Every few minutes one or another ran back to a nearby station house to report what the speakers were saying. Waiting in the station were almost 200 policemen, fully armed, and under the command of none other than John Bonfield.

Parsons and Spies probably did not notice Mayor Carter Harrison in the crowd, either. Only the mayor's presence had kept Bonfield from breaking up the meeting. As Parsons finished, the mayor left; it was obvious to him that everything was peaceful. It was almost ten o'clock and rain was in the air. Most of the crowd, too, began to drift off as the third speaker, Samuel Fielden, began to speak.

Suddenly, 180 policemen (a group almost as large as the crowd itself) marched into the square and up to the wagon where Fielden was speaking. One of the captains turned to the crowd and said: "In the name of the people of the State of Illinois, I command this meeting immediately and peaceably to disperse." After a moment the police captain repeated his order. The crowd was already starting to melt away (it was almost 10:30 by now). Fielden had stopped speaking and was climbing down from the wagon platform. "We are peaceable," Fielden said to Bonfield.

At that moment, without any warning, a dynamite bomb was thrown (it is not known from where or by whom) at the police. The fuse burned for a second or two after the bomb struck the ground. Then it went off with a deafening roar. Screams split the air as people ran in all directions. A number of policemen lay on the ground, one dead and the others wounded. Quickly, the police reformed their ranks, and some of them began to fire into the crowd. Other policemen waded into the confusion swinging their clubs. The uproar lasted only a minute or two. Then suddenly the square was empty.

In addition to the dead policeman, seventy-three of his colleagues were wounded, six of whom died later. Four civilians were killed, and the official reports listed twelve as wounded. The twelve were those who had been too badly hurt to leave the square. Probably several times as many limped or struggled home and never became official statistics.

Like most such incidents, the Haymarket affair had been short. And considering what could have happened, very few people were hurt. But it occurred on the heels of trouble at the McCormick plant, in the midst of the strike for an eight-hour day, with 80,000 Chicago workingmen off the job. Thus the Haymarket bomb touched off a near-panic in the city and much of the rest of the nation. Thousands of respectable citizens convinced themselves that a dangerous conspiracy of anarchists, socialists, and communists was at work to overthrow the government and carry out a bloody revolution. One of the leading business magazines of the day, *Bradstreets'*, spoke for thousands of Americans when it said of the Haymarket incident:

> This week's happenings at Chicago go to show that the threats of the anarchists against the existing order are not idle. In a time of disturbance, desperate men have a power for evil out of proportion to their numbers. They are desperate fanatics who are opposed to all laws. There is no room for anarchy in the political system of the United States.

Also important was the fact that many people had been frightened and angered by a recent flood of immigration from Europe to America—and many of the "anarchists" were also foreigners. Not only in Chicago but all over the nation, newspaper editorialists and public speakers demanded the immediate arrest and conviction of the alien "radicals" who had conspired to murder honest policemen and subvert law and order. The result was a swift and efficient series of illegal raids by the Chicago police. They searched property without warrants. They imprisoned people without charging them and threatened potential witnesses. All in all, the authorities arrested and questioned about 200 "suspects"—probably none of whom had anything at all to do with the bombing.

In this heated atmosphere, fueled by journalists who whipped up unreasonable fears of an anarchist conspiracy, a jury met to determine whether indictments could be brought against anyone for the violence. It decided that although the specific person who threw the bomb could not be identified, anyone who urged violence was a "conspirator" and was as guilty of murder as the bomb thrower. On the basis of this decision, another jury met and indicted thirty-one persons on counts of murder. Of the thirty-one, eight were eventually tried, all of them political radicals. Most had not even been present at the Haymarket bombing.

The effect of the Haymarket affair had now become clear. What had begun weeks before as an ordinary strike at the McCormick works had been transformed into a crusade against political radicalism, most of which was said to be foreign in origin. Only Parsons and Samuel Fielden were not German or of German descent. The names of the other six would have been as natural in Berlin or Hamburg as in Chicago: August Spies, Michael Schwab, Adolph Fischer, George Engel, Louis Lingg, and Oscar Neebe.

In one way or another, all the defendants had some connection with the labor movement and with political agitation for revolution. Several of them were anarchists, though their ideas about anarchism as a philosophy were vague. They might as well have called themselves socialists, as several of them did at one time or another. In general, they were intellectuals. Their jobs were connected with radical journalism in either the English-or German-language press. They did not all know one another, but by the time their trial was over, most of them were probably "comrades," a word they used more and more in the months ahead.

On the other side of the battle were all the forces of law, order, and authority. True, some agreed with Mayor Harrison that the Haymarket meeting had been peaceful, that the whole idea of a conspiracy was a false and legally incorrect notion. But most of Chicago society (including even many elements of the labor movement) favored a quick conviction and the hanging of all eight defendants. The judge who tried the case, the prosecuting attorney, most business leaders, almost all the local clergymen—almost everyone who had anything to say in Chicago—were convinced even before the trial began that the defendants were guilty. Moreover, most of Chicago's leading citizens, and their counterparts in the rest of the country, agreed that the trial was a struggle to the death between American republicanism and foreign anarchism. The entire established order of American society, with very few exceptions, was determined to make an example of the "conspirators."

The Haymarket trial began June 21, 1886. The first three weeks of the seven-week trial were spent selecting a jury. Under Illinois law, the defense had the right to reject a total of 160 jurors on peremptory challenges—that is, without having to discuss a juror's qualifications and abide by the judge's decision. As one prospective juror after another was called, it became clear that most of them were extremely prejudiced against the defendants. The defense attorneys quickly used up their 160 challenges. They then had to show cause for turning down a juror and depend on the judge, Joseph Gary, to rule fairly. Again and again, plainly biased jurors were accepted by the judge—whose own prejudice against the defendants became apparent as the process went on. The result was a jury composed of twelve citizens who obviously wished to hang the defendants.

In his opening statement, prosecuting attorney Julius Grinnell set the tone of the entire trial:

> Gentlemen, for the first time in the history of our country people are on trial for endeavoring to make anarchy the rule. I hope that while the youngest of us lives this will be the last and only time when such a trial shall take place. In the light of the 4th of May, we now know that the preachings of anarchy by these defendants, hourly and daily for years, have been sapping our institutions. Where they have cried murder, bloodshed, anarchy, and dynamite, they have meant what they said. The firing on Fort Sumter was a terrible thing to our country, but it was open warfare. I think it was nothing compared with this insidious, infamous plot to ruin our laws and our country.

It was obvious that this would not be an ordinary murder trial. The defendants would be judged by their words and beliefs. A ninth "conspirator," Rudolph Schnaubelt, had fled. The prosecution would try to prove that he had thrown the bomb. The next step would be to convict the other eight of conspiracy, which would carry the same penalty as murder itself. And they would be convicted by the fact that they had made speeches and written newspaper articles urging violent revolution. Day after day the prosecution offered evidence about the defendants' beliefs, their writings, and even pamphlets they had not written but supposedly helped to sell.

The prosecution had weak cases against the individual defendants. They were able to prove that one, Lingg, had actually made bombs. But Lingg was a stranger to most of the others, and he had not even been at Haymarket Square. Parsons, Spies, Fischer, and Schwab had left the square before the bomb was thrown. George Engel proved that he had been home drinking a glass of beer with his wife. In the end the prosecution's case rested on a theory of "general conspiracy to promote violence." No evidence of a single violent act was brought into court that could withstand even the mildest cross-examination by the frustrated defense attorneys.

After four weeks of testimony the jury retired. The jury members had been instructed by Judge Gary in such a way as to make conviction almost inevitable, and they needed only three hours to discuss the matter. After this short deliberation the jury filed solemnly back into the courtroom. It was ten o'clock, August 19, 1886, when the foreman read the verdict.

> We the jury find the defendants Spies, Schwab, Fielden, Parsons, Fischer, Engel, and Lingg guilty of murder in the manner and form as charged, and fix the penalty at death. We find Oscar Neebe[2] guilty of murder in the manner and form as charged, and fix the penalty at imprisonment in the penitentiary for fifteen years.

Years later Judge Gary recalled that "the verdict was received by the friends of social order with a roar of almost universal approval."

Before they were sentenced, each of the defendants made a speech to the court. Spies spoke for all of them when he said, in the German accent he had never lost:

> There was not a syllable said about anarchism at the Haymarket meeting. But "anarchism is on trial," foams Mr. Grinnell. If that is the case, your honor, very well; you may sentence me, for I am an anarchist. I believe that the state of classes—the state where one class dominates and lives upon the labor of another class—is doomed to die, to make room for a free society, voluntary association, or universal brotherhood,

---

2. Neebe was the youngest defendant; almost no evidence had been presented against him. Most of the jury's three-hour deliberation was devoted to this case.

if you like. You may pronounce the sentence upon me, honorable judge, but let the world know that in A.D. 1886, in the state of Illinois, eight men were sentenced to death because they believed in a better future.

There were appeals, of course, first to state courts and then to the Supreme Court of the United States. One by one the appeals failed. Then there were pleas to the governor of Illinois for mercy, and the sentences of Fielden and Schwab were commuted to life. Lingg, the bomb maker, who was probably half mad, committed suicide in jail—using dynamite set off by a fuse that he lit with his jail-cell candle. The other four condemned men—Engel, Spies, Parsons, and Fischer—were hanged on November 11. As the four stood on the scaffold, ropes around their necks and hoods over their heads, Spies broke the deep silence by shouting: "There will come a time when our silence will be more powerful than the voices you strangle today!"

At the McCormick works the situation had returned to normal months earlier. On May 7, 1886, three days after the Haymarket bombing, Cyrus McCormick was able to write in his diary: "A good force of men at the works today, and things are resuming their former appearance." Three days later, taking full advantage of the public outrage over the "devilish plot," as McCormick called it, at Haymarket Square, the McCormick works quietly resumed the ten-hour day. On Monday, May 10, McCormick wrote: "Things going smoothly. We returned to 5:30 closing hour today, instead of 3:30."

IV

THE FIRST CHAPTER OF CHILDREN'S RIGHTS

Peter Stevens and Marian Eide

Nothing seems more horrible than stories of the plight of abused children. Modern media coverage of such events prompt outpourings of public sympathy, concern and offers of aid. At the same time, however, a great debate is building between the advocates of child protection on the one hand and the antigovernment fundamentalists on the other hand who see no role for government in the child parent relationship. This is not a new debate. In 1874 a young girl would enter the New York legal system as a victim of child abuse. The compelling case of little Mary Ellen would begin the legal struggle to provide protection through the law and the courts for the victims of child abuse. Peter Stevens and Marian Eide provide a captivating story in this article of not only the sad tale of a little girl but also an account of the legal and charitable efforts that would be united to come to her relief.

In the quiet New York courtroom, the little girl began to speak. "My name is Mary Ellen Mc-Cormack. I don't know how old I am. . . . I have never had but one pair of shoes, but can't recollect when that was. I have had no shoes or stockings on this winter. . . . I have never had on a particle of flannel. My bed at night is only a piece of carpet, stretched on the floor underneath a window, and I sleep in my little undergarment, with a quilt over me. I am never allowed to play with any children or have any company whatever. Mamma has been in the habit of whipping and beating me almost every day. She used to whip me with a twisted whip, a raw hide. The whip always left black and blue marks on my body. I have now on my head two black and blue marks which were made by mamma with the whip, and a cut on the left side of my forehead which was made by a pair of scissors in mamma's hand. She struck me with the scissors and cut me. I have no recollection of ever having been kissed, and have never been kissed by mamma. I have never been taken on my mamma's lap, or caressed or petted. I never dared to speak to anybody, because if I did I would get whipped. . . . Whenever mamma went out I was locked up in the bedroom . . . I have no recollection of ever being in the street in my life."

At the beginning of 1874 there were no legal means in the United States to save a child from abuse. Mary Ellen's eloquent testimony changed that, changed our legal system's view of the rights of the child.

Yet more than a century later the concerns that arose from Mary Ellen's case are still being battled over in the courts. The classic dilemmas of just how deeply into the domestic realm the governmental arm can reach and what the obligations of public government are to the private individual take on particular urgency in considering child abuse.

Early in 1989, in the case of *DeShaney vs. Winnebago County*, the Supreme Court declared that the government is not obligated to protect its citizens against harm inflicted by private individuals. DeShaney brought the case before the court in a suit against county social service agencies that had failed to intervene when her estranged husband abused their son, Joshua, who, as a result of his father's brutality, suffered permanent brain damage. The father was convicted, but his former wife believes that fault also lies with the agencies, whose failure to intercede violated her son's Fourteenth Amendment right not to be deprived of life or liberty without due process of the law. Chief Justice William H. Rehnquist wrote that intervening officials are often charged with "improperly intruding into the parent-child relationship." Justice William J. Brennan, Jr., dissenting, wrote: "Inaction can be every bit as abusive of power as action, [and] oppression can result when a State undertakes a vital duty and then ignores it."

The difficulty in bringing Mary Ellen McCormack into the New York Supreme Court in 1874 grew from similar controversy over the role of government in family matters, and Mary Ellen's sad history is not so different from Joshua DeShaney's.

When Mary Ellen's mother, Frances Connor, immigrated to the United States from England in 1858, she took a job at the St. Nicholas Hotel in New York City as a laundress. There she met an Irishman named Thomas Wilson who worked in the hotel kitchen shucking oysters. They were married in April 1862, shortly after Wilson had been drafted into the 69th New York, a regiment in the famous Irish Brigade. Early in 1864 she gave birth to their daughter, whom she named Mary after her mother and Ellen after her sister.

The birth of her daughter seems to have heralded the beginning of Frances Wilson's own decline. Her husband was killed that same year in the brutal fighting at Cold Harbor, Virginia, and with a diminished income she found it necessary to look for a job. In May 1864, unable to pay someone to watch the baby while she was at work, she gave Mary Ellen over to the care of a woman named Mary Score for two dollars a week, the whole of her widow's pension. Child farming was a common practice at that time, and many women made a living taking in unwanted children just as others took in laundry. Score lived in a tenement in the infamous warrens of Mulberry Bend, where thousands of immigrants crowded into small, airless rooms, and it is likely that providing foster care was her only means of income.

Finally Frances Wilson became unable to pay for the upkeep of her child; three weeks after the payments ceased, Score turned Mary Ellen over to the Department of Charities. The little girl—whose mother was never to see her again—was sent to Blackwells Island in July 1865. Her third home was certainly no more pleasant than Mulberry Bend. Mary Ellen was among a group of sick and hungry foundlings; fully two-thirds of them would die before reaching maturity.

The same slum-bred diseases that ravaged the children on Blackwells Island had also claimed all three children of a couple named Thomas and Mary McCormack. So when Thomas frequently bragged of the three children he had fathered by another woman, his wife was more receptive to the idea of adopting them than she might otherwise have been. Those children, he told her, were still alive, though their mother had turned them over to the care of the city.

On January 2, 1866, the McCormacks went to the Department of Charities to reclaim one of the children Thomas's mistress had abandoned. The child they chose as their own was Mary Ellen Wilson. Because the McCormacks were not asked to provide any proof of relation to the child and gave only the reference of their family doctor, there is no evidence that

Thomas was in any way related to the child he brought home that day. More than a month later an indenture was filed for Mary Ellen in which the McCormacks promised to report on her condition each year. There were no other requirements.

Shortly after bringing the child home, Thomas McCormack died, and his widow married a man named Francis Connolly. Little more than that is known of the early childhood of Mary Ellen. She came to her new home in a flannel petticoat, and when her clothing was removed from Connolly's home as evidence six years later, there was barely enough to fill a tiny suitcase. She was beaten, set to work, deprived of daylight, and locked in closets for days at a time; she was rarely bathed, never kissed, and never addressed with a gentle word. During the six years she lived with Connolly, only two reports on her progress were filed with the Commissioners of Charities and Correction.

Late in 1873 Etta Angell Wheeler, a Methodist caseworker serving in the tenements of New York City, received a disturbing report. It came from Margaret Bingham, a landlord in Hell's Kitchen, and told of a terrible case of child abuse. The child's parents had been tenants of Bingham for about four years, and almost immediately after they moved in, Bingham began to observe how cruelly they treated their child, Mary Ellen. They confined her in close quarters during hot weather, kept her severely underdressed in cold, beat her daily, and left her unattended for hours at a time. On several occasions Bingham tried to intervene; each time the child's mother said she would call upon the fullest resources of the law before she would allow any interference in her home. Finally Bingham resorted to threat: The beatings and ill treatment would have to stop, or the family would be evicted. When her plan backfired and the family left, Bingham, in a last-ditch effort, sent for Etta Wheeler. In order to observe Mary Ellen's predicament, Wheeler went to the Connollys' neighbor, an ailing tubercular woman named Mary Smitt. Enlisting Smitt's aid, she proposed that Mary Ellen be sent over each day to check on the patient. Smitt reluctantly agreed, and on the pretext of inquiring about this sick neighbor, Wheeler knocked on Mary Connolly's door.

Inside she saw a "pale, thin child, bare-foot, in a thin, scanty dress so tattered that I could see she wore but one garment besides.

"It was December and the weather bitterly cold. She was a tiny mite, the size of five years, though, as afterward appeared, she was then nine. From a pan set upon a low stool she stood washing dishes, struggling with a frying pan about as heavy as herself. Across the table lay a brutal whip of twisted leather strands and the child's meager arms and legs bore many marks of its use. But the saddest part of her story was written on her face in its look of suppression and misery, the face of a child unloved, of a child that had seen only the fearsome side of life . . . I never saw her again until the day of her rescue, three months later. . . . "

Though social workers often witnessed scenes of cruelty, poverty, and grief, Wheeler found Mary Ellen's plight especially horrifying. She went first to the police; they told her she must be able to furnish proof of assault in order for them to act. Charitable institutions she approached offered to care for the child, but first she must be brought to them through legal means. There were none. Every effort Wheeler made proved fruitless. Though there were laws to protect children—laws, in fact, to prevent assault and battery to any person—there were no means available for intervention in a child's home.

Finally Wheeler's niece had an idea. The child, she said, was a member of the animal kingdom; surely Henry Bergh, the founder of the American Society for the Prevention of Cruelty to Animals, who was famous for his dramatic rescue of mistreated horses in the streets of New York, might be willing to intervene. Within the hour Wheeler had arranged a meeting with Bergh. Despite its apparent strangeness, this sort of appeal was not new to

Bergh. Once before he had tried to intervene in a case of child abuse and had failed. This time he was more cautious.

"Very definite testimony is needed to warrant interference between a child and those claiming guardianship," Bergh told Wheeler. "Will you not send me a written statement that, at my leisure, I may judge the weight of the evidence and may also have time to consider if this society should interfere? I promise to consider the case carefully."

Wheeler provided a statement immediately, including in it the observations of neighbors to whom she had spoken. Bergh was convinced. "No time is to be lost," he wrote his lawyer, Elbridge T. Gerry. "Instruct me how to proceed."

The next day Wheeler again visited the sick woman in Hell's Kitchen and found in her room a young man who, on hearing Wheeler's name, said, "I was sent to take the census in this house. I have been in every room." Wheeler then knew him to be a detective for Bergh.

On the basis of the detective's observations and the testimony provided by Etta Wheeler, Bergh's lawyers, Gerry and Ambrose Monell, appeared before Judge Abraham R. Lawrence of the New York Supreme Court to present a petition on behalf of Mary Ellen. They showed that Mary Ellen was held illegally by the Connollys, who were neither her natural parents nor her lawful custodians, and went on to describe the physical abuse Mary Ellen endured, the marks and bruises on her body, and the general state of deprivation that characterized her existence. They offered a list of witnesses willing to testify on behalf of the child and concluded by stating that there was ample evidence to indicate that she was in clear danger of being maimed or even killed. The lawyers requested that a warrant be issued, the child removed from her home and placed in protective custody, and her parents brought to trial.

Bergh testified that his efforts on behalf of the child were in no way connected to his work with abused animals and that they did not make use of the special legal provisions set up for that purpose. Because of Bergh's association with animal rescue, to this day the case is often described as having originated in his conviction that the child was a member of the animal kingdom. Bergh, however, insisted that his actions were merely those of any humane citizen and that he intended to prevent cruelties inflicted on children through any legal means available.

Judge Lawrence issued a warrant under Section 65 of the Habeas Corpus Act as requested. This provision read in part: "Whenever it shall appear by satisfactory proof that any one is held in illegal confinement or custody, and that there is good reason to believe that he will . . . suffer some irreparable injury, before he can be relieved by the issuing of a *habeas corpus* or *certiorari*, any court or officer authorized to issue such writs, may issue a warrant . . . [and] bring him before such court or officer, to be dealt with according to law."

The press of the day hailed Gerry's use of Section 65 of the Habeas Corpus Act as brilliant. The act was rarely invoked, and the legal means for removing a child from its home were nonexistent. In using the little-known law, Gerry created a new method for intervention.

That same day, April 9, 1874, Mary Ellen was taken from her home and brought into Judge Lawrence's court. Having no adequate clothing of her own, the child had been wrapped in a carriage blanket by the policemen who held her in custody. A reporter on the scene described her as "a bright little girl, with features indicating unusual mental capacity, but with a care-worn, stunted, and prematurely old look. . . . no change of custody or condition could be much for the worse."

The reporter Jacob Riis was present in the court. "I saw a child brought in . . . at the sight of which men wept aloud, and I heard the story of little Mary Ellen told . . . that stirred the soul of a city and roused the conscience of a world that had forgotten, and as I looked, I knew I was where the first chapter of children's rights was being written." Her body and face were terribly bruised; her hands and feet "showed the plain marks of great exposure." And in what almost instantly seemed to condemn Mrs. Connolly before the court, the child's face bore a fresh gash through her eyebrow and across her left cheek that barely missed the eye itself. Mary Ellen was to carry this scar throughout her life. Interestingly, there is no further mention in the ample reports surrounding Mary Ellen's case of her foster father, Francis Connolly. He was never brought into court, never spoke publicly concerning the child. All her life Mary Ellen exhibited a frightened timidity around men, yet it was against her foster mother that she testified.

On the evening of her detention, Mary Ellen was turned over to the temporary custody of the matron of police headquarters. The next day, April 10, the grand jury read five indictments against Mary Connolly for assault and battery, felonious assault, assault with intent to do bodily harm, assault with intent to kill, and assault with intent to maim. Once the stepmother had been brought into the legal system, there were ample means to punish her.

Mary Ellen herself was brought in to testify against the woman she had called her mother. On her second appearance in court she seemed almost wholly altered. She was clothed in a new suit, and her pale face reflected the kindness that surrounded her. She carried with her a new picture book, probably the first she had ever owned. She acted open and uninhibited with strangers, and interestingly, seemed to show no great fear of her mother or any apparent enmity toward her.

The lawyers Gerry and Monell gathered several witnesses against Mary Connolly, among them neighbors, Wheeler, and Mary Ellen herself. Margaret Bingham said she had seen the child locked up in a room and had told other neighbors, but they said there was no point in interfering since the police would do nothing. Bingham had tried to open the window of the child's room to let in some air, but it would not lift more than an inch. As a constant presence and reminder, a cowhide whip was locked in the room with the child. Wheeler recounted her first visit to Mary Ellen, during which the child washed dishes that seemed twice her size and was apparently oblivious of the visitor's presence. The whip lay on the table next to her. The next day, when Wheeler came by again, the child was sewing, and the whip lay on a chair near her.

Then it was the mother's turn to testify. On the witness stand Mary Connolly showed herself to be a woman of some spirit. Despite her treatment of the child, there is something compelling in Connolly's strength and humor. At one point the prosecutor asked if she had an occupation beyond housekeeping. "Well," she said, "I sleep with the boss." As the trial wore on, she became enraged at Gerry's prodding questions; finally she accused him of being "ignorant of the difficulties of bringing up and governing children." Yet she admitted that contrary to regulations, in the six years she had Mary Ellen in her custody, she had reported on her condition to the Commissioners of Charities and Correction only twice.

Two indictments were brought against Connolly, the first for her assault on the child with scissors on April 7, the second for the continual assaults inflicted on the child throughout the years 1873 and 1874. After twenty minutes of deliberation the jury returned a verdict of guilty of assault and battery. Connolly was sentenced to one year of hard labor in the city penitentiary, then known as the Tombs. In handing down this sentence, the judge defined it not only as a punishment to Connolly but also as a statement of precedence in child-abuse cases.

Mary Ellen never returned to the Connollys' home. In the ensuing months the publicity that her case received brought in many claims of relation. But on investigating, her guardian, Judge Lawrence, discovered the stories were fictions, and he finally placed the child in the Sheltering Arms, a home for grown girls; soon after, she was moved to the Woman's Aid Society and Home for Friendless Girls. This mirrors another critical problem in the system's treatment of

minors. All juveniles were handled by the Department of Charities and Correction, and whether they were orphaned or delinquent, their treatment was the same. And so it was that the ten-
year-old Mary Ellen was placed in a home with mostly delinquent adolescents.

Etta Wheeler knew this was wrong for Mary Ellen, and she expressed her hesitations to
Judge Lawrence. He, in turn, consulted with Henry Bergh, and eventually they agreed to turn
the girl over to Etta Wheeler herself. Unable to imagine giving up her work in the slums of
New York City but believing that Mary Ellen deserved a better environment, Wheeler
brought the child to her mother in North Chili, New York. Wheeler's mother became ill
shortly afterward, and Mary Ellen was raised mostly by Wheeler's sister.

"Here began a new life," Wheeler wrote. "The child was an interesting study, so long shut
within four walls and now in a new world. Woods, fields, 'green things growing,' were all
strange to her, she had not known them. She had to learn, as a baby does, to walk upon the
ground,—she had walked only upon floors, and her eye told her nothing of uneven
surfaces. . . . But in this home there were other children and they taught her as children alone
can teach each other. They taught her to play, to be unafraid, to know her rights and to claim
them. She shared their happy, busy life from the making of mud pies up to charming birthday
parties and was fast becoming a normal child."

The happiness of her years in the upstate New York countryside lies in stark contrast to
her early childhood. And indeed, as Wheeler wrote, she learned by example the ways of normal childhood. She grew up strong and well, learning how to read and playing with friends
and pet kittens. In 1875 Wheeler reported to Gerry that Mary Ellen was growing up as a normal child. "She has some faults that are of the graver sort. She tells fibs and sticks to them
bravely, steals lumps of sugar & cookies and only confesses when the crumbs are found in her
pocket—in short she is very much like other children, loving—responding to kindness &
praise, hating a task unless there be a play, or a reward thereof, and inevitably 'forgetting' what
she does not wish to remember—what children do not do some or all of these forbidden
things! She is a favorite with nearly all the people who have come to know her."

When she was twenty-four, Mary Ellen married a widower named Louis Schutt and with
him had two children, Etta—named after the woman who had rescued her—and Florence.
She adopted a third, orphaned child, Eunice. She also raised Louis Schutt's three children
from his first wife.

In 1911 Wheeler visited her protégé in her home, "finding her well and happy. . . . The
family income is small, but Mary Ellen is a prudent housewife & they are comfortable. The two
daughters are promising girls." The eldest daughter, Etta, worked industriously through that
summer, finished high school, and became a teacher. Florence followed her sister's path, teaching first grade for thirty-eight years. When she retired, the elementary school in North Chili was
renamed in her honor. Eunice earned a business degree, married, and raised two sons.

Florence remembers her mother as a solemn woman who came alive whenever she listened to Irish jigs and especially to "The Irish Washerwoman." She was unfailingly generous
with her time and her affection. Her years in North Chili had saved her from the vicious cycle
abused children often suffer of becoming abusers themselves. According to Florence her
mother was capable of sternness and certainly willing to punish her daughters, but the terrible
experiences of her early childhood never spilled into her own child rearing. As Etta Wheeler
wrote, "To her children, two bright, dutiful daughters, it has been her joy to give a happy
childhood in sharp contrast to her own."

Etta and Florence often asked their mother about the Connollys, but Mary Ellen was reluctant to speak of her early years. She did show her daughters the scars on her arms where she
had been burned with a hot iron, and of course they could see the scissors scar across her face.

Florence distinctly recalls that in the few times they spoke of her mother's years in New York City, she never mentioned a woman inflicting her injuries; it was always a man.

In October of 1913 Mary Ellen Schutt attended a meeting of the American Humane Society in Rochester. She was accompanied by Etta Wheeler, who was there to present a paper entitled "The Finding of Mary Ellen." The paper concluded: "If the memory of her earliest years is sad, there is this comfort that the cry of her wrongs awoke the world to the need of organized relief for neglected and abused children."

Mary Ellen died on October 30, 1956, at the age of ninety-two. She was survived by her two daughters, her adopted daughter, three stepchildren, three grandchildren, and five great-grandchildren. More important, she was survived by the beginning of a movement to prevent the repetition of tragedies like her own. On December 15, 1874, Henry Bergh, Elbridge Gerry, and James Wright founded the New York Society for the Prevention of Cruelty to Children (SPCC) with the ample assistance of Cornelius Vanderbilt. It was the first organization of its kind in America. At the outset of their work the founders signed a statement of purpose: "The undersigned, desirous of rescuing the unprotected children of this city and State from the cruelty and demoralization which neglect and abandonment engender, hereby engage to aid, with their sympathy and support, the organization and working of a Children's Protective Society, having in view the realization of so important a purpose."

The SPCC saw its role essentially as a legal one. As an agent or a friend of the court, the society endeavored to intervene on the behalf of children, enforcing the laws that were in existence to prevent cruelty toward them and at the same time introducing new legislation on their behalf.

At the first meeting of the SPCC on December 16, 1874, Gerry stressed the fact that the most crucial role of the society lay in the rescue of children from abusive situations. From there, he pointed out, there were many excellent groups available to care for and shelter children and many state laws to punish abusive parents. He went on to predict that as soon as abusers learned that the law could reach them, there would be few cases like that of Mary Ellen.

Bergh was less optimistic. At the same meeting, he pointed out that neglected and abused children were to become the mothers and fathers of the country and that unless their interests were defended, the interests of society in general would suffer.

In its first year the SPCC investigated more than three hundred cases of child abuse. Many people felt threatened by the intrusion of the government into their private lives; discipline, they believed, was a family issue, and outside influence was not only unwelcome but perhaps even unconstitutional. When, with the aid of a state senator, James W. Booth, Gerry introduced in the New York legislature a law entitled "An Act to Prevent and Punish Wrongs to Children," the proposal was immediately and vigorously attacked. The *New York World* wrote that Bergh was to be authorized to "break into the garrets of the poor and carry off their children upon the suspicion of spanking." According to the *World*, the law would give Bergh "power to discipline all the naughty children of New York. . . . We sincerely hope that it may not be finally kicked out of the legislature, as it richly deserves to be, until the public mind shall have had time to get itself thoroughly enlightened as to the state of things in which it has become possible for such a person as Mr. Bergh to bring the Legislature to the point of seriously entertaining such an impudently senseless measure. This bill is a bill to supersede the common law in favor of Mr. Bergh, and the established tribunals of justice in favor of an irresponsible private corporation." The bill was passed in 1876, however, and became the foundation upon which the SPCC performed its work.

From its initial concentration on preventing abuse in the home, the society broadened its franchise to battle neglect, abandonment, and the exploitation of children for economic gain.

In 1885, after considerable effort by the SPCC and in the face of yet more opposition, Gerry secured passage of a bill that made labor by children under the age of fourteen illegal.

As the explosive story of the death of Lisa Steinberg in the home of her adoptive parents revealed to the nation in 1987, abuse still haunts American society. There are still legal difficulties in removing a child from an abusive situation. In 1987 the House Select Committee on Children, Youth, and Families reported that the incidence of child abuse, particularly sexual abuse and neglect, is rising; in 1985 alone almost two million children were referred to protective agencies. In part, the committee said, this increase was due to a greater awareness of the issue, and there has also been an increased effort to educate children themselves about situations that constitute abuse or molestation and about ways to get help.

Despite a plethora of programs designed to address abuse, the committee concluded that not enough is being done. The most effective programs were found to be those that worked to prevent the occurrence of abuse at the outset through education in parenting techniques, through intervention in high-risk situations, such as unwanted pregnancies, and through screening for mental and emotional difficulties. However, funding for public welfare programs has fallen far below the demands, and what funding there is must frequently be diverted to intervene in more and more sensational and hopeless cases.

If there is still much hard, sad work ahead, there is also much that has been accomplished. And all of it began when Mary Ellen McCormack spoke and, in speaking, freed herself and thousands of other children from torment.

V

RIDE-IN:
A CENTURY OF PROTEST BEGINS

Alan F. Westin

After more than 250 years of slavery, African Americans saw the end of that evil institu-
tion with the ratification of the 13th amendment to the U.S. Constitution in 1865. Then
came the 14th and 15th amendments as well as Civil Rights laws that seemed to signal the
end of the horror that had plagued the nation since the early days of the Jamestown colony.
With the passage of the Civil Rights Act of 1875 it appeared that African Americans
would indeed be integrated into all aspects of American life. But the law was challenged,
and the Supreme Court's decision would open the door to what would become known as
the Jim Crow society of the old South, America's system of apartheid. This article describes
the background to the 1875 law and the actions of the court in dealing with it.

It began one day early in January when a black named Robert Fox boarded a streetcar in Louisville, Kentucky, dropped his coin into the fare box, and sat down in the white section of the car. Ordered to move, he refused, and the driver threw him off the car. Shortly after, Fox filed a charge of assault and battery against the streetcar company in the federal district court, claiming that separate seating policies were illegal and the driver's actions were therefore improper. The district judge instructed the jury that under federal law common carriers must serve all passengers equally without regard to race. So instructed, the jury found the company rules to be invalid and awarded damages of fifteen dollars (plus $72.80 in legal costs) to Mr. Fox.

Immediately there was sharp criticism of the Fox decision from the city and state administrations, both Democratic; the company defied the court's ruling and continued segregated seating. After several meetings with local federal officials and white attorneys cooperating with them, Louisville black leaders decided to launch a full-scale "ride-in." At 7 P.M. on May 12, a young black boy boarded a streetcar near the Willard Hotel, walked past the driver, and took a seat among the white passengers. The driver, under new company regulations, did not attempt to throw him off but simply stopped the car, lit a cigar, and refused to proceed until he moved to "his place." While the governor, the Louisville chief of police, and other prominent citizens looked on from the sidewalks, a large crowd which included an increasingly noisy mob of jeering white teenagers gathered around the streetcar.

Before long, there were shouts of "Put him out!" "Hit him!" "Kick him!" "Hang him!" Several white youths climbed into the car and began yelling insults in the face of the young black rider. He refused to answer—or to move. The youths dragged him from his seat, pulled him off the car, and began to beat him. Only when the boy started to defend himself did the city police intervene: they arrested him for disturbing the peace and took him to jail.

This time the trial was held in Louisville city court, not the federal court. The magistrate ruled that streetcar companies were not under any obligation to treat blacks exactly as they treated whites, and that any federal measures purporting to create such obligations would be "clearly invalid" under the constitutions of Kentucky and the United States. The defendant was fined, and the judge delivered a warning to Louisville blacks that further ride-ins would be punished.

But the ride-in campaign was not halted that easily. In the following days, streetcar after streetcar was entered by blacks who took seats in the white section. Now the drivers got off the cars entirely. On several occasions, the black riders drove the cars themselves, to the sound of cheers from black spectators. Then violence erupted. Bands of white youths and men began to throw black riders off the cars; windows were broken, cars were overturned, and for a time a general race riot threatened. Moderate Kentucky newspapers and many community leaders deplored the fighting; the Republican candidate for governor denounced the streetcar company's segregation policies and blamed the violence on Democratic encouragement of white extremists.

By this time, newspapers across the country were carrying reports of the conflict, and many editorials denounced the seating regulations. In Louisville, federal marshals and the United States attorney backed the rights of the black riders and stated that federal court action would be taken if necessary. There were even rumors that the President might send troops.

Under these threats, the streetcar company capitulated. Soon, all the city transit companies declared that "it was useless to try to resist or evade the enforcement by the United States authorities of the claim of blacks to ride in the cars." To "avoid serious collisions," the company would thereafter allow all passengers to sit where they chose. Although a few disturbances took place in the following months, and some white intransigents boycotted the streetcars, mixed seating became a common practice. The Kentucky press soon pointed with pride to the spirit of conciliation and harmony which prevailed in travel facilities within the city, calling it a model for good race relations. Never again would Louisville street cars be segregated.

The event may have the familiar ring of recent history, but it is not, for it occurred in 1871. The streetcars were horse-drawn. The President who considered ordering troops to Louisville was ex-General Grant, not ex-General Eisenhower. The Republican gubernatorial candidate who supported the black riders, John Marshall Harlan, was not a post-World War II leader of the G.O.P. but a former slaveholder from one of Kentucky's oldest and most famous political families. And the "new" blacks who waged this ride-in were not members of the Congress of Racial Equality and the National Association for the Advancement of Colored People, or followers of Dr. Martin Luther King, but former slaves who were fighting for civil rights in their own time, and with widespread success.

And yet these dramatic sit-ins, ride-ins, and walk-ins of the 1870s are almost unknown to the American public today. The standard American histories do not mention them, providing only thumbnail references to "bayonet-enforced" racial contacts during Reconstruction. Most commentators view the black citizens' resort to direct action as an invention of the last decade. Clearly, then, it is time that the civil-rights struggle of the 1870s and 1880s was rescued from newspaper files and court archives, not only because it is historically important but also because it has compelling relevance for our own era.

Contrary to common assumptions today, no state in the Union during the 1870s, including those south of the Mason-Dixon line, required separation of whites and blacks in places of public accommodation. Admission and arrangement policies were up to individual owners. In the North and West, many theatres, hotels, restaurants, and public carriers served black patrons without hesitation or discrimination. Some accepted blacks only in second-class accommodations, such as smoking cars on railroads or balconies in theatres, where they sat among whites who did not have first-class tickets. Other northern and western establishments, especially the more exclusive ones, refused black patronage entirely.

The situation was similar in the larger cities of the southern and border states. Many establishments admitted blacks to second-class facilities. Some gave first-class service to those of privileged social status—government officials, army officers, newspapermen, and clergymen. On the other hand, many places of public accommodation, particularly in the rural areas and smaller cities of the South, were closed to blacks whatever their wealth or status.

From 1865 through the early 1880s, the general trend in the nation was toward wider acceptance of black patronage. The federal Civil Rights Act of 1866, with its guarantee to blacks of "equal benefit of the laws," had set off a flurry of enforcement suits—for denying berths to blacks on a Washington-New York train; for refusing to sell theatre tickets to blacks in Boston; and for barring black women from the waiting rooms and parlor cars of railroads in Virginia, Illinois, and California. Ratification of the Fourteenth Amendment in 1868 had spurred more challenges. Three northern states, and two southern states under Reconstruction regimes, passed laws making it a crime for owners of public-accommodation businesses to discriminate. Most state and federal court rulings on these laws between 1865 and 1880 held in favor of black rights, and the rulings built up a steady pressure on owners to relax racial bars.

Nevertheless, instances of exclusion and segregation continued throughout the 1870s. To settle the issue once and for all (thereby reaping the lasting appreciation of the black voters), congressional Republicans led by Senator Charles Sumner pressed for a federal statute making discrimination in public accommodations a crime. Democrats and conservative Republicans warned in the congressional debates that such a law would trespass on the reserved powers of the states and reminded the Sumner supporters that recent Supreme Court decisions had taken a narrow view of federal power under the Civil War amendments.

After a series of legislative compromises, however, Sumner's forces were able to enact the statute; on March 1, 1875, "An Act to Protect all Citizens in their Civil and Legal Rights" went into effect. "It is essential to just government," the preamble stated, that the nation "recognize the equality of all men before the law, and . . . it is the duty of government in its dealings with the people to mete out equal and exact justice to all, of whatever nativity, race, color, or persuasion, religious or political . . . "

Section 1 of the act declared that "All persons within the jurisdiction of the United States shall be entitled to the full and equal enjoyment of the accommodations . . . of inns, public conveyances on land or water, theaters and other places of public amusement; subject only to the conditions and limitations established by law, and applicable alike to citizens of every race or color. . . . " Section 2 provided that any person violating the act could be sued in federal district court for a penalty of $500, could be fined $500 to $1,000, or could be imprisoned from thirty days to one year. (A separate section forbade racial discrimination in the selection of juries.)

Reaction to the law was swift. Two black men were admitted to the dress circle of Macauley's Theatre in Louisville and sat through the performance without incident. In Washington, blacks were served for the first time at the bar of the Willard Hotel, and a black man broke the color line when he was seated at McVicker's Theatre in Chicago. But in other instances, blacks were rejected despite "Sumner's law." Several hotels in Chattanooga turned in their licenses, became private boardinghouses, and accepted whites only. Restaurants and barber shops in Richmond turned away black customers.

Suits challenging refusals were filed *en masse* throughout the country. Perhaps a hundred were decided in the federal district courts during the late 1870s and early 1880s. Federal judges in Pennsylvania, Texas, Maryland, and Kentucky, among others, held the law to be constitutional and ruled in favor of black complainants. In North Carolina, New Jersey, and California, however, district judges held the law invalid. And when other courts in New York, Tennessee, Missouri, and Kansas put the issue to the federal circuit judges, the judges divided on the question, and the matter was certified to the United States Supreme Court.

But the Supreme Court did not exactly rush to make its ruling. Though two cases testing the 1875 act reached it in 1876 and a third in 1877, the Justices simply held them on their docket. In 1879, the Attorney General filed a brief defending the constitutionality of the law, but still the Court reached no decisions. In 1880, three additional cases were filed, but two years elapsed before the Solicitor General presented a fresh brief supporting the statute. It was not until late in 1883 that the Supreme Court passed upon the 1875 act, in what became famous as the *Civil Rights Cases* ruling. True, the Court was badly behind in its work in this period, but clearly the Justices chose to let the civil-rights cases "ripen" for almost eight years.

When they finally came to grips with the issue, six separate test suits were involved. The most celebrated had arisen in New York City in November of 1879. Edwin Booth, the famous tragedian and brother of John Wilkes Booth, had opened a special Thanksgiving week engagement at the Grand Opera House. After playing *Hamlet, Othello,* and *Richelieu* to packed houses, he was scheduled to perform Victor Hugo's *Ruy Blas* at the Saturday matinee on November 22.

One person who had decided to see Booth that Saturday was William R. Davis, Jr., who was later described in the press as a tall, handsome, and well-spoken black man of twenty-six. He was the business agent of the *Progressive-American*, a black weekly published in New York City. At 10 o'clock Saturday morning, Davis' girl friend ("a bright octoroon, almost white," as the press put it), purchased two reserved seats at the box office of the Grand Opera House. At 1:30 P.M., Davis and his lady presented themselves at the theatre, only to be told by the doorkeeper, Samuel Singleton, that "these tickets are no good." If he would step out to the box office, Singleton told Davis, his money would be refunded.

It is unlikely that Davis was surprised by Singleton's action, for this was not the first time he had encountered such difficulties. Shortly after the passage of the 1875 act, Davis had been refused a ticket to the dress circle of Booth's Theatre in New York. He had sworn out a warrant against the ticket seller, but the failure of his witnesses to appear at the grand jury proceedings had led to a dismissal of the complaint. This earlier episode, as well as Davis' activity as a black journalist, made it probable that this appearance at the Opera House in 1879 was a deliberate test of the management's discriminatory policies.

Though Davis walked out of the lobby at Singleton's request, he did not turn in his tickets for a refund. Instead, he summoned a young white boy standing near the theatre, gave him a dollar (plus a dime for his trouble), and had him purchase two more tickets. When Davis and his companion presented these to Singleton, only the lady was allowed to pass.

Again Davis was told that his ticket was "no good." When he now refused to move out of the doorway, Singleton called a policeman and asked that Davis be escorted off the theatre property. The officer told Davis that the Messrs. Poole and Donnelly, the managers of the Opera House, did not admit colored persons. "Perhaps the managers do not," Davis retorted, "but the laws of the country [do]."

The following Monday, November 24, Davis filed a criminal complaint; on December 9, this time with witnesses in abundance, Singleton was indicted in what the press described as the first criminal proceeding under the 1875 act to go to trial in New York. When the case opened on January 14, 1880, Singleton's counsel argued that the 1875 law was unconstitutional. "It interferes," he said, "with the right of the State of New York to provide the means under which citizens of the State have the power to control and protect their rights in respect to their private property." The assistant United States attorney replied that such a conception of states' rights had been "exploded and superseded long ago." It was unthinkable, he declared, that "the United States could not extend to one citizen of New York a right which the State itself gave to others of its citizens—the right of admission to places of public amusement."

The presiding judge decided to take the constitutional challenge under advisement and referred it to the circuit court, for consideration at its February term. This left the decision up to Justice Samuel Blatchford of the Supreme Court, who was assigned to the circuit court for New York, and District Judge William Choate. The two judges reached opposite conclusions and certified the question to the United States Supreme Court.

Davis' case, under the title of *United States vs. Singleton*, reached the Supreme Court in 1880. Already lodged on the Court's docket were four similar criminal prosecutions under the act of 1875. *U.S. vs. Stanley* involved the refusal of Murray Stanley in 1875 to serve a meal at his hotel in Topeka, Kansas, to a black man, Bird Gee. *U.S. vs. Nichols* presented the refusal in 1876 of Samuel Nichols, owner of the Nichols House in Jefferson City, Missouri, to accept a black man named W. H. R. Agee as a guest. *U.S. vs. Ryan* involved the conduct of Michael Ryan, doorkeeper of Maguire's Theatre in San Francisco, in denying a black man named George M. Tyler entry to the dress circle on January 4, 1876. In *U.S. vs. Hamilton*, James Hamilton, a conductor on the Nashville, Chattanooga, and St. Louis Railroad, had on April 21, 1879, denied a black woman with a first-class ticket access to the ladies' car.

There was a fifth case, with a somewhat different setting. On the evening of May 22, 1879, Mrs. Sallie J. Robinson, a twenty-eight-year-old black woman, purchased two first-class tickets at Grand Junction, Tennessee, for a trip to Lynchburg, Virginia, on the Memphis and Charleston Railroad. Shortly after midnight she and her nephew, Joseph C. Robinson, described as a young black man "of light complexion, light hair, and light blue eyes," boarded the train and started into the parlor car. The conductor, C. W. Reagin, held Mrs. Robinson back ("bruising her arm and jerking her roughly around," she alleged) and pushed her into the smoker.

A few minutes later, when Joseph informed the conductor that he was Mrs. Robinson's nephew and was black , the conductor looked surprised. In that case, he said, they could go into the parlor car at the next stop. The Robinsons finished the ride in the parlor car but filed complaints with the railroad about their treatment and then sued for $500 under the 1875 act. At the trial, Reagin testified that he had thought Joseph to be a white man with a black woman, and his experience was that such associations were "for illicit purposes."

Counsel for the Robinsons objected to Reagin's testimony, on the ground that his actions were based on race and constituted no defense. Admitting the constitutionality of the 1875 law for purposes of the trial, the railroad contended that the action of its conductor did not fall within the statute. The district judge ruled that the motive for excluding persons was the decisive issue under the act: if the jury believed that the conductor had acted because he thought Mrs. Robinson "a prostitute travelling with her paramour" whether "well or ill-founded" in that assumption, the exclusion was not because of race and the railroad was not liable. The jury found for the railroad, and the Robinsons appealed.

These, with William Davis' suit against the doorkeeper of New York's Grand Opera House, were the six cases to which the Supreme Court finally turned in 1882. The Justices were presented with a learned and eloquent brief for the United States submitted by Solicitor General Samuel F. Phillips, who reviewed the leading cases, described the history of the Civil War amendments to the Constitution, and stressed the importance to the rights of citizens of equal access to public accommodation. Four times since 1865, Phillips noted, civil-rights legislation had been enacted by a Congress filled with men who had fought in the Civil War and had written the war amendments. These men understood that "every rootlet of slavery has an individual vitality, and, to its minutest hair, should be anxiously followed and plucked up. . . . " They also knew that if the federal government allowed blacks to be denied accommodation "by persons who notably were sensitive registers of local public opinion," then "what upon yesterday was only 'fact' will become 'doctrine' tomorrow."

The Supreme Court Justices who considered Phillips' brief and the six test cases were uncommonly talented, among them being Chief Justice Morrison R. Waite, a man under-rated today; Joseph P. Bradley, that Court's most powerful intellect; and Stephen J. Field, a *laissez-faire* interpreter of American constitutional law. John Marshall Harlan, the youngest man on the Court, had already started on the course which was to mark him as the most frequent and passionate dissenter in the Gilded Age.

As a whole, the Court might have appeared to be one which would have looked favorably on the 1875 Act. All were Republicans except Justice Field, and he was a Democrat appointed by Abraham Lincoln. All except Justice Harlan, who was the Court's only southerner, had made their careers primarily in the northern and western states. Without exception, all had supported the Northern cause in the war, and none had any hostility toward blacks as a class.

Yet on the afternoon of October 15, 1883, Justice Bradley announced that the Court found Sections 1 and 2 of the Civil Rights Act of 1875 to be unconstitutional. (This disposed of five of the cases; the sixth, *U.S. vs. Hamilton*, was denied review on a procedural point.) There was added irony in the fact that Bradley delivered the majority opinion for eight of the Justices. A one-time Whig, Bradley had struggled for a North-South compromise in the darkening months of 1860–61, then had swung to a strong Unionist position after the firing on Fort Sumter. He had run for Congress on the Lincoln ticket in 1862 and in 1868 headed the New Jersey electors for Grant. When the Thirteenth and Fourteenth Amendments were adopted, he had given them firm support, and his appointment to the Supreme Court by Grant in 1870 had drawn no criticism from friends of black citizens, as had the appointment of John Marshall Harlan seven years later.

Bradley's opinion had a tightly reasoned simplicity. The Thirteenth Amendment forbade slavery and involuntary servitude, he noted, but protection against the restoration of bondage could not be stretched to cover federal regulation of "social" discriminations such as those dealt with in the 1875 statute. As for the Fourteenth Amendment, that was addressed only to deprivations of rights by the *states*; it did not encompass *private* acts of discrimination. Thus there was no source of constitutional authority for "Sumner's law"; it had to be regarded as an unwarranted invasion of an area under state jurisdiction. Even as a matter of policy, Bradley argued, the intention of the war amendments to aid newly freed blacks had to have some limits. At some point, the black citizen must cease to be "the special favorite of the law" and take on "the rank of a mere citizen."

At the Atlanta Opera House on the evening of the Court's decision, the end man of Haverly's Minstrels interrupted the performance to announce the ruling. The entire orchestra and dress circle audience rose and cheered. Blacks sitting in the balcony kept their seats, "stunned," according to one newspaper account. A short time earlier, a black denied entrance to the dress circle had filed charges against the Opera House management under the 1875 Act. Now his case—their case—was dead.

Of all the nine Justices, only John Marshall Harlan, a Kentuckian and a former slave-holder, announced that he dissented from the ruling. He promised to give a full opinion soon.

Justice Harlan's progress from a supporter of slavery to a civil-rights dissenter makes a fascinating chronicle. Like Bradley, he had entered politics as a Whig and had tried to find a middle road between secessionist Democrats and anti-slavery Republicans. Like Bradley, he became a Unionist after the firing on Fort Sumter. But there the parallels ended. Although Harlan entered the Union Army, he was totally opposed to freeing the slaves, and his distaste for Lincoln and the Radicals was complete. Between 1863 and 1868, he led the Conservative party in Kentucky, a third-party movement which supported the war but opposed pro-black and civil-rights measures as "flagrant invasions of property rights and local government."

By 1868, however, Harlan had become a Republican. The resounding defeat of the Conservatives in the 1867 state elections convinced him that a third party had no future in Kentucky. His antimonopoly views and his general ideas about economic progress conflicted directly with state Democratic policies, and when the Republicans nominated his former field commander, Ulysses S. Grant, for President, in 1868, Harlan was one of the substantial number of Conservatives who joined the G.O.P.

His views on black rights also changed at this time. The wave of vigilante activities against white Republicans and blacks that swept Kentucky in 1868-70, with whippings and murders by the scores, convinced Harlan that federal guarantees were essential. He watched blacks in Kentucky moving with dignity and skill toward useful citizenship, and his devout Presbyterianism led him to adopt a "brotherhood-of-man" outlook in keeping with his church's national position. Perhaps he may have been influenced by his wife, Mallie, whose parents were New England abolitionists. As a realistic Republican politician, he was also aware that 60,000 Kentucky blacks would become voters in 1870.

Thus a "new" John Harlan took the stump as Republican gubernatorial candidate in 1871, the year of the Louisville streetcar ride-ins. He opened his rallies by confessing that he had formerly been anti-black. But "I have lived long enough," he said, "to feel that the most perfect despotism that ever existed on this earth was the institution of African slavery." The war amendments were necessary "to place it beyond the power of any State to interfere with . . . the results of the war. . . . " The South should stop agitating the race issue, and should turn to rebuilding itself on progressive lines. When the Democrats laughed at "Harlan the Chameleon" and read quotations from his earlier anti-black speeches, Harlan replied: "Let it be said that I am right rather than consistent."

Harlan soon became an influential figure in the Republican party and, when President Rutherford B. Hayes decided to appoint a southern Republican to the Supreme Court in 1877, he was a logical choice. Even then, the black issue rose to shake Harlan's life again. His confirmation was held up because of doubts by some senators as to his "real" civil-rights views. Only after Harlan produced his speeches between 1871 and 1877 and party leaders supported his firmness on the question was he approved.

Once on the Supreme Court, Harlan could have swung back to a conservative position on civil rights. Instead, he became one of his generation's most intense and uncompromising defenders of black citizens. Perhaps his was the psychology of the convert who defends his new faith more passionately, even more combatively, than the born believer. Harlan liked to think that he had changed because he knew the South and realized that any relaxation of federal protection of the rights of blacks would encourage the "white irreconcilables" first to acts of discrimination and then to violence, which would destroy all hope of accommodation between the races.

When Harlan sat down in October of 1883 to write his dissent in the *Civil Rights Cases*, he hoped to set off a cannon of protest. But he simply could not get his thoughts on paper. He worked late into the night, and even rose from half-sleep to write down ideas that he was afraid would elude him in the morning. "It was a trying time for him," his wife observed. "In point of years, he was much the youngest man on the Bench; and standing alone, as he did in regard to a decision which the whole nation was anxiously awaiting, he felt that . . . he must speak not only forcibly but wisely."

After weeks of drafting and discarding, Harlan seemed to reach a dead end. The dissent would not "write." It was at this point that Mrs. Harlan contributed a dramatic touch to the history of the *Civil Rights Cases*.

When the Harlans had moved to Washington in 1877, the Justice had acquired from a collector the inkstand which Chief Justice Roger Taney had used in writing all his opinions. Harlan was fond of showing this to guests and remarking that "it was the very inkstand from which the infamous *Dred Scott* opinion was written." Early in the 1880s, however, a niece of Taney's, who was engaged in collecting her uncle's effects, visited the Harlans. When she saw the inkstand she asked Harlan for it, and the Justice agreed. The next morning Mrs. Harlan, noting her husband's reluctance to part with his most prized possession, quietly arranged to have the inkstand "lost." She hid it away, and Harlan was forced to make an embarrassed excuse to Taney's niece.

Now, on a Sunday morning, probably early in November of 1883, after Harlan had spent a sleepless night working on his dissent, Mallie Harlan remembered the inkstand. While the Justice was at church, she retrieved it from its hiding place, filled it with a fresh supply of ink and pen points, and placed it on the blotter of his desk. When her husband returned from church, she told him, with an air of mystery, that he would find something special in his study. Harlan was overjoyed to recover his symbolic antique. Mrs. Harlan's gesture was successful, for as she relates:

> The memory of the historic part that Taney's inkstand had played in the Dred Scott decision, in temporarily tightening the shackles of slavery upon the negro race in those antebellum days, seemed, that morning, to act like magic in clarifying my husband's thoughts in regard to the law . . . Intended by Sumner to protect the recently emancipated slaves in the enjoyment of equal 'civil rights.' His pen fairly flew on that day and, with the running start he then got, he soon finished his dissent.

How directly the recollection of Dred Scott pervaded Harlan's dissent is apparent to anyone who reads the opinion. He began by noting that the pre-Civil War Supreme Court had upheld congressional laws forbidding individuals to interfere with recovery of fugitive slaves. To strike down the Act of 1875 meant that "the rights of freedom and American citizenship cannot receive from the Nation that efficient protection which heretofore was unhesitatingly accorded to slavery and the rights of masters."

Harlan argued that the Civil Rights Act of 1875 was constitutional on any one of several grounds. The Thirteenth Amendment had already been held to guarantee "universal civil freedom"; Harlan stated that barring blacks from facilities licensed by the state and under legal obligation to serve all persons without discrimination restored a major disability of slavery days and violated that civil freedom. As for the Fourteenth Amendment, its central purpose had been to extend national citizenship to black s, reversing the precedent upheld in the Dred Scott decision; its final section gave Congress power to pass appropriate legislation to enforce that affirmative grant as well as to enforce the section barring any state action which might deny liberty or equality. Now, the Supreme Court was deciding what legislation was appropriate and necessary for those purposes, although that decision properly belonged to Congress.

Even under the "State action" clause of the Fourteenth Amendment, Harlan continued, the 1875 act was constitutional; it was well established that "railroad corporations, keepers of inns and managers of places of public accommodation are agents or instrumentalities of the State." Finally, Harlan attacked the unwillingness of the Court's majority to uphold the public-carrier section of the act under Congress' power to regulate interstate trips. That was exactly what was involved in Mrs. Robinson's case against the Memphis and Charleston Railroad, he reminded his colleagues; it had not been true before that Congress had had to cite the section of the Constitution on which it relied.

In his peroration, Harlan replied to Bradley's comment that blacks had been made "a special favorite of the law." The war amendments had been passed not to "favor" black citizens, he declared, but to include them as "part of the people for whose welfare and happiness government is ordained."

> Today, it is the colored race which is denied, by corporations and individuals wielding public authority, rights fundamental in their freedom and citizenship. At some future time, it may be that some other race will fall under the ban of race discrimination. If the constitutional amendments be enforced, according to the intent with which, as I conceive, they were adopted, there cannot be in this republic, any class of human beings in practical subjection to another class. . . .

The *Civil Rights Cases* ruling did two things. First, it destroyed the delicate balance of federal guarantee, black protest, and private enlightenment which was producing a steadily widening area of peacefully integrated public facilities in the North and South during the 1870s and early 1880s. Second, it had an immediate and profound effect on national and state politics as they related to black citizens. By denying Congress power to protect the black citizen's rights to equal treatment, the Supreme Court wiped the issue of civil rights from the Republican party's agenda of national responsibility. At the same time, those southern political leaders who saw anti-black politics as the most promising avenue to power could now rally the "poor whites" to the banner of segregation.

If the Supreme Court had stopped with the *Civil Rights Cases* of 1883, the situation of blacks would have been bad but not impossible. Even in the South, there was no immediate imposition of segregation in public facilities. During the late 1880s, blacks could be found sharing places with whites in many southern restaurants, streetcars, and theatres. But increasingly, Democratic and Populist politicians found blacks an irresistible target. As Solicitor General Phillips had warned the Supreme Court, what had been tolerated as the "fact" of discrimination was now being translated into "doctrine": between 1887 and 1891, eight southern states passed laws requiring railroads to separate all white and black passengers. The Supreme Court upheld these laws in the 1896 case of *Plessy vs. Ferguson*. Then in the Berea College case of 1906, it upheld laws forbidding private schools to educate black and white children together. Both decisions aroused Harlan's bitter dissent. In the next fifteen or twenty years, the chalk line of Jim Crow was drawn across virtually every area of public contact in the South.

Today, as this line is slowly and painfully being erased, we may do well to reflect on what might have been in the South if the Civil Rights Act of 1875 had been upheld, in whole or in part. Perhaps everything would have been the same. Perhaps forces at work between 1883 and 1940 were too powerful for a Supreme Court to hold in check. Perhaps "Sumner's law" was greatly premature. Yet it is difficult to believe that total, state-enforced segregation was inevitable in the South after the 1880s. If in these decades the Supreme Court had taken the same *laissez-faire* attitude toward race relations as it took toward economic affairs, voluntary integration would have survived as a counter-tradition to Jim Crow and might have made the transition of the 1950s less painful than it was. At the very least, one cannot help thinking that Harlan was a better sociologist than his colleagues and a better southerner than the "irreconcilables." American constitutional history has a richer ring to it because of the protest that John Marshall Harlan finally put down on paper from Roger Taney's inkwell in 1883.

VI

POPULISM AND MODERN AMERICAN POLITICS

Peter Frederick

In the 1890s the United States was hit with one of the worst economic setbacks of the century. Out of that economic crisis a new political force emerged. The Populists, or People's Party, was made up primarily of farmers. America's agrarian yeomen had always been the backbone of American society. But in the late 19th century age of big business and increasing urbanization, America's farmers were being forgotten and abused by the economic system and its decline. Angry at the excesses of the railroads and banks and seeing no response to their plight from either political party, they organized their own movement. Their efforts to change fundamentally America's political and economic systems would reach their apex with the election of 1896. Though their efforts failed at the time, their legacy and the things they fought for would eventually lead to many of the changes they sought. This interview with Peter Frederick reveals the struggles of the Populists as well as their impact on American politics and society.

Interview with Peter Frederick

Q. *Were the Populists at all perceived to be a threat to the political and economic establishment in 1892?*

A. They're going to do pretty well in the election of 1892. Populists will get a million votes in a third party candidacy in 1892 and win a few state representatives and three governors. So they become finally a threat because they are forcing issues to the American people that have been ignored for 20 years by the two major parties. And that's scary, and that's threatening. You get the two major parties beginning to recognize and notice. Here is a grassroots people's movement that's threatening because the two major parties are avoiding the issues.

Q. *Sort of a follow-up to that, how successful was the Populist party in 1892? What factors limited their success? And how did the Populist leaders themselves respond to the 1892 election results?*

A. Populists were, by their expectations, enormously successful in 1892. They won a million votes. Won a few state houses, governors, state representatives and senators. They were hopeful that they could look to doing even better in '94 and '96 and they began to say,

"Hey, politics is the way we're going to be heard." And they see the emergence of a third party as a strong force. It was not known then that third parties were anathema in American politics. The last third party had been the Republican party and it had become one of the two dominant ones. So, they had every expectation that they might work. One of the problems with the Populists as they moved into the post '92 election was the depression.

Q. *What factors limited the success of the Populist party in 1892?*

A. Populists were limited in '92 by the fact that they just did [not] make a dent into the labor vote in the cities. Nor did they make a big dent in the black vote. Not many blacks are voting. But there were issues of race, particularly among southern Populists between white and black. There were differences between the perspectives of northern Populists and southern Populists. They began to see rifts in their own movement on political issues. The biggest failure really was not connecting with urban workers.

Q. *How did the depression of 1893 affect the Democratic, the Republican and the Populist parties?*

A. The depression of 1893 was devastating. First of all, it was devastating to people's lives. But it especially had its impact on politics, as depressions will. And Populists saw the depression as a chance to expand their membership and expand their power. And they saw urban workers unemployed and hurting and they thought perhaps they could undo the failures of '92 in reaching the urban workers and add them to their rolls for '94 and '96. The depression had a big effect on the Democratic party. Cleveland was in power and he was totally immobilized. He turned to gold. He'd always been [as] conservative as the Republican party had been on issues. He was a sound money man. He repealed the Silver Purchase Act, and just went wholesale towards sound money politics. That wasn't going to do him any good. The Democrats were split into gold and silver parts of the party. They were in shambles. The Republicans gained enormously in the election of 1894. And 1894 is a very significant election even before the presidential election, because the Republican party emerges as a dominant party and it's going to be dominant until the 1930s.

Q. *Why did the Populists endorse Bryan in 1896? Did they have any alternatives? To what extent had they accomplished their mission when the Democrats picked up on so many of their issues in 1986?*

A. Approaching the election of 1896, the Populists had a serious dilemma. They had not made [an] impact in connection with urban workers. They were divided on race questions between white and black farmers and sharecroppers. The basic question the Populists faced was to continue to push their many issues, to keep pushing a multiple issue campaign, or to focus increasingly on a single issue with a lot of popular appeal, the coinage of free silver. Populists increasingly in '93, '94, '95, even in '96 were a party captured by western silver miners. And it was the power of simplicity, a single issue, an issue that could be turned into a moral issue. They lost the power of focusing on the complex array of a capitalist society that was trampling on the rights of the people as they saw it, and turned increasingly to silver. They saw elements in [the] Democratic party also pushing toward silver, and there was some pressure among the leadership as they moved toward their own political convention in '96 to go along with the Democrats. So the big question they faced was fusion on one issue, that is connect with the Democratic party, or maintain their autonomy and their integrity as a third party with the many issues that had defined the culture that had been emerging in the late 1880s. They are going to make a very disastrous choice for their future.

Q. *Why did Bryan lose the 1896 presidential election? Why did McKinley win? Why was this election significant?*

A. The election of 1896 is one of the most significant elections in the history of American politics. It changes the shape of politics. It does in third party movements and mass democratic movements in a very significant and thorough way. Populists didn't just shoot themselves in the foot, they self-destructed by the decision to fuse with the Democrats and with the very popular young [William Jennings] Bryan of Nebraska. Bryan didn't lose the election so much as the Republicans won it. And they won it by conducting the first modern highly financed political campaign. McKinley sat home in Ohio and just let the money from Standard Oil and J. P. Morgan and the corporations flow in and he spent enormous amounts of money. And he also wrapped himself in the flag. It was very much like the election of '88 with Bush. McKinley was quite silent, but the McKinley people talked about peace, prosperity, progress and patriotism. And every one of his campaign posters had the American flag and a big gold symbol. They just poured money into that campaign. Bryan, who had very little money, traveled a lot and spoke and spoke and spoke. And it wasn't enough to counteract a really thoroughly modern campaign.

Q. *What was the legacy of the Populist party?*

A. The Populist party died as a result of the election of 1896. They joined the Democrats and they were already dead by the time they decided at their own convention to fuse. And yet in many ways, they forced the two major parties to try and address some of the issues. In a sense, the Populists set the agenda for American politics for the next 20 to 30 years. A number of the items in the Omaha platform become implemented in the next 20 years, direct election of senators, graduated income tax, women's suffrage, [recall and] referendum, a number of the direct democracy programs, and so they had an impact on American politics. And yet in a fundamental way, they failed, because what the two major parties do, and what they learn is that when a third party forces issues on us that we've been ignoring, one of the two major parties or both will adapt those issues, but they adapt them to maintain the current established order and the dominant forces in society at an even stronger level. So the Populists, like a bee, they sting and leave a little stinger, but the body is unharmed and essentially unchanged, in fact, strengthened.

Q. *What did the Populist experience show us about how political change comes about in America, and what does it show us about the limits of bringing about political change?*

A. The Populist experience shows that change comes about in America very, very slowly, and that it is always inherently limited. For example, [the] women's movement for the right to vote began in 1848. It's 1920 before they even get that little piece of the agenda. Change also works to further entrench the unequal distribution of wealth and power in the hands of the two major parties and of the established order, in this case, the corporations and the railroads [which emerge] even stronger than when the third party began making so much noise. Also, the Populist experience shows that serious structural changes in American society are impossible. The changes that are made in the aftermath of the Populists further strengthen the established order and the unequal distribution of power, and the underclass remains an underclass in even worse relationship to what they consider their oppressors.

Q. *To what extent was the Populist movement the last serious challenge to the dominance of big corporations in American life?*

A. The Populist movement was really the last serious challenge to the two major parties and to the two party system in America. It was a moment of a very highly energized and idealistic optimism about the power of the people to shape their own destinies. And it's sad that its ultimate fate was to show that that power was not going to happen, and that they couldn't do that. And [there] has not been a significant attempt at a democratic grassroots political movement with as much potential as the Populists in the last 90 years.

Q. *In further analyzing the 1896 election, why didn't more lower and middle income voters support the Populist/Democratic ticket? Why do such voters tend to vote against what we might perceive to be their self-interests?*

A. In 1896, the American voters voted against their self-interests as people often do. Race, for example. Southern white Democrats are going to vote against blacks, against their self-interests because race is a more powerful influence on their lives than economic issues are. Populists in 1896 and the Democrats did not win the votes of the workers. They didn't win the votes of the midwest. Silver had nothing to say to a worker in a factory. And silver was all that Bryan was talking about throughout that campaign, and it scared the workers who saw it as inflating prices. And so the interests ultimately between the farmer and the urban worker were too dissimilar.

Q. *To what extent were the philosophical positions and the constituencies of the two major parties set after the 1896 election?*

A. After 1896, the Republican party entrenched itself as a party of whites, Yankee northerners, rich corporations, Protestants, and the Democratic party became a sectional southern party. Bryan won electoral votes only in the south [and the west]. The Republican swept the north, the northeast and the midwest and so a solid south Democratic party was entrenched and a party that represented Irish, Catholic southerners. A more significant outcome of the election, I think, is that, even though Bryan won more votes than any Democrat had in twenty years, the Republican established themselves as the dominant party in the White House until the 1930s. And the Democrats established themselves as the really out party and a sectional party and a minority party.

Q. *Is it fair to say that the Democratic party from the time of 1896, even though they did become a minority party for a long time, did they in some ways become a party of reform because they had picked up on some of the reform ideas of the Populists?*

A. It's interesting. Another outcome of the election of 1896 is that until that point, the Republicans, insofar as they had any claim to moral issues, were the party of Lincoln and the party that supported the freedmen and Reconstruction and the Reconstruction amendments. And it was the party of morality. It had really started before, but after 1896 it lost its moral claims, and becomes the party of established interests. Interestingly enough, the Democratic party, because Bryan was such a moralist, such a pious person, becomes a party that has the promise of reform in it. Now, it's going to be a restrained reform because that's the nature of American politics, but Bryan's moralism and Protestant piety [pervade] the Democratic party and his stance and style are going to dominate it for the next twenty years. Woodrow Wilson will emerge as the president in many ways in the style of Bryan. And there are reforms, admittedly non-structural ones, not fundamental ones, but insofar as [there is] a party that looks to the interests of the workers and the farmers it's going to be the Democratic party. That will come about in a big way in the 1930s.

VII

THE NEEDLESS WAR WITH SPAIN

William E. Leuchtenburg

"It wasn't much of a war, but it was the only war we had." That was a pat description of America's "Splendid Little War" with Spain. It was brief, and unlike the bloody horror of the Civil War, had relatively few casualties. But what was it all about? Why did the United States go to war with the aged empire of Spain? There was no real threat to American security, and even our interests in Cuba were fairly minimal. In this article Professor Leuchtenburg describes how the U.S. found itself drawn into a war by forces more social and political than diplomatic.

The United States in the 1890s became aggressive, expansionist, and jingoistic as it had not been since the 1850s. In less than five years, we came to the brink of war with Italy, Chile, and Great Britain over three minor incidents in which no American national interest of major importance was involved. In each of these incidents, our secretary of state was highly aggressive, and the American people applauded. During these years, we completely overhauled our decrepit Navy, building fine new warships like the *Maine*. The martial virtues of Napoleon, the imperial doctrines of Rudyard Kipling, and the naval theories of Captain Alfred T. Mahan all enjoyed a considerable vogue.

There was an apparently insatiable hunger for foreign conquest. Senator Shelby M. Cullom declared in 1895: "It is time that some one woke up and realized the necessity of annexing some property. We want all this northern hemisphere, and when we begin to reach out to secure these advantages we will begin to have a nation and our lawmakers will rise above the grade of politicians and become true statesmen." When, in 1895, the United States almost became involved in a war with Great Britain over the Venezuelan boundary, Theodore Roosevelt observed: "The antics of the bankers, brokers and anglo-maniacs generally are humiliating to a degree. . . . Personally I rather hope the fight will come soon. The clamor of the peace faction has convinced me that this country needs a war." The *Washington Post* concluded: "The taste of Empire is in the mouth of the people. . . . "

In the early nineteenth century, under the leadership of men like Simon Bolivar, Spain's colonies in the New World had launched a series of successful revolutions; of the great Spanish empire that Cortes and Pizarro had built, the island of Cuba, "the Ever Faithful Isle," was the only important Spanish possession to stay loyal to the Crown. Spain exploited the economy of the island mercilessly, forcing Cubans to buy Spanish goods at prices far above the world market, and Madrid sent to Cuba as colonial officials younger sons who had no interest in the island other than making a quick killing and returning to Spain. High taxes to support Spanish officialdom crippled the island; arbitrary arrests and arbitrary trials made a mockery of justice; and every attempt at public education was stifled.

The island of Cuba had been in a state of political turbulence for years when in 1894 the American Wilson-Gorman Tariff placed duties on Cuban sugar which, coupled with a worldwide depression, brought ruin to the economy of the island. The terrible hardship of the winter was the signal for revolution; on February 24, 1895, under the leadership of a junta in New York City headed by José Martí, rebels once more took the field against Spain. At first, the American people were too absorbed with the Venezuelan crisis to pay much attention to another revolt in Cuba. Then, in September, 1895, came the event which changed the course of the Cuban rebellion: William Randolph Hearst, a young man of 32 who had been operating the *San Francisco Examiner* in a sensational fashion, purchased the *New York Morning Journal,* and immediately locked horns with Joseph Pulitzer and the *World* in a circulation war that was to make newspaper history.

Hearst capitalized on the fact that the American people had only the most romantic notions of the nature of the Cuban conflict. The rebels under General Máximo Gómez, a tough Santo Domingan guerrilla fighter, embarked on a program of burning the cane fields in the hope not only of depriving the government of revenue but also of so disrupting the life of the island that the government would be forced to submit. Although there were some noble spirits in the group, much of the rebellion had an unsavory odor; one of the main financial supports for the uprising came from American property owners who feared that their sugar fields would be burned unless protection money was paid.

While Gómez was putting Cuba to the torch, American newsmen were filing reports describing the war in terms of nonexistent pitched battles between the liberty-loving Cubans and the cruel Spaniards. The war was presented, in short, as a Byronic conflict between the forces of freedom and the forces of tyranny, and the American people ate it up. When Hearst bought the *Journal* in late 1895, it had a circulation of 30,000; by 1897 it had bounded to over 400,000 daily, and during the Spanish-American War it was to go well over a million.

The sensational newspapers had influence, yet they represented no more than a minority of the press of the country; and in the South and the Middle West where anti-Spanish feeling became most intense, the representative newspaper was much more conservative. Certainly the yellow press played a tremendous part in whipping up sentiment for intervention in Cuba, but these feelings could not be carried into action unless American political leaders of both parties were willing to assume the terrible responsibility of war.

By the beginning of 1896 the rebels had achieved such success in their guerrilla tactics that Madrid decided on firmer steps and sent General Don Valeriano Weyler y Nicolau to Cuba. When Weyler arrived in February, he found the sugar industry severely disrupted and the military at a loss to meet the rebel tactic of setting fire to the cane fields. Weyler declared martial law and announced that men guilty of incendiarism would be dealt with summarily; he was promptly dubbed "The Butcher" by American newspapermen.

By late 1896 Weyler still had not succeeded in crushing the insurrection, and his measures became more severe. On October 21 he issued his famous *reconcentrado* order, directing the "reconcentration" of the people of Pinar del Rio in the garrison towns, and forbidding the export of supplies from the towns to the countryside. Reasoning that he could never suppress the rebellion so long as the rebels could draw secret assistance from people in the fields, Weyler moved the people from the estates into the towns and stripped the countryside of supplies to starve out the rebellion. Since many of the people had already fled to the towns, the *recon-centrado* policy was not as drastic as it appeared; yet the suffering produced by the policy was undeniable. Lacking proper hygienic care, thousands of Cubans, especially women and children, died like flies.

When William McKinley entered the White House in 1897, he had no intention of joining the War Hawks. "If I can only go out of office . . . with the knowledge that I have done what lay in my power to avert this terrible calamity," McKinley told Grover Cleveland on the eve of his inauguration, "I shall be the happiest man in the world." McKinley came to power as the "advance agent of prosperity," and business interests were almost unanimous in opposing any agitation of the Cuban question that might lead to war. Contrary to the assumptions of Leninist historians, it was Wall Street which, first and last, resisted a war which was to bring America its overseas empire.

The country had been gripped since 1893 by the deepest industrial depression in its history, a depression that was to persist until the beginning of 1897. Each time it appeared recovery might be on its way, a national crisis had cut it off: first the Venezuelan boundary war scare of December, 1895, then the bitter free silver campaign of 1896. What business groups feared more than anything else was a new crisis. As Julius Pratt writes: "To this fair prospect of a great business revival the threat of war was like a specter at the feast."

McKinley was not a strong President, and he had no intention of being one. Of all the political figures of his day, he was the man most responsive to the popular will. It was his great virtue and, his critics declared, his great weakness. Uncle Joe Cannon once remarked: "McKinley keeps his ear to the ground so close that he gets it full of grasshoppers much of the time." If McKinley was not one of our greatest Presidents, he was certainly the most representative and the most responsive. Anyone who knew the man knew that, although he was strongly opposed to war, he would not hold out against war if the popular demand for war became unmistakable. "Let the voice of the people rule"—this was McKinley's credo, and he meant every word of it.

The threat to peace came from a new quarter, from the South and West, the strongholds of Democracy and free silver. Many Bryanite leaders were convinced that a war would create such a strain on the currency system that the opposition to free silver would collapse. Moreover, with the opposition to war strongest in Wall Street, they found it easy to believe that Administration policy was the product of a conspiracy of bankers who would deny silver to the American people, who would deny liberty to the people of Cuba, who were concerned only with the morality of the countinghouse. Moreover, Bryan was the spokesman for rural Protestantism, which was already speaking in terms of a righteous war against Spain to free the Cubans from bondage. These were forces too powerful for McKinley to ignore. McKinley desired peace, but he was, above all, a Republican partisan, and he had no intention of handing the Democrats in 1900 the campaign cry of Free Cuba and Free Silver.

While McKinley attempted to search out a policy that would preserve peace without bringing disaster to the Republican party, the yellow press made his job all the more difficult by whipping up popular anger against Spain. On February 12 the *Journal* published a dispatch from Richard Harding Davis, reporting that as the American steamship *Olivette* was about to leave Havana Harbor for the United States, it was boarded by Spanish police officers who searched three young Cuban women, one of whom was suspected of carrying messages from the rebels. The *Journal* ran the story under the headline, "Does Our Flag Protect Women?" with a vivid drawing by Frederic Remington across one half a page showing Spanish plainclothes men searching a wholly nude woman. War, declared the *Journal*, "is a dreadful thing, but there are things more dreadful than even war, and one of them is dishonor." It shocked the country, and Congressman Amos Cummings immediately resolved to launch a congressional inquiry into the *Olivette* outrage. Before any steps could be taken, the true story was revealed. The *World* produced one of the young women who indignantly protested the *Journal*'s version of the incident. Pressured by the *World*, the *Journal* was forced to print a letter from Davis explaining that his article had not said that male policemen had searched the women and that, in fact, the search had been conducted quite properly by a police matron with no men present.

The *Olivette* incident was manufactured by Hearst, but by the spring of 1897 the American press had a new horror to report which was all too true. Famine was stalking the island. Cuba had been in a serious economic state when the rebellion broke out in 1895; two years of war would, under any circumstances, have been disastrous, but the deliberate policies pursued both by the insurgents and by the government forces made the situation desperate. It was a simple matter of Hearst and Pulitzer reporters to pin the full responsibilities on Weyler.

By the middle of July, McKinley had formulated a policy which he set down in a letter of instructions to our new American minister to Spain, General Stewart L. Woodford. The letter emphasized the need of bringing the Cuban war to an end and said that this could be done to the mutual advantage of both Spain and the Cubans by granting some kind of autonomy to Cuba. If Spain did not make an offer to the rebels and if the "measures of unparalleled severity" were not ended, the United States threatened to intervene.

On August 8 an Italian anarchist assassinated the Spanish premier: and when Woodford reached Madrid in September, a new government was about to take over headed by Señor Sagasta and the Liberals, who had repeatedly denounced the "barbarity" of the previous government's policy in Cuba. Sagasta immediately removed General Weyler, and the prospects for an agreement between the United States and Spain took a decided turn for the better.

While Woodford was carrying on skillful diplomatic negotiations for peace in Madrid, the Hearst press was creating a new sensation in this country with the Cisneros affair. Evangelina Cisneros was a young Cuban woman who had been arrested and imprisoned in the Rocojidas in Havana, guilty, according to the American press, of no other crime than protecting her virtue from an unscrupulous Spanish colonel, an aide to Butcher Weyler. The Rocojidas, Hearst's reporter told American readers, was a cage where the innocent beauty was herded with women criminals of every type, subject to the taunts and vile invitations of men who gathered outside.

When it was reported that Señorita Cisneros, whose father was a rebel leader, was to be sent for a long term to a Spanish penal colony in Africa or in the Canaries, the *Journal* launched one of the most fabulous campaigns in newspaper history. "Enlist the women of America!" was the Hearst war cry, and the women of America proved willing recruits. Mrs. Julia Ward Howe signed an appeal to Pope Leo XIII, and Mrs. Jefferson Davis, the widow of the president of the Confederacy, appealed to the queen regent of Spain to "give Evangelina Cisneros to the women of America to save her from a fate worse than death." When the *Journal* prepared a petition on behalf of Señorita Cisneros, it obtained the names of Mrs. Nancy McKinley, the mother of the President, and Mrs. John Sherman, the wife of the secretary of state, as well as such other prominent ladies as Julia Dent Grant and Mrs. Mark Hanna.

It was a startling coup for Mr. Hearst, but he had not yet even begun to display his ingenuity. On October 10, 1897, the *Journal* erupted across its front page with the banner headline: "An American Newspaper Accomplishes at a Single Stroke What the Best Efforts of Diplomacy Failed Utterly to Bring About in Many Months." Hearst had sent Karl Decker, one of his most reliable correspondents, to Havana in late August with others to rescue the Cuban Girl Martyr "at any hazard"; and Decker had climbed to the roof of a house near the prison, broken the bar of a window of the jail, lifted Evangelina out, and, after hiding her for a few days in Havana, smuggled her onto an American steamer. Decker, signing his dispatch to the *Journal* "Charles Duval," wrote: "I have broken the bars of Rocojidas and I have set free the beautiful captive of monster Weyler. Weyler could blind the Queen to the real character of Evangelina, but he could not build a jail that would hold against *Journal* enterprise when properly set to work." The Cuban Girl Martyr was met at the pier by a great throng, led up Broadway in a triumphal procession, taken to a reception at Delmonico's where 120,000 people milled about the streets surrounding the restaurant, and hailed at a monster reception in Madison Square Garden. The Bishop of London cabled his congratulations to the *Journal,* while Governor Sadler of Missouri proposed that the *Journal* send down 500 of its reporters to free the entire island.

On October 23 Sagasta announced a "total change of immense scope" in Spanish policy in Cuba. He promised to grant local autonomy to the Cubans immediately, reserving justice, the armed forces, and foreign relations to Spain. On November 13 Weyler's successor, Captain-General Blanco, issued a decree modifying considerably the *reconcentrado* policy, and on November 25 the queen regent signed the edicts creating an autonomous government for the island. In essence, Madrid had acceded to the American demands.

While Woodford was conducting negotiations with a conciliatory Liberal government in Madrid and while there was still hope for peace, the fatal incident occurred which made war virtually inevitable. On January 12, 1898, a riot broke out in Havana, and Spanish officers attacked newspaper offices. The nature of the riot is still not clear; it was over in an hour, and it had no anti-American aspects. If the United States now sent a naval vessel to Havana, it might be buying trouble with Spain. Yet if a riot did break out and Americans were killed, the Administration would be stoned for not having a ship there to protect them. For several days McKinley wavered; then he ordered the *Maine* to Havana, but with the explanation that this was a courtesy visit demonstrating that so nonsensical were the rumors of danger to American citizens that our ships could again resume their visits to the island.

As the *Maine* lay at anchor in Havana Harbor, the rebels, with a perfect sense of timing, released a new propaganda bombshell. In December, 1897, in a private letter, Señor Enrique Dupuy de Lôme, the Spanish minister at Washington, had set down his opinions of President McKinley's annual message to Congress: "Besides the ingrained and inevitable bluntness (*groseria*) with which it repeated all that the press and public opinion in Spain have said about Weyler," De Lôme wrote, "it once more shows what McKinley is, weak and a bidder for the admiration of the crowd, besides being a would-be politician (*politicastro*) who tries to leave a door open behind himself while keeping on good terms with the jingoes of his party." De Lôme added: "It would be very advantageous to take up, even if only for effect, the question of commercial relations, and to have a man of some prominence sent here in order that I may make use of him to carry on a propaganda among the Senators and others in opposition to the junta."

De Lôme had, to be sure, written all this in a private letter (which was stolen by an insurgent spy in the Havana post office), not in his official capacity, and his characterization of McKinley was not wholly without merit, but it was a blunder of the highest magnitude. Not only had De Lôme attacked the President, but he had gone on to suggest that the negotiations then going on over a commercial treaty were not being conducted in good faith. Throughout the letter ran precisely the tone which Hearst had been arguing expressed the Spanish temper—a cold, arrogant contempt for democratic institutions. The State Department immediately cabled Woodford to demand the recall of the Spanish minister, but Madrid had the good

fortune of being able to tell Woodford that De Lôme, informed of the disaster the night before, had already resigned.

A week after the publication of the De Lôme indiscretion, at 9:40 on the night of February 15, 1898, came the terrible blow which ended all real hope for peace. In the harbor of Havana, the *Maine* was blown up by an explosion of unknown origin. In an instant, the ship was
filled with the sounds of shrieking men and rushing water. The blast occurred in the forward
part of the ship where, a half hour before, most of the men had turned in for the night; they
were killed in their hammocks. Of the 350 officers and men on board, 260 were killed. By
morning the proud *Maine* had sunk into the mud of Havana Harbor.

"Public opinion should be suspended until further report," Captain Sigsbee cabled to
Washington, but even Sigsbee could not down his suspicions. The *Maine* had gone to a Spanish possession on a courtesy call, and the *Maine* now lay at the bottom of Havana Harbor.
What could it mean but war! "I would give everything if President McKinley would order the
fleet to Havana tomorrow," wrote Theodore Roosevelt. "The *Maine* was sunk by an act of
dirty treachery on the part of the Spaniards." Volunteers lined up for war service, even though
there was no one to enlist them; in New York 500 sharpshooting Westchester businessmen
volunteered as a unit for the colors. The *Journal* reported: "The Whole Country Thrills With
War Fever."

The cause of the explosion of the *Maine* has never been finally established. That Spain deliberately decided to blow up the *Maine* is inconceivable, although it is possible that it might
have been the work of unauthorized Spanish extremists. The one group which had everything
to gain from such an episode was the rebels; yet it seems unlikely that either they or Spanish hot-
heads could have carried out such an act and remained undetected. The most likely explanation
is that it was caused by an explosion of internal origin; yet the evidence for this is not conclusive.
In any event, this was the explanation that the Navy in 1898 was least willing to consider since
it would reflect seriously on the care with which the Navy was operating the *Maine*.

The move towards war seemed relentless. On March 9 Congress unanimously voted
$50,000,000 for war preparations. Yet the days went by and there was no war, in part because
important sectors of American opinion viewed Hearst's stories of the atrocious conditions on
the island with profound skepticism. Senator Redfield Proctor of Vermont decided to launch
his own investigation into conditions on the island. On March 17, after a tour of Cuba, Proctor
made one of the most influential speeches in the history of the United States Senate.

Proctor, who Roosevelt reported was "very ardent for the war," had not generally been regarded as a jingo, and no man in the Senate commanded greater respect for personal integrity.
Proctor declared that he had gone to Cuba skeptical of reports of suffering there, and he had
come back convinced. "Torn from their homes, with foul earth, foul air, foul water, and foul
food or none, what wonder that one-half have died and that one-quarter of the living are so
diseased that they can not be saved?" Proctor asked. "Little children are still walking about
with arms and chest terribly emaciated, eyes swollen, and abdomen bloated to three times the
natural size. . . . I was told by one of our consuls that they have been found dead about the
markets in the morning, where they had crawled, hoping to get some stray bits of food from
the early hucksters."

The question of peace or war now lay with McKinley. The Spaniards, Woodford had conceded, had gone about as far as they could go; but with the *Maine* in the mud of Havana Harbor, with the country, following Proctor's speech, crying for war, how much longer could
McKinley hold out? The jingoes were treating his attempt to preserve peace with outright contempt; McKinley, Roosevelt told his friends, "has no more backbone than a chocolate éclair."

"We will have this war for the freedom of Cuba," Roosevelt shouted at a Gridiron Dinner on March 26, shaking his fist at Senator Hanna, "in spite of the timidity of the commercial interests." Nor was McKinley permitted to forget the political consequences. The *Chicago Times-Herald* warned: "Intervention in Cuba, peacefully if we can, forcibly if we must, is immediately inevitable. Our own internal political conditions will not permit its postponement. . . . Let President McKinley hesitate to rise to the just expectations of the American people, and who can doubt that 'war for Cuban liberty' will be the crown of thorns the free silver Democrats and Populists will adopt at the elections this fall?"

On March 28 the President released the report of the naval court of inquiry on the *Maine* disaster. "In the opinion of the court the *Maine* was destroyed by the explosion of a submarine mine, which caused the partial explosion of two or more of the forward magazines," the report concluded. Although no one was singled out for blame, the conclusion was inescapable that if Spain had not willfully done it, Spain had failed to provide proper protection to a friendly vessel on a courtesy visit in its waters. Overnight a slogan with the ring of a child's street chant caught the fancy of the country:

> *Remember the Maine!*
> *To hell with Spain!*

"I have no more doubt than that I am now standing in the Senate of the United States," declared Henry Cabot Lodge, "that that ship was blown up by a government mine, fired by, or with the connivance of, Spanish officials."•

Desiring peace yet afraid of its consequences, McKinley embarked on a policy of attempting to gain the fruits of war without fighting. On March 29 Woodford demanded that Spain agree to an immediate armistice, revoke the reconcentration order, and co-operate with the United States to provide relief; Spain was given 48 hours to reply. On March 31 Spain replied that it had finally revoked the reconcentration orders in the western provinces; that it had made available a credit of three million pesetas to resettle the natives; that it was willing to submit the *Maine* controversy to arbitration; and that it would grant a truce if the insurgents would ask for it. In short, Spain would yield everything we demanded, except that it would not concede defeat; the appeal for a truce would have to come from the rebels. Since the rebels would not make such an appeal, since they were confident of ultimate American intervention, the situation was hopeless; yet Spain had come a long way. Woodford cabled to Washington: "The ministry have gone as far as they dare go to-day. . . . No Spanish ministry would have dared to do one month ago what this ministry has proposed to-day."

For a week the Spaniards attempted to cling to their last shreds of dignity. On Saturday, April 9, Madrid surrendered. Driven to the wall by the American demands, the Spanish foreign minister informed Woodford that the government had decided to grant an armistice in Cuba immediately. Gratified at achieving the final concession, Woodford cabled McKinley: "I hope that nothing will now be done to humiliate Spain, as I am satisfied that the present Government is going, and is loyally ready to go, as fast and as far as it can."

It was too late. McKinley had decided on war. Spain had conceded everything, but Spain had waited too long. Up until the very last moment, Spanish officials had feared that if they yielded to American demands in Cuba, it might mean the overturn of the dynasty, and they preferred even a disastrous war to that. Proud but helpless in the face of American might, many Spanish officials appeared to prefer the dignity of being driven from the island in a heroic defensive war to meek surrender to an American ultimatum. In the end they surrendered and promised reforms. But they had promised reforms before—after the Ten Years' War which ended in 1878—and they had not kept these promises. Throughout the nineteenth century, constitutions had been made and remade, but nothing had changed. Even in the last hours of negotiations with the American minister, they had told Woodford that the President had asked the Pope to intervene, when the President had done nothing of the sort. Even if their intentions were of the best, could they carry them out? Spain had had three full years to end the war in Cuba and, with vastly superior numbers of troops, had not been able to do it. And the insurgents would accept nothing from Madrid, not even peace.

On Monday, April 11, McKinley sent his message to Congress, declaring that "the forcible intervention of the United States as a neutral to stop the war, according to the large dictates of humanity and following many historical precedents" was "justifiable on rational grounds." The fact that Spain had met everything we had asked was buried in two paragraphs of a long plea for war. It took Congress a full week to act. On Monday night, April 18, while the resolution shuttled back and forth between the two chambers and the conference room, congressmen sang "The Battle Hymn of the Republic" and "Dixie" and shook the chamber with the refrain of "Hang General Weyler to a Sour Apple Tree." At three o'clock the next morning the two houses reached an agreement—the United States recognized the independence of Cuba, asserted that we would not acquire Cuba for ourselves, and issued an ultimatum to Spain to withdraw within three days. On April 20 President McKinley signed the resolution. War had come at last. But not quite. Although hostilities had begun, not until four days later did Congress declare war. When it did declare war, it dated it from McKinley's action in establishing a blockade four days before. To the very end, we protested our peaceful intentions as we stumbled headlong into war.

We entered a war in which no vital American interest was involved, and without any concept of its consequences. Although McKinley declared that to enter such a war for high purposes, and then annex territory, would be "criminal aggression," we acquired as a result of the war the Philippines and other parts of an overseas empire we had not intended to get and had no idea how to defend. Although we roundly attacked Spain for not recognizing the rebel government, we, in our turn, refused to recognize the rebels. Although we were shocked by Weyler's policies in Cuba, we were soon in the unhappy position of using savage methods to put down a rebel uprising in the Philippines, employing violence in a measure that easily matched what Weyler had done.

It would be easy to condemn McKinley for not holding out against war, but McKinley showed considerable courage in bucking the tide. McKinley's personal sympathy for the Cubans was sincere; only after his death was it revealed that he had contributed $5,000 anonymously for Cuban relief. It would be even easier to blame it all on Hearst; yet no newspaper can arouse a people that is not willing to be aroused. At root lay the American gullibility about foreign affairs, with the penchant for viewing politics in terms of a simple morality play; equally important were the contempt of the American people for Spain as a cruel but weak Latin nation and the desire for war and expansion which permeated the decade. The American people were not led into war; they got the war they wanted. "I think," observed Senator J. C. Spooner, "possibly the President could have worked out the business without war, but the current was too strong, the demagogues too numerous, the fall elections too near."

PART TWO

1900–1945

In the first half of the twentieth century the United States emerged as the world's leading industrial power, played a decisive role in two world wars, survived a harrowing depression, and found itself in 1945 poised to lead the free world in the long Cold War struggle that lay ahead. The growth of unions and a new emphasis on workers' rights and consumer protection assured that the American work force would enjoy the fruits of its labor. Women asserted their political and legal rights as never before. In Franklin Roosevelt, the United States found an inspiring leader who could sustain the morale of the public during the hard times of the Great Depression and a statesman of vision who saw more clearly than most what the world would look like after 1945. His successor, Harry S. Truman, who was derided in his own times as a mediocre president, has now been ranked by historians in the top tier of chief executives, in no small part for his tough decisions to use the atomic bomb and to fight in Korea.

HELL ON SATURDAY AFTERNOON

John F. McCormack, Jr.

The Great Triangle Fire of 1911 tragically illustrates the darker side of the growth of American industry. The Triangle Shirtwaist Company in New York City employed over 500 people, most of them young women, to produce the shirtwaist garment so popular with American women at the turn of the century. Wages (when there was work) ranged from $4.00 to $10.00 a week, hours were long, safety conditions were appalling, unions had been brutally and systematically defeated, and the factory owners, Isaac Harris and Max Blanck, had grown wealthy over the years.

As is often the case, it took a disaster, in this case a spectacular fire that consumed 146 lives, for the public and lawmakers to begin to address the working conditions of America's laboring class. As McCormack notes, ultimately the terrible loss of life was not in vain, as New York state added 36 pieces of legislation to its labor laws. Equally important, the tragedy energized a wide spectrum of labor leaders, social workers, and politicians.

It was payday for the girls working at the Triangle Shirtwaist Company. A gentle early spring breeze wafted in the open windows of the ten-story Asch Building, situated on the northwest corner of Greene Street and Washington Place, New York City. The machines hummed along as they stitched the lace, lawn and silk into shirtwaists. At 4:30 P.M. they were shut down and the garment workers prepared to leave. Suddenly, flames burst forth from a cluttered rag bin. Efforts to extinguish the fire failed and hell on Saturday afternoon, March 25, 1911 was less than minutes away for over 500 factory employees.

As the eighth story fire began to spread, a bookkeeper alerted the New York City Fire Department at approximately 4:45 P.M.. She also tried to warn those on the two floors above to evacuate the building. At first some of the girls thought the message was a prank. After all, the building was fire-proof. However, flames drawn in the open windows from the eighth floor below soon brought panic to the disbelievers. A babble of foreign languages added to the confusion since a large proportion of the workers were Jewish and Italian immigrants. There were 146 lives lost in what National Fire Protection Association figures show to be the worst factory fire in history.

Life was difficult for all blue collar workers at the beginning of the twentieth century. Organized labor had made few gains and these concerned skilled laborers. Semi-skilled garment workers spent their lives living in tenements and working in sweatshops. One of these girls who worked in Brownsville (Brooklyn) described her work:

The machines go like mad all day, because the faster you work the more money you get. Sometimes in my haste I get my finger caught and the needle goes right through it. It goes so quick though, that it does not hurt much. I bind the finger up with a piece of cotton and go on working. We all have accidents like that. Where the needle goes through the nail it makes for a sore finger, or where it splinters a bone it does much harm. Sometimes a finger has to come off. . . .

This same woman earned $4.50 per week, paying out $2.00 of that for room and board near the factory.

The shirtwaist industry at the time of the Triangle fire employed over 40,000 workers in about 450 New York City factories. About eighty percent of these were single women between the ages of eighteen and twenty-five. These girls worked between fifty-six and fifty-nine hours a week and as high as seventy during the busy season. Wages ranged from $4.00 to as high as $10.00 per week. Idle periods, however, could last as long as three months.

Moreover, substantial reductions were made in the workers' wages for use of electric power, needles and thread. If an operator was a few minutes late to work, she was docked a half-day's pay. Frequently, factory managers would actually lock employees in to force them to work overtime. Very few ill workers were permitted to leave before the day's work was finished. Lunch hours were habitually cut short and known union members were summarily dismissed.

It was the latter action which led to an unexpected and spectacular strike against Triangle Shirtwaist Company and another firm in 1909. The Shirtwaist Makers Union ordered the strike when some of its members were fired because of their union affiliation. The strike spread to the whole industry. The Triangle Company then decided to physically break the union by hiring toughs with criminal records as "special police" to "protect" its property. The *Jewish Daily Forward* printed some photos of the brutalized strikers and public opinion forced Triangle to find a new solution. It did. The company now came up with one of the most unique solutions ever employed to settle a strike. The toughs were replaced outside the factory by prostitutes!

Meanwhile, the shirtwaist makers managed to secure some powerful allies of their own: Mary Dreier, President of the Women's Trade Union League, Mrs. Alva E. Belmont, Mrs. Mary Beard, Anne Morgan, Inez Milholland, Lenora O'Reilly, Victoria Pike, John Mitchell of the United Mine Workers, Rabbi Stephen S. Wise and lawyer Samuel Untermeyer. Rallies and benefits were held under the guidance of these persons and others. The girls from Vassar College worked on behalf of the strikers. After a delegation of New Yorkers visited Philadelphia, the shirtwaist makers there walked off the job. The Philadelphians were visited by Helen Taft, the U.S. President's daughter, a student at nearby Bryn Mawr College. She felt sorry for them and would "speak to papa about the terrible conditions" there. She then left for the opera.

The strike ended with the employees gaining much of what they had asked: better working conditions, a fifty-two hour week with no more than two hours per day overtime and time and a half for that with a fixed wage scale. Unfortunately, the issue of union recognition was never accepted by the manufacturers and there were no guarantees that the employers would not revert to form when they felt they could get away with it.

Among the most obstinate of the employers were Isaac Harris and Max Blanck, owners of the Triangle Shirtwaist Co. The firing of union members by their firm had precipitated the great strike of 1909. As the largest shirtwaist manufacturers, they intended to maintain their leadership in the field by any means possible. For instance, during the strike they hired strike breakers, thugs and prostitutes to cow the strikers. They also set up a phonograph on the ninth floor of the Asch Building so that their workers could dance during lunch time. Blanck even gave out prizes to the best dancers. When the strike ended, so did the dancing.

The owners were constantly concerned that their employees were trying to steal yard goods. In 1907 an incident occurred which indicated the great lengths to which the management would go to safeguard the company from such thefts. Two sisters were accused of taking materials by Samuel Bernstein, superintendent. They were returned to the building and forced to disrobe before two female employees. The sisters further charged that three men watched the proceedings through a transom. No stolen items were found. Nevertheless, this obsession that employees were stealing was to cost many lives in the fire. As a matter of course, the eighth and ninth floor doors on the Washington Place side of the building were locked. This forced the girls to go through a narrow passageway to the freight elevators on the Greene Street side. It also afforded an opportunity for the management to make certain no one was pilfering yard goods.

Other factors contributed to the disaster. There were large bins filled with scraps of cloth waiting for the rag man to come for them. He had last appeared in January. Wicker baskets filled with finished goods lined the aisles. Finished garments hung on racks. Cardboard and wooden boxes were stacked on the tenth floor. Gasoline, used to heat the pressing irons, was stored on the eighth floor. The ninth floor tables had wooden wells where oil drippings from the machines collected just above the knees of the operators. In addition, a large barrel of oil was stored by a door. Stairwells were not illuminated. A small fire escape led to a back courtyard. Fire officials later estimated that it would have taken three hours for the five hundred people on the top three floors to go down this way. Water valves were corroded shut with their attached hoses rotting in the folds. The Asch Building was fire proof, yet events showed it to be as fire proof as any furnace is, consuming all combustibles within it.

When the bookkeeper tried to alarm the two floors above her, the workday had just ended. The unbelieving girl who answered on the tenth floor finally comprehended and reported the fire to Mr. Blanck. On the ninth floor Max Hochfield was the first one to learn of the fire. He worked near the forelady. As she reached out to ring the quitting bell, he dashed past her into the stairwell and down the stairs. He saw the flames as he passed the eighth floor. He turned to go back for his sister when a hand grabbed him and pushed him downward. The first fireman had penetrated the burning building.

Flames had lapped in the open windows of the two floors above and panic gripped those frantically trying to escape. Girls tried in vain to leave by the locked doors. Others bunched up against the doors to the elevator shafts. Still others horrified the crowds now gathering on the street below by appearing on window ledges. "Don't jump!" "Don't jump!" they screamed. The horses of Hook and Ladder Company 20 soon appeared pulling their apparatus behind them. Quickly the firemen raised their ladders, the tallest in New York City. The crowds gasped! The ladders, when fully extended, could only reach the sixth story. Other firemen and citizen volunteers grasped life nets. Garment workers jumped for them. The men were simply bowled over by the impact of the plummeting figures, some of them already aflame. It was of little use since the distance was too great for the life nets to perform their purpose. Bodies had to be removed from atop fire hoses as these were stretched into the building.

At one point a man emerged at a ninth floor window. He helped a young woman to the window then lifted her outwards and let go. He performed this act three times before the horrified onlookers below. A fourth girl came to the window. The two figures embraced and kissed. He then held her out and dropped her. Thereupon, he climbed upon the window sill and leaped to the pavement. It was an act of love never to be forgotten by the witnesses to the Triangle holocaust.

There were others amidst the panic that Saturday afternoon who kept their wits about them. Among these no praise too high could be extended to the elevator operators. In grave danger, themselves, they continued to operate their life-saving machinery until no longer able to raise the elevators. Joseph Zito guessed he had personally brought over a hundred people to safety. Gaspar Mortillalo had his elevator jam when too many forced their way into it and atop it. Men and women slid down the cables to safety while others jumped down the shafts to serious injury and death. One, Herman Meshel, had slid down the cables under an elevator. He was found almost four hours later in water up to his neck still in the shaft, dazed, bleeding and whimpering pathetically.

Those trapped on the tenth floor owed their lives to a quick thinking college professor and his students. Professor Frank Sommer, former Essex County, N. J., sheriff, was lecturing to a class of fifty New York University Law School students on the tenth floor of the New York University-American Bank Company building next door to the Triangle concern. The fire gongs disrupted the class and Sommer rushed to the faculty room which looked across an areaway at the Asch Building. What he saw he described as a "building that was fast becoming a roaring furnace." He swiftly led his students to the roof of the N. Y. U. structure, which was about fifteen feet higher than its neighbor. They found two ladders left around by painters who were redecorating the building. These were lowered to the roof of the Asch Building. Some fifty persons, including Harris and Blanck and the latter's two children, who were visiting their father, were saved by the college students. Several rooms in the college building were scorched and firemen had to be directed there. Hundreds of valuable books were carried to safety by the students before the firemen put out the smoldering college rooms.

By this time all who could get out of the Asch Building had left. Only the doomed remained to be found by shaken fire fighters.

The Edison Company of New York strung lights along Greene Street and Washington Place and throughout the burned-out floors of the Asch Building. Firemen slowly lowered the wrapped bundles which had once been human beings. Bodies were removed to the Twenty-sixth Street pier where the city's morgue attendants and a number of derelicts were pressed into service. Soon grieving families came to identify, if possible, their loved ones. The police were hard-pressed to keep back the grief-stricken. When the latter were let in, the officers had to watch out for suicides and the hysterical. Seven victims would remain unidentified. Meanwhile, the ghouls were at work near the Asch Building. Among other sounds on Monday morning were those of young street hawkers selling alleged "dead girls' earrings" and "finger rings from the fire."

However, most Americans were stunned by the disaster. Officials sought to place the blame—somewhere, anywhere. Charitable organizations appealed for aid for families of the victims. Mayor William J. Gaynor issued a call for public contributions. The respondents ranged from the great of the land to the insignificant. Andrew Carnegie immediately gave $5,000. A little boy and his cousin donated $10, the proceeds of their "savings bank . . . to use it for somebody whose littel (sic) girl jumped out of a window. . . ." The Red Cross was the official agency designated by the mayor to receive funds through its well-known treasurer, investment banker Jacob H. Schiff. As frequently happens, the theatrical community in New York City was quick to respond. Marcus Loew, Guilio Gatti-Casazza, the Shuberts, the Hammersteins, Sam Harris, Al Jolson and George M. Cohan among others responded at once. Their benefit performances raised $15,000. In all, the gigantic sum (for those days) of $120,000 was raised. The major difficulty was getting the people to accept the money. The Red Cross found even the most destitute to be maddeningly independent.

Several protest meetings were held during the days following the tragedy. These ranged from threats of withholding tuition from frightened N. Y. U. students to calls for violent action from leftist orators. Perhaps the most poignant of all protests was the funeral parade called for April 5, after the city decided to bury the seven remaining unidentified victims in Evergreen Cemetery, East New York (Brooklyn).

Mayor Gaynor decided to bury these unfortunates because he feared that the release of their remains would lead to violence. Nevertheless, the Women's Trade Union League called for a public memorial parade on the same day. Rain drenched the marchers, as if the elements, themselves, mourned the victims. The parade consisted of two processions, one beginning uptown on Fourth Avenue between 19th and 22nd Streets; the other started at Seward Park where East Broadway and Canal Street meet. They joined at Washington Square Park and when the Asch Building was sighted a bone chilling wail was emitted by the marchers. Little Rose Schneiderman, the outspoken enemy of the exploiters, felt queasy in her stomach.

A reporter asked if she was ill. She was, for good reason. "As we marched up Fifth Avenue, there they were. Girls right at the top of hundreds of buildings, looking down on us. The structures were no different from the Asch Building . . . many were . . . worse. . . . There they were, leaning out of the upper windows, watching us. This, not the rain, is making me sick."

On April 11 the grand jury investigating the fire handed up indictments for first and second degree manslaughter against Messrs. Harris and Blanck. Judge O'Sullivan released them on $25,000 bail each. The main evidence against them was a bolted lock attached to a charred piece of wood. It came from the ninth floor of the Asch Building. The owners were charged with the deaths of a girl aged sixteen and a woman of twenty-two whose bodies were found among fifty jammed up at the locked door.

The "Shirtwaist Kings," as they were known in the trade, had made a fortune manufacturing the tops made famous by the illustrator, Charles Dana Gibson. The "Gibson Girl" was the epitome of American womanhood of the time, with her upswept hair, slender figure, long skirt and trim shirtwaist. Harris and Blanck catered to the demands of the American woman through their New York and Philadelphia factories. Now all that they had built up was threatened.

Their trial did not begin until December, 1911. When they entered the New York Criminal Court Building on December 5, a crowd of 300 women surged at them, waving photographs of lost loved ones and crying, "Murderers, murderers! Kill the murderers!" Max D. Steuer, their attorney and some court officers managed to get them to the courtroom. Police cleared the corridors. The next day both men were again mobbed as they entered and left a nearby restaurant at lunch time. The trial dragged on with much contradictory testimony until the embattled owners received a belated holiday gift on December 27. After an hour and three-quarters, the jury found them innocent of the charges. Both the acquitted and the jurors were smuggled out of the courtroom for fear for their lives. Incomprehensibly, the next day's *New York Times* printed the names and addresses of the jurymen!

Nonetheless, reform elements in New York continued to press for measures which would protect factory workers. They were following the admonition pronounced by Rabbi Wise: "The lesson of the hour is that while property is good, life is better, that while possessions are valuable, life is priceless."

New York State authorized a Factory Investigating Commission of nine members during the early summer of 1911. The chairman was Robert F. Wagner, Sr., later U.S. Senator from New York, who sponsored much labor and safety legislation. Vice-Chairman was Alfred E. Smith, later governor of the state and 1928 Democratic candidate for President. Sam Gompers, A. F. L. President, and Mary Dreier were other members. Among the commission's inspectors were Rose Schneiderman and Frances Perkins, who became Franklin D. Roosevelt's Secretary of Labor. Henry Morgenthau provided free top legal counsel in Abram Elkus and Bernard Shientag because the state had not appropriated enough money for legal fees. Within three years, thirty-six new pieces of legislation bolstered the state's labor laws. All were the result of findings by the commission. The sacrifices of the 146 had not been in vain, after all.

Frances Perkins stated later that much of the philosophy and legislation of the New Deal rose, like a phoenix, from the ashes of that hell on a Saturday afternoon almost three quarters of a century ago, the "Great Triangle Fire."

WHO PUT THE BORAX IN DR. WILEY'S BUTTER?

Gerald H. Carson

As the United States changed to an urban society in the late nineteenth century, an unexpected (although perfectly logical) consequence was the separation of the consumer of food from the producer. When once most Americans lived on farms and grew their own foodstuffs, now the consumer was at the end of a vast and impersonal food chain. The need to preserve foods for long periods, added to competition for the consumer's dollar, had produced an abundant but unregulated food supply laced with dangerous, addictive, and sometimes fatal additives. This colorful essay by social historian Gerald H. Carson shows how the Progressive movement combined the power of scientific investigation, the spotlight of media publicity, and the influence of a committed President, Theodore Roosevelt, to begin the long process of cleaning up the nation's food supply.

On a hot and humid July morning in 1902, a burly, 200-pound scientist and connoisseur of good food and drink sat hunched over his desk in a red brick building in Washington and planned deliberately to feed twelve healthy young men a diet containing borax. Dr. Harvey W. Wiley, chief chemist of the Department of Agriculture, had in mind a double objective: first, to determine the effects upon human beings of certain chemicals then commonly used to preserve processed foods; and, more broadly, to educate the public in the need for a federal "pure food" law. Food preparation was becoming industrialized and subject to more complicated processing, products were traveling longer distances, passing through many hands. Manufacturers, facing a novel situation, turned to dubious additives to make their products appear more appetizing or to preserve them. Borax compounds, the first object of Dr. Wiley's investigations, were used to make old butter seem like new.

Volunteers for the experiment were recruited from the Department of Agriculture. They pledged themselves to obey the rules. A small kitchen and dining room were fitted out in the basement of the Bureau of Chemistry offices with the assistant surgeon-general in attendance to see to it that the subjects of the experiment did not get too much borax, and Dr. Wiley to see that they got enough. A bright reporter, George Rothwell Brown, of the *Washington Post*, gave the volunteers an enduring handle, "the poison squad"; and before long the public began referring to Wiley, affectionately or otherwise according to the point of view, as "Old Borax."

Six of Dr. Wiley's co-operators at the hygienic table got a normal ration plus measured doses of tasteless, odorless, invisible boracic acid. The other six also enjoyed a wholesome diet, with equally tasteless, odorless, invisible borate of soda added to their menu. The resulting chemical and physiological data was quite technical. But the meaning was clear. The effects of borax included nausea and loss of appetite, symptoms resembling those of influenza and over-burdened kidneys. The feeding experiments continued over a five year period. After the borax initiation, which made a popular sensation, the squad subsequently breakfasted, lunched, and dined on dishes containing salicylates, sulfurous acid and sulfites, benzoates, formaldehyde, sulfate of copper, and saltpeter. Seldom has a scientific experiment stirred the public imagination as did Dr. Wiley's novel procedures in, as he said, "trying it on the dog."

"My poison squad laboratory," said Dr. Wiley, "became the most highly advertised boarding-house in the world."

A popular versifier wrote a poem about it, the "Song of the Pizen Squad." Lew Dockstader introduced a topical song into his minstrel show. The chorus closed with the prediction:

> *Next week he'll give them mothballs à la Newburgh or else plain:*
> *O they may get over it but they'll never look the same!*

The *New York Sun* sourly handed Wiley the title of "chief janitor and policeman of the people's insides," an expression of one line of attack which the opposition was to take—invasion of personal liberty.

The movement to protect the health and pocketbook of the consumer was directed no less at "the patent medicine evil" than it was at the chaotic situation in the food manufacturing field. The "cures" for cancer, tuberculosis, "female weakness," the dangerous fat reducers and "Indian" cough remedies were a bonanza for their proprietors, and many an advertising wizard who knew little enough of drugs or materia medica came to live in a jigsaw mansion and drive a spanking pair of bays because he was a skillful manipulator of hypochondria and mass psychology. Slashing exposés in the popular magazines told of babies' soothing syrups containing morphine and opium, of people who became narcotic addicts, of the use of tonics that depended upon alcohol to make the patient feel frisky.

"Gullible America," said Samuel Hopkins Adams in an angry but thoroughly documented series of articles, "will spend this year [1905] some seventy-five millions of dollars" in order to "swallow huge quantities of alcohol . . . narcotics . . . dangerous heart depressants . . . insidious liver stimulants."

The nostrum vendors at first looked upon the Food and Drugs Act as a joke. In time the manufacturers of Pink Pills for Pale People learned the hard way that they were living dangerously when they ignored the precept, "Thou shalt not lie on the label."

As public interest rose in "the food question," powerful groups took their places in the line of battle to contest the pure food and drug bills which appeared, and died, in Congress with monotonous regularity. On the one side were aligned consumer groups—the General Federation of Women's Clubs, the National Consumers' League, the Patrons of Husbandry, and the labor unions. With them stood food chemists who had had experience in state control work, the American Medical Association, important periodicals (*Collier's Weekly*, Bok's *Ladies' Home Journal*, *World's Work*, *The Independent*, *Cosmopolitan*), President Theodore Roosevelt, and Dr. Wiley.

In opposition were the food manufacturers and manufacturers of articles used in the adulteration of foods and drugs such as cottonseed oil, the proprietary medicine industry, the distillers, canners, *Leslie's Weekly* (to which Dr. Wiley was anathema), newspaper publishers opposed for business reasons, Chicago meat packers, and powerful lobbyists holed up at the Willard and the Raleigh Hotel; also an obdurate Senate, responsive to pressures from big business. Wiley, as the leading personality in the fight for a food bill, achieved the uncommon distinction of acquiring almost as many enemies as did President Roosevelt himself.

When the average member of Congress, newspaper publisher, or pickle manufacturer smelled socialism and deplored the effects of the proposed legislation upon business, he was only responding normally to two powerful stimuli: self-interest and the nostalgic memory of his lost youth. Most mature Americans of the 1880–1900 period were born on farms or in rural areas and knew the conditions of life of a scattered population. The close-knit farm family was the dominant economic unit. It raised, processed, cured, and stored what it ate, and there is abundant evidence that it ate more and better food than the common man of Europe had ever dreamed of tasting. There was no problem of inspection or of deceptive labels. No "Short-weight Jim" invaded the home kitchen or smoke-house. If the preparation was unsanitary, it was no one else's business. What wasn't raised locally was obtained by barter. There were adequate forces of control over that simple transaction—face-to-face bargaining, community of interest, fear of what the neighbors would say.

As to drugs and medicines, grandma could consult the "family doctor" book and compound her home remedies from roots, herbs, and barks gathered along the edge of forest, meadow, and stream: catnip for colic, mullein leaf for asthma, the dandelion for dyspepsia, and so on through the list of simples, essences, flowers, tinctures, and infusions, whose chief merit was that they did not interfere with the tendency of the living cell to recover.

When Americans were called to the cities by the factory whistle, a dramatic change took place in their food supply. No longer was there personal contact between the producer and consumer, nor could the buyer be wary even if he would. For how could a city man candle every egg, test the milk, inquire into the handling of his meat supply, analyze the canned foods which he consumed in increasing quantities?

Since foodstuffs had to stand up in their long transit from the plant to the home, it is not surprising that unhealthy practices developed. During the "embalmed beef" scandal, for example, there was a debate as to whether a little boric acid in fresh beef was after all only an excusable extension of the ancient and accepted use of saltpeter in corning beef. Analytical chemistry was called upon increasingly to make cheap foods into expensive ones, to disguise and simulate, to arrest the processes of nature. The food manufacturers raided the pharmacopoeia. But the salicylic acid that was approved in the treatment of gout or rheumatism was received with mounting indignation on the dining room table where it proved to be a depressant of the processes of metabolism. It was objectionable on another ground too—that it led to carelessness in the selection, cleansing, and processing of foodstuffs.

It is difficult to picture today the vast extent of adulteration at the beginning of this century. More than half the food samples studied in the Indiana state laboratory were sophisticated. Whole grain flour was "cut" with bran and corn meal. The food commissioner of North Dakota declared that his state alone consumed ten times as much "Vermont maple syrup" as Vermont produced. The *Grocer's Companion and Merchant's Hand-Book* (Boston, 1883), warned the food retailer, in his own interest, of the various tricks used to alter coffee and tea, bread and flour, butter and lard, mustard, spices, pepper, pickles, preserved fruits, sauces, potted meats, cocoa, vinegar, and candies. A New York sugar firm was proud to make the point in its advertising of the 1880s that its sugar contained "neither glucose, muriate of tin, muriatic acid, nor any other foreign, deleterious or fraudulent substance whatever." The canned peas looked garden-fresh after treatment with $CuSO_4$ by methods known as "copper-greening." The pork and beans contained formaldehyde, the catsup benzoic acid. As a capstone of inspired fakery, one manufacturer of flavored glucose (sold as pure honey) carefully placed a dead bee in every bottle to give verisimilitude.

The little man of 1900 found himself in a big, big world, filled with butterine and mapleine.

This is not to suggest that the pioneer food manufacturer was as rascally as his contemporaries, the swamp doctor and the lightning rod peddler. What was occurring was less a collapse of human probity than an unexpected testing of human nature in a new context. Someone has said that all morality is based upon the assumption that somebody might be watching. In the milieu of late nineteenth-century business, nobody seemed to be watching. Thus the food crusade became necessary as a means of redressing the balance in the market which had turned so cruelly against the ordinary American and, indeed, against the honest manufacturer.

The ensuing controversy was symptomatic of the passing—painful, nostalgic to many, including no doubt many a big business senator—of the old, simple life of village and farm which was doomed by the expanding national life. It was, one feels, not solely in defense of the hake (sold as genuine codfish with boric acid as a preservative) that Senator George Frisbie Hoar of Massachusetts rose in the Senate to exalt "the exquisite flavor of the codfish, salted, made into balls, and eaten on a Sunday morning by a person whose theology is sound, and who believes in the five points of Calvinism."

The friends of food reform needed all the courage and public discussion they could muster. Since 1879, when the first federal bill was proposed, 190 measures to protect the consumer had been introduced in Congress, of which 49 had some kind of a subsequent history, and 141 were never heard of again. Meanwhile the states did what they could. About half of them had passed pure food laws by 1895. But there was no uniformity in their regulations. Foods legal in one state might be banned in another. Some of the laws were so loosely drawn that it was quite conceivable that Beechnut Bacon might be seized by the inspectors because no beechnuts were involved in its curing. Was Grape-Nuts misbranded because the great Battle Creek "brain food" had only a fanciful connection with either grapes or nuts? One bill actually proposed a numerical count of the contents of a package—the grains of salt, the cherries in a jar of preserves. What if Mr. Kellogg had to count every corn flake which went into his millions of packages?

Conflicts and foolish regulations could be ironed out over a period of time. The fatal flaw was that individual states had no power to get at the real problem: interstate traffic in the "patented" bitters, cancer cures, and strawberry jellies made out of dyed glucose, citric acid, and timothy seed.

The act which Wiley drew up was first introduced in 1902. It was successfully sidetracked in one legislative branch or the other for four years. The provisions were simple. In essence, it was a labeling act.

"Tell the truth on the label," Dr. Wiley said, "and let the consumer judge for himself."

Some of the legislators who opposed the act were states' rights Democrats, concerned about constitutional interpretation, who in the end fortunately saw the wisdom of sacrificing principle for expediency. Others were Old Guard Republicans who were special custodians of the *status quo* and highly sensitive to the sentiments of the business community: men like Senators Aldrich of Rhode Island (wholesale groceries), Kean of New Jersey (preserving and canning), Platt of Connecticut (home of the great Kickapoo Indian remedies), Hale and Frye of Maine, along whose rock-bound coast the familiar Maine herring became "imported French sardines," packaged in boxes with French labels.

The tactic in the Senate was one of unobtrusive obstruction and lip service to the idea of regulation. Open opposition was never much of a factor. "The 'right' to use deceptive labels," observed *The Nation*, "is not one for which impassioned oratory can be readily invoked." When a serious try was made to pass a general pure food law in 1902–3, Senator

Lodge was able to direct the attention of the Senate to legislation more urgently needed, such as a Philippine tariff bill. In the last session of the 59th Congress (1904–5) the food bill was considered less pressing than a proposal to award naval commissions to a couple of young men who had been expelled from the Academy for hazing but still wanted very much to become officers in the United States Navy.

President Roosevelt finally decided to push the issue. "Mr. Dooley" offered a version of how it happened. "Tiddy," he said, was reading Upton Sinclair's novel, *The Jungle*, a grisly sociological tract on "Packingtown." "Tiddy was toying with a light breakfast an' idly turnin' over th' pages iv th' new book with both hands. Suddenly he rose fr'm th' table, an' cryin': 'I'm pizened,' begun throwin' sausages out iv th' window. Th' ninth wan sthruck Sinitor Biv'ridge on th' head an' made him a blond. It bounced off, exploded, an' blew a leg off a secret-service agent, an' th' scatthred fragmints desthroyed a handsome row iv ol' oak-trees. Sinitor Biv'ridge rushed in, thinkin' that th' Prisidint was bein' assassynated be his devoted followers in th' Sinit, an' discovered Tiddy engaged in a hand-to-hand conflict with a potted ham. Th' Sinitor fr'm Injyanny, with a few well-directed wurruds, put out th' fuse an' rendered th' missile harmless. Since thin th' Prisidint, like th' rest iv us, has become a viggytaryan. . . . " At any rate, in his annual message to Congress, December 5, 1905, Roosevelt recommended in the interest of the consumer and the legitimate manufacturer "that a law be enacted to regulate interstate commerce in misbranded and adulterated foods, drinks and drugs," and the bill was re-introduced in the Senate by Senator Weldon B. Heyburn of Idaho. Pressure from the American Medical Association, the graphic exposé of revolting conditions in the Chicago packing houses, and Roosevelt's skillful use of the report of an official commission which investigated the stockyards, finally forced a favorable vote in the Senate and then the House on the Pure Food and Drugs Bill. The meat inspection problem was, actually, a different matter. But an angry public was in no mood to make fine distinctions. Meat, processed foods, and fake medicines all tapped the family pocketbook, all went into the human stomach, and all smelled to high heaven in the spring of 1906. Roosevelt signed the bill into law on June 30, 1906.

The enforcement of the law was placed in the hands of Dr. Wiley. According to the Doctor, it was after the bill became law that the real fight began. Most food and drug manufacturers and dealers adjusted their operations to the new law, and found themselves in a better position because of it, with curtailment of the activities of fly-by-night competition and re-establishment of the consumers' confidence in goods of known quality. But there were die-hards like the sugar and molasses refiners, the fruit driers, whisky rectifiers, and purveyors of wahoo bitters, Peruna and Indian Doctor wonder drugs.

The administration of the Food and Drugs Act involved the Bureau of Chemistry in thousands of court proceedings, *United States vs. Two Barrels of Desiccated Eggs*, *United States vs. One Hundred Barrels of Vinegar*; and one merciful judge noted that Section 6 extended the protection of the act to our four-footed friends. Pure food inspectors had seized 620 cases of spoiled canned cat food. When the case of the smelly tuna fish turned up in the western district court of the state of Washington, the judge cited man's experience with cats throughout recorded time: "Who will not feed cats must feed mice and rats." He confirmed the seizure and directed an order of condemnation.

The law was subsequently strengthened both by legal interpretations and by legislative action, as experience developed needs not met by the original act. Government technicians worked with private industry in the solution of specific problems such as refrigeration and the handling of food. When Dr. Wiley retired from public service in 1912, a revolution had occurred in food processing in only six years' time. Yet the food industry had hardly begun to grow.

"The conditions created by the passage of the act," said Clarence Francis, former president and chairman of the board of General Foods Corporation, "invited responsible business men to put real money into the food business."

The next 25 years saw the decline of the barrel as a food container and its replacement by the consumer unit package; the setting of official standards for the composition of basic food products; and the banning of quack therapeutic mechanical devices such as the electric belt, whose galvanic properties were once presented so vividly to the "Lost Manhood" market. We still have with us in some measure the "horse beef" butcher and the "butterlegger." Tap water remains a tempting means of "extending" many foods. But there is no question about the general integrity of our food supply, the contribution to the national well-being of the original food law, as amended, and the readiness of today's food industry leaders to accept what is now called the Food, Drug, and Cosmetic Act as a proper blueprint of their obligation to the nation's consumers.

| | |

1918

John Lukacs

In many ways World War I ushered in the twentieth century—the end of monarchy as a ruling force in the Western world, the introduction of modern wartime weaponry, the beginning of the end of European colonialism, the entrance onto the world scene of Communism as an international force, and above all, the rise of the United States to superpower status at the dawn of what has come to be called the "American century."

Historian John Lukacs shows here how for a brief glimmering moment President Woodrow Wilson and American ideals of democracy, world peace, and internationalism fired the inspiration of a war-weary world. But then came the disillusionment with the disastrous Versailles treaty, "one of the worst botched peace treaties in modern history," according to Lukacs, followed by a decade and a half of American retreat from European affairs. As historian Bruce Catton once noted, history doesn't usually make sense until long afterward, and the frenzied optimism, joy, and idealism of 1918 now appear all too ephemeral. The author closes with a final pregnant question: Was 1918 the "zenith year" of the American century—or 1945?

In many ways 1918 is closer to us than we are inclined to think. Look at Fifth Avenue in New York (or Regent Street in London, or the Champs-Elysées). Most of their present buildings were there seventy-five years ago. Automobiles, telephones, elevators, electric power, electric lights, specks of droning airplanes in the sky—there they were in 1918. Now count back seventy-five years from 1918. That was 1843, when just about everything looked different. Everything *was* different: the cities, their buildings, the lives of the men and women outside and inside their houses, as well as the furniture of their minds. But many of the ideas current in 1918 are still current in 1993: Making the World Safe for Democracy; the Self-Determination of Peoples; the Emancipation of Women; International Organizations; a World Community of Nations; "Progress." Seventy-five years is a long time; but then, the twentieth century was a short century, also exactly seventy-five years long, having burst forth in 1914, formed and marked by two world wars and the Cold War, ending in 1989.

In many ways 1918 is farther from us than we are inclined to think. After taking comfort—and, more important, pleasure—from a picture of Fifth Avenue in 1918 (I am thinking of that splendid painting by Childe Hassam, with all those Allied flags waving, dramatic poppies in a wheat-colored field of sun-bleached architecture), look closer; lean downward; try to look inside. The people are different from us, and I do not mean only the difference of two or three generations: They *look* different, because their composition and their clothes and their manners and their attitudes and aspirations are different. So are the interiors of those still-standing buildings, what there is and what goes on inside them: their furnishings, in most cases not only their inhabitants but the functions of their rooms. Yes, Fifth Avenue is different, New York is different, America is different, the world is different. The twentieth century is over.

It was—and in many ways it still is—the American century. In 1898 the United States became a world power—not because of some kind of geopolitical constellation, not because of the size of its armed forces, but because that was what the American government and the majority of the American people wanted. Before 1898 the United States was the greatest power in the Western Hemisphere. Twenty years later the United States chose to enter the greatest of European wars (the very term *world war* was an American invention, circa 1915). In 1918 it decided the outcome of the war. By Armistice Day the United States was more than a World Power; it was the greatest power in the world.

That was more than a milestone in the history of the United States. It was a turning point: the greatest turning point in its history since the Civil War and perhaps the greatest turning point since its very establishment. For more than three centuries the colonists and Americans were moving westward, away from Europe. The trickle, and later the flow, of immigrants moved westward too, across the Atlantic, away from Europe. When foreign armies crossed the Atlantic, it was westward, from the Old World to the New. Now, for the first time in history, this was reversed. Two million American soldiers were sent eastward through the Atlantic, to help decide a great war in Europe.

That was an event far more important—and decisive—than was the Russian Revolution in 1917, both in the short and in the long run. In early 1918 Russia dropped out of the war. The United States entered it. Russia abandoned its European allies. The United States came in to join them. In 1918 the Allies were able to defeat Germany and win the war, even without Russia (something that would not be possible in another world war). The presence of an American army on the battlefield proved to be more decisive than the absence of the Russians. In the long run, too, the twentieth century turned out to be the American century, on all levels, ranging from world politics to popular democracy and mass culture. Compared with this, the influence of communism and the emulation of the Soviet Union were minimal. The exaggeration of the importance of communism blinded, willfully, not only many intellectuals but many Americans, pro-Communists and anti-Communists, developing into a popular ideological view of the world. In 1967 I was astonished to find how here, in America, article after article, book after book was devoted to commemorating and analyzing the importance of the Russian Communist Revolution on its fiftieth anniversary, while hardly any notice was paid to the commemoration of the American entry into World War I in 1917.

For a long time Americans believed that the destiny of their country was to differ from the Old World. Beginning in the 1890s, and culminating in 1918, this fundamental creed changed subtly. Many Americans were now inclined to believe that it was the destiny of the United States to provide a model for the Old World. For a while these two essentially contradictory beliefs resided together in many American minds. In 1918 the second belief had temporarily overcome the first. This was the result of a revolution of American attitudes that—on the popular, rather than on the political, level—still awaits a profound treatment by a masterful historian. In 1914 not one American in a thousand thought that the United States would, or should, intervene in the great European war. In less than three years that changed. By 1917 most Americans were willing—and many were eager—to go Over There, to decide and win a war through the employment of American muscle, American practices, American ideas.

After that the tide of American confidence rose, and in November 1918 came the moment of victory. All over the world, but especially in Europe, admiration and gratitude and hope in the United States were suddenly at their zenith—a powerful ray of a faraway sunbeam breaking through those grayest of leaden skies in November 1918. Unlike after 1945, there was no trace of radical, or intellectual, anti-Americanism. The youngest and one of the most promising and most avant-garde of French writers, Raymond Radiguet, wrote about a romantic rendezvous in the spring of 1917 in "an American Bar in the rue Daunou." His lover "went into ecstasies, like a schoolgirl, over the barman's white jacket, the grace with which he shook the silver goblets and the poetic and bizarre names of the concoctions." An old goateed French academician, Henri Lavedan, wrote about President Wilson, "He will remain one of the legends of history . . . he will appear in the poetry of coming ages, like that Dante whom he resembles in profile." Lavedan needed better glasses than his pincenez, but that is beside the point. "Future generations will see him guiding through the dangers of the infernal world that white-robed Beatrice whom we call Peace. . . . " Whether Dante or Beatrice, when Woodrow Wilson landed in France, little girls in white frocks threw rose petals from baskets at his large feet. Harold Nicolson, then a young British diplomat and budding aesthete, had the highest hopes for Wilson and his new ideas—although they would vanish soon. The hope that Wilson and the United States would dominate and design the coming settlement of peace, with principles vastly superior to the petty and vengeful practices of European statesmanship in the past, existed not only in France and Britain but also in Germany, Austria, Hungary. In Vienna and Budapest governments and peoples welcomed the presence of American officers, members of the Allied military missions, some of whom were to distinguish themselves by their impartiality and humaneness. A great Hungarian writer, Gyula Krúdy, found it remarkable how the hapless and ephemeral president of the new Hungarian Republic, Count Károlyi, kept pronouncing—oddly—Wilson's name to his anxious entourage, again and again: "Uilson! Uilson!" Of all the foreign officers, the Americans were the smartest, in their well-cut uniforms, with their Sam Browne belts and superb boots. In France a war-worn, tired population had thronged the streets when the first American troops, fresh, grinning, confident, arrived in their villages and towns. They looked modern. They *were* modern—a wondrous adjective then, though it has lost much of its shine since.

Soon the high tide of enthusiasm receded—and the neap tide of disillusion came in: disillusion with Wilson abroad, disillusion among Americans themselves. The reaction to the war, to peacemaking, to Wilsonianism has been recorded often since. Even about 1918 some questions remain. Was the American intervention decisive? Yes, but the British and the French armies, weary and torn as they were, had halted the great German spring offensive by June 1918, before the mass of the Americans moved up to combat. The training and the transporting and the provisioning and the disposition of the American army had taken very long—almost too long. They did not go into battle until about fifteen months after the American declaration of war. It is arguable that their first great battle in Belleau Wood may have been a mistake, costing too many American lives, misestimating its tactical value. General Pershing had virtues, but he was not a great general, occasionally hardly better than some of his British colleagues, whose generalship was often famously poor. Still—the freshness and the courage of the American soldier in 1918 remain unarguable.

The trouble was with their President, about whom his Postmaster General once wrote that Woodrow Wilson was "a man of high ideals but no principles." That, too, is arguable, but then so many of his ideals were to be proved wrong—again, in both the short and the long runs. In the short run—that is, 1918 and 1919—during that extraordinary chapter in the history of the American Presidency, his absence from Washington for long months in Paris showed up many of his weaknesses. "Open diplomacy" was one thing that men such as Harold Nicolson admired, but Nicolson was abashed to learn that there was no such thing in Paris. Before Versailles Wilson made compromise after compromise involving his principles or his ideas, whatever we call them. He was no match for Clemenceau or Lloyd George, and the result was one of the worst botched peace treaties in modern history. As Chesterson once wrote, the best things are lost in victory and not in defeat. That would dawn on the American people only later. That was not why their elected representatives repudiated him in late 1919 and 1920. But Wilson's failure to bring the United States into the League of Nations was not that important in the long run. Had he had his way at home, had the United States entered the League, it would have made some difference, but not much. The source of the Second World War (and of Adolf Hitler's career) was not American nonparticipation in the League of Nations. It was Versailles, for which Wilson was as responsible as for the former. He also bequeathed to the American people a philosophy of internationalism (enthusiastically espoused by such different Americans as Herbert Hoover and Eleanor Roosevelt, Richard Nixon and Dean Rusk, Jimmy Carter and Ronald Reagan) that, because of its legalistic (and therefore insubstantial) moralism, including its promotion of National Self-Determination, has been rather disastrous. But that is another story.

One year after the armistice, American influence in Europe was receding fast. Within the United States, too, a great national hangover set in—in part a reaction to some of the exaggerations and fever of the earlier war propaganda. It was a return of sorts—but neither to innocence nor to "normalcy" (a word coined by Warren Gamaliel Harding). There followed a decade or more of American isolationism (in regard to Europe, though not to the Caribbean or the Pacific), together with the self-righteous belief, expressed in one of Barton W. Currie's editorials in *The Ladies' Home Journal*: "There is only one first–class civilization in the world today. It's right here in the United States. . . . Europe is hardly second-class." For the first time in American history a very restrictive Immigration Act was passed. It had something to do with the obsession with communism (from which the Republican party knew how to profit, from Harding to Reagan), though there was more to it. Many people, too, forgot that while one out of every one thousand Americans died in World War I, thirty-five of every one thousand Frenchmen died. The French did not forget. Those memories maimed them. They fell out of World War II in the summer of 1940. Soon after that Americans were beginning to ready themselves to enter it and to help liberate France again.

This brings me to a last question that I, and presumably many others, have pondered often. Which was the zenith year of the American century, 1918 or 1945? Perhaps it was 1918—when the United States did not have to share the victory with Russia (although it had to share it with Britain and France, Italy, Japan). Perhaps it was 1945—when the United States, alone among the Great Powers, could wage a war on two vast fronts and conclude it victoriously, across the Atlantic and Pacific alike. In 1918 the Western democracies had all the cards—the ace, the king, the queen, and the jack, with Germany defeated and Russia down and out. In 1945 the United States had the ace (and what an ace!), but Stalin had at least the king. Yet in 1918 America and its Allies played their cards badly and lost the peace almost immediately afterward. In 1945 they let Stalin cash in his winnings, but further than that they did not let him go. The world order (or disorder) shaping up in 1945 was more lasting than that in 1918. The effect of World War II was greater. It transformed the structure of American government and much of American life. A few years after 1918 the American military presence in Europe was gone. After 1945 it remained there. No American general of World War I became a permanent national figure or President. After World War II there was Eisenhower—and also Patton and MacArthur and Kennedy and Bush, whose impressive war records helped form their popular images. Yet there was more enthusiasm in 1918 than in 1945. There was no popular song in World War II comparable to "Over There." Sergeant York was a real soldier, unlike John Wayne. Harry Truman fought in the Argonne, not in Hollywood. Perhaps, if only for a moment, 1918 may have been the highest point, with all of that new American presence in Europe, with all of those great expectations.

And now, seventy-five years later, the United States is the only superpower left in the world, but everything else is different.

IV

"I WAS ARRESTED, OF COURSE . . ."

Robert S. Gallagher

It is always easy to look back through history and say that "this law was passed" or "that amendment was ratified," making it all sound very simple. This revealing interview shows just how complicated, frustrating, and time-consuming it is to enact significant legislation.

Alice Paul, born in 1885, earned a Ph. D. from the University of Pennsylvania in 1912, itself a rare achievement for a woman of that time. But her life's calling was as an indefatigable laborer in the women's rights movement. A veteran of the British suffrage struggle, she returned to the United States in 1910, took up the cause of voting rights for American women, and was soon chair of the Congressional Committee of the National American Woman Suffrage Association. As interviewer Robert Gallagher notes, her "single-minded devotion to The Cause is . . . legendary in the women's movement . . . " Her comments reveal the many strategies necessary to enact the Nineteenth Amendment, first in the Congress and then in the state legislatures. Women marched in parades, picketed day and night in front of the White House, met with President Woodrow Wilson, congressmen, senators, and former President Theodore Roosevelt, were jailed and sometimes force-fed, and methodically lobbied state legislators to get the necessary three-fourth of the states on board. One activist, Inez Milholland Boissevain, literally gave her life for the movement. With the final passage of the suffrage amendment, as if all this were not enough, Alice Paul and her compatriots then threw themselves into the cause, still unfulfilled, of an equal rights amendment to the Constitution.

Q. *How did you first become interested in woman suffrage?*

A. It wasn't something I had to think about. When the Quakers were founded in England in the 1600s, one of their principles was and is equality of the sexes. So I never had any other idea. And long before my time the Yearly Meeting in Philadelphia, which I still belong to, formed a committee to work for votes for women. The principle was always there.

Q. *Then you had your family's encouragement in your work?*

A. My father—he was president of the Burlington County [New Jersey] Trust Company—died when I was quite young, but he and Mother were both active in the Quaker movement. Mother was the clerk of the Friend's Meeting in our hometown. I would say that my parents supported all the ideals that I had.

Q. *In 1912 wasn't it a bit unusual for a woman to receive a Ph.D. degree?*

A. Oh, no. There were no women admitted, of course, to the undergraduate school at the University of Pennsylvania, but there were a number of women graduate students.

Q. *When did you actually become involved in suffrage work?*

A. Well, after I got my master's in 1907, my doctoral studies took me to the School of Economics in London. The English women were struggling hard to get the vote, and everyone was urged to come in and help. So I did. That's all there was to it. It was the same with Lucy Burns.

Q. *You met Miss Burns in London?*

A. Yes, we met in a police station after we were both arrested. I had been asked to go on a little deputation that was being led by Mrs. [Emmeline] Pankhurst to interview the Prime Minister. I said I'd be delighted to go, but I had no idea that we'd be arrested. I don't know what the charge was. I suppose they hadn't made all the preparations for the interview with the Prime Minister or something. At any rate, I noticed that Miss Burns had a little American flag pin on her coat, so I went up to her, and we became great friends and allies and comrades. Well, we got out of that, and, of course, afterwards we were immediately asked to do something else. And that way you sort of get into the ranks.

Q. *What sort of things were you asked to do?*

A. The next thing I was asked to do was to go up to Norwich and "rouse the town," as they say. Winston Churchill was in the British cabinet and was going to make a speech there. Well, the English suffragists knew that the government was completely opposed to suffrage, and they conceived this plan to publicly ask all the cabinet members what they were going to do about votes for women. For that moment at least, the whole audience would turn to the subject of suffrage. We considered it an inexpensive way of advertising our cause. I thought it was a very successful method.

Q. *What happened at Norwich?*

A. I went to Norwich with one other young woman, who was as inexperienced as I was, and we had street meetings in the marketplace, where everyone assembled for several nights before Mr. Churchill's speech. I don't know whether we exactly "roused the town," but by the time he arrived, I think Norwich was pretty well aware of what we were trying to do. The night he spoke, we had another meeting outside the hall. We were immediately arrested. You didn't have to be a good speaker, because the minute you began, you were arrested.

Q. *Were you a good speaker?*

A. Not particularly. Some people enjoyed getting up in public like that, but I didn't. I did it, though. On the other hand, Lucy Burns was a very good speaker—she had what you call that gift of the Irish—and she was extremely courageous, a thousand times more courageous than I was. I was the timid type, and she was just naturally valiant. Lucy became one of the pillars of our movement. We never, never, never could have had such a campaign in this country without her.

Q. *In her book about the suffrage movement Inez Haynes Irwin tells about your hiding over-night on the roof of St. Andrew's Hall in Glasgow, Scotland, in order to break up a politi-cal rally the next day.*

A. Did Mrs. Irwin say that? Oh, no. I never hid on any roof in my life. In Glasgow I was ar-rested, but it was at a street meeting we organized there. Maybe Mrs. Irwin was referring to the Lord Mayor's banquet in London. I think it was in December of 1909, and Miss Burns and I were asked to interrupt the Lord Mayor. I went into the hall, not the night before but early in the morning when the charwomen went to work, and I waited up in the gallery all day. That night Lucy went in down below with the banquet guests. I don't remember whether she got up and interrupted the mayor. I only remember that I did.

Q. *What happened?*

A. I was arrested, of course.

Q. *Was this the time you were imprisoned for thirty days and forcibly fed to break your hunger strike?*

A. I can't remember how long I was in jail that time. I was arrested a number of times. As for forcible feeding, I'm certainly not going to describe that.

Q. *The whole concept of forcible feeding sounds shocking.*

A. Well, to me it was shocking that a government of men could look with such extreme con-tempt on a movement that was asking nothing except such a simple little thing as the right to vote. Seems almost unthinkable now, doesn't it? With all these millions and mil-lions of women going out happily to work today, and nobody, as far as I can see, thinking there's anything unusual about it. But, of course, in some countries woman suffrage is still something that has to be won.

Q. *Do you credit Mrs. Pankhurst with having trained you in the militant tactics you subsequently introduced into the American campaign?*

A. That wasn't the way the movement was, you know. Nobody was being trained. We were just going in and doing the simplest little things that we were asked to do. You see, the movement was very small in England, and small in this country, and small everywhere, I suppose. So I got to know Mrs. Pankhurst and her daughter, Christabel, quite well. I had, of course, a great veneration and admiration for Mrs. Pankhurst, but I wouldn't say that I was very much trained by her. What happened was that when Lucy Burns and I came back, having both been imprisoned in England, we were invited to take part in the cam-paign over here; otherwise nobody would have ever paid any attention to us.

Q. *That was in 1913?*

A. I came back in 1910. It was in 1912 that I was appointed by the National American Woman Suffrage Association to the chairmanship of their Congressional Committee in Washington, which was to work for the passage of the amendment that Susan B. Antho-ny had helped draw up. And Lucy Burns was asked to go with me. Miss Jane Addams, who was on the national board, made the motion for our appointments. They didn't take the work at all seriously, or else they wouldn't have entrusted it to us, two young girls. They did make one condition, and that was that we should never send them any bills, for as much as one dollar. Everything we did, we must raise the money ourselves. My prede-cessor, Mrs. William Kent, the wife of the congressman from California, told me that she had been given ten dollars the previous year by the national association, and at the end of her term she gave back some change.

Q. *Weren't you discouraged by the national association's attitude?*

A. Well, when we came along, we tried to do the work on a scale which we thought, in our great ignorance, might bring some success. I had an idea that it might be a one year's campaign. We would explain it to every congressman, and the amendment would go through. It was so clear. But it took us seven years. When you're young, when you've never done anything very much on your own, you imagine that it won't be so hard. We probably wouldn't have undertaken it if we had known the difficulties.

Q. *How did you begin?*

A. I went down to Washington on the seventh of December, 1912. All I had at the start was a list of people who had supported the movement, but when I tried to see them, I found that almost all of them had died or moved, and nobody knew much about them. So we were left with a tiny handful of people.

Q. *With all these obstacles how did you manage to organize the tremendous parade that greeted President-elect Wilson three months later?*

A. Well, it wasn't such a tremendous parade. We called it a procession. I don't know whether there were five thousand or ten thousand marchers, maybe, but it wasn't a very big one. The idea for such a parade had been discussed at the 1912 suffrage convention, although some of the delegates thought it was too big an undertaking. It was unusual. There had never been a procession of women for any cause under the sun, so people did want to go and see it.

Q. *The press estimated the crowd at a half million. Whose idea was it to have the parade the day before Wilson's inaugural?*

A. That was the only day you could have it if you were trying to impress the new President. The marchers came from all over the country at their own expense. We just sent letters everywhere, to every name we could find. And then we had a hospitality committee headed by Mrs. Harvey Wiley, the wife of the man who put through the first pure-food law in America. Mrs. Wiley canvassed all her friends in Washington and came up with a tremendous list of people who were willing to entertain the visiting marchers for a day or two. I mention these names to show what a wonderful group of people we had on our little committee.

Q. *Did you have any trouble getting a police permit?*

A. No, although in the beginning the police tried to get us to march on Sixteenth Street, past the embassies and all. But from our point of view Pennsylvania Avenue was the place. So Mrs. Ebenezer Hill, whose husband was a Connecticut congressman and whose daughter Elsie was on our committee, she went to see the police chief, and we got our permit. We marched from the Capitol to the White House, and then on to Constitution Hall, which was the hall of the Daughters of the American Revolution, which many of our people were members of.

Q. *Didn't the parade start a riot?*

A. he press reports said that the crowd was very hostile, but it wasn't hostile at all. The spectators were practically all tourists who had come for Wilson's inauguration. We knew there would be a large turnout for our procession, because the company that put up the grandstands was selling tickets and giving us a small percentage. The money we got—it was a gift from heaven—helped us pay for the procession. I suppose the police thought we were only going to have a couple of hundred people, so they made no preparations. We were worried about this, so another member of our committee, Mrs. John Rogers, went the night before to see her brother-in-law, Secretary of War [Henry L.] Stimson, and he promised to send over the cavalry from Fort Myer if there was any trouble.

Q. *Did you need his help?*

A. Yes, but not because the crowd was hostile. There were just so many people that they poured into the street, and we were not able to walk very far. So we called Secretary Stimson, and he sent over the troops, and they cleared the way for us. I think it took us six hours to go from the Capitol to Constitution Hall. Of course, we did hear a lot of shouted insults, which we always expected. You know, the usual things about why aren't you home in the kitchen where you belong. But it wasn't anything violent. Later on, when we were actually picketing the White House, the people did become almost violent. They would tear our banners out of our hands and that sort of thing.

Q. *Were you in the front ranks of the 1913 parade?*

A. No. The national board members were at the head of it. I walked in the college section. We all felt very proud of ourselves, walking along in our caps and gowns. One of the largest and loveliest sections was made up of uniformed nurses. It was very impressive. Then we had a foreign section, and a men's section, and a Negro women's section from the National Association of Colored Women, led by Mary Church Terrell. She was the first colored woman to graduate from Oberlin, and her husband was a judge in Washington. Well, Mrs. Terrell got together a wonderful group to march, and then, suddenly, our members from the South said they wouldn't march. Oh, the newspapers just thought this was a wonderful story and developed it to the utmost. I remember that that was when the men's section came to the rescue. The leader, a Quaker I knew, suggested that the men march between the southern delegations and the colored women's section, and that finally satisfied the southern women. That was the greatest hurdle we had.

Q. *If the parade didn't cause any real trouble, why was there a subsequent congressional investigation that resulted in the ouster of the district police chief?*

A. The principal investigation was launched at the request of our women delegates from Washington, which was a suffrage state. These women were so indignant about the remarks from the crowd. And I remember that Congressman Kent was very aroused at the things that were shouted at his daughter, Elizabeth, who was riding on the California float, and he was among the first in Congress to demand an investigation into why the police hadn't been better prepared. As I said, the police just didn't take our little procession seriously. I don't think it was anything intentional. We didn't testify against the police, because we felt it was just a miscalculation on their part.

Q. *What was your next move after the parade?*

A. A few weeks after Mr. Wilson became President, four of us went to see him. And the President, of course, was polite and as much of a gentleman as he always was. He told of his own support, when he had been governor of New Jersey, of a state referendum on suffrage, which had failed. He said that he thought this was the way suffrage should come, through state referendums, not through Congress. That's all we accomplished. We said we were going to try and get it through Congress, that we would like to have his help and needed his support very much. And then we sent him another delegation and another and another and another and another and another and another—every type of women's group we could get. We did this until 1917, when the war started and the President said he couldn't see any more delegations.

Q. *So you began picketing the White House?*

A. We said we would have a perpetual delegation right in front of the White House, so he wouldn't forget. Then they called it picketing. We didn't know enough to know what picketing was, I guess.

Q. *How did you finance all this work?*

A. Well, as I mentioned, we were instructed not to submit any bills to the National American. Anything we did, we had to raise the money for it ourselves. So to avoid any conflict with them we decided to form a group that would work exclusively on the Susan B. Anthony amendment. We called it the Congressional Union for Woman's Suffrage. You see, the Congressional Committee was a tiny group, so the Congressional Union was set up to help with the lobbying, to help with the speechmaking, and especially to help in raising money. The first year we raised $27,000. It just came from anybody who wanted to help. Mostly small contributions. John McLean, the owner of the Washington *Post,* I think, gave us a thousand dollars. That was the first big gift we ever got.

Q. *The records indicate that you raised more than $750,000 over the first eight years. Did your amazing fund-raising efforts cause you any difficulties with the National American?*

A. I know that at the end of our first year, at the annual convention of the National American, the treasurer got up—and I suppose this would be the same with any society in the world—she got up and made a speech, saying, "Well, this group of women has raised a tremendous sum of money, and none of it has come to my treasury," and she was very displeased with this. Then I remember that Jane Addams stood up and reminded the convention that we had been instructed to pay our own debts, and so that was all there was to it. Incidentally, the Congressional Union paid *all* the bills of that national convention, which was held in Washington that year. I remember we paid a thousand dollars for the rent of the hall. If you spend a hard time raising the money, you remember about it.

Q. *Were you upset about not being reappointed chairman of the Congressional Committee?*

A. No, because they asked me to continue. But they said if I were the committee chairman, I would have to drop the Congressional Union. I couldn't be chairman of both. Some of the members on the National American board felt that all the work being put into the federal amendment wasn't a good thing for the entire suffrage campaign. I told them I had formed this Congressional Union and that I wanted to keep on with it.

Q. *Was it true, as some historians of the movement maintain, that the National American's president, Dr. Anna Shaw, was "suspicious" of unusual activity in the ranks?*

A. No, I don't think she was. She came down to Washington frequently and spoke at our meetings, and she walked at the head of our 1913 procession. But I think we did make the mistake perhaps of spending too much time and energy just on the campaign. We didn't take enough time, probably, to go and explain to all the leaders why we thought [the federal amendment] was something that could be accomplished. You see, the National American took the position—not Miss Anthony, but the later people—that suffrage was something that didn't exist anywhere in the world, and therefore we would have to go more slowly and have endless state referendums to indoctrinate the men of the country.

Q. *Obviously you didn't agree with this. Was this what caused the Congressional Union to break with the National American?*

A. We didn't break with the National American. In a sense we were expelled. At the 1913 convention they made lots and lots of changes in the association's constitution. I don't recall what they were, and I didn't concern myself with the changes at the time. At any rate, the Congressional Union was affiliated with the National American under one classification, and they wrote to us and said if we would resign from that classification and apply for another classification, there would be a reduction in our dues. So we did what they told us, and then when we applied for the new classification, they refused to accept us, and we were out.

Q. *Why did the National American do this to your group?*

A. The real division was over the Shafroth-Palmer amendment that the National American decided to substitute for the Anthony amendment in the spring of 1914. Under this proposal each state would hold a referendum on woman suffrage *if* more than 8 per cent of the legal voters in the last preceding election—males, of course—signed a petition for it. This tactic had been tried without much success before, and with all the time and money such campaigns involve, I don't think many women would have ever become voters. Our little group wanted to continue with the original amendment, which we called the Susan B. Anthony because the women of the country, if they knew anything about the movement, had heard the name Susan B. Anthony. Now the great part of the American women were very loyal to this amendment, and when the National American suddenly switched to Shafroth-Palmer, we thought that the whole movement was going off on a sidetrack. And that is the reason we later formed the National Woman's Party, because if we hadn't continued, there would have been nobody in Washington speaking up for the original amendment.

Q. *You didn't have much faith in state referendums?*

A. The first thing I ever did—after I graduated from Swarthmore, I did some social work in New York City—one of the suffragists there asked me to go with her to get signatures for a suffrage referendum in New York State. So I went with her, and she was a great deal older and much more experienced than I was. I remember going into a little tenement room with her, and a man there spoke almost no English, but he could vote. Well, we went in and tried to talk to this man and ask him to vote for equality for women. And almost invariably these men said, "No, we don't think that it is the right thing. We don't do that in Italy, women don't vote in Italy." You can hardly go through one of those referendum campaigns and not think what a waste of the strength of women to try and convert a majority of men in the state. From that day on I was convinced that the way to do it was through Congress, where there was a smaller group of people to work with.

Q. *Then the National Woman's Party was formed to continue the work on the federal amendment?*

A. We changed our name from the Congressional Union to the National Woman's Party in 1916, when we began to get so many new members and branches. Mainly people who disagreed with the National American's support of the Shafroth-Palmer. And the person who got us to change our name was Mrs. [Alva E.] Belmont.

Q. *Would you tell me about Mrs. Belmont?*

A. She was, of course, a great supporter of the suffrage movement financially, and we didn't even know her the first year we were in Washington. People said to me that she was a wonderfully equipped person who was very fond of publicity, and they suggested that I invite her to come down and sit on one of the parade floats. Well, I didn't know who she was at all, but I wrote her an invitation, and I remember thinking what a queer person she must be to want to sit on a float. She turned out to be anything but the type she was described, and, of course, she didn't sit on any float. Anyway, a year later, after we had been expelled from the National American and couldn't have been more alone and more unpopular and more unimportant, one of our members, Crystal Eastman [Benedict], contacted Mrs. Belmont. And Mrs. Belmont invited me to come have dinner and spend the night at her home in New York City. Well, I like to go to bed early, but Mrs. Belmont was the type that liked to talk all night. So all night we talked about how we could probably get suffrage. A little later Mrs. Belmont withdrew entirely from the old National American and threw her whole strength into our movement. The first thing she did was give us five thousand dollars. We had never had such a gift before.

Q. *Why do you think Mrs. Belmont crossed over to your group?*

A. She was entirely in favor of our approach to the problem. She wanted to be immediately put on our national board, so she could have some direction. And then, after suffrage was won, she became the president of the Woman's Party, and at that time she gave us most of the money to buy the house in Washington that is still the party's headquarters. Over the years Mrs. Belmont did an enormous amount for the cause of women's equality. She was just one of those people who were born with the feeling of independence for herself and for women.

Q. *Did Mrs. Belmont have something to do with the decision to campaign against the Democrats in the November, 1914, elections?*

A. Yes. You see, here we had an extremely powerful and wonderful man—I thought Woodrow Wilson was a very wonderful man—the leader of his party, in complete control of Congress. But when the Democrats in Congress caucused, they voted against suffrage. You just naturally felt that the Democratic Party was responsible. Of course, in England they were up against the same thing. They couldn't get this measure through Parliament without getting the support of the party that was in complete control.

Q. *Didn't this new policy of holding the party in power responsible represent a drastic change in the strategy of the suffrage movement?*

A. Up to this point the suffrage movement in the United States had regarded each congressman, each senator, as a friend or a foe. It hadn't linked them together. And maybe these men were individual friends or foes in the past. But we deliberately asked the Democrats to bring it up in their caucus, and they did caucus against us. So you couldn't regard them as your allies anymore. I reported all this to the National American convention in 1913, and I said that it seemed to us that we must begin to hold this party responsible. And nobody objected to my report. But when we began to put it into operation, there was tremendous opposition, because people said that this or that man has been our great friend, and here you are campaigning against him.

Q. *Would you have taken the same position against the Republicans if that party had been in power in 1914?*

A. Of course. You see, we tried very hard in 1916—wasn't it [Charles Evans] Hughes running against Wilson that year?—to get the Republicans to put federal suffrage in their platform, and we failed. We also failed with the Democrats. Then we tried to get the support of Mr. Hughes himself. Our New York State committee worked very hard on Mr. Hughes, and they couldn't budge him. So we went to see former President [Theodore] Roosevelt at his home at Oyster Bay to see if *he* could influence Mr. Hughes. And I remember so vividly what Mr. Roosevelt said. He said, "You know, in political life you must always remember that you not only must be on the right side of a measure, but you must be on the right side at the right time." He told us that that was the great trouble with Mr. Hughes, that Mr. Hughes is certainly for suffrage, but he can't seem to know that he must do it in time. So Mr. Hughes started on his campaign around the country, and when he came to Wyoming, where women were already voting, he wouldn't say he was for the suffrage amendment. And he went on and on, all around the country. Finally, when he came to make his final speech of the campaign in New York, he had made up his mind, and he came out strongly for the federal suffrage amendment. So it was true what Mr. Roosevelt had said about him.

Q. *Do you think Hughes might have beaten Wilson in 1916 if he had come out for suffrage at the beginning of his campaign?*

A. Oh, I don't know about that. I was just trying to show you that we were always trying to get the support of both parties.

Q. *Well, this decision to politically attack the party in power, could this be attributed to the influence of Mrs. Pankhurst and your experience in England?*

A. Maybe, although I didn't ever really think about it as being that. The key was really the two million women who were already enfranchised voters in the eight western suffrage states. One fifth of the Senate, one seventh of the House, and one sixth of the electoral votes came from the suffrage states, and it was really a question of making the two political parties aware of the political power of women. This was also part of my report to the 1913 National American convention. I said that this was a weapon we could use—taking away votes in the suffrage states from the party in power—to bring both parties around to the federal amendment more quickly.

Q. *In the 1914 elections women voted for forty-five members of Congress, and the Democrats won only nineteen of these races, often by drastically reduced pluralities. Weren't you at all concerned about defeating some of your strongest Democratic supporters in Congress?*

A. Not really. Whoever was elected from a suffrage state was going to be prosuffrage in Congress anyway, whether he was Republican or Democrat. But how else were we going to demonstrate that women could be influential, independent voters? One of the men we campaigned against was Representative—later Senator—Carl Hayden of Arizona, and he finally became a very good friend of the movement, I thought. But it is true that most of them really did resent it very much.

Q. *You mean like Representative Taggart of Kansas?*

A. Who? I don't remember him.

Q. *Taggart was the man who attacked you personally at the Judiciary Committee hearings on December 16, 1914. His election majority had been cut from 3,000 in 1912 to 300 in 1914, and when you appeared before the committee to testify on the federal amendment, he said, "Are you here to report the progress of your efforts to defeat Democratic candidates?" He was very upset.*

A. Evidently. But I really don't remember that, although I know that that feeling was fairly general among the men we had campaigned against. You see, we had so many, many of these hearings. I don't try to remember them. I sort of wiped them all out of my mind because all of that is past.

Q. *I mentioned this particular hearing because the man who came to your defense that day was Representative Volstead, the author of Prohibition, which had a great impact on woman suffrage by removing one of your most vigorous enemies, the liquor lobby.*

A. Oh? I wouldn't know what you call the liquor lobby, but certainly the liquor interests in the country were represented at the hearings against us. They had some nice dignified name, but they were always there, and I suppose they are still in opposition to our equal-rights amendment. People have the idea that women are the more temperate half of the world, and I hope they are, although I don't know for sure. The prohibitionists supported our efforts, but I didn't have any contact with them. And I wasn't a member of the Women's Christian Temperance Union at that time. I've since become a member.

Q. *By the way, what was the significance of the movement's official colors?*

A. The purple, white, and gold? I remember the person who chose those colors for us, Mrs. John J. White. She noticed that we didn't have a banner at the 1913 procession, so she said, "I am going to have a banner made for you, a beautiful banner that will be identified with the women's movement." So she had a banner made with these colors, and we agreed to it. There wasn't any special significance to the choice of colors. They were just beautiful. It may be an instinct, it is with me anyway, when you're presenting something to the world, to make it as beautiful as you can.

Q. *You were once quoted to the effect that in picking volunteers you preferred enthusiasm to experience.*

A. Yes. Well, wouldn't you? I think everybody would. I think every reform movement needs people who are full of enthusiasm. It's the first thing you need. I was full of enthusiasm, and I didn't want any lukewarm person around. I still am, of course.

Q. *One of your most enthusiastic volunteers was Inez Milholland Boissevain, wasn't she?*

A. Inez Milholland actually gave her life for the women's movement. I think Inez was our most beautiful member. We always had her on horseback at the head of our processions. You've probably read about this, but when Inez was a student at Vassar, she tried to get up a suffrage meeting, and the college president refused to let her hold the meeting. So she organized a little group, and they jumped over a wall at the edge of the college and held the first suffrage meeting at Vassar in a cemetery. Imagine such a thing happening at a women's college so short a time ago. You can hardly believe such things occurred. But they did.

Q. *How did Miss Milholland give her life for the movement?*

A. After college Inez wanted to study law, but every prominent law school refused to admit a girl. She finally went to New York University, which wasn't considered much of a university then, and got her law degree. Then she threw her whole soul into the suffrage movement and really did nothing else but that. Well, in 1916, when we were trying to prevent the re-election of Woodrow Wilson, we sent speakers to all the suffrage states, asking people not to vote for Wilson, because he was opposing the suffrage which they already had. Inez and her sister, Vita, who was a beautiful singer, toured the suffrage states as a team. Vita would sing songs about the women's movement, and then Inez would speak. Their father, John Milholland, paid all the expenses for their tour, which began in Wyoming. Well, when they got to Los Angeles, Inez had just started to make her speech when she suddenly collapsed and fell to the floor, just from complete exhaustion. Her last words were "Mr. President, how long must women wait for liberty?" We used her words on picket banners outside the White House. I think she was about twenty-eight or twenty-nine.

Q. *What happened then?*

A. She was brought back and buried near her family home in New York State. We decided to have a memorial service for her in Statuary Hall in the Capitol on Christmas Day. So I asked Maud Younger, who was our congressional chairman and a great speaker, if she would make the principal speech at the ceremony. Maud said she had never made this kind of speech before and asked me how to do it. I remember telling her, "You just go and read Lincoln's Gettysburg Address and then you will know just how." Maud made a wonderful speech, as she always did.

Q. *Did you have any difficulties getting permission to hold the Milholland service in Statuary Hall?*

A. When you have a small movement without much support, you sometimes run into difficulties. I don't remember any particular difficulty, but we always had them. You just take things in your stride, don't you think? If you come up against all these obstacles, well, you've got to do something about them if you want to get through to the end you have in view. In this case we wanted to show our gratitude to Inez Milholland, and we wanted the world to realize—and I think they did—the importance of her contribution by holding it in the Capitol and having so many people of national importance attend.

Q. *Did you invite President Wilson and his family?*

A. Oh, no. We did send a delegation to him from the meeting, but he wouldn't receive them. Finally on January 9, 1917, he agreed to meet with women from all over the country who brought Milholland resolutions. The women asked him once more to lend the weight and influence of his great office to the federal amendment, but the President rejected the appeal and continued to insist that he was the follower, not the leader, of his party. The women were quite disappointed when they returned to Cameron House, where we had established our headquarters across Lafayette Square from the White House. That afternoon we made the decision to have a perpetual delegation, six days a week, from ten in the morning until half past five in the evening, around the White House. We began the next day.

Q. *And this perpetual delegation, or picketing, continued until the President changed his position?*

A. Yes. Since the President had made it clear that he wouldn't see any more delegations in his office, we felt that pickets outside the White House would be the best way to remind him of our cause. Every day when he went out for his daily ride, as he drove through our picket line he always took off his hat and bowed to us. We respected him very much. I always thought he was a great President. Years later, when I was in Geneva [Switzerland] working with the World Woman's Party, I was always so moved when I would walk down to the League of Nations and see the little tribute to Woodrow Wilson.

Q. *Do you think that the President's daughters, Jessie and Margaret, who were strong supporters of the suffrage movement, exerted any pressure on the President?*

A. Well, I think if you live in a home and have two able daughters—the third daughter was younger, and I didn't know much about what she was doing—it would almost be inevitable that the father would be influenced. Also, I think the first Mrs. Wilson was very sympathetic to us, but we never knew Mrs. Galt, his second wife. Someone told me that she wrote a book recently about her life in the White House in which she spoke in the most derogatory terms about the suffragists.

Q. *Do you want to talk about the violence that occurred on the White House picket line?*

A. Not particularly. It is true that after the United States entered the war [April 6, 1917], there was some hostility, and some of the pickets were attacked and had their banners ripped out of their hands. The feeling was—and some of our own members shared this and left the movement—that the cause of suffrage should be abandoned during wartime, that we should work instead for peace. But this was the same argument used during the Civil War, after which they wrote the word "male" into the Constitution. Did you know that "male" appears three times in the Fourteenth Amendment? Well, it does. So we agreed that suffrage came *before* war. Indeed, if we had universal suffrage throughout the world, we might not even have wars. So we continued picketing the White House, even though we were called traitors and pro-German and all that.

Q. *Mrs. Irwin wrote in her book that on one occasion a sailor tried to steal your suffrage sash on the picket line and that you were dragged along the sidewalk and badly cut.*

A. Oh, no. She wrote *that?* No, that never happened. You know, when people become involved in a glorious cause, there is always a tendency, perhaps, to enlarge on the circumstances, to magnify situations and incidents.

Q. *And is there, perhaps, on your part a tendency to be overmodest about your activities?*

A. I wouldn't know about that. All this seems so long ago and so unimportant now, I don't think you should be taking your precious lifetime over it. I try always, you know, to vanquish the past and try to be a new person.

Q. *But it is true, isn't it, that you were arrested outside the White House on October 20, 1917, and sentenced to seven months in the District of Columbia jail?*

A. Yes.

Q. *And that when you were taken to the cell-block where the other suffragists were being held, you were so appalled by the stale air that you broke a window with a volume of Robert Browning's poetry you had brought along to read?*

A. No. I think Florence Boeckel, our publicity girl, invented that business about the volume of Browning's poetry. What I actually broke the window with was a bowl I found in my cell.

Q. *Was this the reason you were transferred to solitary confinement in the jail's psychopathic ward?*

A. I think the government's strategy was to discredit me. That the other leaders of the Woman's Party would say, well, we had better sort of disown this crazy person. But they didn't.

Q. *During the next three or four weeks you maintained your hunger strike. Was this the second or third time you underwent forcible feeding?*

A. Probably, but I'm not sure how many times.

Q. *Is this done with liquids poured through a tube put down through your mouth?*

A. I think it was through the nose, if I remember right. And they didn't use the soft tubing that is available today.

Q. *While you were held in solitary confinement your own lawyer, Dudley Field Malone, could not get in to see you. And yet one day David Lawrence, the journalist, came in to interview you. How do you explain this?*

A. I think he was a reporter at that time, but anyway he was a very great supporter of and, I guess, a personal friend of President Wilson's. I didn't know then what he was, except that he came in and said he had come to have an interview with me. Of course, a great many people thought that Lawrence, because of his close connection with the White House, had been encouraged to go and look into what the women were doing and why they were making all this trouble and so on.

Q. *You and all the other suffragist prisoners were released on November 27 and 28, just a few days after Lawrence's visit. Could this action have been based on his report to the President?*

A. I wouldn't know about that. Of course, the only way we could be released would be by act of the President.

Q. *And on January 9, 1918, President Wilson formally declared for federal suffrage. The next day the House passed the amendment 274–136, and the really critical phase of the legislative struggle began.*

A. Yes. Well, when we began, Maud Younger, our congressional chairman, got up this card catalogue, which is now on loan to the Library of Congress. We had little leaflets printed, and each person who interviewed a congressman would write a little report on where this or that man stood. We knew we had the task of winning them over, man by man, and it was important to know what our actual strength was in Congress at all times. These records showed how, with each Congress, we were getting stronger and stronger, until we finally thought we were at the point of putting the Anthony amendment to a vote. And of course this information was very helpful to our supporters in Congress.

Q. *Yet when the Senate finally voted on October 1, 1918, the amendment failed by two votes of the necessary two thirds. What happened?*

A. We realized that we were going to lose a few days before the vote. We sat there in the Senate gallery, and they talked on and on and on, and finally Maud Younger and I went down to see what was going on, why they wouldn't vote. People from all over the country had come. The galleries were filled with suffragists. We went to see Senator Curtis, the Republican whip, and the Republican leader, Senator Gallinger. It was then a Republican Senate. And there they stood, each with a tally list in their hands. So we said, why don't you call the roll. And they said, well, Senator Borah has deserted us, he has decided to oppose the amendment, and there is no way on earth we can change his mind.

Q. *You thought Borah was on your side?*

A. Oh, yes. He wanted our support for his re-election campaign that year out in Idaho, and our organizer out there, Margaret Whittemore, had a statement signed by him that he would vote for the suffrage amendment. But then he changed. He never gave any reason for changing.

Q. *Did you then oppose him in the November election?*

A. We opposed him, yes. We cut his majority, but he was reelected, and from a suffrage state.

Q. *Was it about this time that your members began burning the President's statements in public?*

A. I'm not sure when it started. We had a sort of perpetual flame going in an urn outside our headquarters in Lafayette Square. I think we used rags soaked in kerosene. It was really very dramatic, because when President Wilson went to Paris for the peace conference, he was always issuing some wonderful, idealistic statement that was impossible to reconcile with what he was doing at home. And we had an enormous bell—I don't recall how we ever got such an enormous bell—and every time Wilson would make one of these speeches, we would toll this great bell, and then somebody would go outside with the President's speech and, with great dignity, burn it in our little caldron. I remember that Senator Medill McCormick lived just down the street from us, and we were constantly getting phone calls from him saying they couldn't sleep or conduct social affairs because our bell was always tolling away.

Q. *You had better results from the next Congress, the Sixty-sixth, didn't you?*

A. Yes. President Wilson made a magnificent speech calling for the amendment as a war measure back in October, 1918, and on May 20, 1919, the House passed the amendment. Then on June 4 the Senate finally passed it.

Q. *Did you go to hear the President?*

A. I don't believe we were there, because when the President spoke, everybody wanted tickets, and the Woman's Party has never asked for tickets, because we still don't want to be in any way under any obligation. I know we were in the gallery when the Senate actually voted, because nobody wanted tickets then. Our main concern was that the Senate might try to reinstate the seven-year clause that had been defeated in the House.

Q. *The seven-year clause?*

A. This clause required the amendment to be ratified by the states within seven years or else the amendment would be defeated. We got the clause eliminated on the suffrage amendment, but we were unable to stop Congress from attaching it to the present equal-rights amendment.

Q. *Were you relieved when the Anthony amendment finally passed?*

A. Yes, for many reasons. But we still had to get it ratified. We went to work on that right away and worked continuously for the fourteen months it took. But that last state . . . we thought we never would get that last state. And, you know, President Wilson really got it for us. What happened was that Wilson went to the governor of Tennessee, who was a Democrat. The President asked him to call a special session of the state legislature so the amendment could be ratified in time for women to vote in the 1920 Presidential election.

Q.   *That was on August 18, 1920, and there is a well-known photograph of you, on the balcony of your headquarters, unfurling the suffrage flag with thirty-six stars. What were your feelings that day?*

A.   You know, you are always so engrossed in the details that you probably don't have all the big and lofty thoughts you should be having. I think we had this anxiety about how we would pay all our bills at the end. So the first thing we did was to just do nothing. We closed our headquarters, stopped all our expenses, stopped publishing our weekly magazine, *The Suffragist,* stopped everything and started paying off the bills we had incurred. Maud Younger and I got the tiniest apartment we could get, and she took over the housekeeping, and we got a maid who came in, and we just devoted ourselves to raising this money.

Q.   *What happened to Lucy Burns, your co-leader?*

A.   Well, she went back, I guess, to her home in Brooklyn. Everybody went back to their respective homes. Then the following year, on February 15, 1921, we had our final convention to decide what to do. Whether to disband or whether to continue and take up the whole equality program—equality for women in all fields of life—that had been spelled out at the Seneca Falls Convention in 1848. We decided to go on, and we elected a whole new national board, with Elsie Hill as our new chairman. We thought we ought to get another amendment to the Constitution, so we went to many lawyers—I remember we paid one lawyer quite a large sum, for us, at least—and asked them to draw up an amendment for equal rights. We had another meeting up in Seneca Falls on the seventy-fifth anniversary of the original meeting, and there we adopted the program we have followed ever since on the equal-rights amendment. That was 1923. So that is when we started.

Q.   *Was that the year the first equal-rights amendment was introduced?*

A.   We hadn't been able to get any lawyer to draft an amendment that satisfied us, so I drafted one in simple ordinary English, not knowing anything much about law, and we got it introduced in Congress. But at the first hearing our little group was the only one that supported it. All these other organizations of women that hadn't worked to get the vote, these professional groups and so on, opposed the amendment on the grounds that it would deprive them of alimony and force them to work in the mines, and they would lose these special labor laws that protect women. So it was obvious to us—and to the Congress—that we were going to have to change the thinking of American women first. So we began going to convention after convention of women, trying to get them to endorse E.R.A. It took many years. The American Association of University Women just endorsed it in 1972. Imagine, all the years and years and years that women have been going to universities. But the new generation of college women were so hopeless on this subject.

Q.   *It was like forty years in the wilderness, wasn't it?*

A.   Yes, more or less. But during that time we opened—and by "we" I mean the whole women's movement—we opened a great many doors to women with the power of the vote, things like getting women into the diplomatic service. And don't forget we were successful in getting equality for women written into the charter of the United Nations in 1945.

Q.   *Do you think the progress of the equal-rights amendment has been helped by the women's liberation movement?*

A.   I feel very strongly that if you are going to do anything, you have to take one thing and do it. You can't try lots and lots of reforms and get them all mixed up together. Now, I think the liberation movement has been a good thing, because it has aroused lots of women from their self-interest, and it has made everyone more aware of the inequalities that exist. But the ratification of the equal-rights amendment has been made a bit harder by these people who run around advocating, for instance, abortion. As far as I can see, E.R.A. has nothing whatsoever to do with abortion.

Q. *How did abortion become involved with equal rights?*

A. At the 1968 Republican convention our representative went before the platform committee to present our request for a plank on equal rights, and as soon as she finished, up came one of the liberation ladies, a well-known feminist, who made a great speech on abortion. So then all the women on the platform committee said, well, we're not going to have the Republican Party campaigning for abortion. So they voted not to put *anything* in the party platform about women's rights. That was the first time since 1940 that we didn't get an equal-rights plank in the Republican platform. And then that feminist showed up at the Democratic convention, and the same thing happened with their platform. It was almost the same story at the 1972 conventions, but this time we managed to get equal rights back into the platforms.

Q. *It's really the principle of equal rights that you're concerned with, isn't it, not the specific applications?*

A. I have never doubted that equal rights was the right direction. Most reforms, most problems are complicated. But to me there is nothing complicated about ordinary equality. Which is a nice thing about our campaign. It really is true, at least to my mind, that only good will come to everybody with equality. If we get to the point where everyone has equality of opportunity—and I don't expect to see it, we have such a long, long way ahead of us—then it seems to me it is not our problem how women use their equality or how men use their equality.

Q. *Miss Paul, how would you describe your contribution to the struggle for women's rights?*

A. I always feel . . . the movement is a sort of mosaic. Each of us puts in one little stone, and then you get a great mosaic at the end.

THE DAYS OF BOOM
AND BUST

John Kenneth Galbraith

Economics has long had the unflattering nickname of the "dismal science," both for its complexity and for the impenetrable style of much of the writing on the subject. Yet in the case of the great stock market crash of 1929, even citizens totally uninterested in economics know that something dramatic and far-reaching occurred. Although it did not by itself cause the worst economic depression in American history, the crash nonetheless dramatically and disastrously signalled its onset.

No one has written more lucidly about the stock market in the 1920s than John Kenneth Galbraith, Professor Emeritus of Economics at Harvard University. He sees maldistribution of personal income, corporate pyramid schemes, and unsustainable optimism about ever-increasing stock prices as three of the major weaknesses of the market. Most serious, however, was the poor leadership of presidents and other public leaders in the face of this Wall Street frenzy. This disastrous episode goes far to explain why later generations have seen fit to put in place governmental controls on the economy and the stock market that business leaders of the twenties would have found unacceptable.

The decade of the twenties, or more precisely the eight years between the postwar depression of 1920–21 and the stock market crash in October of 1929, were prosperous ones in the United States. The total output of the economy increased by more than 50 percent. The preceding decades had brought the automobile; now came many more and also roads on which they could be driven with reasonable reliability and comfort. There was much building. The downtown section of the mid-continent city—Des Moines, Omaha, Minneapolis—dates from these years. It was then, more likely than not, that what is still the leading hotel, the tallest office building, and the biggest department store went up. Radio arrived, as of course did gin and jazz.

These years were also remarkable in another respect, for as time passed it became increasingly evident that the prosperity could not last. Contained within it were the seeds of its own destruction. The country was heading into the gravest kind of trouble. Herein lies the peculiar fascination of the period for a study in the problem of leadership. For almost no steps were taken during these years to arrest the tendencies which were obviously leading, and did lead, to disaster.

At least four things were seriously wrong, and they worsened as the decade passed. And knowledge of them does not depend on the always brilliant assistance of hindsight. At least three of these flaws were highly visible and widely discussed. In ascending order, not of importance but of visibility, they were as follows:

First, income in these prosperous years was being distributed with marked inequality. Although output per worker rose steadily during the period, wages were fairly stable, as also were prices. As a result, business profits increased rapidly and so did incomes of the wealthy and the well-to-do. This tendency was nurtured by assiduous and successful efforts of Secretary of the Treasury Andrew W. Mellon to reduce income taxes with special attention to the higher brackets. In 1929 the 5 percent of the people with the highest incomes received perhaps a third of all personal income. Between 1919 and 1929 the share of the one percent who received the highest incomes increased by approximately one-seventh. This meant that the economy was heavily and increasingly dependent on the luxury consumption of the well-to-do and on their willingness to reinvest what they did not or could not spend on themselves. Anything that shocked the confidence of the rich either in their personal or in their business future would have a bad effect on total spending and hence on the behavior of the economy.

This was the least visible flaw. To be sure, farmers, who were not participating in the general advance, were making themselves heard; and twice during the period the Congress passed far-reaching relief legislation which was vetoed by Coolidge. But other groups were much less vocal. Income distribution in the United States had long been unequal. The inequality of these years did not seem exceptional. The trade-union movement was also far from strong. In the early twenties the steel industry was still working a twelve-hour day and, in some jobs, a seven-day week. (Every two weeks when the shift changed a man worked twice around the clock.) Workers lacked the organization or the power to deal with conditions like this; the twelve-hour day was, in fact, ended as the result of personal pressure by President Harding on the steel companies, particularly on Judge Elbert H. Gary, head of the United States Steel Corporation. Judge Gary's personal acquaintance with these working conditions was thought to be slight, and this gave rise to Benjamin Stolberg's now classic observation that the Judge "never saw a blast furnace until his death." In all these circumstances the increasingly lopsided income distribution did not excite much comment or alarm. Perhaps it would have been surprising if it had.

But the other three flaws in the economy were far less subtle. During World War I the United States ceased to be the world's greatest debtor country and became its greatest creditor. The consequences of this change have so often been described that they have the standing of a cliché. A debtor country could export a greater value of goods than it imported and use the difference for interest and debt repayment. This was what we did before the war. But a creditor must import a greater value than it exports if those who owe it money are to have the wherewithal to pay interest and principal. Otherwise the creditor must either forgive the debts or make new loans to pay off the old.

During the twenties the balance was maintained by making new foreign loans. Their promotion was profitable to domestic investment houses. And when the supply of honest and competent foreign borrowers ran out, dishonest, incompetent, or fanciful borrowers were invited to borrow and, on occasion, bribed to do so. In 1927 Juan Leguia, the son of the then dictator of Peru, was paid $450,000 by the National City Company and J. & W. Seligman for his services in promoting a $50,000,000 loan to Peru which these houses marketed. Americans lost and the Peruvians didn't gain appreciably. Other Latin American republics got equally dubious loans by equally dubious devices. And, for reasons that now tax the imagination, so did a large number of German cities and municipalities. Obviously, once investors awoke to the character of these loans or there was any other shock to confidence, they would no longer be made. There would be nothing with which to pay the old loans. Given this arithmetic, there would be either a sharp reduction in exports or a wholesale default on the outstanding loans, or more likely both. Wheat and cotton farmers and others who depended on exports would suffer. So would those who owned the bonds. The buying power of both would be reduced. These consequences were freely predicted at the time.

The second weakness of the economy was the large-scale corporate thimblerigging that was going on. This took a variety of forms, of which by far the most common was the organization of corporations to hold stock in yet other corporations, which in turn held stock in yet other corporations. In the case of the railroads and the utilities, the purpose of this pyramid of holding companies was to obtain control of a very large number of operating companies with a very small investment in the ultimate holding company. A $100,000,000 electric utility, of which the capitalization was represented, half by bonds and half by common stock, could be controlled with an investment of a little over $25,000,000—the value of just over half the common stock. Were a company then formed with the same capital structure to hold *this* $25,000,000 worth of common stock, it could be controlled with an investment of $6,250,000. On the next round the amount required would be less than $2,000,000. That $2,000,000 would still control the entire $100,000,000 edifice. By the end of the twenties, holding-company structures six or eight tiers high were a commonplace. Some of them—the utility pyramids of Insull and Associated Gas & Electric, and the railroad pyramid of the Van Sweringens—were marvelously complex. It is unlikely that anyone fully understood them or could.

In other cases companies were organized to hold securities in other companies in order to manufacture more securities to sell to the public. This was true of the great investment trusts. During 1929 one investment house, Goldman, Sachs & Company, organized and sold nearly a billion dollars' worth of securities in three interconnected investment trusts—Goldman Sachs Trading Corporation; Shenandoah Corporation; and Blue Ridge Corporation. All eventually depreciated virtually to nothing.

This corporate insanity was also highly visible. So was the damage. The pyramids would last only so long as earnings of the company at the bottom were secure. If anything happened to the dividends of the underlying company, there would be trouble, for upstream companies had issued bonds (or in practice sometimes preferred stock) against the dividends on the stock of the downstream companies. Once the earnings stopped, the bonds would go into default or the preferred stock would take over and the pyramid would collapse. Such a collapse would have a bad effect not only on the orderly prosecution of business and investment by the operating companies but also on confidence, investment, and spending by the community at large. The likelihood was increased because in any number of cities—Cleveland, Detroit, and Chicago were notable examples—the banks were deeply committed to these pyramids or had fallen under the control of the pyramiders.

Finally, and most evident of all, there was the stock market boom. Month after month and year after year the great bull market of the twenties roared on. Sometimes there were setbacks but more often there were fantastic forward surges. In May of 1924 the *New York Times* industrials stood at 106; by the end of the year they were 134; by the end of 1925 they were up to 181. In 1927 the advance began in earnest—to 245 by the end of that year and on to 331 by the end of 1928. There were some setbacks in early 1929, but then came the fantastic summer explosion when in a matter of three months the averages went up another 110 points. This was the most frantic summer in our financial history. By its end, stock prices had nearly quadrupled as compared with four years earlier, transactions on the New York Stock

Exchange regularly ran to 5,000,000 or more shares a day. Radio Corporation of America went to 573¾ (adjusted) without ever having paid a dividend. Only the hopelessly eccentric, so it seemed, held securities for their income. What counted was the increase in capital values.

And since capital gains were what counted, one could vastly increase his opportunities by extending his holdings with borrowed funds—by buying on margin. Margin accounts expanded enormously, and from all over the country—indeed from all over the world—money poured into New York to finance these transactions. During the summer, brokers' loans increased at the rate of $400,000,000 a month. By September they totaled more than $7,000,000,000. The rate of interest on these loans varied from 7 to 12 percent and went as high as 15.

This boom was also inherently self-liquidating. It could last only so long as new people, or at least new money, were swarming into the market in pursuit of the capital gains. This new demand bid up the stocks and made the capital gains. Once the supply of new customers began to falter, the market would cease to rise. Once the market stopped rising, some, and perhaps a good many, would start to cash in. If you are concerned with capital gains, you must get them while the getting is good. But the getting may start the market down, and this will one day be the signal for much more selling—both by those who are trying to get out and those who are being forced to sell securities that are no longer safely margined. Thus it was certain that the market would one day go down, and far more rapidly than it went up. Down it went with a thunderous crash in October of 1929. In a series of terrible days, of which Thursday, October 24, and Tuesday, October 29, were the most terrifying, billions in values were lost, and thousands of speculators—they had been called investors—were utterly and totally ruined.

This too had far-reaching effects. Economists have always deprecated the tendency to attribute too much to the great stock market collapse of 1929: this was the drama: the causes of the subsequent depression really lay deeper. In fact, the stock market crash was very important. It exposed the other weakness of the economy. The overseas loans on which the payments balance depended came to an end. The jerry-built holding-company structures came tumbling down. The investment-trust stocks collapsed. The crash put a marked crimp on borrowing for investment and therewith on business spending. It also removed from the economy some billions of consumer spending that was either based on, sanctioned by, or encouraged by the fact that the spenders had stock market gains. The crash was an intensely damaging thing.

And this damage, too, was not only foreseeable but foreseen. For months the speculative frenzy had all but dominated American life. Many times before in history—the South Sea Bubble, John Law's speculations, the recurrent real-estate booms of the last century, the great Florida land boom earlier in the same decade—there had been similar frenzy. And the end had always come, not with a whimper but a bang. Many men, including in 1929 the President of the United States, knew it would again be so.

The increasingly perilous trade balance, the corporate buccaneering, and the Wall Street boom—along with the less visible tendencies in income distribution—were all allowed to proceed to the ultimate disaster without effective hindrance. How much blame attaches to the men who occupied the presidency?

Warren G. Harding died on August 2, 1923. This, as only death can do, exonerates him. The disorders that led eventually to such trouble had only started when the fatal blood clot destroyed this now sad and deeply disillusioned man. Some would argue that his legacy was bad. Harding had but a vague perception of the economic processes over which he presided. He died owing his broker $180,000 in a blind account—he had been speculating disastrously while he was President, and no one so inclined would have been a good bet to curb the coming boom. Two of Harding's Cabinet officers, his secretary of the interior and his attorney general, were to plead the Fifth Amendment when faced with questions concerning their official acts, and the first of these went to jail. Harding brought his fellow townsman Daniel R. Crissinger to be his comptroller of the currency, although he was qualified for this task, as Samuel Hopkins Adams has suggested, only by the fact that he and the young Harding had stolen watermelons together. When Crissinger had had an ample opportunity to demonstrate his incompetence in his first post, he was made head of the Federal Reserve System. Here he had the central responsibility for action on the ensuing boom. Jack Dempsey, Paul Whiteman, or F. Scott Fitzgerald would have been at least equally qualified.

Yet it remains that Harding was dead before the real trouble started. And while he left in office some very poor men, he also left some very competent ones. Charles Evans Hughes, his secretary of state; Herbert Hoover, his secretary of commerce; and Henry C. Wallace, his secretary of agriculture, were public servants of vigor and judgment.

The problem of Herbert Hoover's responsibility is more complicated. He became President on March 4, 1929. At first glance this seems far too late for effective action. By then the damage had been done, and while the crash might come a little sooner or a little later, it was now inevitable. Yet Hoover's involvement was deeper than this—and certainly much deeper than Harding's. This he tacitly concedes in his memoirs, for he is at great pains to explain and, in some degree, to excuse himself.

For one thing, Hoover was no newcomer to Washington. He had been secretary of commerce under Harding and Coolidge. He had also been the strongest figure (not entirely excluding the President) in both Administration and party for almost eight years. He had a clear view of what was going on. As early as 1922, in a letter to Hughes, he expressed grave concern over the quality of the foreign loans that were being floated in New York. He returned several times to the subject. He knew about the corporate excesses. In the latter twenties he wrote to his colleagues and fellow officials (including Crissinger) expressing his grave concern over the Wall Street orgy. Yet he was content to express himself—to write letters and memoranda, or at most, as in the case of the foreign loans, to make an occasional speech. He could with propriety have presented his views of the stock market more strongly to the Congress and the public. He could also have maintained a more vigorous and persistent agitation within the Administration. He did neither. His views of the market were so little known that it celebrated his election and inauguration with a great upsurge. Hoover was in the boat and, as he himself tells, he knew where it was headed. But, having warned the man at the tiller, he rode along into the reef.

And even though trouble was inevitable, by March, 1929, a truly committed leader would still have wanted to do something. Nothing else was so important. The resources of the Executive, one might expect, would have been mobilized in a search for some formula to mitigate the current frenzy and to temper the coming crash. The assistance of the bankers, congressional leaders, and the Exchange authorities would have been sought. Nothing of the sort was done. As secretary of commerce, as he subsequently explained, he had thought himself frustrated by Mellon. But he continued Mellon in office. Henry M. Robinson, a sympathetic Los Angeles banker, was commissioned to go to New York to see his colleagues there and report. He returned to say that the New York bankers regarded things as sound. Richard Whitney, the vice-president of the Stock Exchange, was summoned to the White House for a conference on how to curb speculation. Nothing came of this either. Whitney also thought things were sound.

Both Mr. Hoover and his official biographers carefully explained that the primary responsibility for the goings on in New York City rested not with Washington but with the governor of New York State. That was Franklin D. Roosevelt. It was he who failed to rise to his responsibilities. The explanation is far too formal. The future of the whole country was involved. Mr. Hoover was the President of the whole country. If he lacked authority commensurate with this responsibility, he could have requested it. This, at a later date, President Roosevelt did not hesitate to do.

Finally, while by March of 1929 the stock market collapse was inevitable, something could still be done about the other accumulating disorders. The balance of payments is an obvious case. In 1931 Mr. Hoover did request a one-year moratorium on the inter-Allied (war) debts. This was a courageous and constructive step which came directly to grips with the problem. But the year before, Mr. Hoover, though not without reluctance, had signed the Hawley-Smoot tariff. "I shall approve the Tariff Bill. . . . It was undertaken as the result of pledges given by the Republican Party at Kansas City. . . . Platform promises must not be empty gestures." Hundreds of people—from Albert H. Wiggin, the head of the Chase National Bank, to Oswald Garrison Villard, the editor of the *Nation*—felt that no step could have been more directly designed to make things worse. Countries would have even more trouble earning the dollars of which they were so desperately short. But Mr. Hoover signed the bill.

Anyone familiar with this particular race of men knows that a dour, flinty, inscrutable visage such as that of Calvin Coolidge can be the mask for a calm and acutely perceptive intellect. And he knows equally that it can conceal a mind of singular aridity. The difficulty, given the inscrutability, is in knowing which. However, in the case of Coolidge the evidence is in favor of the second. In some sense, he certainly knew what was going on. He would not have been unaware of what was called the Coolidge market. But he connected developments neither with the well-being of the country nor with his own responsibilities. In his memoirs Hoover goes to great lengths to show how closely he was in touch with events and how clearly he foresaw their consequences. In his *Autobiography*, a notably barren document, Coolidge did not refer to the accumulating troubles. He confines himself to such unequivocal truths as "Every day of Presidential life is crowded with activities" (which in his case, indeed, was not true); and "The Congress makes the laws, but it is the President who causes them to be executed."

At various times during his years in office, men called on Coolidge to warn him of the impending trouble. And in 1927, at the instigation of a former White House aide, he sent for William Z. Ripley of Harvard, the most articulate critic of the corporate machinations of the period. The President became so interested that he invited him to stay for lunch, and listened carefully while his guest outlined (as Ripley later related) the "prestidigitation, double-shuffling, honey-fugling, hornswoggling, and skulduggery" that characterized the current Wall Street scene. But Ripley made the mistake of telling Coolidge that regulation was the responsibility of the states (as was then the case). At this intelligence Coolidge's face lit up and he dismissed the entire matter from his mind. Others who warned of the impending disaster got even less far.

And on some occasions Coolidge added fuel to the fire. If the market seemed to be faltering, a timely statement from the White House—or possibly from Secretary Mellon—would often brace it up. William Allen White, by no means an unfriendly observer, noted that after one such comment the market staged a 26-point rise. He went on to say that a careful search "during these halcyon years . . . discloses this fact: Whenever the stock market showed signs of weakness, the President or the Secretary of the Treasury or some important dignitary of the administration . . . issued a statement. The statement invariably declared that business was 'fundamentally sound,' that continued prosperity had arrived, and that the slump of the moment was 'seasonal.'"

Such was the Coolidge role. Coolidge was fond of observing that "if you see ten troubles coming down the road, you can be sure that nine will run into the ditch before they reach you and you have to battle with only one of them." A critic noted that "the trouble with this philosophy was that when the tenth trouble reached him he was wholly unprepared. . . . The outstanding instance was the rising boom and orgy of mad speculation which began in 1927." The critic was Herbert Hoover.

Plainly, in these years, leadership failed. Events whose tragic culmination could be foreseen—and was foreseen—were allowed to work themselves out to the final disaster. The country and the world paid. For a time, indeed, the very reputation of capitalism itself was in the balance. It survived in the years following perhaps less because of its own power or the esteem in which it was held, than because of the absence of an organized and plausible alternative. Yet one important question remains. Would it have been possible even for a strong President to arrest the plunge? Were not the opposing forces too strong? Isn't one asking the impossible?

No one can say for sure. But the answer depends at least partly on the political context in which the Presidency was cast. That of Coolidge and Hoover may well have made decisive leadership impossible. These were conservative Administrations in which, in addition, the influence of the businessman was strong. At the core of the business faith was an intuitive belief in *laissez faire*—the benign tendency of things that are left alone. The man who wanted to intervene was a meddler. Perhaps, indeed, he was a planner. In any case, he was to be regarded with mistrust. And, on the businessman's side, it must be borne in mind that high government office often nurtures a spurious sense of urgency. There is no more important public function than the suppression of proposals for unneeded action. But these should have been distinguished from action necessary to economic survival.

A bitterly criticized figure of the Harding-Coolidge-Hoover era was Secretary of the Treasury Andrew W. Mellon. He opposed all action to curb the boom, although once in 1929 he was persuaded to say that bonds (as distinct from stocks) were a good buy. And when the depression came, he was against doing anything about that. Even Mr. Hoover was shocked by his insistence that the only remedy was (as Mr. Hoover characterized it) to "liquidate labor, liquidate stocks, liquidate the farmers, liquidate real estate." Yet Mellon reflected only in extreme form the conviction that things would work out, that the real enemies were those who interfered.

Outside of Washington in the twenties, the business and banking community, or at least the articulate part of it, was overwhelmingly opposed to any public intervention. The tentative and ineffective steps which the Federal Reserve did take were strongly criticized. In the spring of 1929 when the Reserve system seemed to be on the verge of taking more decisive action, there was an anticipatory tightening of money rates and a sharp drop in the market. On his own initiative Charles E. Mitchell, the head of the National City Bank, poured in new funds. He had an obligation, he said, that was "paramount to any Federal Reserve warning, or anything else" to avert a crisis in the money market. In brief, he was determined, whatever the government thought, to keep the boom going. In that same spring Paul M. Warburg, a distinguished and respected Wall Street leader, warned of the dangers of the boom and called for action to restrain it. He was deluged with criticism and even abuse and later said that the subsequent days were the most difficult of his life. There were some businessmen and bankers—like Mitchell and Albert Wiggin of the Chase National Bank—who may have vaguely sensed that the end of the boom would mean their own business demise.

Many more had persuaded themselves that the dream would last. But we should not compli-
cate things. Many others were making money and took a short-run view—or no view—either of their own survival or of the system of which they were a part. They merely wanted to
be left alone to get a few more dollars.

And the opposition to government intervention would have been nonpartisan. In 1929
one of the very largest of the Wall Street operators was John J. Raskob. Raskob was also
chairman of the Democratic National Committee. So far from calling for preventive
measures, Raskob in 1929 was explaining how, through stock market speculation, literally
anyone could be a millionaire. Nor would the press have been enthusiastic about, say, legislation to control holding companies and investment trusts or to give authority to regulate
margin trading. The financial pages of many of the papers were riding the boom. And even
from the speculating public, which was dreaming dreams of riches and had yet to learn that it
had been fleeced, there would have been no thanks. Perhaps a President of phenomenal power
and determination might have overcome the Coolidge-Hoover environment. But it is easier
to argue that this context made inaction inevitable for almost any President. There were too
many people who, given a choice between disaster and the measures that would have prevented it, opted for disaster without either a second or even a first thought.

On the other hand, in a different context a strong President might have taken effective
preventive action. Congress in these years was becoming increasingly critical of the Wall Street
speculation and corporate piggery-pokery. The liberal Republicans—the men whom Senator
George H. Moses called the Sons of the Wild Jackass—were especially vehement. But conservatives like Carter Glass were also critical. These men correctly sensed that things were going
wrong. A President such as Wilson or either of the Roosevelts (the case of Theodore is perhaps
less certain than that of Franklin) who was surrounded in his Cabinet by such men would
have been sensitive to this criticism. As a leader he could both have reinforced and drawn
strength from the contemporary criticism. Thus he might have been able to arrest the destruc-
tive madness as it became recognizable. The American government works far better—perhaps
it only works—when the Executive, the business power, and the press are in some degree at
odds. Only then can we be sure that abuse or neglect, either private or public, will be given
the notoriety that is needed.

Perhaps it is too much to hope that by effective and timely criticism and action the Great
Depression might have been avoided. A lot was required in those days to make the United
States in any degree depression-proof. But perhaps by preventive action the ensuing depression might have been made less severe. And certainly in the ensuing years the travail of bankers and businessmen before congressional committees, in the courts, and before the bar of
public opinion would have been less severe. Here is the paradox. In the full perspective of history, American businessmen never had enemies as damaging as the men who grouped themselves around Calvin Coolidge and supported and applauded him in what William Allen
White called "that masterly inactivity for which he was so splendidly equipped."

VI

"Shut the Goddam Plant"

Stephen W. Sears

Although the union movement can trace its origins to the years immediately after the Civil War, unions made little headway because of the refusal of most factory owners to recognize them as the exclusive bargaining agent of the workers—to engage in "collective bargaining," in other words. Moreover, the American Federation of Labor, the most successful of the early unions, concentrated on organizing highly skilled craftsmen rather than entire plant work forces.

Legislation passed during the early 1930s guaranteed workers the right of collective bargaining, but the Big Three automakers—Chrysler, Ford, and General Motors—were adamant in their refusal to obey the law. As the most visible example of big industry in early twentieth-century America, the automakers were the logical target for the union movement, and mighty GM was the first to feel the pain of the highly effective tactic of the sit-down strike.

This essay tells the dramatic story of the 1937 Flint, Michigan Fisher Body Number One strike against General Motors. Worker solidarity, some fumbles by GM, a state governor sympathetic to the workers and skillful in getting the two sides to negotiate, and public opinion not altogether supportive of GM's property rights, all combined to win the United Auto Workers a stunning victory against the mighty auto company. Within five years, Chrysler, Ford, and several independent automakers would also succumb to the union movement. Today, when many Americans view unions as unnecessary or archaic, it is fitting to remember their courageous efforts to win the many rights that American workers now take for granted.

At General Motors' Flint, Michigan, Fisher Body Number One, the largest auto-body factory in the world, it was early evening of a chill winter day. Suddenly a bright red light began flashing in the window of the United Automobile Workers union hall across the street from the plant's main gate. It was the signal for an emergency union meeting.

When the swing shift took its dinner break at 8:00 P.M., excited workers crowded into the hall. UAW organizer Robert C. Travis confirmed the rumor crackling through the huge plant: dies for the presses that stamped out car body panels were being loaded into freight cars on a Fisher One spur track. Two days earlier, he reminded the men, fellow unionists had struck the Fisher Body plant in Cleveland; now, fearing Flint would be next, General Motors was trying to transfer the vital stamping dies to its other plants. "Well, what are we going to do about it?" Travis asked.

"Well, them's our jobs," a man said. "We want them left right here in Flint." There was a chorus of agreement. " What do you want to do?" Travis asked.

"Shut her down! Shut the goddam plant!" In a moment the hall was a bedlam of cheering.

As the dinner break ended, the men streamed back into Fisher One. Travis was watching anxiously in front of the union hall when the starting whistle blew. Instead of the usual answering pound of machinery, there was only silence. For long minutes nothing seemed to be happening. Then a third-floor window swung open and a worker leaned out, waving exultantly to Travis. "She's ours!" he shouted.

Thus began, on December 30, 1936, the great Flint sit-down strike, the most momentous confrontation between American labor and management in this century. For the next six weeks Flint would be a lead story in newspapers, newsreels, and radio newscasts. Events there dramatized the new militancy of the American worker, a mass movement that was to produce basic changes in the relationship of capital and labor. To those in sympathy with labor's goal of unionizing the auto industry, the rambunctious young United Automobile Workers union was David challenging the General Motors Goliath. To those dedicated to the sanctity of property, the UAW and its methods posed a radical, revolutionary threat to industrial capitalism. Few observers were neutral about the Flint sit-down.

There was no disputing the fact that the UAW faced a giant. Auto making was America's number-one industry, and General Motors was the number one auto maker. Indeed, it was the largest manufacturing concern in the world. GM's 1936 sales of 1,500,000 Chevrolets, Pontiacs, Buicks, Oldsmobiles, La Salles, and Cadillacs represented better than 43 per cent of the domestic passenger-car market. It had sixty-nine auto plants in thirty-five cities. Business analysts regarded GM President Alfred P. Sloan, Jr., as a genius and his company as the best managed in America. It was unquestionably the most profitable—$284,000,000 in 1936 pretax profits on $1,400,000,000 in sales. This was a matter of great satisfaction to its 342,384 stockholders, and to one in particular. E. I. Du Pont de Nemours & Company owned nearly one-quarter of GM's common stock, good that year for nearly $45,000,000 in dividends. In short, General Motors was the paragon of industrial capitalism, and there was heavy pressure, both from within and without, to maintain the *status quo* that produced so many golden eggs.

One fundamental tenet of the *status quo* was a fiercely anti-union stance. In this General Motors acted in perfect unanimity with its competitors. Nineteen thirty-six marked the fortieth anniversary of the American automobile industry, and never in those four decades had the open shop seriously been threatened. The very notion of unionism was anathema to captains of the auto industry. "As a businessman, I was unaccustomed to the whole idea," Alfred Sloan wrote blandly in his memoirs.

Before the Great Depression, unionism was in truth not much of an issue in Detroit. The vast labor army recruited during the auto boom of the twenties—white dirt farmers, poor city dwellers, southern blacks, recent immigrants—was docile and innocent of trade-union experience. Any labor grievances were defused by pay scales higher than those in most other industries and by a system of "welfare capitalism" (group insurance, savings programs, housing subsidies, recreational facilities, and the like) in which General Motors was a pioneer. Open-shop Detroit had little to fear from the nation's largest union, the American Federation of Labor. The craft-minded AFL devoted itself to horizontal unionism—organizing all the machinists, for example, regardless of industry. It studiously ignored industrial unionism, the vertical organization of the unskilled or semiskilled workers within a particular industry such as autos, steel, or rubber.

Then the Depression knocked everything haywire. In the early 1930s Detroit auto workers found themselves powerless as the industry collapsed like a punctured balloon. Welfare capitalism was silent on job security. Wages and work time were slashed. As layoffs mounted, workers with ten or twenty years' experience discovered that their seniority counted for nothing; it counted for nothing, either, in the call-backs that marked an upturn in auto sales beginning in 1933. Assembly lines were speeded up mercilessly to raise productivity and restore profit levels. Bitter men protested. "You might call yourself a man if you was on the street," a Fisher Body worker recalled, "but as soon as you went through the door and punched your card, you was nothing more or less than a robot." "It takes your guts out, that line. The speed-up, that's the trouble," another said. "You should see him come home at night, him and the rest of the men . . . ," a Flint auto worker's wife testified. "So tired like they was dead. . . . And then at night in bed, he shakes, his whole body, he shakes. . . . "

More and more auto workers began to see unionism as their only hope to redress the balance. In this they detected an ally in the New Deal. The National Industrial Recovery Act (1933) recognized labor's right to organize and bargain collectively. The NIRA, however, was too weak a reed to support labor's aspirations, for it was largely unenforceable and easily evaded by management; and in any event, the Supreme Court knocked it down in 1935. But labor's hopes were raised anew by the passage of the National Labor Relations Act—the so-called Wagner Act, named for its chief sponsor, New York Senator Robert F. Wagner. The act established a National Labor Relations Board and gave it teeth to enforce collective bargaining and permit unionization efforts without interference by management.

The auto companies ignored the Wagner Act, confidently expecting the Supreme Court to do its duty. While they waited, they turned increasingly to labor spies to quash unionizing efforts. The most notorious spy system flourished at Ford, where goon squads instituted a bloody reign of terror in the massive River Rouge complex in Dearborn, outside Detroit. The General Motors espionage network was nonviolent but no less widespread. Evidence gathered by a Senate investigating committee chaired by Wisconsin's Robert M. La Follette, Jr., revealed that from 1934 to mid-1936 GM hired no fewer than fourteen private detective and security agencies, at a cost of $994,000, to ferret out and fire employees with union sympathies. This "most colossal super-system of spies yet devised in any American corporation," the La Follette committee charged, enveloped the worker in a web of fear. "Fear harries his every footstep, caution muffles his words. He is in no sense any longer a free American."

Launching an effective union in such turbulent waters would be difficult enough, and it was made no easier by an upheaval in labor's ranks. In 1933, prodded into action by the collective bargaining section of the NIRA, the American Federation of Labor had made a cautious stab at organizing Detroit's work force by chartering the United Automobile Workers union. However, leadership in the AFL-affiliated UAW was far too conservative to suit the rank and file. Three years' work produced a few toeholds among independent auto makers but barely a dent in the Big Three. In GM's Flint factories, for example, there was a grand total of 150 paid-up UAW members in June, 1936, just six months before the great sit-down.

This stumbling effort to organize the auto workers reflected the fratricidal conflict within the AFL. Advocates of industrial unionism, led by John L. Lewis of the United Mine Workers, David Dubinsky of the International Ladies' Garment Workers, and Sidney Hillman of the Amalgamated Clothing Workers, formed a rump group, the Committee (later Congress) of Industrial Organization. In the summer of 1936 the CIO seceded from the AFL ranks, taking with it the United Automobile Workers locals. Marching under the new CIO banner, the UAW prepared to do battle with the auto industry. It would be the first modern test of the theory of industrial unionism.

The revitalized UAW settled on General Motors as its first target. Chrysler's Walter Chrysler, who had climbed Horatio Alger-like up through the ranks, was considered the auto magnate most sympathetic to labor; if number-one GM could be conquered, number-two Chrysler might follow along. Ford was simply too tough a nut to crack yet. In addition, General Motors was particularly vulnerable. All bodies for the low-priced Chevrolet and the medium-priced Pontiac, Buick, and Oldsmobile were built by its Fisher Body division. If it came down to a strike—and no labor leader doubted that it would—the closing of only a few selected Fisher Body plants would immediately cripple the company.

And when the strike came, there was no doubt it would focus on Flint, the General Motors citadel. William C. Durant founded the company there in 1908, and it had remained the center of GM auto production. The Flint of 1936 was a drab gray industrial city of 160,000, some sixty miles northwest of Detroit, ringed by GM installations. Fisher Body One was to the south, a huge Buick assembly plant to the north, Fisher Body Two and a Chevrolet complex to the west, AC Spark Plug to the east. Two out of three of the city's breadwinners—more than 47,000 of them—worked for GM. Four out of five families, directly or indirectly, lived off the company payroll. Virtually every aspect of economic, social, and cultural life revolved around GM. Flint was very much a company town.

The union's first job was what a later generation would call consciousness raising. Wyndham Mortimer, a veteran trade unionist, began this task even before the UAW defected to the CIO, combining the five weak Flint locals into one, Local 156, and planting the seeds of unionism. In October, 1936, however, the quiet, hard-working Mortimer was replaced by twenty-seven-year-old Bob Travis, a more personable and energetic organizer. At Travis' side was Roy Reuther, who, with his brothers Victor and Walter, would become a dominant force in the UAW. The sons of a German immigrant, the Reuthers were, in Victor's words, "born into the labor movement." Eloquent, ambitious, and like his brothers deeply committed to trade unionism, Roy Reuther formed a strong partnership with Travis.

Facing a hostile management with a fearful company town infested with labor spies (the only safe topics of conversation in Flint, according to Mortimer, were "sports, women, dirty stories, and the weather"), UAW organizers did the bulk of their recruiting in workers' homes and at clandestine meetings. The labor journalist Henry Kraus was brought in to edit the *Flint Auto Worker*, an important vehicle for airing worker grievances and spreading the UAW gospel. Much effort was devoted to involving workers' wives in the movement. And rather than spreading themselves thin proselytizing the entire Flint GM work force, Travis and Reuther focused on the men in the city's two key Fisher Body plants. Their efforts were made easier by Franklin D. Roosevelt's overwhelming victory in the November elections, which labor took as a good omen for support from Washington.

By late December, Flint Local 156 had signed up 10 per cent of the city's GM workers, largely in secret to foil the spies and mostly in Fisher One and Fisher Two. On December 22, GM Executive Vice-President William S. Knudsen, meeting with UAW President Homer Martin, denied that issues such as union recognition, job security, pay rates, seniority rights, and the speed-up were "national in scope." Corporate headquarters had no say in such matters, he piously declared: they must be settled on the local level with individual plant managers. Martin recognized this account of the workings of the General Motors Corporation for what it was—pure fiction. It was clear that the company had no intention of obeying the Wagner Act and seriously bargaining with any independent union. The stage was set for a strike.

But what kind of strike? Veteran Flint workers remembered an attempt to close Fisher One in 1930 that had been smashed by local lawmen abetted by the Michigan state police. Pickets were scattered and ridden down by mounted officers, and strike leaders were arrested and subsequently fired. Few UAW officials in Flint had any illusions that their forty-five hundred or so members could long sustain a conventional picket-line strike in the heart of General Motors country. The solution might lie in an entirely different kind of strike—a sit-down.

The tactic was ingeniously simple. Instead of walking off the job, strikers stopped work but stayed at their machines, holding valuable company property hostage to enforce their demands. A sit-down was far less vulnerable to police action than outside picketing, and it neutralized a primary weapon in management's arsenal, the use of strikebreakers to resume production. Even more than a conventional striker, the sit-downer was taking his fight directly to management.

The sit-down was not new—some claimed to have traced its origins back to stone masons in ancient Egypt—but its baptism by fire took place in Europe in the twenties and thirties. Italian metal workers, Welsh coal miners, Spanish copper miners, and Greek rubber workers sat down at their jobs, and in the spring of 1936 mass sit-downs in France took on the proportions of a nationwide general strike. In the United States in 1936 the Bureau of Labor Statistics reported forty-eight sit-down strikes. The ones most closely watched by auto workers took place at Bendix Products (owned in part by GM) in South Bend, Indiana, and at two Detroit parts makers, Midland Steel Products and Kelsey-Hayes Wheel. All three won limited worker gains and deeply impressed UAW militants. Thus far, however, no American sit-down had been played for truly high stakes.

In the midst of the feverish unionizing efforts in Flint's Fisher One, a shop steward named Bud Simons was asked if his men were ready to strike. "Ready?" Simons exclaimed. "They're like a pregnant woman in her tenth month!" Flint's militants, however, were upstaged by militants in the Fisher Body plant in Cleveland. On December 28, 1936, Fisher Cleveland was shut tight by a sit-down. In Flint Bob Travis and his UAW organizers cast about desperately for some excuse to initiate a strike.

The report on December 30 that the company was moving the stamping dies out of Fisher One was the *casus belli* Travis needed. "Okay!" he said happily, "they're asking for it!" By midnight that day the swing shift's capture of the huge plant was complete. Two miles away the smaller Fisher Two was also taken over by sit-downers. As the new year began, production of Chevrolets and Buicks, General Motors' bread-and-butter cars, ground to a halt. Soon other GM marques were effected, for the occupation of the two Fisher Body plants in Flint and the one in Cleveland had the potential for halting fully 75 percent of the company's passenger-car production. The sit-down gave David the weapon to use against Goliath.

Over the next few weeks, strikes would shut down more than a dozen other GM plants. Parts shortages forced many additional plant closings. The total number of idled men would reach 136,000. Yet from first to last, the spotlight remained on Flint. The strike's success or failure—and to the strikers, success meant nothing less than management's recognition of the UAW as exclusive bargaining agent—would be decided at the center of the General Motors empire.

The sit-downers began to organize themselves with military precision. Once all non-strikers (and all female employees) left, the two plants were barricaded and patrolled. "It was like we were soldiers holding the fort," one of them said. "It was like war. The guys with me became my buddies." Everyone served a regular daily shift on a committee to manage such functions as defense, food supply, sanitation, and recreation. Discipline was strict: the strike leaders were determined to show the public that this was no rabble-in-arms take-over. News reporters and other observers who toured the seized factories remarked on the organization and on the absence of wild-eyed fanatics. "We're just here protecting our jobs," a Fisher Two striker told *The New York Times*. "We don't aim to keep the plants or try to run them, but we want to see that nobody takes our jobs. . . . " Petty violations of strike committee rules meant extra cleanup or K. P. duty, serious offenses (possession of guns or liquor, the sabotaging of company property) meant expulsion. Round-the-clock dining halls were established in the plant cafeterias, and sleeping quarters were improvised from car seats and bodies.

Keeping the men occupied during their new six-hour "work shifts" was not difficult, but it required more ingenuity to fill the off-duty periods and keep morale high. Defense committees set up production lines for the making of blackjacks and billy clubs. Many hours were devoted to cards, checkers, and dominoes, and there was a steady flow of newspapers and magazines into the plants. UAW lecturers spoke on parliamentary procedures, collective bargaining, and labor history. There were improvised games of volleyball and Ping-pong, and here and there men could be seen roller skating between the long rows of idle machinery. Amateur theatricals, in which enthusiasm and raucous humor were more evident than acting skill, played to cheering, jeering audiences. A showing of Charlie Chaplin's satire on assembly-line mass production, *Modern Times,* was greeted enthusiastically. Those who played banjos, mandolins, or harmonicas put on impromptu concerts and almost everyone took up community singing, sometimes writing their own lyrics; to the tune of "Gallagher and Shean," for example, they belted out:

Oh! Mr. Sloan! Oh! Mr. Sloan!
Everyone knows your heart was made of stone.
But the Union is so strong That we'll always carry on.
Absolutely, Mr. Travis! Positively, Mr. Sloan!

The population in Fisher One and Fisher Two varied widely during the six-week strike. Local 156 set up outside picket lines as an aid to maintaining traffic into and out of the plants, which enabled sit-downers to take leave and visit friends and families. The number of men in Fisher One varied from a high of something over one thousand to a low of ninety, in Fisher Two from upwards of four hundred and fifty to as few as seventeen. The problem for the Fisher Two strike leaders was the large number of married men in their ranks; concern for the welfare of families eroded their staying power as the strike dragged on. Fisher One had a higher percentage of single men of the "hard, reckless type" (in the words of a New York Times reporter) and who were better able to endure the strike's pressures. Population fluctuated as hopes for a settlement waxed and waned, and when the number of sit-downers fell dangerously low, the UAW called on militant locals from Detroit and Toledo for reinforcements. The arrival of one such group moved Bud Simons to remark, "I have never seen a bunch of guys that were so ready for blood in my life."

On the whole, however, the sit-downers maintained a remarkably strong sense of community. In a letter to his wife, one of them wrote, "I could of came out wen they went on strike But hunny I just thought I join the union and I look pretty yellow if I dident stick with them. . . . " A growing self-esteem strengthened the workers' commitment. As labor historian Sidney Fine writes, they were "transformed from badge numbers and easily replaceable cogs in an impersonal industrial machine into heroes of American labor." A striker remembered that "it started out kinda ugly because the guys were afraid they put their foot in it and all they was gonna do is lose their jobs. But as time went on, they begin to realize they could win this darn thing, 'cause we had a lot of outside people comin' in showin' their sympathy."

Meanwhile, on the outside, Bob Travis and Roy Reuther set up strike headquarters in the Pengelly Building, a down-at-the-heels firetrap in downtown Flint. The place was a beehive, with strikers and volunteer helpers cranking out publicity releases, raising money, mobilizing support, planning strategy. The most immediate problem was food. Dorothy Kraus, wife of the *Flint Auto Worker* editor Henry Kraus, directed a strike kitchen set up in a restaurant near Fisher One that was turned over to the union by its owner. Meals were prepared there three times a day and delivered to the plants in large kettles under heavy union guard. (The menus were the work of Max Gazan, former chef of the Detroit Athletic Club, a favorite haunt of the GM Establishment.) Food stocks were purchased or donated by sympathizers or by Flint merchants pressured to do so by the threat of boycott. As many as two hundred people took part in running the strike kitchen, many of them sit-downers' wives. Wives also formed a Women's Auxiliary and a Women's Emergency Brigade. Kraus's newspaper and the mimeographed *Punch Press*, put out by student volunteers from the University of Michigan, kept the men informed. Cars equipped with loudspeakers allowed instant communication with the sit-downers, and outside picket lines lent moral support.

Despite its espionage network, General Motors was caught flat-footed by the sit-down tactic. At first management tried harassment by sporadically cutting back heat and light to the two plants, but it was feared that any serious attempt to starve out or freeze out the strikers would result in violence—and they were right. Groping for a policy to deal with the crisis, the company discovered that nothing in the Michigan statute books forbade the peaceful occupation of a company's property by its employees. Nor were the trespass laws much help: since the workers had entered the plants at management's "invitation," trespass presented a legal thicket. Nevertheless, GM quickly turned to the courts, petitioning on January 2, 1937, for an injunction to "restrain" the strikers from occupying Fisher One and Fisher Two. County Circuit Court Judge Edward D. Black, an eighty-three-year-old lifelong resident of Flint, granted it the same day.

To its subsequent great embarrassment, the corporation in its haste had failed to do its homework on Judge Black. On January 5 the UAW called a press conference to charge that in issuing the injunction Black was guilty of "unethical conduct," for he owned 3,665 shares of GM stock with a market value of almost $220,000. In the ensuing uproar, the Black injunction became a dead letter.

Round One to the UAW.

Round Two, if General Motors had its way, would find the sit-downers under irresistible pressure from the community. On January 5, GM President Alfred Sloan published an open letter to all employees. "Will a labor organization run the plants of General Motors . . . or will the Management continue to do so?" he asked. "You are being forced out of your jobs by sit-down strikes, by widespread intimidation. . . . You are being told that to bargain collectively you must be a member of a labor organization. . . . Do not be misled. Have no fear that any union or any labor dictator will dominate the plants of General Motors Corporation. No General Motors worker need join any organization to get a job or to keep a job. . . . " A campaign of mass meetings, balloting, and petitions—"I Love My Boss" petitions as strikers derisively tagged them—indicated that by company count four out of five Flint workers wanted to return to their jobs. (Only AC Spark Plug among GM's Flint plants was still operating at full capacity.) The UAW charged that coercion and intimidation produced this outpouring of company loyalty. The truth lay somewhere in between. As Sidney Fine points out, there was in Flint "a large middle group of workers, who, although preferring work to idleness, were uncommitted to either side in the dispute and were awaiting its outcome to determine where their best interests lay."

Two days after Sloan's open letter, a local businessman and former mayor named George E. Boysen announced the formation of the Flint Alliance "for the Security of Our Jobs, Our Homes, and Our Community." Membership was open to all Flint citizens, and within a week Boysen claimed that almost twenty-six thousand had signed up. Evidence that GM sponsored the alliance is sketchy, but it clearly had the company's blessing. The UAW viewed the alliance with concern, seeing it as a possible umbrella group for organizing strikebreakers or triggering violence against the occupied plants.

Several main themes marked this campaign to turn public opinion against the strikers—the oppression of the majority by a militant minority; the presence of "outside agitators" disrupting the General Motors family; and the insistence that the sit-down was a "Red Plot" threatening the capitalist system. This last was one of the most persistent charges. It was pointed out that the seizure of private property was a favorite communist tactic, and that the auto workers' union was honeycombed with Red radicals.

Hindsight has magnified this communist conspiracy theory, for such prominent UAW leaders as Wyndham Mortimer, Bob Travis, and Bud Simons, head of the strike committee in Fisher One, were in fact later involved in various communist or communist front activities. Indeed, the UAW itself, for a decade after 1937, was in constant fratricidal turmoil over the issue of communists within its ranks. It is clear, however, that the Flint sit-down strike was a grassroots revolt owing no allegiance to communist ideology or conspiracy. The sit-downers were men driven to desperation by oppressive working conditions, men convinced that management's attitude toward labor held no hope for improvement. "So I'm a Red?" a worker summed it up for a reporter. "I suppose it makes me a Red because I don't like making time so hard on these goddamned machines. When I get home I'm so tired I can't sleep with my wife."

Tension continued to build in Flint. On January 11, 1937, the thirteenth day of the strike, it exploded into violence. The incident that triggered it was carefully staged. About noon that day General Motors abruptly cut off heat to the Fisher Two plant, where about one hundred sit-downers were holding the second floor. (Unlike more strongly fortified Fisher One two miles away, Fisher Two's first floor and main gate were controlled by company security men.) It was a cold, raw day, with temperatures around sixteen degrees. During the afternoon an unusual number of police cars was seen in the neighborhood. At 6:00 P.M., when the strikers' evening meal was delivered to the Fisher Two main gate, guards refused to let it through. By 8:30, when Victor Reuther drove up in a union sound car to investigate, he found the cold and hungry strikers "in no pleasant mood." It was decided to take over the main gate to link the sit-downers with the pickets outside.

A squad of strikers, armed with homemade billy clubs, marched up to the company guards blocking the gate and demanded the key. When they were refused, a striker yelled, "Get the hell out of there!" and the guards fled to the plant ladies' room, locking themselves in. The head of the security detail telephoned Flint police headquarters to report that his men had been threatened and "captured." Right on cue, squad cars arrived, carrying some thirty riot-equipped city policemen. The police stormed the plant entrance, smashing windows and firing tear gas into the interior. The strikers fought back with a drumfire of bottles, rocks, nuts and bolts, heavy steel car-door hinges, and cascades of water from the plant's fire hoses. Under this barrage, the attackers withdrew to rearm and await reinforcements. The sit-downers put the lull to good use, tossing door hinges and other stocks of "popular ammunition" to pickets outside and rushing a squad to vantage points on the roof.

Soon the police charged a second time, firing their gas guns and hurling gas grenades through the plant windows and among the pickets outside. But now the defensive firepower was doubled as the pickets joined the battle. Fire hoses sent policemen sprawling. Others were felled by hinges, milk bottles, bricks, and pieces of roof coping. The county sheriff's car was tipped over; as he crawled out, a hinge struck him on the head. Tear gas took a toll among the defenders, who were left choking and vomiting and half-blinded. Finally, drenched and bloodied, sliding on pavement icing over from the fire-hose torrents, the attack force fled once more. Watching the "bulls" scramble away, someone gave the struggle a derisive name that stuck—the Battle of the Running Bulls.

Frustrated and humiliated, the police suddenly stopped, turned on a band of strikers pursuing them, and opened fire with pistols and riot guns loaded with buckshot. Then it was the strikers' turn to retreat, dragging their casualties with them. Thirteen suffered gunshot wounds, a dozen struck by buckshot and one hit seriously in the stomach by a pistol bullet. Eleven of the attackers also were hurt, most suffering from gashed heads but one having been hit in the leg by an errant police bullet. Retreating up a hill out of missile range, the police began sniping at the strikers in the plant, their bullets splattering against the walls and shattering windows. Clouds of acrid tear gas drifted across the icy battlefield, and above the shouting and the shooting could be heard the thundering amplified voice of Victor Reuther in the union sound car, directing the defenses and exhorting the men to stand fast. At last it was clear that the recapture effort had failed. Ambulances arrived to carry off the wounded and the injured. About midnight the sniping ceased.

But the battle had turned the sitdown onto a new course.

Hurrying to Flint from the state capital in Lansing, Michigan Governor Frank Murphy ordered in the National Guard troops and the state police. "It won't happen again," Murphy vowed. "Peace and order will prevail. The people of Flint are not going to be terrorized." By January 13 there were almost thirteen hundred Guardsmen in the city; before the strike ended, the number would rise by another two thousand. Whether General Motors had orchestrated every detail of the attempted recapture of Fisher Two, as the UAW charged, remained a matter of heated debate, but Murphy's action ensured that police violence would not "settle" the sit-down.

Organized labor had reason to fear National Guard and state police forces, which in the past had often been used to break strikes. In this instance, however, the union cheered their arrival, for it trusted the man who sent them. Indeed, the timing of the sit-down had been pegged to Democrat Murphy's taking office on January 1, 1937. He had run for governor with strong labor support. "I am heart and soul in the labor movement," he had declared during the campaign. As Wyndham Mortimer later said, "We felt that while he may or may not have been on our side, he at least would not be against us."

It was an accurate assessment. While Murphy disapproved of the sit-down tactic as an invasion of property rights, he strongly approved of the right to organize. Above all, he was determined to defuse the explosive atmosphere in Flint and get the two parties to the bargaining table. At first it appeared he would be quickly and brilliantly successful. On January 15, just four days after the Battle of the Running Bulls, Murphy announced a truce: the union agreed to evacuate Fisher One and Fisher Two, and GM agreed not to resume production while bargaining "in good faith." Then a report leaked out that GM had invited the Flint Alliance, which claimed to speak for the "greatest majority" of the city's idled workers, to attend the talks as a third party. Strike leaders saw this as fatal to their goal of winning exclusive UAW recognition; crying double-cross, they renounced the truce.

As the stalemate continued and positions hardened, new figures joined Frank Murphy in the limelight. On the GM side, Executive Vice President William Knudsen, a bluff, rough-and-ready production genius less concerned with how the strike was settled than when, was joined by two tougher-minded negotiators, Du Pont-trained financial expert Donaldson Brown and company attorney John T. Smith. On the union side, UAW President Homer Martin, an evangelical speaker but a poor negotiator, was eclipsed when the best-known figure in American labor strode onto the scene. John L. Lewis, head of the CIO, was determined to make the Flint sit-down the opening wedge in his crusade for industrial unionism. Supreme orator ("The economic royalists of General Motors—the Du Ponts and Sloans and others—" he thundered, " . . . have their fangs in labor") and a master press agent ("Seeing

John Lewis," said journalist Heywood Broun, "is about as easy as seeing the Washington Monument"), Lewis was a figure to reckon with.

Just how potent a publicist he could be was evident when the spotlight shifted from Flint to Washington. The Roosevelt administration, led by Secretary of Labor Frances Perkins, tried to get the strike off dead center by bringing together Lewis and Alfred Sloan, whom Miss Perkins described as "the real principals." For all his brilliance as an administrator, the GM president was saddled with a colorless personality and did not relish taking on the theatrical Lewis. Furthermore, the intense loathing he felt for the New Deal made any dealings with the administration difficult for him. In the end he called off the talks, angering both the President and Miss Perkins. For Sloan the sticking point was bargaining with "a group that holds our plants for ransom without regard to law or justice." Lewis announced to the nation that the GM high command had "run away" to New York "to consult with their allies [a barb at the GM-Du Pont connection] to determine how far they can go in their organized defiance of labor and the law." GM gained no friends in the exchange.

General Motors, in fact, was not doing as well mustering support as might have been expected of the world's largest corporation. Its disdain for the Wagner Act, the fiasco of the Black injunction, and the violence of the Battle of the Running Bulls did little for its corporate image. Despite strong and widespread public concern over the sit-down's threat to cherished property rights, the company's position won only a fifty-three to forty-seven edge in a Gallup poll published on January 31; apparently there was considerable sympathy for the union's stated—and lawful—goal of organizing and bargaining collectively without management interference. *Business Week* analyzed the public's view as "it's 'not right' for the strikers to stay in or for the company to throw them out."

There is little doubt that the union would have done less well on any poll taken in Flint. The city's blue-collar workers were suffering intensely now. By January 20, a full 88 per cent of the city's GM work force was unemployed. The percentage on the relief rolls was greater than it had been during the depths of the Depression. General Motors also was suffering: its January output was just 60,000 cars, instead of a projected figure of 224,000. Yet neither side would budge. Tension began again to build, fueled by violent incidents at GM plants in Anderson, Indiana, on January 25 and in Saginaw, Michigan, two days later. Then two events occurred that would push the sit-down to its climax.

On January 28 General Motors turned once more to the courts, applying for a second injunction to compel the strikers to leave. This time the company first checked out the circuit court judge, Paul V. Gadola, to be sure he was clean. Flint's strike leaders, meanwhile, planned a move of their own, one considerably more dramatic.

To regain the initiative and to demonstrate to General Motors that none of its properties was safe from seizure by sit-down, Travis, Roy Reuther, and other UAW strategists plotted the capture of Chevrolet Four, the Flint factory that produced all Chevrolet engines. Their plan had to be a daring one, for the engine plant was heavily guarded by GM police. Within hearing of auto workers whom their counterintelligence had identified as company spies, the strike leaders "secretly" revealed their next target to be a bearings plant, Chevrolet Nine. Company security snapped up the bait. On February 1, when the diversionary attempt was made on Chevrolet Nine, it was met by every Chevrolet guard the company could muster. After tear gas and wild, club-swinging melees, the unionists were driven out in apparent defeat. While the battle was raging inside Chevrolet Nine, however, three hundred yards away other strikers had swept through unguarded Chevrolet Four and secured the huge plant. "We have the key plant of the GM . . . ," one of the sit-downers would write to his wife. "We shure done a thing that GM said never could be done. . . . " He was right; the brilliantly executed capture of Chevrolet Four was the turning point.

Events now swiftly combined to bring the United Automobile Workers and General Motors to the negotiating table. On February 2 Judge Gadola issued a sweeping injunction that called for evacuation of the Flint Fisher Body plants within twenty-four hours, and the imposition of a $15,000,000 fine if the UAW did not comply. Although there was nothing like that sum to collect from the union treasury—"If the judge can get fifteen million bucks from us, he's welcome to it," a striker scoffed—the injunction did pressure the UAW to bargain. It also pressured Governor Murphy to find a quick strike-ending formula; as chief executive of the state of Michigan, he was obliged to decide how and when to enforce the injunction and uphold the law. As for GM, a massive demonstration of support by unionists outside Fisher One on February 3 seemed proof enough that any attempt to drive out the sit-downers would produce certain bloodshed and probable destruction of three of its most important plants. Reluctantly, like "a skittish virgin" in *Fortune's* irreverent phrase, the company surrendered to collective bargaining.

The talks were held in Detroit. On the GM side were Knudsen, Donaldson Brown, and John T. Smith. John L. Lewis headed the union delegation, seconded by CIO counsel Lee Pressman and UAW President Homer Martin. (The bumbling Martin was soon dispatched on a tour of faraway union locals to get him out of the way.) Murphy acted as chief negotiator, jumping back and forth between the parties "like a jack rabbit," seeking leverage for a settlement. Machinery was agreed to for later bargaining on such specific issues as wages and working conditions, and the union agreed to give up the plants and return to work while those issues were hammered out. GM agreed to take the sit-downers back without penalty or prejudice. The stiffest battle was fought over GM's recognition of the UAW as exclusive bargaining agent.

Hanging threateningly over the talks was the Gadola injunction. The very mention of using the National Guard to enforce the injunction provoked Lewis to one of his characteristic oratorical flights. According to his later recollection (perhaps embellished), he announced to Murphy: "Tomorrow morning, I shall personally enter General Motors plant Chevrolet Number Four. I shall order the men to disregard your order, to stand fast. I shall then walk up to the largest window in the plant, open it, divest myself of my outer raiment, remove my shirt, and bare my bosom. Then when you order your troops to fire, mine will be the first breast those bullets will strike!" In fact, the governor never had any notion of carrying out Judge Gadola's ruling with National Guard arms: "I'm not going down in history as 'Bloody Murphy'!" He did hint, however, at sealing off the captured plants with Guardsmen to prevent food deliveries unless the union made concessions. GM was pushed into concessions of its own by a painful economic fact. In the first ten days of February, the nation's largest auto maker produced exactly 151 cars.

Finally, at 2:35 on the morning of February 11, after sixteen grueling hours of final negotiating, the forty-four-day Flint sit-down strike came to an end. The agreement applied only to the seventeen plants that had gone out on strike, but they were GM's most important plants. As a face-saving gesture, the company did not have to state categorically that it was recognizing the union. But in fact it was: the UAW had six months to sign up auto workers before a representational election, during which time management could not interfere or deal with any other workers' body. "Well, Mr. Lewis," GM negotiator Smith said, "you beat us, but I'm not going to forget it." Production man Knudsen was not one to hold grudges. "Let us have peace and make automobiles," he proclaimed.

Late on the afternoon of February 11 the sit-downers came out. Carrying American flags, surrounded by throngs of cheering, horn-tooting supporters, the men of Fisher One marched the two miles across town to collect their compatriots in Fisher Two and Chevrolet Four. Then, thousands strong, they held a spectacular torchlight parade through downtown Flint. As they tramped along, they sang what had become their anthem:

Solidarity forever!
Solidarity forever!
Solidarity forever!
For the Union makes us strong!

They had every reason to sing and celebrate; they had won a major victory. UAW locals throughout the auto industry were promptly flooded with workers clamoring to sign up; just eight months after the sit-down settlement, the UAW could count nearly four hundred thousand dues-paying members, a five-fold increase. It easily won the representational elections in plants throughout the GM empire. Independents—Packard, Studebaker, Hudson—soon recognized the union, as did leading parts makers. In April, 1937, after a sit-down, Chrysler also succumbed. Ford held out the longest, but in 1941 it too acknowledged the UAW as exclusive bargaining agent. An important factor in all this was the Supreme Court decision, in April, 1937, upholding the Wagner Act. Unionization without interference by management was confirmed as the law of the land.

The United Automobile Workers failed to handle its success gracefully, however. From the moment of its birth, the union's high command had been rent with problems; its most decisive leaders, like those of Flint Local 156, came from the bottom. Rifts at the top were papered over during the sit-down by the overriding need for a united front, but with victory came chaos. Not until after World War II would the UAW, under the strong hand of Walter Reuther, finally put its house in order, purge itself of communists, and reach stable maturity. As for the CIO, the Flint victory, as John L. Lewis predicted, was industrial unionism's foot in the door. Beginning with Big Steel in March, 1937, the CIO successfully organized one basic industry after another. Union membership in the United States spurted 156 per cent between 1936 and 1941, most of it CIO gains.

The Flint sit-down inspired a rash of imitators. In the early months of 1937 workers of every stripe, from garbage men and dogcatchers to rug weavers and pie bakers, tried the tactic. Public irritation mounted swiftly. Many Americans had accepted the UAW's argument that the sit-down was the sole weapon it possessed to force intransigent General Motors to obey the law and permit union organizing and collective bargaining. Such an argument lost force after the Supreme Court upheld the Wagner Act; now, with both government and law behind it, organized labor was seen as achieving parity with management. Increasingly, the sitdown was condemned as an irresponsible act, and by 1939, when the Supreme Court outlawed the practice as a violation of property rights, it had long since gone out of vogue.

Victory in the Flint sit-down by no means ended the discontents of the auto worker. Yet now, for the first time, he could envision himself as something more than simply an insignificant part of a great impersonal machine; as "Solidarity" phrased it, the union had made him strong. "Even if we got not one damn thing out of it other than that," a Fisher Body worker said, "we at least had a right to open our mouths without fear."

VII

MAN OF THE CENTURY

Arthur Schlesinger, Jr.

Civil War historian David Donald has noted how, for decades after that conflict, politi-cians of all stripes felt the need to "get right with Lincoln"—to assure the public that their principles were solidly in line with those of the Great Emancipator. First it was fel-low Republicans, but then New Deal Democrats jumped on the Lincoln bandwagon, and finally the Progressives of 1948 and even the American Communist Party, with its "Lincoln-Lenin rallies."

Similarly, in the five decades since Franklin D. Roosevelt's death, politicians and pres-idents across the political spectrum—from Democrats like Truman, Kennedy, Johnson, and Clinton, to Republicans such as Eisenhower, Nixon, and Reagan (especially Reagan!)—have tried to cast themselves as disciples of our only four-term president. What is it about Roosevelt that has so dominated the politics of a generation?

In this article, noted historian and Roosevelt biographer Arthur Schlesinger, Jr. con-centrates on the often-overlooked foreign policy of the Roosevelt years. The President who led the United States through the fiery trial of World War II realized earlier than most that the world could not live with a Hitler. No leader of his generation—not Churchill, not Stalin—had a clearer and more accurate vision of what the postwar world would look like. According to Schlesinger, "FDR deserves supreme credit as the twentieth-century statesman who saw most deeply into the grand movements of history." Little wonder that his successors in the Oval Office have struggled to "get right" with the supreme political and military leader of the twentieth century.

After half a century it is hard to approach Franklin D. Roosevelt except through a minefield of clichés. Theories of FDR, running the gamut from artlessness to mystification, have long pa-raded before our eyes. There is his famous response to the newspaperman who asked him for his philosophy: "Philosophy? I am a Christian and a Democrat—that's all"; there is Robert E. Sherwood's equally famous warning about "Roosevelt's heavily forested interior"; and we weakly conclude that both things were probably true.

FDR's Presidency has commanded the attention of eminent historians at home and abroad for fifty years or more. Yet no consensus emerges, especially in the field of foreign af-fairs. Scholars at one time or another have portrayed him at every point across a broad spec-trum: as an isolationist, as an internationalist, as an appeaser, as a warmonger, as an impulsive decision maker, as an incorrigible vacillator, as the savior of capitalism, as a closet socialist, as a Machiavellian intriguer plotting to embroil his country in foreign wars, as a Machiavellian intriguer avoiding war in order to let other nations bear the brunt of the fighting, as a gullible dreamer who thought he could charm Stalin into postwar collaboration and ended by selling Eastern Europe down the river into slavery, as a tightfisted creditor sending Britain down the road toward bankruptcy, as a crafty imperialist serving the interests of American capitalist hegemony, as a high-minded prophet whose vision shaped the world's future. Will the real FDR please stand up?

Two relatively recent books illustrate the chronically unsettled state of FDR historiography—and the continuing vitality of the FDR debate. In *Wind Over Sand* (1988) Frederick W. Marks III finds a presidential record marked by ignorance, superficiality, inconsistency, random prejudice, erratic impulse, a man out of his depth, not waving but drowning, practicing a diplomacy as insubstantial and fleeting as wind blowing over sand. In *The Juggler* (1991), Warren F. Kimball finds a record marked by intelligent understanding of world forces, astute maneuver, and a remarkable consistency of purpose, a farsighted statesman facing dilemmas that defied quick or easy solutions. One-third of each book is given over to endnotes and bibliography, which suggests that each portrait is based on meticulous research. Yet the two historians arrive at diametrically opposite conclusions.

So the debate goes on. Someone should write a book entitled *FDR: For and Against*, modeled on Pieter Geyl's *Napoleon: For and Against*. "It is impossible," the great Dutch historian observed, "that two historians, especially two historians living in different periods, should see any historical personality in the same light. The greater the political importance of a historical character, the more impossible this is." History, Geyl (rightly) concluded, is an "argument without end."

I suppose we must accept that human beings are in the last analysis beyond analysis. In the case of FDR, no one can be really sure what was going on in that affable, welcoming, reserved, elusive, teasing, spontaneous, calculating, cold, warm, humorous, devious, mendacious, manipulative, petty, magnanimous, superficially casual, ultimately decent, highly camouflaged, finally impenetrable mind. Still, if we can't as historians puzzle out what he *was*, we surely must as historians try to make sense out of what he *did*. If his personality escapes us, his policies must have some sort of pattern.

What Roosevelt wrote (or Sam Rosenman wrote for him) in the introduction to the first volume of his *Public Papers* about his record as governor of New York goes, I believe, for his foreign policy too: "Those who seek inconsistencies will find them. There were inconsistencies of methods, inconsistencies caused by ceaseless efforts to find ways to solve problems for the future as well as for the present. There were inconsistencies born of insufficient knowledge. There were inconsistencies springing from the need of experimentation. But through them all, I trust that there also will be found a consistency and continuity of broad purpose."

Now purpose can be very broad indeed. To say that a statesman is in favor of peace, freedom, and security does not narrow things down very much. Meaning resides in the details, and in FDR's case the details often contradict each other. If I may invoke still another cliché, FDR's foreign policy seems to fit Churchill's description of the Soviet Union: "a riddle wrapped in a mystery inside an enigma." However, we too often forget what Churchill said next: "But perhaps there is a key. That key is Russian national interest." German domination of Eastern Europe, Churchill continued, "would be contrary to the historic life-interests of Russia." Here, I suggest, may be the key to FDR, the figure in his carpet: his sense of the historic life-interests of the United States.

Of course, "national interest" narrows things down only a little. No one, except a utopian or a millennialist, is against the national interest. In a world of nation-states the assumption that governments will pursue their own interests gives order and predictability to international affairs. As George Washington said, "No nation is to be trusted farther than it is bound by [its] interest." The problem is the substance one pours into national interest. In our own time, for example, Lyndon Johnson and Dean Rusk thought our national interest required us to fight in Vietnam; William Fulbright, Walter Lippmann, Hans Morgenthau thought our national interest required us to pull out of Vietnam. The phrase by itself settles no arguments.

How did FDR conceive the historic life-interests of the United States? His conception emerged from his own long, if scattered, education in world affairs. It should not be forgotten that he arrived in the White House with an unusual amount of international experience. He was born into a cosmopolitan family. His father knew Europe well and as a young man had marched with Garibaldi. His elder half-brother had served in American legations in London and Vienna. His mother's family had been in the China trade; his mother herself had lived in Hong Kong as a little girl. As FDR reminded Henry Morgenthau in 1934, "I have a background of a little over a century in Chinese affairs."

FDR himself made his first trip to Europe at the age of three and went there every summer from his ninth to his fourteenth year. As a child he learned French and German. As a lifelong stamp collector he knew the world's geography and politics. By the time he was elected President, he had made thirteen trips across the Atlantic and had spent almost three years of his life in Europe. "I started . . . with a good deal of interest in foreign affairs," he told a press conference in 1939, "because both branches of my family have been mixed up in foreign affairs for a good many generations, the affairs of Europe and the affairs of the Far East."

Now much of his knowledge was social and superficial. Nor is international experience in any case a guarantee of international wisdom or even of continuing international concern. The other American politician of the time who rivaled FDR in exposure to the great world was, oddly, Herbert Hoover. Hoover was a mining engineer in Australia at twenty-three, a capitalist in the Chinese Empire at twenty-five, a promoter in the City of London at twenty-seven. In the years from his Stanford graduation to the Great War, he spent more time in the British Empire than he did in the United States. During and after the war he supervised relief activities in Belgium and in Eastern Europe. Keynes called him the only man to emerge from the Paris Peace Conference with an enhanced reputation.

Both Hoover and Roosevelt came of age when the United States was becoming a world power. Both saw more of that world than most of their American contemporaries. But international experience led them to opposite conclusions. What Hoover saw abroad soured him on foreigners. He took away from Paris an indignant conviction of an impassable gap between his virtuous homeland and the European snake pit. Nearly twenty years passed before he could bring himself to set foot again on the despised continent. He loathed Europe and its nationalist passions and hatreds. "With a vicious rhythm," he said in 1940, "these malign forces seem to drive [European] nations like the Gadarene swine over the precipice of war." The less America had to do with so degenerate a place, the Quaker Hoover felt, the better.

The patrician Roosevelt was far more at home in the great world. Moreover, his political genealogy instilled in him the conviction that the United States must at last take its rightful place among the powers. In horse breeder's parlance, FDR was by Woodrow Wilson out of Theodore Roosevelt. These two remarkable Presidents taught FDR that the United States was irrevocably a world power and poured substance into his conception of America's historic life-interests.

FDR greatly admired TR, deserted the Democratic party to cast his first presidential vote for him, married his niece, and proudly succeeded in 1913 to the office TR had occupied fifteen years earlier, assistant Secretary of the Navy. From TR and from that eminent friend of both Roosevelts, Admiral Mahan, young Roosevelt learned the strategic necessities of international relations. He learned how to distinguish between vital and peripheral interests. He learned why the national interest required the maintenance of balances of power in areas that, if controlled by a single power, could threaten the United States. He learned what the defense of vital interests might require in terms of ships and arms and men and production and resources. His experience in Wilson's Navy Department during the First World War consolidated these lessons.

But he also learned new things from Wilson, among them that it was not enough to send young men to die and kill because of the thrill of battle or because of war's morally redemptive qualities or even because of the need to restore the balance of power. The awful sacrifices of modern war demanded nobler objectives. The carnage on the Western Front converted FDR to Wilson's vision of a world beyond war, beyond national interest, beyond balances of power, a world not of secret diplomacy and antagonistic military alliances but of an organized common peace, founded on democracy, self-determination, and the collective restraint of aggression.

Theodore Roosevelt had taught FDR geopolitics. Woodrow Wilson now gave him a larger international purpose in which the principles of power had a strong but secondary role. FDR's two mentors detested each other. But they joined to construct the framework within which FDR, who cherished them both, approached foreign affairs for the rest of his life.

As the Democratic vice presidential candidate in 1920, he roamed the country pleading for the League of Nations. Throughout the twenties he warned against political isolationism and economic protectionism. America would commit a grievous wrong, he said, if it were "to go backwards towards an old Chinese Wall policy of isolationism." Trade wars, he said, were "symptoms of economic insanity." But such sentiments could not overcome the disillusion and disgust with which Americans in the 1920s contemplated world troubles. As President Hoover told the Italian foreign minister in 1931, the deterioration of Europe had led to such "despair . . . on the part of the ordinary American citizen [that] now he just wanted to keep out of the whole business."

Depression intensified the isolationist withdrawal. Against the national mood, the new President brought to the White House in 1933 an international outlook based, I would judge, on four principles. One was TR's commitment to the preservation of the balance of world power. Another was Wilson's vision of concerted international action to prevent or punish aggression. The third principle argued that lasting peace required the free flow of trade among nations. The fourth was that in a democracy foreign policy must rest on popular consent. In the isolationist climate of the 1930s, this fourth principle compromised and sometimes undermined the first three.

Diplomatic historians are occasionally tempted to overrate the amount of time Presidents spend in thinking about foreign policy. In fact, from Jackson to FDR, domestic affairs have always been, with a few fleeting exceptions—perhaps Polk, McKinley, Wilson—the presidential priority. This was powerfully the case at the start for FDR. Given the collapse of the economy and the anguish of unemployment, given the absence of obvious remedy and the consequent need for social experiment, the surprise is how much time and energy FDR did devote to foreign affairs in these early years.

He gave time to foreign policy because of his acute conviction that Germany and Japan were, or were about to be, on the rampage and that unchecked aggression would ultimately threaten vital interests of the United States. He packed the State Department and embassies abroad with unregenerate Wilsonians. When he appointed Cordell Hull Secretary, he knew what he was getting; his brain trusters, absorbed in problems at hand, had warned him against international folly. But there they were, Wilsonians all: Hull, Norman Davis, Sumner Welles, William Phillips, Francis B. Sayre, Walton Moore, Breckinridge Long, Josephus Daniels, W. E. Dodd, Robert W. Bingham, Claude Bowers, Joseph E. Davies. Isolationists like Raymond Moley did not last long at State.

Roosevelt's early excursions into foreign policy were necessarily intermittent, however, and in his own rather distracting personal style. Economic diplomacy he confided to Hull, except when Hull's free-trade obsessions threatened New Deal recovery programs, as at the London Economic Conference of 1933. He liked, when he found the time, to handle the political side of things himself. He relished meetings with foreign leaders and found himself in advance of most of them in his forebodings about Germany and Japan. He invited his ambassadors, especially his political appointees, to write directly to him, and nearly all took advantage of the invitation.

His diplomatic style had its capricious aspects. FDR understood what admirals and generals were up to, and he understood the voice of prophetic statesmanship. But he never fully appreciated the professional diplomat and looked with some disdain on the career Foreign Service as made up of tea drinkers remote from the realities of American life. His approach to foreign policy, while firmly grounded in geopolitics and soaring easily into the higher idealism, always lacked something at the middle level.

At the heart of Roosevelt's style in foreign affairs was a certain incorrigible amateurism. His off-the-cuff improvisations, his airy tendency to throw out half-baked ideas, caused others to underrate his continuity of purpose and used to drive the British especially wild, as minutes scribbled on Foreign Office dispatches make abundantly clear. This amateurism had its good points. It could be a source of boldness and creativity in a field populated by cautious and conventional people. But it also encouraged superficiality and dilettantism.

The national mood, however, remained FDR's greatest problem. Any U.S. contribution to the deterrence of aggression depended on giving the government power to distinguish between aggressors and their victims. He asked Congress for this authority, first in cooperating with League of Nations sanctions in 1933, later in connection with American neutrality statutes. Fearing that aid to one side would eventually involve the nation in war, Congress regularly turned him down. By rejecting policies that would support victims against aggressors, Congress effectively nullified the ability of the United States to throw its weight in the scales against aggressors.

Roosevelt, regarding the New Deal as more vital for the moment than foreign policy and needing the support of isolationists for his domestic program, accepted what he could not change in congressional roll calls. But he did hope to change public opinion and began a long labor of popular education with his annual message in January 1936 and its condemnation of "autocratic institutions that beget slavery at home and aggression abroad."

It is evident that I am not persuaded by the school of historians that sees Roosevelt as embarked until 1940 on a mission of appeasement, designed to redress German grievances and lure the Nazi regime into a constructive role in a reordered Europe. The evidence provided by private conversations as well as by public pronouncements is far too consistent and too weighty to permit the theory that Roosevelt had illusions about coexistence with Hitler. Timing and maneuver were essential, and on occasion he tacked back and forth like the small-boat sailor that Gaddis Smith reminds us he was. Thus, before positioning the United States for entry into war, he wanted to make absolutely sure there was no prospect of negotiated peace: hence his interest in 1939–40 in people like James D. Mooney and

William Rhodes Davis and hence the Sumner Welles mission. But his basic course seems pretty clear: one way or another to rid the world of Hitler.

I am even less persuaded by the school that sees Roosevelt as a President who rushed the nation to war because he feared German and Japanese economic competition. America "began to go to war against the Axis in the Western Hemisphere," the revisionist William Appleman Williams tells us, because Germany was invading U.S. markets in Latin America. The Open Door cult recognizes no geopolitical concerns in Washington about German bases in the Western Hemisphere. Oddly, the revisionists accept geopolitics as an O.K. motive for the Soviet Union but deny it to the United States. In their view American foreign policy can never be aimed at strategic security but must forever be driven by the lust of American business for foreign markets.

In the United States, of course, as any student of American history knows, economic growth has been based primarily on the home market, not on foreign markets, and the preferred policy of American capitalists, even after 1920, when the United States became a creditor nation, was protection of the home mar ket, not freedom of trade. Recall Fordney-McCumber and Smoot-Hawley. The preference of American business for high tariffs was equally true in depression. When FDR proposed his reciprocal trade agreements program in 1934, the American business community, instead of welcoming reciprocal trade as a way of penetrating foreign markets, denounced the whole idea. Senator Vandenberg even called the bill "Fascist in its philosophy, Fascist in its objectives." A grand total of two Republicans voted for reciprocal trade in the House, three in the Senate.

The "corporatism" thesis provides a more sophisticated version of the economic interpretation. No doubt we have become a society of large organizations, and no doubt an associational society generates a certain momentum toward coordination. But the idea that exporters, importers, Wall Street, Main Street, trade unionists, and farmers form a consensus on foreign policy and impose that consensus on the national government is hard to sustain.

It is particularly irrelevant to the Roosevelt period. If Roosevelt was the compliant instrument of capitalist expansion, as the Open Door ideologies claim, or of corporate hegemony, as the corporatism thesis implies, why did the leaders of American corporate capitalism oppose him so viciously? Business leaders vied with one another in their hatred of "that man in the White House." The family of J. P. Morgan used to warn visitors against mentioning Roosevelt's name lest fury raise Morgan's blood pressure to the danger point. When Averell Harriman, one of that rare breed, a pro-New Deal businessman, appeared on Wall Street, old friends cut him dead. The theory that Roosevelt pursued a foreign policy dictated by the same corporate crowd that fought him domestically and smeared him personally belongs, it seems to me, in the same library with the historiography of Oliver Stone.

What was at stake, as FDR saw it, was not corporate profits or Latin American markets but the security of the United States and the future of democracy. Basking as we do today in the glow of democratic triumph, we forget how desperate the democratic cause appeared half a century ago. The Great War had apparently proved that democracy could not produce peace; the Great Depression that it could not produce prosperity. By the 1930s contempt for democracy was widespread among elites and masses alike: contempt for parliamentary methods, for government by discussion, for freedoms of expression and opposition, for bourgeois individualism, for pragmatic muddling through. Discipline, order, efficiency, and all-encompassing ideology were the talismans of the day. Communism and fascism had their acute doctrinal differences, but their structural similarities—a single leader, a single party, a single body of infallible dogma, a single mass of obedient followers—meant that each in the end had more in common with the other than with democracy, as Hitler and Stalin acknowledged in August 1939.

The choice in the 1930s seemed bleak: either political democracy with economic chaos or economic planning with political tyranny. Roosevelt's distinctive contribution was to reject this either/or choice. The point of the New Deal was to chart and vindicate a middle way between laissez-faire and totalitarianism. When the biographer Emil Ludwig asked FDR to define his "political motive," Roosevelt replied, "My desire to obviate revolution. . . . I work in a contrary sense to Rome and Moscow."

Accepting renomination in 1936, FDR spoke of people under economic stress in other lands who had sold their heritage of freedom for the illusion of a living. "Only our success," he continued, "can stir their ancient hope. They begin to know that here in America we are waging a great and successful war. It is not alone a war against want and destitution and economic demoralization. It is more than that: it is a war for the survival of democracy. We are fighting to save a great and precious form of government for ourselves and for the world."

Many people around the world thought it a futile fight. Let us not underestimate the readiness by 1940 of Europeans, including leading politicians and intellectuals, to come to terms with a Hitler-dominated Europe. Even some Americans thought the downfall of democracy inevitable. As Nazi divisions stormed that spring across Scandinavia, the Low Countries, and France, the fainthearted saw totalitarianism, in the title of a poisonous little book published in the summer by Anne Morrow Lindbergh, a book that by December 1940 had rushed through seven American printings, as "the wave of the future." While her husband, the famous aviator, predicted Nazi victory and opposed American aid to Britain, the gentle Mrs. Lindbergh lamented "the beautiful things . . . lost in the dying of an age," saw totalitarianism as democracy's predestined successor, a "new, and perhaps even ultimately good, conception of humanity trying to come to birth," discounted the evils of Hitlerism and Stalinism as merely "scum on the wave of the future," and concluded that "the wave of the future is coming and there is no fighting it." For a while Mrs. Lindbergh seemed to be right. Fifty years ago there were only twelve democracies left on the planet.

Roosevelt, however, believed in fighting the wave of the future. He still labored under domestic constraints. The American people were predominantly against Hitler. But they were also, and for a while more strongly, against war. I believe that FDR himself, unlike the hawks of 1941—Stimson, Morgenthau, Hopkins, Ickes, Knox—was in no hurry to enter the European conflict. He remembered what Wilson had told him when he himself had been a young hawk a quarter-century before: that a President could commit no greater mistake than to take a divided country into war. He also no doubt wanted to minimize American casualties and to avoid breaking political promises. But probably by the autumn of 1941 FDR had finally come to believe that American participation was necessary if Hitler was to be beaten. An increasing number of Americans were reaching the same conclusion. Pearl Harbor in any case united the country, and Hitler then solved another of FDR's problems by declaring war on the United States.

We accepted war in 1941, as we had done in 1917, in part because, as Theodore Roosevelt had written in 1910, if Britain ever failed to preserve the European balance of power, "the United States would be obliged to get in . . . in order to restore the balance." But restoration of the balance of power did not seem in 1941, any more than it had in 1917, sufficient reason to send young men to kill and die. In 1941 FDR provided higher and nobler aims by resurrecting the Wilsonian vision in the Four Freedoms and the Atlantic Charter and by proceeding, while the war was on, to lay the foundations for the postwar reconstruction of the world along Wilsonian lines.

I assume that it will not be necessary to linger with a theory that had brief currency in the immediate postwar years, the theory that Roosevelt's great failing was his subordination of political to military objectives, shoving long-term considerations aside in the narrow interest of victory. FDR was in fact the most political of politicians, political in every reflex and to his fingertips—and just as political in war as he had been in peace. As a virtuoso politician he perfectly understood that there could be no better cloak for the pursuit of political objectives in wartime than the claim of total absorption in winning the war. He had plenty of political objectives all the same.

The war, he believed, would lead to historic transformations around the world. "Roosevelt," Harriman recalled, "enjoyed thinking aloud on the tremendous changes he saw ahead—the end of colonial empires and the rise of newly independent nations across the sweep of Africa and Asia." FDR told Churchill, "A new period has opened in the world's history, and you will have to adjust yourself to it." He tried to persuade the British to leave India and to stop the French from returning to Indochina, and he pressed the idea of UN trusteeships as the means of dismantling empires and preparing colonies for independence.

 Soviet Russia, he saw, would emerge as a major power. FDR has suffered much criticism in supposedly thinking he could charm Stalin into postwar collaboration. Perhaps FDR was not so naive after all in concentrating on Stalin. The Soviet dictator was hardly the helpless prisoner of Marxist-Leninist ideology. He saw himself not as a disciple of Marx and Lenin but as their fellow prophet. Only Stalin had the power to rewrite the Soviet approach to world affairs; after all, he had already rewritten Soviet ideology and Soviet history. FDR was surely right in seeing Stalin as the only lever capable of overturning the Leninist doctrine of irrevocable hostility between capitalism and communism. As Walter Lippmann once observed, Roosevelt was too cynical to think he could charm Stalin. "He distrusted everybody. What he thought he could do was to outwit Stalin, which is quite a different thing."

Roosevelt failed to save Eastern Europe from communism, but that could not have been achieved by diplomatic methods alone. With the Red Army in control of Eastern Europe and a war still to be won against Japan, there was not much the West could do to prevent Stalin's working his will in countries adjacent to the Soviet Union. But Roosevelt at Yalta persuaded Stalin to sign American-drafted Declarations on Liberated Europe and on Poland—declarations that laid down standards by which the world subsequently measured Stalin's behavior in Eastern Europe and found it wanting. And FDR had prepared a fallback position in case things went wrong: not only tests that, if Stalin failed to meet them, would justify a change in policy but also a great army, a network of overseas bases, plans for peacetime universal military training, and the Anglo-American monopoly of the atomic bomb.

In the longer run Roosevelt anticipated that time would bring a narrowing of differences between democratic and Communist societies. He once told Sumner Welles that marking American democracy as one hundred and Soviet communism as zero, the American system, as it moved away from laissez-faire, might eventually reach sixty, and the Soviet system, as it moved toward democracy, might eventually reach forty. The theory of convergence provoked much derision in the Cold War years. Perhaps it looks better now.

So perhaps does his idea of making China one of the Four Policemen of the peace. Churchill, with his scorn for "the pigtails," dismissed Roosevelt's insistence on China as the "Great American Illusion." But Roosevelt was not really deluded. As he said at Teheran, he wanted China there "not because he did not realize the weakness of China at present, but he was thinking farther into the future." At Malta he told Churchill that it would take "three generations of education and training . . . before China could become a serious factor." Today, two generations later, much rests on involving China in the global web of international institutions.

As for the United States, a great concern in the war years was that the country might revert to isolationism after the war just as it had done a quarter-century before—a vivid memory for

FDR's generation. Contemplating Republican gains in the 1942 midterm election, Cordell Hull told Henry Wallace that the country was "going in exactly the same steps it followed in 1918." FDR himself said privately, "Anybody who thinks that isolationism is dead in this country is crazy."

He regarded American membership in a permanent international organization, in Charles Bohlen's words, as "the only device that could keep the United States from slipping back into isolationism." And true to the Wilsonian vision, he saw such an organization even more significantly as the only device that could keep the world from slipping back into war. He proposed the Declaration of the United Nations three weeks after Pearl Harbor, and by 1944 he was grappling with the problem that had defeated Wilson: how to reconcile peace enforcement by an international organization with the American Constitution. For international peace enforcement requires armed force ready to act swiftly on the command of the organization, while the Constitution requires (or, in better days, required) the consent of Congress before American troops can be sent into combat against a sovereign state. Roosevelt probably had confidence that the special agreements provided for in Article 43 of the UN Charter would strike a balance between the UN's need for prompt action and Congress's need to retain its war-making power and that the great-power veto would further protect American interests.

He moved in other ways to accustom the American people to a larger international role—and at the same time to assure American predominance in the postwar world. By the end of 1944 he had sponsored a series of international conferences designed to plan vital aspects of the future. These conferences, held mostly at American initiative and dominated mostly by American agendas, offered the postwar blueprints for international organization (Dumbarton Oaks), for world finance, trade, and development (Bretton Woods), for food and agriculture (Hot Springs), for relief and rehabilitation (Washington), for civil aviation (Chicago). In his sweeping and sometimes grandiose asides, FDR envisaged plans for regional development with environmental protection in the Middle East and elsewhere, and his Office of the Coordinator for Inter-American Affairs pioneered economic and technical assistance to developing countries. Upon his death in 1945 FDR left an imaginative and comprehensive framework for American leadership in making a better world—an interesting achievement for a President who was supposed to subordinate political to military goals.

New times bring new perspectives. In the harsh light of the Cold War some of FDR's policies and expectations were condemned as naive or absurd or otherwise misguided. The end of the Cold War may cast those policies and expectations in a somewhat different light.

FDR's purpose, I take it, was to find ways to safeguard the historic life-interests of the Republic—national security at home and a democratic environment abroad—in a world undergoing vast and fundamental transformations. This required policies based on a grasp of the currents of history and directed to the protection of U.S. interests and to the promotion of democracy elsewhere. From the vantage point of 1994, FDR met this challenge fairly well.

Take a look at the Atlantic Charter fifty years after. Is not the world therein outlined by Roosevelt and Churchill at last coming to pass? Consider the goals of August 1941—"the right of all peoples to choose the form of government under which they will live," equal access "to the trade and to the raw materials of the world," "improved labor standards, economic advancement and social security," assurance that all "may live their lives in freedom from fear and want," relief from "the crushing burden of armaments," establishment of a community of nations. Is this not the agenda on which most nations today are at last agreed?

Does not most of the world now aspire to FDR's Four Freedoms? Has not what used to be the Soviet Union carried its movement toward the West even more rapidly than FDR dared contemplate? Has not China emerged as the "serious factor" FDR predicted? Did not the Yalta accords call for precisely the democratic freedoms to which Eastern Europe aspires today? Has not the UN, at last liberated by the end of the Cold War to pursue the goals of the founders, achieved new salience as the world's best hope for peace and cooperation?

Consider the world of 1994. It is manifestly not Adolf Hitler's world. The thousand-year Reich turned out to have a brief and bloody run of a dozen years. It is manifestly not Joseph Stalin's world. That world disintegrated before our eyes, rather like the Deacon's one-hoss shay. Nor is it Winston Churchill's world. Empire and its glories have long since vanished into the past.

The world we live in today is Franklin Roosevelt's world. Of the figures who, for good or for evil, bestrode the narrow world half a century ago, he would be the least surprised by the shape of things at the end of the century. Far more than the rest, he possessed what William James called a "sense of futurity." For all his manifold foibles, flaws, follies, and there was a sufficiency of all of those, FDR deserves supreme credit as the twentieth-century statesman who saw most deeply into the grand movements of history.

VIII

THE BIGGEST DECISION: WHY WE HAD TO DROP THE ATOMIC BOMB

Robert James Maddox

On August 6, 1945 the world was changed forever with the detonation of an atomic over the Japanese city of Hiroshima, followed three days later with the use of another bomb over Nagasaki. For the next fifty years mankind would live under the threat and fear that these terrible weapons of destruction would be used again. In the age of the Cold War with its reliance on the MAD (mutually assured destruction) policy of the United States and the Soviet Union, it became fashionable among historical revisionists and politically correct pundits to condemn the president who made the decision to use the bombs in 1945. Harry Truman, the plain spoken man from Missouri, never second guessed his decision. For Truman the bombs brought a swift end to the war against Japan and prevented the massive loss of American lives that would have occurred in an invasion of the Japanese islands. Robert James Maddox, author of Weapons of War: Hiroshima Fifty Years Later, *gives an accurate account in this article of the reasons for Truman's decision and the efforts that went into the making of that decision*

On the morning of August 6, 1945, the American B-29 *Enola Gay* dropped an atomic bomb on the Japanese city of Hiroshima. Three days later another B-29, *Bock's Car*, released one over Nagasaki. Both caused enormous casualties and physical destruction. These two cataclysmic events have preyed upon the American conscience ever since. The furor over the Smithsonian Institution's *Enola Gay* exhibit and over the mushroom-cloud postage stamp last autumn are merely the most obvious examples. Harry S. Truman and other officials claimed that the bombs caused Japan to surrender, thereby avoiding a bloody invasion. Critics have accused them of at best failing to explore alternatives, at worst of using the bombs primarily to make the Soviet Union "more manageable" rather than to defeat a Japan they knew already was on the verge of capitulation.

By any rational calculation Japan was a beaten nation by the summer of 1945. Conventional bombing had reduced many of its cities to rubble, blockade had strangled its importation of vitally needed materials, and its navy had sustained such heavy losses as to be powerless to interfere with the invasion everyone knew was coming. By late June advancing American forces had completed the conquest of Okinawa, which lay only 350 miles from the southernmost Japanese home island of Kyushu. They now stood poised for the final onslaught.

Rational calculations did not determine Japan's position. Although a peace faction within the government wished to end the war—provided certain conditions were met—militants were prepared to fight on regardless of consequences. They claimed to welcome an invasion of the home islands, promising to inflict such hideous casualties that the United States would retreat from its announced policy of unconditional surrender. The militarists held effective power over the government and were capable of defying the emperor, as they had in the past, on the ground that his civilian advisers were misleading him.

Okinawa provided a preview of what invasion of the home islands would entail. Since April 1 the Japanese had fought with a ferocity that mocked any notion that their will to resist was eroding. They had inflicted nearly 50,000 casualties on the invaders, many resulting from the first large-scale use of kamikazes. They also had dispatched the superbattleship *Yamato* on a suicide mission to Okinawa, where, after attacking American ships offshore, it was to plunge ashore to become a huge, doomed steel fortress. *Yamato* was sunk shortly after leaving port, but its mission symbolized Japan's willingness to sacrifice everything in an apparently hopeless cause.

The Japanese could be expected to defend their sacred homeland with even greater fervor, and kamikazes flying at short range promised to be even more devastating than at Okinawa. The Japanese had more than 2,000,000 troops in the home islands, were training millions of irregulars, and for some time had been conserving aircraft that might have been used to protect Japanese cities against American bombers.

Reports from Tokyo indicated that Japan meant to fight the war to a finish. On June 8 an imperial conference adopted "The Fundamental Policy to Be Followed Henceforth in the Conduct of the War," which pledged to "prosecute the war to the bitter end in order to uphold the national polity, protect the imperial land, and accomplish the objectives for which we went to war." Truman had no reason to believe that the proclamation meant anything other than what it said.

Against this background, while fighting on Okinawa still continued, the President had his naval chief of staff, Adm. William D. Leahy, notify the Joint Chiefs of Staff (JCS) and the Secretaries of War and Navy that a meeting would be held at the White House on June 18. The night before the conference Truman wrote in his diary that "I have to decide Japanese strategy—shall we invade Japan proper or shall we bomb and blockade? That is my hardest decision to date. But I'll make it when I have all the facts."

Truman met with the chiefs at three-thirty in the afternoon. Present were Army Chief of Staff Gen. George C. Marshall, Army Air Force's Gen. Ira C. Eaker (sitting in for the Army Air Force's chief of staff, Henry H. Arnold, who was on an inspection tour of installations in the Pacific), Navy Chief of Staff Adm. Ernest J. King, Leahy (also a member of the JCS), Secretary of the Navy James Forrestal, Secretary of War Henry L. Stimson, and Assistant Secretary of War John J. McCloy. Truman opened the meeting, then asked Marshall for his views. Marshall was the dominant figure on the JCS. He was Truman's most trusted military adviser, as he had been President Franklin D. Roosevelt's.

Marshall reported that the chiefs, supported by the Pacific commanders Gen. Douglas MacArthur and Adm. Chester W. Nimitz, agreed that an invasion of Kyushu "appears to be the least costly worthwhile operation following Okinawa." Lodgment in Kyushu, he said, was necessary to make blockade and bombardment more effective and to serve as a staging area for the invasion of Japan's main island of Honshu. The chiefs recommended a target date of November 1 for the first phase, code-named Olympic, because delay would give the Japanese more time to prepare and because bad weather might postpone the invasion "and hence the end of the war" for up to six months. Marshall said that in his opinion, Olympic was "the only course to pursue." The chiefs also proposed that Operation Cornet be launched against Honshu on March 1, 1946.

Leahy's memorandum calling the meeting had asked for casualty projections which that invasion might be expected to produce. Marshall stated that campaigns in the Pacific had been so diverse "it is considered wrong" to make total estimates. All he would say was that casualties during the first thirty days on Kyushu should not exceed those sustained in taking Luzon in the Philippines—31,000 men killed, wounded, or missing in action. "It is a grim fact," Marshall said, "that there is not an easy, bloodless way to victory in war." Leahy estimated a higher casualty rate similar to Okinawa, and King guessed somewhere in between.

King and Eaker, speaking for the Navy and the Army Air Forces respectively, endorsed Marshall's proposals. King said that he had become convinced that Kyushu was "the key to the success of any siege operations." He recommended that "we should do Kyushu now" and begin preparations for invading Honshu. Eaker "agreed completely" with Marshall. He said he had just received a message from Arnold also expressing "complete agreement." Air Force plans called for the use of forty groups of heavy bombers, which "could not be deployed without the use of airfields on Kyushu." Stimson and Forrestal concurred.

Truman summed up. He considered "the Kyushu plan all right from the military standpoint" and directed the chiefs to "go ahead with it." He said he "had hoped that there was a possibility of preventing an Okinawa from one end of Japan to the other," but "he was clear on the situation now" and was "quite sure" the chiefs should proceed with the plan. Just before the meeting adjourned, McCloy raised the possibility of avoiding an invasion by warning the Japanese that the United States would employ atomic weapons if there were no surrender. The ensuing discussion was inconclusive because the first test was a month away and no one could be sure the weapons would work.

In his memoirs Truman claimed that using atomic bombs prevented an invasion that would have cost 500,000 American lives. Other officials mentioned the same or even higher figures. Critics have assailed such statements as gross exaggerations designed to forestall scrutiny of Truman's real motives. They have given wide publicity to a report prepared by the Joint War Plans Committee (JWPC) for the chiefs' meeting with Truman. The committee estimated that the invasion of Kyushu, followed by that of Honshu, as the chiefs proposed, would cost approximately 40,000 dead, 150,000 wounded, and 3,500 missing in action for a total of 193,500 casualties.

That those responsible for a decision should exaggerate the consequences of alternatives is commonplace. Some who cite the JWPC report profess to see more sinister motives, insisting that such "low" casualty projections call into question the very idea that atomic bombs were used to avoid heavy losses. By discrediting that justification as a cover-up, they seek to bolster their contention that the bombs really were used to permit the employment of "atomic diplomacy" against the Soviet Union.

The notion that 193,500 anticipated casualties were too insignificant to have caused Truman to resort to atomic bombs might seem bizarre to anyone other than an academic, but let it pass. Those who have cited the JWPC report in countless op-ed pieces in newspapers and in magazine articles have created a myth by omitting key considerations: First, the report itself is studded with qualifications that casualties "are not subject to accurate estimate" and that the projection "is admittedly only an educated guess." Second, the figures never were conveyed to Truman. They were excised at high military echelons, which is why Marshall cited only estimates for the first thirty days on Kyushu. And indeed, subsequent Japanese troop buildups on Kyushu rendered the JWPC estimates totally irrelevant by the time the first atomic bomb was dropped.

Another myth that has attained wide attention is that at least several of Truman's top military advisers later informed him that using atomic bombs against Japan would be militarily unnecessary or immoral, or both. There is no persuasive evidence that any of them did so. None of the Joint Chiefs ever made such a claim, although one inventive author has tried to make it appear that Leahy did by braiding together several unrelated passages from the admiral's memoirs. Actually, two days after Hiroshima, Truman told aides that Leahy had "said up to the last that it wouldn't go off."

Neither MacArthur nor Nimitz ever communicated to Truman any change of mind about the need for invasion or expressed reservations about using the bombs. When first informed about their imminent use only days before Hiroshima, MacArthur responded with a lecture on the future of atomic warfare and even after Hiroshima strongly recommended that the invasion go forward. Nimitz, from whose jurisdiction the atomic strikes would be launched, was notified in early 1945. "This sounds fine," he told the courier, "but this is only February. Can't we get one sooner?" Nimitz later would join Air Force generals Carl D. Spaatz, Nathan Twining, and Curtis LeMay in recommending that a third bomb be dropped on Tokyo.

Only Dwight D. Eisenhower later claimed to have remonstrated against the use of the bomb. In his *Crusade in Europe*, published in 1948, he wrote that when Secretary Stimson informed him during the Potsdam Conference of plans to use the bomb, he replied that he hoped "we would never have to use such a thing against any enemy," because he did not want the United States to be the first to use such a weapon. He added, "My views were merely personal and immediate reactions; they were not based on any analysis of the subject."

Eisenhower's recollections grew more colorful as the years went on. A later account of his meeting with Stimson had it taking place at Ike's headquarters in Frankfurt on the very day news arrived of the successful atomic test in New Mexico. "We'd had a nice evening at headquarters in Germany," he remembered. Then, after dinner, "Stimson got this cable saying that the bomb had been perfected and was ready to be dropped. The cable was in code . . . 'the lamb is born' or some damn thing like that." In this version Eisenhower claimed to have protested vehemently that "the Japanese were ready to surrender and it wasn't necessary to hit them with that awful thing." "Well," Eisenhower concluded, "the old gentleman got furious."

The best that can be said about Eisenhower's memory is that it had become flawed by the passage of time. Stimson was in Potsdam and Eisenhower in Frankfurt on July 16, when word came of the successful test. Aside from a brief conversation at a flag-raising ceremony in Berlin on July 20, the only other time they met was at Ike's headquarters on July 27. By then orders already had been sent to the Pacific to use the bombs if Japan had not yet surrendered. Notes made by one of Stimson's aides indicate that there was a discussion of atomic bombs, but there is no mention of any protest on Eisenhower's part. Even if there had been, two factors must be kept in mind. Eisenhower had commanded Allied forces in Europe, and his opinion on how close Japan was to surrender would have carried no special weight. More important, Stimson left for home immediately after the meeting and could not have personally conveyed Ike's sentiments to the President, who did not return to Washington until after Hiroshima.

On July 8 the Combined Intelligence Committee submitted to the American and British Combined Chiefs of Staff a report entitled "Estimate of the Enemy Situation." The committee predicted that as Japan's position continued to deteriorate, it might "make a serious effort to use the USSR [then a neutral] as a mediator in ending the war." Tokyo also would put out "intermittent peace feelers" to "weaken the determination of the United Nations to fight to the bitter end, or to create inter-allied dissension." While the Japanese people would be willing to make large concessions to end the war, "For a surrender to be acceptable to the Japanese army, it would be necessary for the military leaders to believe that it would not entail discrediting warrior tradition and that it would permit the ultimate resurgence of a military Japan."

Small wonder that American officials remained unimpressed when Japan proceeded to do exactly what the committee predicted. On July 12 Japanese Foreign Minister Shigenori Togo instructed Ambassador Naotaki Sato in Moscow to inform the Soviets that the emperor wished to send a personal envoy, Prince Fuminaro Konoye, in an attempt "to restore peace with all possible speed." Although he realized Konoye could not reach Moscow before the Soviet leader Joseph Stalin and Foreign Minister V. M. Molotov left to attend a Big Three meeting scheduled to begin in Potsdam on the fifteenth, Togo sought to have negotiations begin as soon as they returned.

American officials had long since been able to read Japanese diplomatic traffic through a process known as the magic intercepts. Army intelligence (G-2) prepared for General Marshall its interpretation of Togo's message the next day. The report listed several possible constructions, the most probable being that the Japanese "governing clique" was making a coordinated effort to "stave off defeat" through Soviet intervention and an "appeal to war weariness in the United States." The report added that Undersecretary of State Joseph C. Grew, who had spent ten years in Japan as ambassador, "agrees with these conclusions."

Some have claimed that Togo's overture to the Soviet Union, together with attempts by some minor Japanese officials in Switzerland and other neutral countries to get peace talks started through the Office of Strategic Services (OSS), constituted clear evidence that the Japanese were near surrender. Their sole prerequisite was retention of their sacred emperor, whose unique cultural/religious status within the Japanese polity they would not compromise. If only the United States had extended assurances about the emperor, according to this view, much bloodshed and the atomic bombs would have been unnecessary.

A careful reading of the MAGIC intercepts of subsequent exchanges between Togo and Sato provides no evidence that retention of the emperor was the sole obstacle to peace. What they show instead is that the Japanese Foreign Office was trying to cut a deal through the Soviet Union that would have permitted Japan to retain its political system and its prewar empire intact. Even the most lenient American official could not have countenanced such a settlement.

Togo on July 17 informed Sato that "we are not asking the Russians' mediation in *anything like unconditional surrender* [emphasis added]." During the following weeks Sato pleaded with his superiors to abandon hope of Soviet intercession and to approach the United States directly to find out what peace terms would be offered. "There is . . . no alternative but immediate unconditional surrender," he cabled on July 31, and he bluntly informed Togo that "your way of looking at things and the actual situation in the Eastern Area may be seen to be absolutely contradictory." The Foreign Ministry ignored his pleas and continued to seek Soviet help even after Hiroshima.

"Peace feelers" by Japanese officials abroad seemed no more promising from the American point of view. Although several of the consular personnel and military attachés engaged in these activities claimed important connections at home, none produced verification. Had the Japanese government sought only an assurance about the emperor, all it had to do was grant one of these men authority to begin talks through the OSS. Its failure to do so led American officials to assume that those involved were either well-meaning individuals acting alone or that they were being orchestrated by Tokyo. Grew characterized such "peace feelers" as "familiar weapons of psychological warfare" designed to "divide the Allies."

Some American officials, such as Stimson and Grew, nonetheless wanted to signal the Japanese that they might retain the emperorship in the form of a constitutional monarchy. Such an assurance might remove the last stumbling block to surrender, if not when it was issued, then later. Only an imperial rescript would bring about an orderly surrender, they argued, without which Japanese forces would fight to the last man regardless of what the government in Tokyo did. Besides, the emperor could serve as a stabilizing factor during the transition to peacetime.

There were many arguments against an American initiative. Some opposed retaining such an undemocratic institution on principle and because they feared it might later serve as a rallying point for future militarism. Should that happen, as one assistant Secretary of State put it, "those lives already spent will have been sacrificed in vain, and lives will be lost again in the future." Japanese hard-liners were certain to exploit an overture as evidence that losses sustained at Okinawa had weakened American resolve and to argue that continued resistance would bring further concessions. Stalin, who earlier had told an American envoy that he favored abolishing the emperorship because the ineffectual Hirohito might be succeeded by "an energetic and vigorous figure who could cause trouble," was just as certain to interpret it as a treacherous effort to end the war before the Soviets could share in the spoils.

There were domestic considerations as well. Roosevelt had announced the unconditional surrender policy in early 1943, and it since had become a slogan of the war. He also had advocated that peoples everywhere should have the right to choose their own form of government, and Truman had publicly pledged to carry out his predecessor's legacies. For him to have formally *guaranteed* continuance of the emperorship, as opposed to merely accepting it on American terms pending free elections, as he later did, would have constituted a blatant repudiation of his own promises.

Nor was that all. Regardless of the emperor's actual role in Japanese aggression, which is still debated, much wartime propaganda had encouraged Americans to regard Hirohito as no less a war criminal than Adolf Hitler or Benito Mussolini. Although Truman said on several occasions that he had no objection to retaining the emperor, he understandably refused to make the first move. The ultimatum he issued from Potsdam on July 26 did not refer specifically to the emperorship. All it said was that occupation forces would be removed after "a peaceful and responsible" government had been established according to the "freely expressed will of the Japanese people." When the Japanese rejected the ultimatum rather than at last inquire whether they might retain the emperor, Truman permitted the plans for using the bombs to go forward.

Reliance on MAGIC intercepts and the "peace feelers" to gauge how near Japan was to surrender is misleading in any case. The army, not the Foreign Office, controlled the situation. Intercepts of Japanese military communications, designated ULTRA, provided no reason to believe the army was even considering surrender. Japanese Imperial Headquarters had correctly guessed that the next operation after Okinawa would be Kyushu and was making every effort to bolster its defenses there.

General Marshall reported on July 24 that there were "approximately 500,000 troops in Kyushu" and that more were on the way. ULTRA identified new units arriving almost daily. MacArthur's G-2 reported on July 29 that "this threatening development, if not checked, may grow to a point where we attack on a ratio of one (1) to one (1) which is not the recipe for victory." By the time the first atomic bomb fell, ULTRA indicated that there were 560,000 troops in southern Kyushu (the actual figure was closer to 900,000), and projections for November 1 placed the number at 680,000. A report, for medical purposes, of July 31 estimated that total battle and nonbattle casualties might run as high as 394,859 *for the Kyushu operation alone.* This figure did not include those men expected to be killed outright, for obviously they would require no medical attention. Marshall regarded Japanese defenses as so formidable that even after Hiroshima he asked MacArthur to consider alternate landing sites and began contemplating the use of atomic bombs as tactical weapons to support the invasion.

The thirty-day casualty projection of 31,000 Marshall had given Truman at the June 18 strategy meeting had become meaningless. It had been based on the assumption that the Japanese had about 350,000 defenders in Kyushu and that naval and air interdiction would preclude significant reinforcement. But the Japanese buildup since that time meant that the defenders would have nearly twice the number of troops available by "X-day" than earlier assumed. The assertion that apprehensions about casualties are insufficient to explain Truman's use of the bombs, therefore, cannot be taken seriously. On the contrary, as Winston Churchill wrote after a conversation with him at Potsdam, Truman was tormented by "the terrible responsibilities that rested upon him in regard to the unlimited effusions of American blood."

Some historians have argued that while the first bomb *might* have been required to achieve Japanese surrender, dropping the second constituted a needless barbarism. The record shows otherwise. American officials believed more than one bomb would be necessary because they assumed Japanese hard-liners would minimize the first explosion or attempt to explain it away as some sort of natural catastrophe, precisely what they did. The Japanese minister of war, for instance, at first refused even to admit that the Hiroshima bomb was atomic. A few hours after Nagasaki he told the cabinet that "the Americans appeared to have one hundred atomic bombs . . . they could drop three per day. The next target might well be Tokyo."

Even after both bombs had fallen and Russia entered the war, Japanese militants insisted on such lenient peace terms that moderates knew there was no sense even transmitting them to the United States. Hirohito had to intervene personally on two occasions during the next few days to induce hard-liners to abandon their conditions and to accept the American stipulation that the emperor's authority "shall be subject to the Supreme Commander of the Allied Powers." That the militarists would have accepted such a settlement before the bombs is farfetched, to say the least.

Some writers have argued that the cumulative effects of battlefield defeats, conventional bombing, and naval blockade already had defeated Japan. Even without extending assurances about the emperor, all the United States had to do was wait. The most frequently cited basis for this contention is the *United States Strategic Bombing Survey,* published in 1946, which stated that Japan would have surrendered by November 1 "even if the atomic bombs had not been dropped, even if Russia had not entered the war, and even if no invasion had been planned or contemplated." Recent scholarship by the historian Robert P. Newman and others has demonstrated that the survey was "cooked" by those who prepared it to arrive at such a conclusion. No matter. This or any other document based on information available only after the war ended is irrelevant with regard to what Truman could have known at the time.

What often goes unremarked is that when the bombs were dropped, fighting was still going on in the Philippines, China, and elsewhere. Every day that the war continued thousands of prisoners of war had to live and die in abysmal conditions, and there were rumors that the Japanese intended to slaughter them if the homeland was invaded. Truman was Commander in Chief of the American armed forces, and he had a duty to the men under his command not shared by those sitting in moral judgment decades later. Available evidence points to the conclusion that he acted for the reason he said he did: to end a bloody war that would have become far bloodier had invasion proved necessary. One can only imagine what would have happened if tens of thousands of American boys had died or been wounded on Japanese soil and then it had become known that Truman had chosen not to use weapons that might have ended the war months sooner.

PART THREE

1945–PRESENT

After 1945 the United States was preoccupied for four decades with the long struggle with the Soviet Union and Communism known as the Cold War. Punctuating this war of words, economies, and ideologies were two very real "hot" wars. The Korean war in the early 1950s ended in a stalemate in which communist expansion from the north was checked; the Vietnamese conflict bedeviled Americans for a quarter of a century and ended much less satisfactorily. While triumph came in the larger battle with Communism, at home Americans weathered a series of challenges—the modern civil rights movement, political scandals that undermined citizen trust in the very foundations of government, an energy crisis, and the assassinations of several national leaders. Perhaps the greatest challenge, as the nation approaches a new century and millennium, is the age old question of whether the great variety of cultures, races, and ethnic groups that make up the United States today will continue to interact for the larger good of the nation as a whole or will fragment into competing and mutually exclusive pieces of an incomplete mosaic.

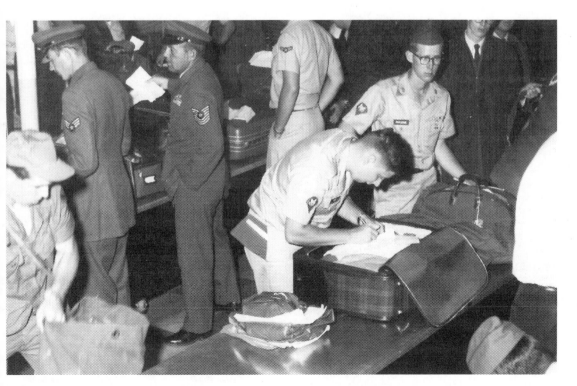

LEAVING FOR KOREA

James Brady

Americans in 1945 confidently assumed that victory in World War II would bring a peaceful world presided over by the military, political, and economic hegemony of the United States. Yet just five years later the nation found itself in another hot war, this time on the rugged Korean peninsula. Journalist James Brady was a 21-year old college gradu-ate in 1950, fresh to the ways of the world. His moving, often funny memoir of his halcy-on days before shipping off to the war is a poignant account of the introduction of young men to the experience of war, the loss of comrades, and the end of innocence.

We sat over beer on rough-hewn cedar benches at a big old table in the shade of trees that only California grows, young men talking away the hot November afternoon, a November such as we rarely had in the East, all of us in proper uniform, the forest green, and we were pared lean and very fit by the hills and the forced marches and the heat, burned cordovan by the California sun.

It was my birthday, November 15, and tomorrow we were going to the war.

A dozen Marine officers, lieutenants like me, and about ninety master sergeants and gunnery sergeants and other NCOs, men of enormous dignity who made me uneasy when they saluted, had flown north at dawn from Camp Pendleton to the Navy airfield outside San Francisco to take a plane across the Pacific. We were replacements for men dead or wounded in Korea.

"Fresh meat," one of the sergeants remarked pleasantly.

The division was short of sergeants and platoon leaders—young lieutenants—after the September and October fighting on the ridges. They were in a hurry to get us, and that's why we were being flown over. The rest of the replacement draft, maybe two thousand officers and men, including most of our friends, would cross the Pacific in troopships. In the plane flying north to San Francisco I wrote to Sheila Collins, who was going to marry somebody else, wishing her well and telling her what a great girl she was and what fun we'd had. And mean-ing it. That letter accomplished, I mentioned to the man sitting alongside that today was my birthday, that I was twenty-three. He wished me well.

"You know," he said then, "George Custer was a major general at twenty-three."

That rather put me in my place. The other man sensed it and tried to make it up.

"Well, brevet general. Not permanent rank. He was really only a colonel, and after Appomattox they reduced him back."

"I'd take colonel," I said. "I'd take major."

"Different kind of war. Promotion came quick."

"He had another advantage over me, Custer," I said.

"Oh?"

"Yeah, I can't ride a horse."

At Moffett Field outside San Francisco they discovered something wrong with the plane that was to take us to Korea, and they were going to have to find another. That would take until tomorrow morning, so we were free until then. 6:00 A.M. That was luck: a day to kill in San Francisco. And on my birthday. Bob Phelps said we ought to drive down to Palo Alto, where he'd played football the year before at Stanford.

"You've never seen such a place," Phelps said.

Bob Doran and Lou Faust had friends to visit or errands to run, but Mack Allen and a few of us piled into a borrowed car with Phelps and drove down. He was right about Stanford. Even Mack said so, and he was a Virginian, and you know how they are, restraining enthusiasm, but you could see pleasure in Mack's grin.

Stanford happened that week to be the top football team in the country in the wire polls, and when Phelps took us to practice, the coach, Chuck Taylor, whose photo was in Life magazine, came over to shake hands. He made a fuss over Phelps and the rest of us. Bob Mathias came over too, the big all-American end who was the decathlon champion from the 1948 Olympics and who would, like us, be in the Marines in another year. Then all the others came over, seeing it was okay to break from practice, and we met most of them, including a couple of those unpronounceable Armenians who ran so well in the backfield, Hugasian and one other.

After watching the football for a while, we went back to the car and drove over under the trees to this beer garden where students went.

"There might be some girls coming by," Phelps said, "you know, after class."

There were no girls, but that was okay. When men of the Round Table set off seeking the Holy Grail, they always prayed the night away before an altar. I felt some of that about going to Korea, about joining the division. Besides, remembering New York Novembers, raw and cold and dank, I realized that after just six weeks in California I'd fallen in love. Not with a girl but with a state. And I suspected privately this was precisely what the 1950s were meant to be, maybe the best time there ever was in America.

By 1950 the big war had been over for five years, and people again had cars and jobs, and all the soldiers were home and going to college on the GI Bill or apprenticing at their trades and buying those neat little seven-thousand-dollar houses that Mr. Levitt was putting up spanking bright with carpeting and washers and dryers anywhere there was a bit of green lawn. The Germans and the Japanese were finished, and unless the Russians did something stupid, there would never again be a Big War, and in the meantime the United States would pretty much run the world.

That was how it had been in 1950. I was twenty-one that year and graduated from college and got my first job as a professional writer, doing advertising copy for Macy's, my specialty being household appliances and unpainted furniture and area rugs.

"Our last day," Mack Allen said abruptly, interrupting silence, which was odd because Mack talked less than any of us. But it was what we all were thinking. I wished Taffy Sceva was there, but he'd been left behind at Pendleton to take the troopship. Taffy was a ginger-haired first lieutenant, big-shouldered, funny. He was married and might have pulled strings to stay home, but he was going too.

"The Marine Corps is always interrupting my Christmases," he'd said one night over beers in the officers' club, quite cheerful about it. "In 1942, American Samoa. In '43, Bougainville. And 1944 was Guam. We thought that would be cake, but it wasn't. In 1945, the good news, I was back in the States; the bad news, it was the Hospital for Tropical Diseases, Klamath Falls, Oregon. Now it'll be Christmas in Korea."

Taffy ran the fish cannery at Olympia, Washington, and Lou Faust's wife had gone up there to sit out the war with Sceva's wife. I wished that Taffy was here now, that we were going over together, that I'd have him to look to when I got there.

Lou was a big, rawboned guy who sold radio time. He had broken a man's jaw with one punch when we were back at Quantico, and after that people edged around him with a degree of caution.

Mack Allen had been an enlisted man in the war too, fighting on Okinawa and then service up in North China, occupation duty, rounding up Japanese stragglers and shooting bandits, keeping the rail lines open and trying to keep the locals from starving. After that came the Virginia Military Institute and then the Harvard "B" School. Mack was an engineer and couldn't wait to get to Korea and the division.

Phelps, like me, had never been in combat. We were the babies. But Phelps was a large, smooth young man, arrogant with strength and money. He was hardly a close friend, but I was glad we'd come down here with him to Stanford. You could see, with Coach Taylor and Mathias and the others, how Phelps carried himself, fond of his own opinion. Though he said little now.

"Brady," someone called, "share that pitcher a little, will you, like a good fellow?"

"Sure."

But it was nearly empty, and the girl brought another one, and as she walked away, flatbacked and with hips moving gracefully under a cotton dirndl skirt, we remarked on her look, the tan legs and honeyed hair. November 15, with winter coming, yet the sun was hot even under the trees, dappled by leaves, condensation beading our pitcher.

"A few days from now, a week . . . ," Mack said.

We all could finish the thought. This would be the second winter of the war, and we all knew what had happened in November exactly a year before, when the Chinese came in and nearly destroyed the division up at Koto-ri and the Chosin Reservoir. As replacement officers we'd read the reports. I remembered what Colonel Litzenberg had written back, warning us: ". . . men came down to the sick bay suffering from what appeared to be shock. Some of them would come in crying; some were extremely nervous; and the doctors said it was simply the sudden shock of the terrific cold."

Another officer lectured us at Quantico in Virginia, saying his Marines came off the line "just like zombies . . . a sort of paralysis . . . that sets in in extreme cold."

And these were Marines, the best men MacArthur had that first winter.

Phelps spoke on it for the first time. "Today's the fifteenth. Last November twelfth Colonel Davis reported it was sixteen below zero Fahrenheit, and with wind."

The waitress came back then, asking if we wanted another. "My, my, my," Mack Allen said in admiration, his soft Virginia voice paying courtly tribute.

"Just the check." Phelps said. "It's time to go."

He meant to leave Palo Alto. But he meant something more than that, and we all knew it.

At six tomorrow morning, if they had found a plane, we would be going to the war, to fight the Chinese and the cold and to lead men into combat. The others seemed ready; I wondered about myself. Suddenly I remembered a story from Freddie Grosse, who lived next door, the art director of a tobacco trade journal and a man who'd fought in World War I, so long ago.

"We were very cocky, and they marched us up into the trenches at night, all very secret, no one was to know. And in the morning, when we looked out over the trenches and through the barbed wire, there was a sign out there, hand-painted, and in perfect English. It was the Germans, welcoming us to the war, and getting our regiment and battalion exactly right, and I thought, 'Oh—oh, we may be in trouble here . . . '"

Sheepshead Bay, Brooklyn, where Mr. Grosse still lived and where I was born and my family was, seemed a long way off, in time and distance.

Funny, Korea, some six thousand miles away, seemed closer.

Phelps had tossed some money on the tray, and now he said, "Come on, it's time."

We drove slowly through the vast, lovely college campus in the autumn afternoon, toward the highway north, passing pretty girls and young men carrying books and tennis rackets, past touch football games and track men in sweats loping around an oval, past cyclists and parked convertibles, all the delicious accessories of peacetime America. Then, as Stanford fell behind and we rolled onto the Palo Alto entrance to the highway, Phelps's borrowed car leaped powerfully ahead, surging and speeding up.

Hurrying us toward war.

I was in that car because of the Cold War that had started a few years earlier. When the damned Russians began raising hell and blockading Berlin while the Commies in China were chasing old Chiang around and one country after another in Eastern Europe and Asia and Africa and even some in Latin America were caving in—and all this just a couple of years after V-J Day—it really began to look as if we might have to fight all over again, this time out against the Russians, this time with nuclear weapons. So President Truman proposed that we revive the draft, and Congress went along, and the day you turned eighteen you had to go down to your local Selective Service board, which was usually your local layabouts and political hacks and middle-aged men who sneered a lot and ordered you around. Like everybody else, I registered for the draft. Then, early in my sophomore year, my friend Gene Martin came back with a terrific suntan and stories about an officer-candidate program the Marine Corps had established called the Platoon Leaders Class. If you spent two summers training down at the Marine Corps Schools in Quantico, Virginia, then on the day you graduated from college, you received a reserve commission as a second lieutenant in the Marines.

I didn't want to be drafted, I rather liked the idea of being an officer, and the Marines had an undeniable cachet. A bunch of us signed up.

I left for Quantico and the Marine Corps on a summer's Sunday morning in 1948. My father took the bus with me to New Jersey, where I caught the train south. He was very excited. All his life he'd fantasized about going to war; now his eldest son would play out the dream.

At the railroad station he shook my hand. "If you run short of money . . . "

"I won't. They're paying us the rate of corporals."

"That's fine, just fine," he said. I assume he was broke, and the promise was as well meant, and as empty, as most of his.

I got a window seat and read the paper and watched the country rolling past. I'd never been to Washington and there was an hour's stopover at Union Station, where I transferred to another train, the Richmond, Fredericksburg & Potomac, for the forty miles into Virginia to the Marine Corps base. There were other young men in the car, crew-cut and tanned, wearing khaki pants and sport shirts or sweaters. There were a couple of Marines, as young as we but looking bored and condescending. It was dusk before we pulled into Quantico, not stopping at a station but on a siding, where we jumped down onto the right of way with our bags.

"All right, you peepul . . . "

The Southern voice cracked through the night. It was neither friendly nor encouraging.

I'd expected the South to be hot and muggy, and it was. The few men from the train who wore suits or sports jackets now got down to shirtsleeves along with the rest of us, while uniformed men in khaki, sleeves buttoned to the wrist and neckties snugly tied, barked, and chivvied us into a primitive formation and marched us through the rail yards and across a grassy field onto a street that ran between red-brick buildings that looked like college dorms. There was little traffic, only a couple of men on the sidewalks. Few Marines returned early on Sunday evening from a weekend.

The corporals and sergeants fell us in by alphabet. I met the man who had the next cot, a redhead with a broken nose and flat grin.

"Doug Bradlee," he said. The voice suggested Boston. He was maybe six-four and with shoulders. Jesus, I hoped they weren't all this big.

That first night none of us got into those cots before two in the morning. We were fallen out and issued clothing, bedding, helmets, boots, shoes, socks, underwear, mattresses, blankets, mess kits, canteens, cartridge belts, bayonets. Before we slept, the clothing all had to be stenciled, a sloppy, inky job. By midnight I was ready to quit and go home. And I wasn't alone.

They had us up by five the next morning. "Come on, come on, come on, you peepul . . . ."

We were fed and then marched off for a physical exam and shots. By mid-morning we'd been issued rifles left over from the war, packed since 1945 in Cosmoline, a Vaseline-like grease. They marched us out into an alleyway behind the barracks.

"Wear your boots and skivvies," the sergeant said.

For the next three or four hours we squatted, cleaning the rifles as our arms swelled from the vaccinations and the sun beat down. I'd never had a rifle in my hands before and didn't know where to start. When I asked a corporal, he grabbed my arm. "You see that there fella."

"Yes."

"He seems to know a leetle bit. You watch him. Do what he does."

The sergeants and corporals were DIs, drill instructors. Terrible people. Our officer was a Captain Finlayson, slender, blond, an aviator. He didn't come near us. Sunburned, exhausted, both arms throbbing, a low-grade fever working at me, I fell into bed that evening very nearly ready to cry. Most of us seemed to feel that way. At five they got us up again.

It wasn't like that at Parris Island, old salts assured us—Parris Island, where enlisted men went through boot camp. This was soft, this was plush compared with Parris Island.

That first time when I met Bradlee I asked the usual dumb question, what school he went to.

"St. Mark's," he said.

I said that was quite a coincidence, that I'd gone to St. Mark's grammar school. I didn't realize his St. Mark's was something quite different, and that while there Bradlee had been the captain of the hockey team and a star on the football team and that now he played varsity tackle for Harvard. I learned that after a while.

Quantico, with its single main street easing its way down to the Potomac, which along here was a big, slow Southern river, was boring, a two-bit garrison town, the dusty street to the river flanked by tailoring shops and the like, where Marines went to have their uniforms cleaned and pressed and custom-tailored, the shirts cut skintight. Regulars, the enlisted men, seemed to spend much of their lives at such things and shining their shoes. The real fun of the garrison took place off base, at Dumfries and Triangle, wide spots in the road along the Shirley Highway, where there were bars and fierce women and fistfights. Such places belonged to the "shifty-eyed" enlisted men and were tacitly off-limits to us, officer candidates.

As our trucks rolled through on the way to field problems, we saw the small, blonde redneck girls in their tight jeans sashaying through Dumfries and Triangle, and I wished I wasn't going to be an officer.

Under Captain Finlayson, who gave off the distinct impression he would rather be up in that cool blue sky flying fighter planes than running a bunch of college kids around in the Virginia heat, we were chivvied about by two drill instructors, both corporals. One of the DIs was weasel-smooth, round-faced, smiling, and currying favor. Oh, he ordered us around and snapped at us sometimes, but he was intelligent enough to realize that in a couple of years, when we had been beatified as lieutenants, he would still be an enlisted man. The other DI was a moron, plump and tightly sewn into his khakis, given to an assiduous scratching of his behind while not actually in formation and standing at attention. When we made sport of him, he reacted angrily. "You peepul [we were always being addressed as "you peepul"], if you be half so f————shop as me, you be pretty f———— shop."

"Shop" was "sharp," and his ultimate adjective of praise. And when he was not chewing us out or scratching, the corporal spent many hours polishing his shoes.

"When you see a Marine what got shop shoes," he would say, "you know he's one shop Marine, every which way. It's the shoes what does it."

If you drew him out, he softened and would go on for twenty or thirty minutes on the best techniques for rendering your shoes truly "shop." I never got very good at it, but shoe shining was quite a fetish with many enlisted Marines and even some of us. Bradlee, for one, the Harvard man, became splendid at shining shoes and on occasion was praised for being "shop."

Each week they issued chits on us: military bearing, discipline, targetry, neatness, physical condition, and so on. Assisted by our two DIs, Captain Finlayson marked up the chits.

After the first few weeks of sheer terror, awe, and self-doubt, we began to become capable once more of critical judgments. After all, we weren't seventeen-year-old recruits off the farm; we were nineteen- and twenty-year-old college men, reasonably mature and in some instances even sophisticated. Although we continued to obey the shouted orders of our DIs (you really had no choice), we permitted contempt to show through. The moron never really got it; the slick one, the politician, did, and curried favor even more. As for Captain Finlayson, what was he, after all, but a flier, an "airdale," while we were training to be rifle platoon leaders, infantry officers. Even in those first weeks as Marines we were already staking out claims to higher rungs in one of the most rigidly structured and ferocious caste systems in the world.

But the Marine Corps was touching and changing me in other ways. I was the product of Irish Catholic schools and of the working-class community of Sheepshead Bay and in part a reflection of friends like Joe Torpey, who became a baseball player and was married at home plate in a minor-league stadium just before the double-header, and like "Beaner" Toomey, whose dream it was to run a bar and grill. I suppose there were more provincial men in the Platoon Leaders program, but I was about as narrowly focused as you could get without being stupid. Now, in the barracks of a military base in a Virginia summer, as I was talking, talking, talking, and, more to the point, occasionally listening, a dormant imagination woke, curious, to look about and take notes. A boy from a small Catholic school was now, suddenly and unexpectedly, living with men from Princeton and the University of Texas and Stanford and Amherst and Yale and Michigan and USC.

A cowboy from Texas, Bobby Ray Something, taught me how to buy and wear jeans, how they had to look and to fit and to fade, distressed and slim. Chuck Brodhead, who played in the University of Michigan marching band (which may have had more members than the entire student body of smaller colleges), taught us all the Michigan fight song, "The Champions," and drilled us in it over and over. A kid from La Jolla told me about surfing and the sun-bleached rituals of the California beaches and the small coast towns I must promise to visit one day. Bradlee spoke lyrically and without self-consciousness of Harvard Yard and what it meant, those football rallies before the Yale game. And Dick Bowers, who was a Yalie and played tailback, talked of western Pennsylvania, where he had grown up in coal-mining towns and where, he assured us solemnly, the football had been harder and meaner and tougher than anything ever experienced in the Ivy League. And Southern boys formed us into ad hoc glee clubs and taught us close harmony, singing late into the Virginia evening the songs of the Old South.

"In the evening/By the moonlight/ You can hear the banjos ringin' . . . "

Someone else, or several someones, taught me occasionally to shut up. Maybe that was the best lesson of all. That, and how to order a bourbon with branch water or to savor a cool glass of beer on a hot day.

I took mental notes, began to absorb a smattering of social graces, to wonder, at least vaguely, about one day becoming a gentleman. I wasn't as methodical about it as James Gatz-becoming-Gatsby, but there was a little of that in it too.

"Brooks Brothers is the place," I was told. "No, J. Press." "Chipp cuts a better shoulder." "Give me Fenn-Feinstein."

I listened. And bought my first blue oxford cloth button-down shirt.

Maybe they learned something as well, all those Yalies and Texans and Harvards. I took Doug Bradlee home with me one weekend to Brooklyn. My brother was away, and Doug slept in his bed, and in the morning my mother gave him breakfast in the kitchen, as she did with all of us (the dining-room table was for dinner!), and I got him a date that Saturday evening with a girl who worked at the phone company, and on Sunday he went to mass with us at the Catholic church even though he was Episcopalian or something, and I showed him the Sheepshead Bay waterfront and he loved that, knowing New England and the lobster boats, and when we took the train back that late afternoon out of Penn Station, Bradlee said that was one of the best weekends he could remember. Ever.

Doug was always polite, but I don't think he lied.

The Korean War began on a Sunday, June 25. It wasn't really clear for a day or two that we would become involved. Then it became very clear.

By a fluke the American delegation was able to ram through a veto-proof resolution calling for United Nations forces to stop the North Koreans. The Soviets were boycotting the session, or they could have killed the resolution on the spot. Within a few days the first American soldiers were in action and MacArthur had been named commander of U.N. forces.

By mid-July the first letters had gone out from the Marine Corps. Get ready to be called up for active duty, we were told. But don't quit your job yet, remain in school, stay put until further word. Get in shape and read your mail.

In 1950 *Life* magazine was what we had instead of television, and it was *Life* that brought us the war.

The newspapers were there, certainly, with Marguerite Higgins of the New York *Herald Tribune* and Drew Middleton of *The New York Times* and wire-service men reporting almost from the very first. But no one could match *Life* with those big pages and slick paper and great photographs, especially ones by a man named David Douglas Duncan who had been a Marine during the big war and was now with the Marines in Korea.

The South Korean army, which was called ROKs for "Republic of Korea," fell apart almost instantly, the way you expected such armies to behave, but the first Americans into the fighting weren't much better. They were soldiers rushed over from Japan, garrison troops fat and slack from years of occupation duty. They weren't precisely Caesar's Tenth Legion, and they were up against a tough little peasant army with lots of mortars and very good artillery. Nevertheless some of them fought, and quite a few of them died, and the thing was a disaster. One of the divisional generals, a man named William Dean, actually ended up fighting as a rifleman when his regiments and battalions disintegrated around him, and he was captured by the North Koreans trying to defend a roadblock like some private dog soldier. Miss Higgins wrote about General Dean, and people clucked and said, "Oh, what a shame, what a gallant man." Later, Marines I talked to said he should have been court-martialed for getting himself and his outfit into such a sorry state.

After a few weeks what was left of the South Koreans and the dribs and drabs MacArthur was sending over had been compressed into a small quadrant of southeastern South Korea up against the sea, behind a river called the Naktong and based on a big port town called Pusan. Pusan was important because our ships could get in there with reinforcements and armor and supplies. If we lost Pusan, the war was over. In Washington some people were starting to talk quietly about withdrawal, remembering Dunkirk.

I was following the fight from Sheepshead Bay and on the subway going to work at Macy's, reading the papers. Unlike most people on the subway, I had more than a rooting interest. The first Marine units went into combat in August in what was being called the Pusan Perimeter. And Duncan's photos started appearing every week in *Life*. The country looked rugged; the Marines looked drained, exhausted; the rice paddies in between the mountains looked hot and wet and perfectly lousy places to die. The photos scared me.

By now the North Koreans had run out of steam and been knocked back from the Naktong, and in September MacArthur pulled out the Marines and ran them around the left flank and landed at Inchon, a brilliant stroke that threatened to cut off the North Koreans from their base.

Then, in October, the war apparently won, MacArthur did a bizarre thing. He split his army and went north, with winter coming and warnings that so too would come the Chinese.

They did, a half-million of them, it was said; they routed the Americans, and MacArthur seemed to panic and started calling out for air strikes north of the Yalu River and, maybe— the newspapers were unclear—for the atomic bomb. The first heavy snow fell in North Korea, and the mercury dropped below zero.

Then my orders arrived. I was to report to Quantico, Virginia, to the Third Special Basic Class (SBC) at the Marine Corps Schools, on January 3, 1951. Charges for transportation would be honored. The orders came to my house on Nineteenth Street in Sheepshead Bay, the house where I'd lived for so long, with my mother and my brother, Tom, with Grandma until she died, with Uncle Tom and Aunt Mary, where I'd once lived in the basement when my dad was still there, and where he put up the electric trains every Christmas. Was that how death came calling? In a routinely delivered letter to a little row house in Brooklyn?

My last day of work for Macy's was the Friday before Christmas. A couple of copywriters took me out to lunch, and afterward we wandered Fifth Avenue, admiring the store windows at Saks and Lord & Taylor and the decorations of Rockefeller Center.

That night there was a college alumni dance, the first since I'd graduated in June and maybe the last I'd ever attend. I took Sheila Collins and wore my new uniform. It was a bit premature since I wasn't going on active duty until January 3, but it saved me the rental of a tuxedo, and I thought it looked pretty good, and anyway, who was going to complain? The dance was in one of the big New York hotels and a smashing affair, a final chance to see some good friends. Sheila was as ever the liveliest, the funniest, the best girl at the table. Sometime after midnight the dance came to its conclusion, winding down and ending, as all dances did then, always with the same last song: "Good night, sweetheart/Till we meet tomorrow? Good night, sweetheart/Parting's such a sorrow. . . ."

And with that corny and rather lovely assumption that we dancers, boys and girls half in love, would now part until tomorrow, would go home to separate beds, the dance ended.

The Marines, again pushed back to the coast, got out of Hungnam on Christmas Eve, the rear guard wading out to the landing barges from the beach through the low surf, and as soon as they were off, four hundred tons of frozen dynamite and hundreds of thousand-pound bombs detonated, destroying the waterfront. Offshore three rocket vessels, seven destroyers, and three cruisers pumped shells into the city. The Chinese would not find much there to comfort them. Between October 26 and mid-December the Marine division lost 604 killed in action, 114 dead of wounds, 192 missing, 3,500 wounded, and another 7,300 nonbattle casualties, mostly frostbite and frozen limbs, many of whom returned after treatment to resume fighting. The division originally numbered about 15,000 men.

Some of this was in the papers, but for security reasons, not all. You didn't need the statistics when you looked at Duncan's pictures in *Life* magazine, the men with icicles hanging from their noses and their hollow, haunted eyes. It turned raw over Christmas and during Christmas week, and I imagined I felt cold more deeply than I ever had before. Nerves. I'd just turned twenty-two in November and felt much younger, wondering if I'd ever see another birthday, another Christmas.

At times like this you focus very narrowly and precisely on yourself.

All through that summer of 1950 and into the autumn and winter, the Marine Corps simply exploded, expanding to twice its size in a few months. Not even Truman's well-publicized distaste for the Marines and their penchant for self-promotion could inhibit the build-up. What the Marine brigade had done to stop the North Koreans along the Naktong River and around Pusan, how the Marine division had swarmed over the sea walls of Inchon, made the Corps virtually criticism-proof. What the Corps wanted, the Corps would get. And what it wanted now were thousands of officers to command the recruits being pumped out of the boot camps of Parris Island and San Diego. Not all these newly mobilized officers would be virgins, freshly minted kid lieutenants like Doug Bradlee and me. Many were hard men from the Pacific battles with the Japanese, officers back for their second war in just five years. Some of these men came reluctantly to Quantico.

But others welcomed the call back.

I met Taffy Sceva as soon as I got back to Quantico. Taffy had done a lot of fighting in the big war and now was out of college with an agriculture degree, working for the Olympia Canning Company up in Washington State. His wife, Barbara, was about to have their first child, and he was ordered to report into the Basic School the same day I got there.

At Quantico their son was born, Taffy and I competed for shortstop on the battalion softball team (I won), and to get out of the Marine Corps Schools and to combat in Korea, Sceva stunned everyone by petitioning Col. Chesty Puller, under whom he'd served in the Big War, to arrange the transfer. Some men we knew pulled strings to avoid being sent to Korea; a few like Sceva pulled strings to go. I'm not sure his wife ever knew that, however. There are limits to what you tell a good woman who loves you.

Gunny Arzt and I often occupied a small but well-sited table in a Washington cocktail lounge from where we could observe both the entrance and the door of the ladies' room. Arzt was big, tough, competent, ugly, hair slicked back and face punctuated by a cigar; I was eager, unsure just what to do or say next if a girl actually joined us, and awed by Arzt's enormous self-assurance.

"Buford, patience is everything."

It might take fifteen minutes. Two young women, government clerical workers by the look of them, would take a neighboring table. Arzt lifted his glass to them, smiling broadly without having to remove the cigar.

"Ladies, Buford here and I have traveled through several of the world's capitals, and not until just now have we gazed upon . . . "

A drink would be sent over next. Eventually, sometimes, the women joined us.

Gunny Arzt was one of the new men, new to us, though not to the Corps. He had a dark brush cut, a pug nose, and an underslung chin, and he sold cars in Yakima, Washington; I believe he owned a dealership and was wealthy. Arzt may have been nearly thirty, and he took me up, patronizing me boisterously, addressing me as "Buford" and informing people how delighted he was to have me in the outfit, else he would be its ugliest man.

Gunny had money and I did not. But I had an old Buick that provided a bond between us. Arzt went often into Washington to get laid; I went along, doing the driving while he paid for the drinks, hoping desperately all the time that some of Gunny's success with women might rub off on me. It never did.

I idolized Arzt.

"Sixty-five landings on hostile beaches," Arzt would remark, "sixty-five." There hadn't been that many invasions during World War II anywhere in the world, and some laughed at Arzt and his loudly proclaimed "sixty-five landings." But Bradlee warned against this, so I never did, which was a good thing because one day during a course we took on reconnaissance patrols they showed a training film left over from World War II and how recon companies sent small teams of men, four or six of them, ashore on Japanese-held islands to snoop about for intelligence and then row back out to a waiting submarine.

In the film, easily recognizable despite a coating of lampblack and the erosion of a half-dozen years, was our own Gunny Arzt. We all broke into applause.

"So you really did make all those f——— landings!" men told Arzt after the film ended and the class broke.

"Course I did," he said with nonchalance, "you could have asked Buford here."

There were men in the class who didn't make quite the impact of a Gunny Arzt or impose their personalities but who gradually took form, growing distinct and recognizable from the mass. You cannot sleep with forty men in the same room for three or four months, shave and brush your teeth side by side each morning, share a group shower, and sit on adjoining toilet seats day after day without becoming aware of just who is who.

Dick Brennan was from Massachusetts, a tall, lean, handsome Irishman with crow's wing hair and high cheekbones. The hair fell over one eye, and women found him something more than attractive, but Brennan was fiercely shy and private and didn't reciprocate. He wanted to be a writer, maybe a Civil War historian, which sounded right because Dick lacked small talk and easy laughter. He'd been in the Big War and never spoke of it.

Mack Allen's square name was Maurice J. Allen and he was a Lynchburg, Virginia, man, about five feet nine, tough, strong, compact, with jug ears and a wide smile. Whether it was V.M.I. or having been an enlisted man in the wartime Marine Corps, Mack was, though quietly, about as ferocious as a man could be about wanting to get into combat, and soon, as a rifle-platoon leader. I mouthed such sentiments too but deep down didn't mean them and hoped to be assigned to something cushy. And safe. Mack meant what he said. Leading men into combat was sort of a religious cause for Mack. Back in 1095 when Pope Urban II preached the First Crusade to liberate Jerusalem, the men who joined up must have been a lot like Mack Allen, though without the Southern accent.

Lou Faust, the rangy, rawboned, married guy in the radio business, had sandy hair and slightly bowed legs. He'd been a Marine before too. Lou was amiable as hell, never boasted or said very much at all, and always wore a wide, easy grin. Then one morning there was this big inspection of barracks laid on, and when we were all through sweeping and swabbing our platoon area and had fallen in outside in the company street waiting for the colonel to come through and look things over, and each platoon had left one man to stay behind a bit, to be sure no one came through and tracked up the newly scrubbed deck, Faust was one of the men assigned. A Marine from another platoon, late for the formation, started to cut through Faust's platoon area on his way out, trying to save a few seconds. He was as tall as Lou and heftier, but Lou told him, "Go around, pal, this area's secured."

"Bullshit!" the guy said, and started to push his way past.

Faust hit him just the once, breaking his jaw.

After that no one messed with Lou, and the guy with the broken jaw came back a few days later and told Lou that he was right to do what he did, that he shouldn't have tried to cut through. At Quantico you took things like newly swabbed barracks floors pretty seriously in that year.

Jim Callan had straw-colored hair and a Western twang and squinting eyes slit against the New Mexico sun. His family had a ranch and raised horses, and naturally his nickname was Wild Horse. Wild Horse said the big problem they had in New Mexico was drought and he hoped to save sufficient money over the next year or so in Korea that he could help his dad get some irrigation in there. If he could put together a few dollars, taking care not to spend anything in Korea (what would there be to spend it on, he reasoned), the ranch could make it. If they got water. How long had the drought been on, I inquired, very much the city boy. How many months?

Jim looked at me. "Nineteen years," he said.

So saving money in the Marine Corps was a priority for Callan. But then Wild Horse fell upon evil days, and in a way it was my fault.

I'd finished reading the B. Traven novel *The Treasure of the Sierra Madre*.

"Wild Horse, you've got to read this. It's a great story. It's set in Mexico, down near where you live."

Callan took the book, promising to get back to me with an informed critique. Then he was caught reading it during a terminally boring lecture on military courtesy or something and called up to the platform, where the book was seized and thrown away and he was given a bad chit.

Callan apologized, but I said it couldn't be helped.

A month later, when our class graduated and we got our assignments, Callan was one of the first men hustled out of there and sent to the division. I always wondered if it was that bad chit he got for reading B. Traven in class.

That winter in Virginia had been very cold. "Getting us ready for the Yalu," men said, a humorless joke. Now, in April, it would come to an end. And with the spring came our assignments. The twelve to thirteen weeks of the Basic School were ending. Some men would go to the division; others to Camp Lejeune and perhaps to the Mediterranean, some more to artillery school or communications or supply. Still others would stay here at Quantico to teach or to ramrod a new class through Basic School. I was one of those.

There were brief good-byes. The men ticketed for Korea wanted to get away swiftly, to enjoy their three weeks of leave before reporting to Camp Pendleton in California. The rest of us got a weekend off. When we got back on Monday, there would be a private room in the bachelor officers' quarters (BOQ). That would be a treat.

On Monday the BOQ wasn't quite ready. Nor had I been assigned to a new platoon. I wandered around, no schedule, no one to order me about, no formation into which I fitted, no friends. The squad bay where I'd spent the past three months was empty, the day hot. I sat on the side of my cot, then I lay down and fell asleep. An irate major woke me.

"Are you ill?"

"No, sir." I was standing at attention.

"Then what the hell are you doing sleeping in an empty barracks on a workday?"

I made my explanations.

"All right, then get the hell out of here and walk around and at least look useful. Nothing worse than a damned young officer looking slack."

I wandered about the main base until my BOQ room was emptied out and policed up so I could move in. I missed Bradlee and Callan and the others already.

Quantico echoed, empty and lorn.

It wouldn't stand vacant long, not with new classes coming into the Basic School every month or so now and more men coming back from Korea to help instruct them. The emptiness was only in those of us left behind.

The Marine Corps was eminently sensible about some matters. No man was to be left in Korea a day beyond what was necessary; there was no testing yardstick of machismo or brute endurance. As soon as there was a qualified replacement for an officer or an enlisted man, he could be rotated home. There was no training as valuable as combat, and since Korea was the only shooting war now available, the Corps had no intention of wasting it. Officers and men were shunted in and out as quickly as possible to learn, or perfect, their trade and then to come home to teach it to others. This was good news to those of us who expected shortly to be heading west. There were to be no marathons as during the last war, when a man might spend thirty-six or forty months in the Pacific with no hope of home until war's end or a bad wound.

So as Mack Allen and Sceva and Faust and others like us took over fresh platoons of new second lieutenants and started to take them through their paces, other men, returning veterans of the fighting in Korea, joined our ranks in the "faculty" of the Basic School. Such men were physically fit, of course. The broken men were parceled out to what is now St. Alban's Hospital in New York City and to other hospitals around the country. The men who came to work alongside us, whom I regarded with considerable awe, had come through whole. They looked whole, and they acted that way too except late on certain nights at the bar of Waller Hall, when their eyes seemed empty and you might draw certain conclusions.

One of those early May weekends, when Mack was in Richmond or somewhere, I drove up to Washington, as Gunny Arzt and I had so often done, and, having found no mischief, drove back alone and Baptist-proper through the warm afternoon of northern Virginia toward the BOQ and an early dinner.

Then, on that quiet, seeking, restless, empty Sunday I saw the sign. MANASSAS 12 miles, it said.

I swung the wheel. How grand it would have been to have had Mack Allen with me, a man who knew about Manassas, born in Virginia, educated there, a man whose people had fought at Manassas, or, as we called it, Bull Run.

My people hadn't fought there. Mack knew Manassas; I'd just read about it.

There were other signs, confusing, and the spring sun sank behind low hills and old trees overhanging the road. I kept going, looking for Manassas, past signs and mile markers and across the narrow runs and through the crossroads hinting of towns somewhere off in the dusk. Perhaps there were historical markers, pointing toward the battlefield, but in the gloom

I couldn't see them, only the occasional lone barn or farmhouse, a white church steeple ghostly, rising, and what seemed to be big farms beyond split-rail fences, and lots of trees, sometimes organized in orchards, row on row, but mostly just stands of wood, thick and mysterious. McClellan had fought here, and Meade and Jeb Stuart and Lee and Hood. Here stood the Army of the Potomac, and toward it came the long gray lines of Southerners, Mack Allen's people, the brigades of cavalry slouching in their saddles and the regiments of Carolinians and Georgians and Texans and the batteries of guns, rattling and lurching along these same roads. Along here just about every mile and at every crossroads they fought for four years, starting here at Manassas in 1861 and ending here, big set-piece battles and small, nasty skirmishes when a detachment of horse stumbled across a woodcutting party in the dark. I wondered if those men, those long-dead men whose wraiths still marched here in the deep Virginia night, felt about war as I did, drawn to it and fearing it at the same time.

Thoroughly lost, I gave up the search and cut back on the first side road toward the Shirley Highway and Quantico.

Letters and postcards began to arrive in Quantico from the West. From Camp Pendleton, from the embarkation ports of San Diego and San Francisco, from Pacific Ocean points en route, finally from Korea itself and the 1st Marine Division.

Bradlee's letters were touched with eloquence, and I thought how pleased his Harvard tutors would have been.

" . . . Had a very interesting talk with Champion as the evening wore on. He's the man who has three children, two purple hearts, and fought through almost the entire last war. He was a lieutenant on Iwo and Okinawa after coming up through the ranks. Very mild, quiet, slim guy who was a refrigerator repairman in Muskegon, Michigan. He was considering moving and I told him my liking for old timers in New England, the rather reduced but satisfactory scale of living of lobstermen. He likes to work with his hands too."

This sure sounded like Doug. During Harvard summers he worked on a lobster boat, setting and lifting the big traps. Probably it was good training for another season of football, keeping him lean and tough. But for a man who lived in some comfort, if not luxury, on Pinckney Street in Boston's Back Bay, the lot of the New England lobsterman had another, more subtle pull. Bradlee really did mean it when he talked of a "reduced but satisfactory" way of life. I'd seen his car with its wooden two-by-fours bridging the rusted-away parts of the floor.

That was Bradlee, of St. Mark's and Harvard and effete Boston.

From Korea and the 1st Mar Div he wrote: "The country is very rugged, almost unbelievably so. We are dug in for the evening around the bottom of a ravine for a change. Stream about 100 yards away, babbling over stones, cold, clear. Washed myself and clothes and feel wonderful. Yesterday my platoon was sent up to seize a ridge. We really pushed hard and found the Chinks had stopped on a ridge 600 to 800 yards away. Small arms and machine gun fire came sporadically but we didn't pay much attention and they gave up in disgust. Marines are far and away the best fighters in Korea but tired out. I've lost five men in the last three days through heat prostration and exhaustion. Platoon very good. Company commander is good and whole outfit and whole first Division very sharp.

"The spirit of the Corps never ceases to amaze me. Walking to our assembly area yesterday it rained all the way. Much singing, horseplay, laughter, even though pretty miserable actually. Spirits kept high and we were rewarded by a beautiful day when we arrived.

"Have impressions of Korean civilians, farmers, as they watch Marines move on to their farms and set up camp. They can only look and hope for the best. No language bridge, so no talk exchanged, except extra rations usually find their way to them. Many houses burn because of thatched roofs. On ridges at night I can usually see two or three burning in valleys below. Usual procedure is to set up in a line around a bowl of terrain, each platoon tied in with one on each side. Fighting holes are on the front slope, sleeping holes on the reverse side.

"Amazing thing here is that there are mocking birds exactly the same as in Colorado."

Now another letter came back. Dick Brennan had been hit on June 10, assaulting a Chinese hill. Someone said he'd been machine-gunned; someone else said it was a burp gun, a sort of submachine gun. Anyway, it stapled both his hands and one arm half-way up. That letter said Dick had been put up for a medal for pushing the assault after he was hit.

In his own letters to us from the naval hospital, Dick wrote us nothing about the war, only about the medical care and how fine it was though the food was tiresome. Brennan said he and another officer were writing a play; it wouldn't be about the war but about the hospital.

"I think it could be a fine play," he said.

And he never wrote anything about the fighting.

Bob Bjornsen was a forest ranger, about as tall and naturally impressive as the trees he tended in Nevada, up north near Reno. He'd been an enlisted man during the war and enjoyed talking about it, not loud and didactic as Gunny Arzt could be, but proud of his being a "mustang," an officer promoted from the ranks. There's one photo of Bjornsen with Mack Allen and me, Bjornsen half a head taller and at the shoulders half again as wide. While Mack and I stayed behind as platoon leaders in the 5th SBC, Bjornsen went early to Korea in a replacement draft, joining the 3d Battalion 1st Marines in May. Jim ("Wild Horse") Callan and Doug Bradlee were with Bob Bjornsen and were both huge men. Wild Horse and Bjornsen too had something in common: Callan would go back to the ranch after the war, he said, and Bjornsen said he'd return to the forests. That was the work he did, and he loved it, the trees and the peace and quiet, and he was good at his work.

"We became buddies," he said of Bradlee. "I've got pictures of Doug and me at Pearl Harbor, Guam, Japan, and in Korea. He, quiet, me, talkative, an old salt with a wife and daughter back home and Doug just a year out of college."

All three men were assigned to the same battalion on the same day, May 20. "Doug was killed June third," Bjornsen said, "and Callan on June tenth. I took over Callan's heavy machine-gun platoon in a firefight on the day he was killed. Doug and I just hit it off together from Quantico days, and how well I remember trudging up the hill that day, thinking sixty-six percent of the three officers who came as replacements were already killed in action and we hadn't been in Korea a month. Neither Doug nor Jim had been in combat before and were killed before they learned the ropes. By contrast I was a World War II enlisted combat Marine and knew how to survive and maneuver troops in a firefight.

"His father wrote me after Doug's death and wanted the particulars. I wrote back that he was killed instantly, which was true, but left out the particulars."

Back in Quantico that spring and summer we got too many reports like this back from men we knew about other men. I'd heard about Doug from his father. The wire arrived at Camp Barrett, where I was a platoon leader training other young officers. It read: "WORD RECEIVED DOUG'S DEATH IN ACTION 3 JUNE NO FURTHER DETAILS." It was signed "Malcolm Bradlee."

In late July from Saunderstown, Rhode Island, Mr. Bradlee wrote me again.

"My dear Jim, I sent you that wire about Doug's death because I sensed at once how close friends you two had become. This picture was taken just before he left home for San Francisco. Also, Mrs. Bradlee and I felt that you would like to have the enclosed reading at the memorial services. I sincerely hope that you will write me about your current news and that you will keep in touch with us in the future. Always sincerely, Malcolm Bradlee."

The memorial service had been held not at Harvard but at St. Mark's School chapel in Southborough, Massachusetts, on June 17, two weeks after he died. A Professor Finlay had presided, and Mr. Bradlee sent along his remarks and the readings.

No one mentioned in letters or at the service how Doug could have stayed behind at Quantico, could have played football this coming fall, and not gone over until 1952, when, as far as we all knew, the fighting might have ended. He was actually pretty sore about being called in and told of the football option. "I mean, why do they think we're here? It's sure not to play tackle against William and Mary or some Navy team from Norfolk."

I guess Doug was fairly brisk with the morale and recreation officer who'd called him in, and his name popped right up on the very next replacement draft. "You don't want to play football for the Marine Corps, son? Okay, then, go fight the Koreans." A lot of officers who'd played in college or the pros took the option and stayed home to play football.

There was one other letter from Doug among the things his family sent us. This one didn't sound as much like him as it did a more spiritual Bradlee than I knew: "As I once said, try not to be overtly upset by my present mission. I have felt during the last seven years or more that I might have been cut out for things away from the beach and the country club . . . not away from business into school teaching but really away. I didn't figure on its being in this form, but this might be a good foundation.

"I look to the world of the spirit and the world of human relationships as the most important thing. No peace treaty, no international government is any good without the spirit underneath it. I look to the principles of a Christian life, not stopping at a 'gentlemanly' Christian life but working towards a saintly one.

"I hope some day to find and work toward God."

There might have been services for Jim Callan out West. But no one wrote to us about them, and we just didn't know.

I wondered why I didn't cry about Doug and Wild Horse. I was the sort who cried at movies or to a rendition of "Danny Boy."

Maybe it was because I would soon go where they had gone. In September Mack Allen and most of us wrapped up the 5th Special Basic Class and got our orders for Korea. Three weeks of leave, then a month or so in California at Camp Pendleton, then across the Pacific to the division. We'd get there late in November, we reckoned.

"Just in time for the first snow," men said cheerfully.

It was a few days after Bobby Thomson had hit the home run to beat Branca and the Dodgers to get the Giants into the 1951 World Series that I flew to Los Angeles en route to Camp Pendleton. I went out a couple of days early to see California before I had to check in, and I got a room in an L.A. hotel a cabdriver from the airport assured me was clean and cheap. I knew nothing of Los Angeles, where it began or ended, and the hotel was in precisely the wrong place, downtown and dull, near City Hall and the Los Angeles *Times* building. Gray office blocks, business streets, no palm trees, men wearing business suits, no beach, very few suntans.

On the day I was to report in to Camp Pendleton I took the train south out of Union Station to Oceanside, past the oil rigs bobbing up and down at Long Beach, occasionally seeing the Pacific through the windows and off to the other side the big, dusty brown mountains and the small towns and crossroads and the highway that sped along beside the tracks with lots of cars going very fast, ragtops most of them, maybe headed for the beach.

I felt very young and very lonely.

That changed at Pendleton. You began to realize that when they talked of the Corps being family, there was something to it and not just chamber of commerce crap. We were in big wooden barracks, officers I'd known at Quantico and some others, and we all were in a replacement draft and were going to the war. Now there was a schedule; now there were dates and rosters and names and faces and sheaves of orders for "duty beyond the seas."

I was no longer lonely. I was again part of something and not an outsider.

In September and October, while I was on leave and then in California, a lot of men died in the eastern mountains. The Marines were sent to attack and seize a series of high, stony ridgelines thrusting up out of the evergreens and the narrow valleys with their streams and marginal rice paddies. They were up against North Koreans who were dug in and well armed and knew what they were doing. This was the fighting that came to be called the "the meat grinder."

I first heard about it at Pendleton.

The barracks were big and bare, barnlike structures on two floors with wooden staircases outside and steel bunks and lockers and bare-plumbing toilets and showers and naked light bulbs, nothing *House & Garden* would have covered. I liked Camp Pendleton. It had a raw feel you didn't get back East at Quantico, which was more like a college campus.

I was always something of a nut about snow. When I was little, I'd vet the weather reports and watch the sky when it was low and gray and the air was cold enough and heavy. I thought I could sense snow coming, almost wish it here. I grew up to be a skier; I loved the cold and the mountains and the deep drifts. Then one day at Pendleton we were issued thermal boots and heavy gloves and piled into school buses with box lunches and driven eleven hours through the rain up Route 395 though Riverside and San Bernardino and past Barstow and through Bishop, where the rain began to change to snow, but most of us were asleep by then and didn't know. And then past Mono Lake and into Alpine County, where the mountains ran ten, eleven thousand feet up, and then we were at Pickle Meadows, flush up against the Nevada line near Tahoe, the new cold-weather warfare training camp the Marines had set up. It was morning, bright with sun, and it was still October, but there were eighteen inches of fresh snow on the ground of the parking area when we piled off the bus.

The replacement draft ahead of us, who'd come up here the week before, was coming down now from the hillsides, moving slowly and looking shocked, some of them, others cursing steadily.

One of them said, "There's three feet of this up there."

Men in our draft turned to look at one another. Were we really going to spend five days up here running field problems? In three feet of snow?

It was cold in the sun at noon. I tried to imagine what it would be like at two in the morning, especially if it snowed again. It didn't snow again, as it turned out, and it never got really cold, nothing lower than fifteen or so, but we were there for five days running field problems day and night, humping our packs and our weapons up and down hillsides and ridgelines. The new thermal boots, vacuum-lined and designed to keep your feet warm well below zero, boots they hadn't had that first winter in Korea, when so many men lost their feet, worked fine. The big problem was the altitude. Nothing I'd skied in New England was higher than four thousand feet. Here we ranged from nine to twelve thousand or so, and we covered miles every day, up and down, digging in and setting up the mortars and the machine guns, simulating a firefight, and then moving on to another position on another hill a thousand feet higher or lower, to do it all over again.

I thought I was going to die.

On the fourth night with the battalion dug into defensive positions, "aggressor troops," Marines stationed up here to help work us out, men accustomed by now to the thin air and the altitude, launched a series of raids on our lines.

"They'll be armed with squirt guns filled with red dye," the war-games umpire warned us, "so tomorrow morning if you wake up with red dye on your puss, you're dead."

I was fast asleep in the down sleeping bag, exhausted from the climbing and the cramps that came with altitude sickness, when the "aggressors" came. One of them peeled back the hood of the sleeping bag.

"Peekaboo," he said, ugly face split in a grin.

"F—— you," I said, but not very energetically.

"Bang!" he said, "you're dead," and squirted me in the face. I wiped it off as best I could with a filthy handkerchief and fell back to sleep. I don't think he knew I was an officer. I hoped not. Even through the fatigue and the pain I retained vestiges of pride.

A few hours later the scoring officers chewed us out for lack of nighttime security. "If those were Chinese up there, a lot of you would be dead this morning." Just before noon the buses rolled up, and we climbed on board. I never thought I'd be happy leaving the mountains and the snow, but I was. I felt like Taffy Sceva; the Marine Corps kept taking me places I'd never seen.

Old salts around Pendleton, regulars, got their laughs out of us. Regular officers were that way too, talking endlessly about "the old Corps." Whatever we were, however well we did, we weren't "old Corps." The talk was all of the Raider battalions that had been in the thick of the worst of the fighting in the Pacific. At the end of every story we'd all have another drink on that, and the major, or another of the salts, would shake his head and say: "They don't make Marines anymore like the Raiders, not by a damn sight."

We all were duly impressed. Or we were until four of us were driving up to Laguna Beach one Saturday noon.

Someone, I forget who, had a car, and we were barreling along the back roads of Pendleton, maybe going seventy down a deserted rural road heading for the Coast Highway and a weekend's liberty at Laguna Beach, when a motorcycle with a Marine aboard it blasted past us on the left as if we were pausing to take the air.

"Wow!" someone said, hushed tribute.

I was in the front next to the driver, watching the motorcycle swiftly dwindling as it pulled away ahead of us, and then noticed the Marine seemed to be doing some sort of trick riding, wobbling his rear wheel.

"Look at that," I said admiringly, "I sure wouldn't be playing games the speed he's going."

"Listen, that's not showing off. He's thrown a bolt or something!"

Within a second or two the motorcycle had started to skid and then go over sideways, and almost instantly the cycle was on its side, the driver still astride the seat but half under his bike now as it skidded along, throwing up a shower of sparks as it went.

"Oh, Jesus."

There was going to be nothing left of the Marine. He was still skidding, still sliding along the blacktop, a hundred yards, maybe two hundred from where he first went over. There wouldn't be any flesh left on him when we got there, when he finally stopped. The sparks were still spraying out to both sides and behind him as bare metal scraped the road at speed.

Then he stopped. We pulled up alongside and jumped out. I turned away, as if looking for other traffic coming along, but the truth was I didn't want to see him, didn't want to see a man's body flayed raw and bleeding.

But when the bike was lifted off him, the Marine stirred, trying to get up. At least he was conscious.

"You okay? You okay? Anything broke?"

"I don't think so," he said. "Jest gimme a hand here."

We got him to his feet now, all of us lending a hand, even me.

"The roll bar saved my leg," he said.

So had a leather jacket and the thick wool uniform and the helmet. We talked to him for a while.

"I thought you were doing stunts back there," I said, "wobbling your wheel."

"Nah, threw a bolt. Wheel jest went. Weren't nawthin' I could do, just try to slow it and go over easy."

Someone asked how fast he was going.

"Oh, not more'n a hunnert, maybe one-oh-five or ten. She'll move better than that on the straight."

You could hear pride in his voice when he talked about the bike.

"You fellas want to drive me back a bit so I can look for that bolt, sirs?" he said, throwing in the "sirs" at the end.

"Maybe we ought to drop you at Main Base, at the sick bay."

"Nah," he said, "I'm okay. Sore is all."

We found the bolt about half a mile back, and when we left him, the Marine had the bike back up and his sleeves rolled up and he was working on the rear axle where the bolt had come loose.

About halfway to Laguna someone said, and meaning it, "I don't want to hear any more shit from these old-timers about the Raiders and how tough they were and how we ain't. Understood?"

We all said, "Understood," and meant that too.

Laguna Beach was our Riviera. It was thirty-five miles up the coast from Oceanside and the main gate to Pendleton, and it was where we went weekends, a small, sunny town on cliffs overlooking crescents of golden sand skirting the dark blue Pacific coves. We took rooms in cheap hotels and motels and boardinghouses along the coast strip, sleeping four or even six men to a room.

This was when I truly fell in love with California, on those weekends at Laguna Beach.

The highway comes up into Laguna from the south, rising slightly until, when you are in the town itself, you are maybe two hundred, three hundred feet high on cliffs that bulwark the narrow beaches. Down every side street and between the houses you could see the Pacific, dark and wonderful, slow and lazy, with kids out there surfing, local boys with sun-bleached hair and baggy shorts on long, polished boards, measuring the big waves coming in, waves that came from Asia, more than six thousand miles away.

On Saturday they let us off at noon, and someone always had a car and we drove up the coast to Laguna Beach and checked into a beachfront hotel and got out of uniform and into shorts and sweatshirts and went down the rocky path to the sand to try to pick up girls and to swim and to play two-man volleyball. We might have a beer or two, and there was a hole-in-the-wall restaurant called My Place where we got burgers. On the portable radios you could hear the big football games back East or in the Midwest, and the announcer, Bill Stern maybe, would say it's colder now and starting to snow and growing dark and . . .

And we were lounging there on beach blankets, chatting with pretty girls and working on our suntans, and the big rollers kept coming in, here and there dark with kelp and sometimes with the sleek, cannonball head of a seal, and it was only two o'clock in California, and the November sun was still high and night a long time off.

To an Easterner there was something almost magical about the time zones, the three-hour differences between here and home, something inexpressibly lovely about the dramatic fall of the sun into the late-afternoon ocean. There are magnificent beaches in the East, but nowhere on the Atlantic does the sun disappear into the ocean as it does in the Pacific.

It was of such things that we spoke with the girls we met, and not of Korea.

When we spoke of Doug Bradlee and Wild Horse Callan or others now dead or in the naval hospitals, men our age and until recently our shipmates, it was always in fun, the silly, inconsequential memories of days and nights at Quantico, not of death and war wounds. To dwell on losses was unhealthy. Nor was there guilt. They had gone to the division, and now our turn had come.

"Who's this Wild Horse you're always talking about?" a girl would say as we lay on an old blanket in the sun after a swim.

"A guy we know, a pal."

"He sounds pretty funny."

"He is."

"Does he actually talk like that, a real cowboy?"

"Absolutely, a real old-fashioned cowboy."

We spoke always in the present tense.

"Smear some more gook on my back, will you, honey? I'm getting burned."

"Sure."

It was intimate but all pretty innocent, these weekend living conditions being what they were, so many men to a room, sharing beds, sleeping on couches or stretched out between two chairs, on the floor, occasionally on a blanket in the tub. There was a great deal of necking, little more serious, though certainly some of us tried. I was twenty-two and a virgin still and making regrettably little progress in becoming anything else. And for all the large talk, I don't believe I was unique.

Before we left Pendleton for the division, I did two last things. One was to seek out a priest at a small parish in Oceanside and go to confession in his office in the rectory one evening (all those necking parties at Laguna!). The other was to buy a .38-caliber Smith & Wesson military and police special with a four-inch barrel and fifty rounds of ammunition.

Then, a few days before we were to go down to San Diego and board ship, new orders were cut. Mack Allen and I and a few others were to fly over.

Trying to sound enthusiastic, I said something about being lucky, that we were going to get there before it was over. We weren't going to miss the war after all.

Mack, who had already attended one war, nodded slowly. "There's no rush, Jim. They're not goin' to run out of Chinamen. They got plenty."

That night some of us who'd been together right from the very first at Quantico got together for a last drink at the O Club.

"Bourbon and branch water," I ordered.

Mack smiled in delight. "Well, well, well, so you finally learned what a gentleman drinks."

"Yes, sir."

Sceva and Faust were there, and Bob Phelps, the big football player from Stanford, and others.

"Hell, you guys flying over are the lucky ones. Do you know what sort of chicken shit they run in on you aboard ship? Inspections every hour on the hour, queuing up for food, for movies, for showers. You line up to get *seasick*."

Some officers had been flown over earlier, late in 1950 and earlier in 1951, and one man knew the drill.

"You fly out of San Francisco . . ."

"Not Dago?"

"No, they use Navy planes, the military equivalent of the DC-6. And you land at Hawaii and lots of other places on the way. So take along some swim shorts and suntan stuff. Maybe a sport shirt. And khakis . . . "

"Khakis? We're going to Korea. It's November, and there's snow."

"I tell you, Hawaii, Kwajalein, Guam. You'll want khakis. It's still the South Pacific."

I was confused. "I thought you always flew the Great Circle route. Why wouldn't we go north, via Alaska, the Aleutians, Japan?"

"Maybe they got MiGs up there, out of Siberia," someone said. Gloom descended on choir practice. MiGs were Soviet fighter planes that the North Koreans and the Chinese flew, fast, competent, deadly. An old Navy DC-6 wouldn't have a prayer with MiGs.

We talked late that night, making our good-byes without ever saying them. In a week, maybe ten days, some of us would be there in Korea, in the snow and the cold and the mountains, holding commands in the division. It was entirely possible, though not likely, one or more of us might be dead. The rest, the majority, ten days from now would be less than halfway across.

"It doesn't matter which way we go," said Taffy Sceva. "We'll all be together again before Christmas."

People began to drift away after that, emptying glasses and exchanging handshakes. It looked pretty casual. Let the doggies, the Army, have the drama. We were the professionals.

Outside the officers' club I walked back to the barracks, enjoying the clear, starry sky, the familiar chill of Southern California when the sun went down, thinking about what Taffy said. Christmas. I hadn't thought about Christmas. Hadn't thought about my birthday, only two days away now. November 15, the day we were to fly out, or so the orders said, and the orders never lied, did they?

I wished I had said a proper good-bye to my mother. I hadn't really. She hated the war so, and the Corps, I didn't want to upset her, so I kept it relaxed, maybe too much so. Maybe we should have hugged and cried together. It's hard to know what to do, what is right and proper, when you have never gone to war before, when it is your first time.

Two mornings later we flew up to San Francisco, and the plane wasn't ready, and we had a day to waste, a birthday to enjoy, and Bob Phelps took us down to Stanford.

We drove north from Palo Alto toward San Francisco, Phelps at the wheel, in the fading November light, no one talking much, most of us thinking, I guess, about this being our last day in America. I know that was what I was thinking.

We'd taken a couple of double rooms at the Mark Hopkins, two double rooms for seven of us who hung together. It was cheaper that way, and we shared beds and flipped for the couch and saved money. We could have gone to a lesser hotel, but on your last night in San Francisco it somehow seemed right to be at the Mark. Only Phelps, who had some style (and money), complained about the room arrangements, remarking it wasn't a very classy way to go to war and was probably against the hotel rules. By the time we had the sleeping arrangements sorted out and had gone upstairs to the cocktail lounge of the Top of the Mark, it was full night, and Faust and Doran had joined us, men leaving wives behind, children.

Out beyond the windows, as we lazed over drinks, the Pacific was dead black except for the lights here and there of fishing boats and coasters. Behind us the Golden Gate Bridge was a necklace slung delicately against the bosom of the dark.

"Nice," someone said. And it was.

Mack and Phelps and I told them about Palo Alto, about meeting the football team and having beers under the trees.

"Sounds good."

I don't know really what the others felt. This was one of those times when we were shy, even among ourselves, men who'd lived together for most of a year suddenly fallen mute. I knew what I was thinking, blend of exultation and pride, fear and inadequacy.

"Another?"

We all had one more. Why not? You could pick out individual stars in the western sky, way out over the ocean. I took a sip of bourbon and shivered. That night in bed, before I slept, listening to the muted sounds of men in sleep, the snores and restless movement, I thought of Freddie Grosse, who lived next door and of the sign the Germans held up that long ago October in the Argonne Forest, said a brief prayer for Wild Horse and Doug. I wished I had a martial tradition on which to call, like Mack Allen or Taffy Sceva, a noble father or grandfather. All I had was an uncle dead on D-day, a man I can't recall having ever seen, who went into the Army and might otherwise have gone to jail.

I was sure that like my father, I would play the fool, and I hoped only that I would not run away or get men killed out of cowardice or weakness, hoped I might accomplish things in which people who knew me might take a modest pride.

They'd found a new plane or repaired the old one. And we climbed on board in the half-light that next morning—all those senior NCOs and officers who'd been to war before, and kids like me who hadn't. They handed us box lunches as we climbed up, sufficient to get us to Hawaii.

"Waikiki next stop!" someone exulted. Men laughed, and there was some tomfoolery and kidding around, what the Marines call "grabass." Mostly, I suspected, it was nerves. Even for the older men.

The interior of the plane had been gutted of its airline seats, and in their place hung rows of stretchers, double-berthed, riveted or bolted to the overhead and to the bulkheads.

"Hey," I said enthusiastically, "we can stretch out, take a nap."

A gunnery sergeant looked at me. "Lieutenant, them's stretchers for the wounded. They fly replacements over, and they use this same plane to fly the woundeds back."

There were rust brown stains in the canvas of the stretchers.

I nodded and shut up.

It took a while to get everyone on board and then a longer time to get the engines started and before we rolled out onto the tarmac, so I wrote a letter to my dad, writing on notepaper in my lap. You know how it is in the service, they're always after you, making work, keeping you busy, sending you this way and that, so you learn to read or think or write a letter whenever there's time, no matter how brief. I wrote to him about these last days in California and how it was now time to go, but mostly about San Francisco and what a great town it was and a lot about Stanford and especially about going to practice and meeting their football team.

He'd enjoy that. He loved football and had never played it. And he'd always wanted to go to war and never had.

We were moving now, rolling slowly over the tarmac, bumping gently, the old plane vibrating slightly, rattling, the wood and canvas stretchers banging against the bulkheads, the motors revving slowly and then faster. I was on the right side, and in the east the sun was climbing but slowly. Then the plane was rolling faster, bumping more, and now very fast.

Now we were off the ground and rising and the sun coming up with us, clear of the horizon, as we banked once over the bay and then banked again so that the Golden Gate arced beneath us. Then California fell behind as we flew west toward Asia.

INVENTING THE COMMERCIAL

Harry Matthei

Micro processor, Internet, the WEB, DOS, MAC, WINDOWS 95 all are terms easily rec-ognizable in the high tech world of the 1990s. It is almost unimaginable that barely a generation ago not only did none of these items exist but television, the almost omnipresent item in every American home, was just entering American life. Although it had existed for decades before, it was not until the 1950s that television would begin its relentless march into its dominance of American society and culture. In its infant days television was a me-dium of live broadcasts. This fact was a challenge not only for performers but for advertis-ers as well. After all, television at the beginning was seen as a wonderful new way to promote the sales of products. Harry Matthei, who spent over 40 years in television adver-tising, presents a fascinating look at the early years of television. He shows how this fasci-nating device captured the American public along with the merchandising and marketing geniuses of American business.

It was 1945, and everybody needed everything. If you knew how to build a car, a house, or a washing machine, you could sell it faster than you could make it. Car dealers, including fine old names that soon would be history—Hudson, Nash, Packard, and Studebaker—all had long waiting lists. Many dealers bluntly quoted not the price of the car but the price of getting on their waiting lists.

In 1945 I had barely heard of either television or the advertising business, and I had no idea what a boom was, even though I was smack in the middle of one. I was thirteen years old, just out of grade school, and my goal was to become an engineer. Instead I spent forty-six years in advertising, mostly as a TV copywriter, later as a writer-producer and agency owner. While it wasn't always fun, it certainly was never dull.

In 1945 on New York's Madison Avenue—Main Street for America's advertising agen-cies—business had never been better. Freed of wartime paper restrictions, the big general-in-terest magazines—*Life, Look, The Saturday Evening Post,* and *Collier's*—swelled with advertisements. So did the major women's magazines: *Good Housekeeping, McCall's,* and *La-dies' Home Journal*. Fifteen percent of the placement cost of every ad went straight into the ad-vertising agencies' pockets.

Of course, every city of any size in 1945 had at least two newspapers: morning and evening. Big cities had three or four of each, plus the foreign language press, and every one of them was stuffed with advertising. Americans once again could buy cigarettes, film, shoes, steaks, nylon stockings, tires, and everything else missing from their lives since December 7, 1941.

Into this giddy, superheated economy, commercial television was born. Again.

Television broadcasting had been launched in the United States in 1928 by the General Electric Company, in Schenectady, New York. The station—today's WRGB, Channel 6—had been licensed to broadcast "experimental" television only. Commercials were expressly forbidden.

According to *Advertising Age*, the industry's trade weekly, the first "legal" television commercial was aired on WNBT, the NBC station in New York, on July 1, 1941, during a Dodgers-Phillies game at Brooklyn's Ebbets Field. The camera focused on a Bulova watch with the second hand ticking as the announcer read the correct time. Bulova time checks ("It's three o'clock, Bulova watch time") were already fixtures in radio advertising; Bulova simply adapted them to TV. For the first time in all of advertising, Bulova was able to combine the stimuli of sight, sound, and motion via television.

Bulova's agency, the Biow Company, billed its client nine dollars: five for airtime and four more for "station charges." Fifteen percent of this ($1.35), we can assume, was profit to the Biow Company as its standard advertising-agency commission. There were then about four thousand TV sets in the New York City area, roughly half of all the sets in the country.

"Illegal" commercials, *Advertising Age* noted, had appeared as early as 1930, when all TV licenses were strictly "experimental"—*i.e.*, noncommercial. On July 1, 1939, General Mills, Procter & Gamble, and Socony Oil (now Mobil), all sponsors of Brooklyn Dodgers' radio coverage, were given free plugs by Red Barber, the Dodgers' announcer, during the first televised major-league baseball game. Red sliced bananas into a bowl of Wheaties, held up a bar of soap, and donned a gas-station attendant's cap. He thereby became the father of the demonstration commercial. The Federal Communications Commission (FCC) apparently missed this debut. Earlier violators of the noncommercial rule had drawn fines and threats of license suspension, but Red got off scot-free.

During the war years commercial television went on hold. The government halted the manufacture of new sets and transmission equipment and stopped issuing station licenses. Established stations provided regular programming, but only a handful of people were equipped to watch it.

In October 1945, less than two months after the war ended, commercial television got two major shots in the arm: The FCC lifted the wartime bans on licensing TV stations and making sets, and RCA demonstrated an improved TV camera that delivered a far crisper, clearer picture. So, after years of sluggish progress, a depression, and a war, television at last was ready to roll.

The major advertising agencies—the "hucksters" that had turned network radio into a money machine—saw the new medium as a natural out-growth of the older, better-established one. The admen ruled radio as they never could newspapers or magazines, controlling the editorial content. Companies like Procter & Gamble, Ford, and General Foods paid advertising agencies to create and produce—or buy from independent producers—hours of network radio programs every day. The broadcasters functioned only as an electronic pipeline. They generally accepted whatever programming the advertisers chose.

Filling the pipe usually began with an independent producer or talent agent proposing a program to an agency. This might be anything from a soap opera to a quiz show. The agency would then sell the idea to one of its clients and negotiate a time slot with a network. The network in turn would offer the show to local affiliate stations, which simply took the network feed via AT&T lines and broadcast it within their areas. The only locally produced radio programming usually was local news, farm and market reports, and fillers for dead times like Sunday mornings, when the audiences were too tiny to attract big advertisers.

With the coming of television the agencies and their clients assumed that the new medium simply would be radio with pictures, commercials included. The agencies would develop the programs, the TV stations would air them, advertising dollars would pay the bills, and everyone would make money. What could be simpler?

Still, from a 1940s advertising viewpoint, television was a feeble medium. It had neither the scope nor the prestige of the big national magazines. It lacked the stars of radio—Jack Benny, Fibber McGee, Bob Hope. It was just radio's baby brother. In 1946 the four radio networks—"webs," they were called—reached more than 90 percent of the homes in the forty-eight states plus about half the cars. By contrast the only television network linked just three cities: Philadelphia, New York, and Schenectady. Period.

As Fred Allen, one of radio's most popular wits—and one of TV's bitterest critics—put it, "In television, coast-to-coast means from here to Passaic." He was in Manhattan at the time; Passaic is barely ten miles away on the opposite side of the Hudson River. All through the forties television continued to be a local medium. As with today's Internet and on-line services, nobody could be sure how fast it would grow, what it could offer, or how advertising agencies could make money from it. In fact, it would be 1948 before a million homes had TV sets and 1951 before coast-to-coast television networks existed. Except for a few major cities, most of the U.S. heartland would have no TV at all until the mid-fifties or later.

George Pryde, a Connecticut advertising man born in Wyoming, remembers his grandparents taking him to visit friends in the little town of Ranchester, a few miles from Sheridan, in 1949. He was ten years old. At one especially nice house, he recalls, "the people seemed pretty well-off. In their living room was a new wooden cabinet like a big radio, with an opaque glass window in the front of it. I asked what it was, because I had no idea. Our host said, 'That's a television set.' And he seemed really pleased with himself. It didn't impress me much because I'd never even heard of television, and the screen was blank." It would be at least five more years before television reached Ranchester, Wyoming.

In the middle of 1946 there were fewer than ten thousand sets in the entire country, half of them still in New York City. This was the age of vacuum tubes and hand-soldered wiring, not printed circuits and transistors, so the sets were not easy to mass-produce. Neither were they cheap. Prices ranged from $350 to $2,000, at a time when a typical family could live nicely on $10,000 a year.

Most major advertising agencies weren't eager to shift dollars out of high-profit, measurable network radio and mass magazines into this highly questionable and uncharted frontier. So the new medium grew slowly through the forties. Even during the early fifties you'd be more likely to find a TV set in a neighborhood bar than in a living room.

Saloonkeepers loved the tube. A televised baseball game or boxing match would pack in the customers and hold them spellbound for hours. In fact, until the sixties, most men probably saw their first TV program in a bar. For advertisers of cigarettes, beer, cars, and the Gillette Safety Razor Company, this was the medium of their dreams. Their best customers were males over eighteen, and saloons and sports were more purely male territory in the fifties than today.

In June 1946 Gillette and NBC staged the first televised sports spectacular: the Joe Louis-Billy Conn heavyweight championship bout at Yankee Stadium in New York. Louis won. So did Gillette. For the first time the blade maker was able to demonstrate its products to a TV audience estimated at 150,000 fans in New York City, plus bonus viewers in Schenectady and Philadelphia. The next year Gillette joined with Ford to televise the first game of the 1947 World Series. Over the following decades, Gillette's "Look Sharp, Be Sharp" march music, its jingle, "How're you fixed for blades? (Do you have plenty?)," and "Sharpie," its animated parrot, became three of television's best-known and longest-lived commercial properties.

By the late forties television sets were beginning to appear in more and more American living rooms. And during commercial television's first postwar decade, no matter what was televised, people watched. Roller derbies. Wrestling. Harness racing. Vaudeville. Amateur shows. The very worst B movies. Like it or not, the new medium seemed to mesmerize people—both sexes and all ages, urban, suburban, and eventually rural. Indeed, viewers couldn't tear themselves away even to eat. Housewives were torn between watching television and cooking dinner. Then along came frozen TV dinners. In many households dinnertime—the nightly ritual with everyone gathered at the table—simply faded away. America preferred to watch TV.

Some advertisers and their agencies dismissed our compulsive viewing habit as little more than a fad. TV equaled free movies. Once the novelty wore off, the whole medium might just dry up and blow away. But more thoughtful and prescient advertising people recognized television as the natural successor to radio. Far more attention-getting and involving and harder-selling, it was radio with teeth.

Radio didn't demand the listener's undivided attention; kids did homework, moms sewed, and dads painted the kitchen to its background babble and steady throb of commercials. Television, by contrast, caught the eye as well as the ear. It seemed to insist, "Look here! Pay attention! Watch this!" Advertisers and their agencies soon realized that TV audiences did pay attention. Products hawked on the tube seemed to sell faster than non-TV brands.

Some of these sales reflected the makeup of the audience. Viewers tended to be more sophisticated and prosperous than average. They all lived in major cities. They were more likely to experiment with new, untried products. What's more—and this is still true—retailers were favorably impressed by the brands advertised on television. With buyers and sellers alike so willing to be wooed, television advertising began flexing its muscles.

Live television today usually means news, sports, and special events. But from 1945 to 1950 *all* television was "live," including most commercials. There were no other options, except for showing motion pictures or kinescopes—poor-quality films made by shooting specially synchronized movies of television images.

Local sponsors and stations usually couldn't afford film, and videotape wasn't available until 1956. So for a few years every night was amateur night. (Daytime TV was almost nonexistent until the 1950s.) Live television was a grab bag of minor-league talent mingled with promising unknowns and recycled radio announcers. The latter were there to open and close the programs and deliver commercials in a suitably dignified manner.

Each performance was, for better or worse, unique and then gone. This ephemeral, spontaneous quality made live television both challenging to produce and fun to watch. For viewers it seemed personal, almost participatory. Audience and performers, together, were partners in an intriguing experiment. And neither was sure what would happen next. For those of us who wrote, directed, and produced live television, it's fair to say we made it up as we went along. We really did. Without quite realizing it, we virtually invented an advertising, news, entertainment, and information medium.

One of the earliest of television's trailblazers was Sy Frolick. Discharged from the U.S. Coast Guard in 1946 and just married, Frolick set out to become an advertising copywriter. In March 1946 he took a job on trial for thirty days writing radio commercials at the Campbell-Ewald Company, in New York. This later became the Fletcher D. Richards agency, then Richards, Calkins & Holden. Frolick's thirty-day trial lasted nearly twenty years, during which he rose to the head of television production and earned awards for his commercials almost every year. In the sixties he joined the William Esty advertising agency. He retired almost twenty years later.

"Every Tuesday night," Sy remembers, "my boss, a senior copywriter named Scotty Kosting, would go down to the old John Wanamaker department store on lower Broadway to produce a TV show with live commercials for our client, the U.S. Rubber Company. We got a free half-hour every week from WABD, Channel 13, New York [then, as no longer, a commercial channel], just to help fill empty airtime. That would be prime time today. In '46 they were giving it away."

The agency had created a science program using Encyclopaedia Britannica films, called "Serving Through Science," which was U.S. Rubber's corporate slogan. The company's U.S. Royal tires and Keds sneakers were promoted on the show. Sy's boss, Scotty, hated this weekly TV assignment. It wiped out every Tuesday night for him. Like most senior copywriters in 1946, Scotty yearned to write big full-color spreads for Life, Look, and The Saturday Evening Post. That was where the money was.

Frolick was younger and frankly curious about television. So one Tuesday night he asked Scotty if he could tag along to Wanamaker's to see TV in the making. As he recalls it, "The studio was behind Wanamaker's music department, in a tiny area rented by WABD, Alan B. DuMont's flag-ship station in New York City. When it came time for the commercials, an announcer stepped up to the camera and read a typewritten script."

Frolick was stunned. "Here we were on television, with moving pictures, and we were doing radio commercials!" The copy chief at the agency sensed Sy's interest in TV and assigned him to relieve Scotty of the Tuesday-night follies at Wanamaker's. Three weeks later Scotty quit his job and moved to another agency to work exclusively on print ads. That left Sy Frolick as Mr. Television at the Richards agency: writer, producer, casting, wardrobe, everything. Mr. Television proceeded to teach himself the business.

One day the U.S. Rubber people said, "Be sure to mention that Keds are washable." Immediately Sy thought, "We should *demonstrate* that." So he asked the WABD production crew, "Why don't we get a washing machine in here and show how clean the Keds come out?"

"Aw, come on, Sy," they all moaned. "We don't have any running water."

"Well," said Sy, "there's a men's room down the hall. We can hook up a hose in there and wash the sneakers while the show's going on. Then at the end we'll show them nice and clean." That's what they did. And it worked.

Soon Keds had a Friday-night show for teenagers broadcast live on WNBT, NBC's New York station. The set design was a simple forties soda shop. Frolick named the show "Campus Hoopla," and the following year it was broadcast on the "network" that now linked Schenectady, New York City, Philadelphia, and Washington.

To give the commercials more pizzazz, Frolick created the Keds Cheerleaders and wrote them a cheer—possibly the only commercial cheer ever written:

Keds are keen. Keds are neat.
Keds are best for your family's feet.
Wear 'em! Keds! Keds! Keds!

Then Frolick canvassed model agencies for teens who looked like cheerleader material. He met one pretty blonde girl who had just come to New York to become an actress. He had her in for an audition and instantly hired the young Eva Marie Saint.

Thirty years later Frolick happened to see Eva Marie Saint appearing on the Johnny Carson show. Carson asked her how she got her start in show business. "I was a Keds Cheerleader," she told him.

"Do you remember the cheers?" Johnny asked. According to Frolick, "She not only remembered the Keds cheer, she remembered every move that went with it. She popped up and did her Keds routine for thirty million Johnny Carson fans and got a huge round of applause."

Television commercials became an important first step for more than one aspiring talent. They paid better than off-Broadway or summer stock, as much as ten dollars a day in pre-union days. They combined the close-up intimacy of the movies with the real-time, real-life spontaneity of the stage. In some ways they were more demanding than either medium.

As always actors had to learn their lines and hit their marks. But they also had to keep one eye peeled for the red light on the cameras—there might be three on the set—that told them which one was live, while staying aware of the countless wires and cables that littered the studio floor, waiting to trip the unwary.

Most important, they had to deliver all their lines "to time." The commercials were almost all exactly sixty seconds long. Not fifty-two. Not sixty-seven. Noncommercial segments were just as rigidly timed. So performers learned to speed up or slow down their speeches. This implacable time discipline was unknown in films and theater. Only radio actors learned to pace themselves so precisely.

A live TV show usually shared its studio with the sets and cast of the sponsor's commercials. During commercial breaks the noncommercial performers were expected to freeze in place and remain absolutely silent for the minute when the commercial players did their turn. This usually took place in a quiet corner of the studio, away from the main action, but even so, an audible background sneeze, squeaky shoes, or a fit of giggles could throw the client into a tantrum. Commercials, lest anyone forget, paid the wages of everyone in the studio.

Julia Meade, a young actress fresh from the Yale University Drama School, remembers working in the tiny, cramped Wanamaker's studio that Sy Frolick used, though the two never met. She would later become the spokesperson for Lincoln and Mercury cars on "The Ed Sullivan Show," as well as for the American Gas Association on "Playhouse 90" and for other sponsors on other shows. She began her television career, which spanned more than thirty years, as a model on a local New York show called "Fashion Parade." Recently she recalled, "The lights in that studio were so hot I was always wringing wet within minutes. My makeup was always running off my face. On one occasion I had my hair pinned up with plastic combs. When I came out of the studio, the lights had melted the combs into my hair. When I finally disentangled them, they'd shriveled into hairy, weird-looking plastic claws. I guess I was lucky I wasn't bald."

TV cameras in the 1940s needed a great deal of light, but TV lighting didn't yet include cool-burning fluorescent tubes, so studio heat was a constant problem. It not only baked the actors but exploded beer bottles, liquefied candles, blistered paint, and made some props too hot to touch, as scorched actors learned firsthand. One producer remembers that his lights once melted the glue bonding the wood veneer to a grand piano. The veneer buckled and peeled off in huge, sticky sheets. The owners of the piano were not amused.

Of course, faster, more sensitive cameras and cooler, brighter lights were on the way, along with more efficient air conditioning. And in 1947 Dr. Frank G. Back invented the revolutionary Zoomar lens. This was the first lens that allowed zooming in for a close-up and zooming out for a long shot without moving the camera or losing the focus. Cameramen and directors wondered how they had ever lived without it. A frenzy of in-and-out zoom shots followed until Dr. Back's Zoomar became just another lens in the cameraman's bag.

During the fall of 1948 Milton Berle burst into television with the "Texaco Star Theater." By November he had achieved a record rating, reaching nearly 90 percent of all the TV homes in the country. That same autumn "The Ed Sullivan Show" made its debut, sponsored by Ford's Lincoln-Mercury Division.

George Burns and Gracie Allen, sponsored by B. F. Goodrich, abandoned radio in 1948 to be among these first stars of the new medium. By this time, Advertising Age reported, more than a hundred new TV licenses had been issued by the FCC, and at least as many more were being processed. Nearly a thousand advertisers bought television time in 1948, five times as many as the year before. For the men who ran the major advertising agencies—there were no women—it was time to take television seriously.

In 1950, coming through the back door as a messenger, I joined the biggest, most buttoned-up agency of all, the J. Walter Thompson Company. WASP-ish, decorous, Ivy League (Yale)-oriented, Thompson had been founded in 1864. At J. Walter Thompson a key to the executive washroom carried almost as much cachet then as a personal limousine would today.

Between 1946 and 1956, according to Advertising Age's estimates, Thompson's billings grew from $78 million to $220 million, and they topped $300 million before 1960. Most of this growth was based on the television boom. With few exceptions Thompson's major competitors grew as fast or faster.

JWT, as it was called, was the very model of a modern advertising firm. At its New York headquarters in the Graybar Building, an appendage of Grand Central Terminal, waves of secretaries arrived each morning in their ladylike hats, fresh white gloves, and stockings in both winter and unair-conditioned summer. JWT men were uniformly tailored by Brooks Brothers, J. Press, Chipp, or at the very least Rogers Peet.

Thompson's tall, patrician president, Stanley Resor, set the tone at the agency from 1917, when he bought it, well into the fifties. With his striking, icy-eyed wife, Helen—a gifted copywriter—Resor devoted his life to making the business responsible, professional, and dignified. In the early 1940s, the legend goes, one of Resor's vice presidents set out to win the Camel cigarette account for JWT. It looked like a sure thing. All the agency had to do to close the deal was submit some speculative advertising. Camel was the biggest cigarette in the business—the best seller and biggest spender. Most agencies would have killed for the account. Stanley Resor felt otherwise.

JWT policy forbade doing speculative work for any prospect. The vice president, Bill Esty, urged Resor to make an exception for Camel. Resor haughtily refused, and Esty departed JWT in what Fortune magazine later described as a "shower of sparks." He opened the William Esty Company a block away. Overnight the William Esty Company was a major agency. Esty launched R. J. Reynolds's Winston and Salem brands in the mid-fifties, and both became gold mines for his agency.

Resor pioneered consumer research with the JWT Consumer Panel, a national list of householders recruited to keep diaries of their everyday purchases. They regularly mailed the diaries to JWT, New York, in exchange for modest rewards, such as coupons for products the agency handled. If a new soap, toothpaste, or food product ignited the sales charts, the JWT Consumer Panel would sound the alarm, so when television arrived, Thompson was quick to sense its selling power. JWT urged its clients to take the lead in sponsoring quality TV programs the agency would create, just as it had for radio.

In 1947 Thompson launched "The Kraft Television Theater," bringing original live drama and star talent to television for the first time. Schlitz beer, Armstrong floors, Philco appliances, Goodyear, and others all launched television theaters of their own. But "Kraft Theater" was the opening curtain. It survived for more than twenty years.

Kraft Theater" also took Red Barber's naive demo commercials to new heights for Kraft foods. During intermissions Ed Herlihy, the voice of Kraft for the next forty years, described the action as viewers saw Miracle Whip, Velveeta, and Cheez Whiz transformed live into an endless menu of culinary delights.

What viewers did not see were the harried "home economists"—they're called "food stylists" today—who heated and stirred, sliced and poured, just out of camera range. Endless rehearsals, truckloads of food, and real human tears went into these live how-to commercials. If the cheese sauce spilled or the lady poked her finger through an egg, well, that was live television. No matter how many rehearsals, nobody's perfect. But JWT became masters of the demo for Kraft, Scott Paper, Lever Brothers, and a long list of others.

The most ingenious demos were usually those promoting consumer goods in highly competitive product categories. This was where a demonstrable difference—even a tiny one— could make a product soar off the sales graph. Only television could turn tiny differences into compelling theater, sixty seconds at a time.

Classic early demos included the egg test (1956), in which a Band-Aid plastic strip with "Super Stick" clung fast to an egg even in boiling water; the Remington shaver peach test of 1954 ("shaves close enough to shave a peach"); the Timex watch torture tests, with John Cameron Swayze ("Timex takes a licking and keeps on ticking"), from 1948 to 1968; RCA's "Impac Case," a plastic portable radio that survived a drop from a twelvefoot ladder (1954); and of course Betty Furness's Westinghouse appliance demos, each of which proved "You can be sure . . . if it's Westinghouse" (1949–1960).

Betty Furness was the undisputed queen of the live demo, first gaining national attention during the 1952 and 1956 Republican and Democratic conventions. Day and night, product after product, in the heat of high summer, Betty coolly sold appliances as nobody has before or since. But one of the most perversely memorable Westinghouse demos—for which Betty has been incorrectly credited—was handled by a bright, unflappable young actress named June Graham.

June was demonstrating an "easy open" Westinghouse "frost-free" refrigerator, the door of which stubbornly refused to yield. She pressed, tapped, and then thumped the "easy open" button. But no luck. So, barely missing a beat, she shifted emphasis to the "frost-free" feature as the camera moved in close on her face, squeezing the fridge out of the picture while someone in the studio crew overcame the traitorous easy-open mechanism. As the camera moved back out again, it revealed a smiling June Graham beside the now open door. Millions who saw the spot never forgot it, and it was reported in newspapers nationwide.

In 1959, in Dayton, Ohio, I nearly electrocuted a lady named Betty Rogge while she was doing a live demo with a Frigidaire electric range. Frigidaire was a client of Dancer-Fitzgerald-Sample, Inc., and I, in my mid-twenties, was the creative director of the DFS Dayton office. When Frigidaire asked me to produce four live commercials at WLW-D, Dayton, on election night, I was delighted. This would be my first solo production. I had written dozens of TV commercials, but in this case I was required to write, direct, and produce the commercials entirely on my own. I never imagined I might threaten somebody's life in the process.

Frigidaire had a new campaign created at DFS, New York: "You'll feel like a queen with Frigidaire." I was told to find a "queen" in Dayton and have her deliver the commercials while balancing a brass coronet on her head. No easy job for live television.

I booked Betty Rogge, a talented local spokesperson, as our queen and had her rehearse with the crown until she could do cartwheels while wearing it. On election night Betty donned her crown and clipped the microphone to her bra beneath her soft, high-necked dress. She was ready: regal, cool, and lovely. When I cued her, she stepped up to the range, draped her hand on it, and delivered her lines flawlessly. But as soon as she heard, "Cut," Betty screamed, "Help! I can't move!" The microphone had somehow short-circuited to her skin when she touched the range. She could not let go. Some quick-witted person disconnected the microphone wire and possibly saved Betty's life.

Until the networks, under agency pressure, began selling thirty-second commercials in 1971, advertisers had sixty seconds to make their demos work. To minimize risk, most demos were filmed or taped. Today's commercials are almost all thirty seconds long. Result: More commercials but fewer demos. Reason: Performing a credible demonstration in thirty seconds is not easy at all.

In 1949 the rules of tv began to change when Sylvester ("Pat") Weaver left the highly respected Young & Rubicam agency to join NBC-TV as its president. Weaver believed that the networks, not the advertisers, should decide what shows to air and at what times to air them. When he took the job with NBC, he made it clear that he would devote himself to programming, not just to selling minutes of commercial time. This was heresy.

Since the days of radio's "A&P Gypsies," "The Ford Sunday Evening Hour," and "The Voice of Firestone," advertisers had owned not only their shows but their time slots too. Pat Weaver rewrote the book. First he launched his "Magazine Concept": Advertisers could participate in shows that NBC would produce just as advertisers participated in magazines. But NBC would own and control the programs' content. A tectonic power shift was at hand.

If Weaver succeeded, NBC would earn a profit from producing shows as well as from the commercials that ran within them. Also, by selling one-minute participations, NBC could bring network TV within the reach of smaller advertisers, companies that couldn't afford to sponsor entire programs on their own.

CBS had taken this tack in radio in 1948 and succeeded, gambling on launching a number of untried shows on its own, unsponsored. Within a year advertisers were lining up to buy participations in them. Two of the shows—"Our Miss Brooks," with Eve Arden, and "My Favorite Husband," with Lucille Ball—became TV hits as well, the latter as "I Love Lucy," which is still running. In 1950 Weaver launched "Today," with Dave Garroway, and "The Home Show," with Arlene Francis. In 1954 he added "The Tonight Show," with Steve Allen. All three were hits with viewers and advertisers. Forty-three years later "Today" and "The Tonight Show" still run.

The shows ran in "fringe" time—early morning, midday, and late night—time that network advertisers normally shunned. But all three offered participations rather than full sponsorships, so an advertiser could buy commercials a minute at a time. NBC also offered "Today"/"Home"/"Tonight" combination buys, giving smaller advertisers a way to pitch their goods to three different audiences at a relatively low cost. Weaver's new concept turned a healthy profit. So he next planted his flag in prime time, 8:00 to 11:00 P.M. NBC launched "Your Show of Shows," starring Sid Caesar and Imogene Coca, on Saturday nights, again selling only participations. And again with success.

Across town at CBS, its president, Frank Stanton, was happy to align his network with Weaver's in the spot-not-sponsorship shift. Stanton had seen it work for CBS radio. So NBC and CBS, independently but in parallel, edged the agencies out of programming. In exchange the networks assumed the risk for buying and creating new shows and for paying for those that flopped.

The agencies resisted surrendering control over programming—and the profits that went with it—but they soon saw the benefits in picking and choosing their spot participations. This gave them new flexibility in how and where to spend their clients' money, and it excused them from facing irate clients when an expensive agency-created show turned out to be a turkey. A few advertisers continued to sponsor shows of their own, regardless of rising costs and network pressure. "Hallmark Hall of Fame" is still a valiant holdout after nearly fifty years, but as a special event, not a weekly regular.

What this change meant for the viewer was that original quality drama and experimental or exploratory television, such as "Omnibus" and "See It Now," disappeared to make room for mass entertainment—Westerns, cop shows, sitcoms, and games. These were hardly all bad, but excellence became rare, greatness even rarer.

Most major agencies and their clients had exited show business entirely by the sixties. Instead they focused their creative energies on building more distinctive commercials. By then the agencies were scattering one-minute spots here, there, and yonder, so it became more important than ever that these messages be noticed and remembered, no matter where viewers might find them. This dictated filmed, not live, commercials. Some advertisers, especially of autos and cigarettes, had been able to afford filmed commercials even during television's barroom epoch in the forties. And when color TV arrived in 1953, they were among the first to switch over to it, swallowing production costs that grew by a third or more.

Chevrolet and Ford filmed their gleaming new beauties swooping about the landscape from coast to coast. The Utah salt flats, surf-washed beaches, and the Pacific Coast Highway came to symbolize emancipated driving, TV-style. Chrysler—pre-Iacocca—used much the same imagery but usually with lower budgets and less panache. And Volkswagen led the way for imports in the early sixties with its memorable commercials from the new agency on the block, Doyle Dane Bernbach.

Such early VW Beetle commercials as "How does the man who drives the snowplow get to the snowplow?" set a new standard for auto advertising. And Doyle Dane Bernbach—non-WASP, informal, and brilliantly creative—began its meteoric ascent.

Cigarette makers—always lavish spenders until banned from the air in 1971—tended toward lighthearted image advertising, most of it on film when film cost too much for most advertisers. Among the first cigarette commercials were square-dancing cigarettes (Lucky Strike, 1948), dancing packs with women inside (Old Gold, 1950), and an animated penguin (Kool, 1954).

As the filter-versus-regular cigarette war sputtered through the fifties, Viceroy thundered about its "filter traps," Parliament introduced its recessed filter, Kent created the Micronite filter (made of asbestos), and Marlboro offered the slinky, seductive Julie London crooning, "You get a lot to like with a Marlboro—filter . . . flavor . . . flip-top box." The Marlboro cowboy and Marlboro Country, created by Chicago's Leo Burnett agency, came later, around 1959. Perhaps the most successful cigarette advertising campaign in history, it still runs worldwide.

Very late in the TV cigarette era, around 1968, when Salem advertising was my responsibility at the William Esty Company, we launched "You can take Salem out of the country but . . . you can't take the country out of Salem." It was a relatively expensive campaign to film, using city and country locations from coast to coast.

One of my commercials called for a white gazebo with a Dixieland band and singers set among flowering trees. A search for just the right location turned up a slightly run-down gazebo in a grove of apple trees at a convent in New York's Hudson River valley. The setting was ideal, and in exchange for a substantial contribution, the mother superior agreed to allow the use of the property for the filming. The gazebo was given a fresh coat of white paint with accents of gold and Salem green, and buses and vans were poised to whisk cast and crew there just as soon as the apple trees reached full flower. Then, the night before the big day, a lashing rainstorm moved in and stripped the apple trees of their blossoms. But the location still looked fresh and springlike, and that was Salem's trademark. As I drove to the convent, dawn broke sunny and warm.

At six that morning a van filled with thousands of plastic apple blossoms rolled up to the convent, and by eight-thirty the trees were beautifully abloom with polyethylene flowers. The mother superior—a tiny sixtyish lady with a saintly smile—watched as a swarm of workers redecorated her denuded apple trees. Then she turned to the film's director, the late Peter Miranda, and said, "Oh, my! I thought only God could make a tree." Miranda—one of the quickest wits in a witty business—clasped his hands, smiled, and replied, "Sister, this is what God would do—if he had our budget."

As the live television era wound down—as Pat Weaver launched his magazine concept and as coast-to-coast networks were born, thanks to the laying of coaxial cable in 1951— Rosser Reeves emerged as the creative maestro of the Ted Bates Agency. For the next twenty years Reeves was Madison Avenue's leading advocate of "hard sell" advertising.

In his 1961 book, *Reality in Advertising*, he claimed that his commercials for Anacin pain reliever had tripled annual sales in less than two years. Trumpeting "Fast . . . fast . . . fast relief" from "tension headache" and replete with lightning bolts and sledgehammers, Anacin's one-minute spots were generally despised by viewers and derided by competitors. But Reeves and Anacin seemed to prove that people needn't like a commercial to be influenced by it. They needed only to understand the message, find its promise appealing, and be willing to believe it. "Fast relief" is, after all, what a painkiller is supposed to deliver. Anacin made "tension headache" its own private ailment, and the spots ran everywhere, ad nauseam.

Rosser Reeves, Southern-born, was a shrewd thinker and marketer and an unabashed salesman. He was indifferent to style, taste, and artistry in advertising. He cared only about clarity, persuasion, and uniqueness. These he refined and distilled into his personal advertising formula—the "Unique Selling Proposition," or U.S.P.—which he considered a virtual reinvention of salesmanship.

The U.S.P. meant describing a product and its benefits so that consumers would feel they had never heard of such a thing before and had to have it, yet no competitor could duplicate it without appearing to be a craven imitator. Once this was accomplished, the advertiser had only to keep hammering away at the same message as often and loudly as possible. On television, of course.

By scattering his spots far and wide, with little regard for what programs they were in, Reeves spent his clients' money efficiently, and he never (well, almost never) changed the commercials, which also saved a few dollars. He insisted, correctly, that even a weak commercial, run again and again, will outperform individually stronger commercials that keep changing.

Under Reeves's guidance the Ted Bates Agency launched TV campaigns for Colgate toothpaste ("Cleans your breath while it cleans your teeth"), M&M's candy ("Melts in your mouth, not in your hand"), Wonder bread ("Builds strong bodies 12 ways"), and a flock of others. In 1952 Reeves wrote, produced, and directed the first TV spots ever used in a presidential election. They were titled "The Man From Abilene." He gave Dwight Eisenhower very few lines to speak on camera, relying on Ike's folksy image rather than his painfully self-conscious acting. By election day "The Man From Abilene" was almost as omnipresent on the tube as Ivory soap or Listerine. Some people were shocked to see Eisenhower peddled like toothpaste, but Adlai Stevenson became the last presidential candidate not to use television.

Rosser Reeves's polar opposite was probably Leo Burnett, of Chicago's Leo Burnett agency. Burnett made commercials that were distinctive and direct but also fun to watch. His agency probably created more animated commercial characters than anyone else in the business: the Jolly Green Giant, Tony the Tiger, the Keebler Elves, Charlie the Tuna, and dozens of others. Many are still performing.

Animated characters make superb salespeople. They never grow old. They never get in trouble with the law or spouses not their own. And they can do anything people can do and more—like baking cookies in hollow trees. Among television's very first animated characters were the pixies created in 1948 by the Sherman & Marquette agency for Colgate's Ajax cleanser. Its singing commercial made Ajax—the first scouring powder to contain detergent—the number one brand. Its ditty was unforgettable:

Try Ajax (Bum Bum),
the foaming cleanser,
(Ba, Ba, Ba, Ba, Ba, Bum, Bum),
Floats the dirt . . .
right down the drain!
(Ba, Ba, Ba, Ba, Ba, Ba, Bum!)

The pixies were too unforgettable, it turned out. When Procter & Gamble's Comet cleanser with chlorine bleach arrived some years later, nobody seemed able to write a television spot for Ajax that could effectively introduce new Ajax with bleach. According to Colgate's consumer-recall tests, housewives remembered nothing about Ajax except (Bum, Bum) pixies! It wasn't until around 1960s when I wrote a "slice of life" commercial using Bess Myerson—a former Miss America and a popular game-show panelist—that the pixies disappeared. But don't be shocked if they reappear one day. It wouldn't be the first time an old commercial idea was resurrected. Speedy Alka-Seltzer came back from the dead after twenty years to replace some very clever Alka-Seltzer advertising: the famous "Bellies" commercial and "Some spicy meatball," both award winners. Trade gossip says Speedy simply sold more Alka-Seltzer.

In 1954, television became the dominant medium for national advertising. At the same time, network radio imploded as the major stars and their audiences abandoned it in favor of TV. Even general magazines grew thinner and thinner as advertisers moved their dollars to television scatter plans, shotgunning one-minute spots throughout prime time.

By the early sixties the ad-lib, ad hoc quality of live television had almost totally disappeared. Fewer live shows and live commercials went on the air. Live hosts—Arthur Godfrey, Garry Moore, Dave Garroway, and Jack Paar—cut their involvement with advertising to live lead-ins to filmed spots: "Here's good news from the folks who make Glass Wax!" or "Don't go 'way, we'll be back in one minute . . . "

Television had matured, become formalized. Shows, time slots, commercials, and even personalities acquired ratings. Each measurement was crucial. The financial stakes had become so enormous that live television was nearly dead. It simply didn't fit the formula. To paraphrase Winston Churchill, this was not the end or even the beginning of the end. But it was certainly the end of the beginning.

THE WEEK THE WORLD WATCHED SELMA

Stephen B. Oates

In the 1950s the U.S. Supreme began through a series of decisions to strike fatal blows to the Southern world of Jim Crow. But despite the legal successes against segregation in the schools, transportation and public facilities, African Americans were still deprived of one of the basic rights of free citizens, the suffrage. In 1965 in Alabama, a struggle developed as civil rights leaders sought to gain this fundamental right in the heart of the Old South. In this article, Stephen Oates shows how the march from Selma to Montgomery, Alabama would capture the attention of a nation and lead to the passage of the Voting Rights Act. He also shows how this major event in the Civil Rights struggle would change the image of the Southern black as it laid to rest the idea of the docile, submissive African American of the deep South.

From the frozen steps of Brown Chapel they could see the car moving toward them down Sylvan Street, past the clapboard homes and bleak, red-brick apartments that dotted the black section of Selma, Alabama. In a moment it pulled up at the chapel, a brick building with twin steeples, and the people on the steps sent word inside, where a mass meeting of local blacks was under way. *He was here. It was Dr. King.* They had waited for him much of the afternoon, singing freedom songs and clapping and swaying to the music. Now they rose in a burst of excitement, and local leaders rushed to greet King and his staff at the doorway. Dressed in an immaculate black suit and tie, he was a short, stocky man with a thin mustache and sad, Oriental eyes. As he mounted the speaker's platform, the crowd broke into such a tumultuous ovation that the entire church seemed to tremble.

It was January 2, 1965, a decade since the Montgomery bus boycott had launched the black protest movement in the South. Martin Luther King, Jr., leader of the boycott and founder and president of the Southern Christian Leadership Conference (SCLC), was here this day to help mount a concerted voting rights drive for Alabama's disenfranchised blacks. And the cheering people in Brown Chapel were ready to follow him. Regardless of the danger, many of them believed, King would show them how to stand and walk with their backs straight, for he was the Moses of the movement and would lead them to the promised land. . . .

The movement had come to Selma two years before, when the Student Nonviolent Coordinating Committeem (SNCC)—which King had helped establish—sent in several young workers as part of a campaign to organize Alabama blacks at the grass roots. But this proved a formidable task in Selma, an old black-belt town on the banks of the murky Alabama River, fifty-odd miles west of Montgomery. The lives of Selma's twenty-nine thousand people, more than half of them black, were regulated by a Jim Crow system that forced blacks to live in an impoverished "colored" section and barred them from white schools, cafés, lunch counters, and theaters—and the polls.

White Selma recoiled from the boycotts and demonstrations and sit-ins and freedom rides that shook Dixie during the fifties and early sixties, recoiled from federal efforts to desegregate schools and public accommodations there. But worst of all was the arrival of the SNCC workers. A local judge, noting that they were racially mixed, wore blue overalls, and came mostly from outside Alabama, branded them "Communist agitators" in the employ of Moscow, Peking, and Havana. And agitate they did. They complained that of the fifteen thousand eligible black voters in Dallas County, just over three hundred were registered. Why? Because the county board of registrars met only two days a month and cheerfully rejected black applicants for reasons no more momentous than failing to cross a *t* on the registration form. The SNCC people also stirred up trouble by leading small, tentative protest marches to the courthouse in downtown Selma. At the same time, a dental hygienist named Marie Foster, a proud, forthright woman who served as secretary of a black organization called the Dallas County Voters League, conducted nighttime citizenship classes for her neighbors. These in turn led to weekly mass meetings at the black churches on Sylvan Street.

As the movement gained momentum in Selma, the white community sharply disagreed over what should be done. Wilson Baker, the hefty new director of the city police and a thoroughly professional lawman who had taught at the University of Alabama, was determined to avoid the kind of racial explosions that had rocked other Southern cities. With the support of Mayor Joe T. Smitherman and Selma's old and affluent families, Baker intended to meet nonviolent protest with nonviolent law enforcement, deal quietly with federal officials, and get around national civil rights laws with minimal compliance. But the die-hard segregationists—particularly the country people of Dallas County—vowed to protect the old ways, come what may.

Their spokesman was Sheriff Jim Clark, a burly fellow who hailed from rural Coffee County, where populism and Negrophobia both ran deep. Clark was out "to preserve our way of life," he told his wife, and "not let the niggers take over the whole state of Alabama." And nobody was going to get in his way.

In July, 1964, a segregationist state judge banned all marches and meetings in Selma, and Sheriff Clark enforced the injunction with a vengeance. By December the movement was paralyzed. In desperation local black leaders contacted SCLC headquarters in Atlanta and implored Dr. King to come and take charge.

So it was that King picked Selma as the next target for his civil rights crusade. Inspired by Gandhi, King had embraced nonviolent direct action as the most effective weapon to combat segregation in Dixie. While the Congress of Racial Equality had actually pioneered direct action in America, King and the SCLC had refined the technique in civil rights battlefields across the South, for the first time drawing the black masses there into the struggle for equality. King and his lieutenants would select some notoriously segregated city, mobilize the local blacks, and lead them on peaceful protest marches. They would escalate the marches, increase their demands, even fill up the jails, until they brought about a moment of "creative tension," when white authorities would either agree to negotiate or resort to violence, thereby laying bare the brutality inherent in segregation and appealing to the national conscience that would force the federal government to intervene. The technique failed in Albany, Georgia, where white authorities handled King's marchers with unruffled decorum ("We killed them with kindness," chuckled one city official). But it succeeded brilliantly in Birmingham, where

Police Commissioner Eugene "Bull" Connor turned police dogs and firehoses on the marchers in full view of reporters and television cameras. Revolted by such scenes, Congress had produced the 1964 Civil Rights Act, which desegregated all public facilities.

And now, hurrying down to Selma in early January, 1965, King would employ nonviolent direct action again, this time against discrimination at the polls. He and his staff would defy Clark, challenge the court injunction, and start a movement that they hoped would force Congress to guarantee Southern blacks the right to vote. And Selma's embattled blacks, thrilled that so celebrated a man would lead them personally, greeted King with the most incandescent mass meeting ever seen in Brown Chapel. They would start marching when the registrars next met, King promised them, and they would keep marching until victory was theirs. "Our cry to the state of Alabama is a simple one: *Give us the ballot!*" He had them shouting out. "We're not on our knees begging for the ballot. *We are demanding the ballot.*" They were on their feet cheering. Then they broke into the great hymn of the civil rights movement, "We Shall Overcome."

And so on January 18 the campaign began as King led four hundred people to the courthouse. Wilson Baker, however, broke them up into small groups. Otherwise, he said, he would have had to arrest them for parading without a permit, and Baker wanted no arrests.

At the courthouse, however, the marchers passed into Clark's jurisdiction. And the sheriff stood there now, in his uniform and braid-trimmed hat, gripping his billy club as King recited the grievances of local blacks and in his most dignified manner asked that they be registered to vote. Going along with Baker for now, Clark simply ushered the demonstrators into a back alley and left them there.

But the next day wave after wave of blacks besieged Clark's courthouse. With the campaign attracting blacks of all ages and occupations, civil rights workers told one another, "Brother, we got a *movement* goin' on in Selma."

On Monday, January 25, they were back at the courthouse again, demanding the right to vote and singing "Ain't Gonna Let Nobody Turn Me 'Round." Now they were protected by a federal court order, just handed down in Mobile over the weekend, that overruled Clark's injunction and barred city and county officials from impeding the "orderly process" of voter registration. Wearing a lapel button that read NEVER, Clark strode angrily down the line. When Mrs. Annie Lee Cooper, a huge woman, remarked that "there ain't nobody scared around here," Clark pushed her so hard that she lost her balance. She rose up, punched the sheriff to his knees, and then slugged him again. A deputy grabbed her from behind, but she stamped on his foot and elbowed him in the stomach and then knocked Clark down a second time. At last three deputies subdued Mrs. Cooper and held her fast as Clark beat her methodically with his billy club, ignoring the newsmen and their cameras.

Several black men started to interfere, but King stopped them. "Don't do it, men. I know how you feel 'cause I know how I feel. But hold your peace." He was determined to have his followers adhere to his philosophy of nonviolence, never hating or fighting their white oppressors but relying on the redemptive power of love and dignity. And it was the only way black men could protest in the South without getting killed. As the SCLC's James Bevel put it later, any man who had the urge to hit white officers was a fool. "That is just what they want you to do. Then they can call you a mob and beat you to death." In any case, a photograph of the beating of Mrs. Cooper was soon circulating across the country.

That Monday night, with passions running high, local blacks crowded into Brown Chapel to hear Ralph Abernathy. A stout, earthy Baptist preacher who had marched and gone to jail with King since the early days of the movement, Abernathy soothed his people with a mixture of droll humor and defiance. He pointed to a radio antenna attached to the pulpit and said the police had installed that "doohickey" and had warned him to watch what he said. "But they forgot something when they said that," Abernathy exclaimed with his jowly face set in a frown. "They forgot that Ralph Abernathy isn't afraid of any white man, or any white man's doohickey either. In fact, I'm not afraid to talk to it, *man to man.*" He held the antenna up and cried, "Doohickey, hear me well!" and shouts and waves of laughter rolled over the sanctuary. "We don't have to spread out when we go down to that courthouse, doohickey. And the next time we go we're going to walk *together*, we're not going to go two together, twenty feet apart. We're not going to have a parade, we're just going to walk down to the courthouse. When we want to have a parade, doohickey, we'll get the R. B. Hudson High School Band and take over the town!"

His speech scared Mayor Smitherman. Convinced that mass demonstrations were afoot, he called in the Alabama state troopers under Colonel Al Lingo, an ally of Governor George C. Wallace and a small-town businessman with firm views about what should be done with "outside agitators." Lingo's troopers rumbled into Selma in their two-tone Fords, with the stars and bars of the Confederacy emblazoned on the front bumpers. Sensing that the moment of "creative tension" was fast approaching, King and his staff called for mass marches and mass arrests and decided that it was time for King himself to go to jail. Accordingly, on February 1, King led 250 people en masse down Selma's streets, forcing a disheartened Wilson Baker to arrest them for parading without a permit. By week's end, more than three thousand demonstrators—King and Abernathy included—were locked up in Dallas County jails, subsisting on a cup of black-eyed peas and a square of cornbread twice a day. King's incarceration, of course, made national headlines and brought reporters and television newsmen swarming into Selma.

Now that he had a national audience, King posted bond and held a news conference about his next step; he would personally ask President Lyndon Johnson to sponsor a voting rights bill for blacks in Dixie. On February 9 King flew off to Washington for a round of talks with administration officials, including Johnson. Although the administration was actually planning some sort of voting legislation, Johnson and Vice President Hubert H. Humphrey doubted that Congress would pass an additional civil rights bill so soon after the 1964 measure. But Humphrey told King that Congress might do so "if the pressure were unrelenting."

In Selma, however, the number of marchers had begun to dwindle, and Baker's hopes were rising. If Clark could be restrained, maybe King's campaign could yet be derailed. But Clark could not be restrained. On February 10 he and his possemen attacked a column of young student marchers and drove them out of town at a run, hitting and shocking them with cattle prods. "You wanted to march, didn't you?" the possemen yelled. "*Now march!*" They chased the youngsters until they stumbled vomiting and crying into ditches.

Back from Washington, King led twenty-eight hundred furious blacks on the biggest protest march of the campaign. At the courthouse a deputy smashed one of King's aides in the mouth with his billy club. As *Time* reported, Clark was the movement's energizing force: every time it faltered, the sheriff and his deputies revived it with some new outrage. *The Nation* proclaimed King himself "the finest tactician the South has produced since Robert E. Lee." And like Lee, *The Nation* observed, King got a lot of help from his opponents.

By now movement leaders had expanded the voting rights drive to contiguous Perry and Wilcox counties. In backwater Wilcox County racial oppression was so grim that blacks on one plantation had never even seen United States currency: they used octagonal tin coins parceled out by the white owners and shopped at a plantation commissary. Conditions were almost as bad in rural Perry County, where, aroused by King, a group of luckless blacks attempted a night march in the county seat of Marion; Lingo's state troopers ambushed the blacks and clubbed them, sending them screaming through the streets. When Jimmie Lee Jackson, a young pulpwood cutter, tried to defend his mother and grandfather, a trooper shot him in the stomach with a revolver. An ambulance rushed him to the black hospital in Selma, and as he hovered near death, Colonel Lingo served Jackson for assault and battery with intent to kill a police officer. On February 26 Jackson died, and King and hundreds of blacks from the area buried him on a rainswept hillside.

After the funeral, King escalated the campaign once again. He announced a mass march to the Alabama capital in Montgomery, to begin in Selma on Sunday, March 7, and to proceed down Highway 80—popularly known as the Jefferson Davis Highway. SCLC's James Bevel, a brooding young minister who wore denim overalls and a skullcap, had conceived the idea for the march. "I can't promise you that it won't get you beaten," King told his followers. "But we must stand up for what is right."

The announcement appalled Alabama officials: the image of hundreds of flag-waving blacks descending on the state capitol was more than they could bear. Wallace banned the march and instructed Lingo to enforce his order "with whatever means are necessary." The governor's aides, though, assured Mayor Smitherman that there would be no violence, and Smitherman in turn promised the full cooperation of the city police. All of this infuriated Police Chief Baker. Smitherman and Wallace were both "crazy," he said, if they thought Lingo and Clark would not molest the marchers, and he threatened to resign before he would let his men participate in what was sure to become a blood bath. At last Smitherman relented and allowed the city police to stay out of the matter. Once the marchers crossed Edmund Pettus Bridge and left Selma, they would be in the hands of Lingo and Clark.

On Saturday, March 6, King was back in Atlanta, where he decided to postpone the march until the following Monday. On a conference phone call with his aides in Selma, he explained that for two straight Sabbaths he had neglected his congregation—he was co-pastor of Atlanta's Ebenezer Baptist Church—and that he really needed to preach there the next day. He would return to Selma on Monday to lead the march. All his staff agreed to the postponement except Hosea Williams, a rambunctious Army veteran with a flair for grass roots organizing. "Hosea," King warned, "you need to pray. You're not with me. You need to get with me."

On Sunday morning, though, King's aides reported that more than five hundred pilgrims were gathered at Brown Chapel and that Williams wanted permission to march that day. In his church office King thought it over and relayed word to Brown Chapel that his people could start without him. Since the march had been prohibited, he was certain that they would get arrested at the bridge. He would simply join them in jail. He expected no mayhem on Highway 80, since even the conservative Alabama press had excoriated Lingo's troopers for their savagery in Marion.

With King's blessings 525 people now left Brown Chapel in Selma and headed for Edmund Pettus Bridge toting bedrolls and blankets. Williams and John Lewis, a SNCC veteran who had been savagely beaten as a Freedom Rider several years earlier, were in the lead; an escort of borrowed ambulances took up the rear. It was gray and hazy, with a brisk March wind gusting up from the Alabama River as the column came over the crest of the bridge and saw a chilling sight. "Wallace's storm troopers," as civil rights workers called the state police, stood three deep across all four lanes of Highway 80, wearing gas masks beneath their sky-blue hard hats and armed with billy clubs. Williams turned to Lewis and asked, "John, can you swim?"

"No," Lewis replied.

"I can't either, and I'm sure we're gonna end up in that river."

As the blacks approached the wall of troopers, Major John Cloud raised a bullhorn and shouted, "You've got two minutes to disperse! Turn around and go back to your church! You will not be allowed to march any further!" Sixty seconds later Cloud ordered a charge, and the troopers waded in with clubs flailing. They shoved the front ranks back, fractured Lewis's skull, hammered women and men alike to the ground. Then they regrouped and attacked again, this time firing canisters. "Tear gas!" a marcher cried. Soon clouds of yellow and white smoke swirled across the highway, and the marchers fell back choking.

As white onlookers cheered, Clark's mounted posse now rode out from between two buildings, their leader bellowing, "Get those goddamn niggers!" With a Rebel yell, the posse-men charged into the blacks, lashing out at them with bullwhips and rubber tubing wrapped in barbed wire. "Please, no!" a marcher cried. "My God, we're being killed." In chaos the blacks retreated to Brown Chapel, the road behind them littered with bedrolls, shoes, and purses. At the chapel some blacks hurled bricks and bottles at the possemen, while Lewis—his head covered with blood—and Williams guided their stricken people inside. The air reeked of tear gas as they huddled in the sanctuary, some groaning and weeping, others in shock.

Outside, Wilson Baker tried to assume jurisdiction, but the sheriff pushed past him, shouting, "I've already waited a month too damned long about moving in!" At that, his posse-men stormed through the black section, beating people, and shoving their way into the First Baptist Church, where they seized a black youth and flung him through a stained-glass window depicting Christ as the Good Shepherd. At last Baker ordered Clark to "get your cowboys the hell out of here," whereupon the possemen raged through downtown Selma, pounding on the hoods of black-owned cars and yelling, "Get the hell out of town. We want all the niggers off the streets." By nightfall seventeen blacks had been hospitalized and seventy others treated for injuries.

That evening, ABC television interrupted its Sunday-night movie, *Judgment at Nuremberg*, to show a film clip of Selma's bloody Sunday. In Washington, President Johnson publicly deplored such brutality; thousands of people in cities all over the country marched in sympathy demonstrations over the next few days.

In Atlanta, Martin Luther King was horrified at the news and guilt-stricken that he had not been there with his people. But the events on Sunday also gave him an inspiration: he had long complained that clergymen "have too often been the taillight rather than the headlight" of the civil rights movement, and here was a tremendous opportunity to enlist them actively in the struggle. Accordingly he sent out a flurry of telegrams, summoning religious leaders across the nation to join him in Selma for "a ministers' march to Montgomery" on Tuesday, March 9.

The response was sensational. Overnight some four hundred ministers, rabbis, priests, nuns, students, and lay leaders—black and white alike—rushed to stand in Selma's streets with King. State authorities branded them all agitators. "Why not?" one retorted. "An agitator is the part of the washing machine that gets the dirt out."

On Monday morning King's attorneys filed into Judge Frank M. Johnson's U.S. District Court in Montgomery and asked that he enjoin Alabama officials from blocking Tuesday's march. King expected a favorable ruling since Johnson was thought to be the most sympathetic to civil rights of all the federal judges in the Deep South. But Judge Johnson refused to hand down an injunction that day. Instead he asked King to postpone the march until after a court hearing on Tuesday. At first King agreed. But when he reached Selma on Monday evening and found all those clergymen prepared to stand with him, he resolved to march as planned.

All that night civil rights leaders debated about what kind of march should be undertaken. Should they attempt to reach Montgomery or settle for a token demonstration here in Selma? Clearly the troopers and possemen would be massed out on Highway 80 tomorrow. Under considerable duress, King argued that it was not the nonviolent way to try to break through an armed wall, and he sold his colleagues on a compromise. They would march to the site of Sunday's beatings and confront the police line, making it clear to all the world that Alabama planned to stop them with violence. Then they would turn back.

Tuesday morning brought an unexpected blow: Judge Johnson officially banned the march that day. For the most part the federal judiciary had been a powerful ally of the movement; but now King would have to proceed in defiance of a federal court order, and some advisers pressed him to cancel the march lest he alienate the very Washington politicians on whom his hopes depended. But King would not cancel the march, he said; he could not cancel it. If he waited until after protracted court hearings, all the clergymen in Selma might leave, public interest evaporate, and a decisive moment in the struggle be irretrievably lost. And there was still another consideration: if he did nothing today, pent-up emotions might explode into "an uncontrollable situation." He had to march at least to the police barrier.

Attorney General Nicholas Katzenbach phoned and asked King not to march. "Mr. Attorney General," King said, "you have not been a black man in America for three hundred years."

At Brown Chapel that afternoon, some fifteen hundred marchers listened quietly as King spoke of his "painful and difficult decision" to defy the court injunction. "I do not know what lies ahead of us. There may be beatings, jailings, and tear gas. But I would rather die on the highways of Alabama than make a butchery of my conscience." He led them through town two abreast, stopping at the Pettus Bridge to hear a U.S. marshal read the court's restraining order. Then he walked them out to the Jefferson Davis Highway, where columns of state troopers, with billy clubs, again barred their way.

"You are ordered to stop and stand where you are," Major Cloud boomed through his bullhorn. "This march will not continue." King shot back, "We have a right to march. There is also a right to march on Montgomery."

When Cloud repeated his order, King asked him to let them pray. "You can have your prayer," Cloud replied, "and then you must return to your church." Behind him the troopers stood sullen and still. As hundreds of marchers knelt in the crisp sunlight, King motioned to Abernathy. "We come to present our bodies as a living sacrifice," Abernathy intoned. "We don't have much to offer, but we do have our bodies, and we lay them on the altar today." In another prayer, a Methodist bishop from Washington, D.C., compared this to the exodus out of Egypt and asked God to part the Red Sea and let them through. As he finished, Cloud turned to his men and shouted, "Clear the road completely—move out!" At that the troopers stood aside, leaving the way to Montgomery clear. The Methodist bishop was awe-struck, certain that God had answered his prayer.

King eyed the troopers suspiciously. He sensed a trap. "Let us return to the church," he said, "and complete our fight in the courts." And the marchers, some singing "Ain't Gonna Let Nobody Turn Me 'Round," headed unmolested back into town.

Back at Brown Chapel, King pronounced the march a victory and promised that he and his people would get to Montgomery one day. Most of his followers were content with the abbreviated march, but the Methodist bishop felt betrayed. And the SNCC people were furious. They wanted to storm on to Montgomery that day, even if it meant crashing through Lingo's line. Many of the students were already jealous of King, feeling that SNCC had begun the Selma movement but King and "slick" had received all the glory. Now they censured him bitterly for turning around at the police barrier, fumed about the white people he had brought into the movement, and denounced his admonitions to love those who oppressed them. "If we can't sit at the table of democracy," raged SNCC executive director James Forman, "we'll knock the - - - -ing legs off." Soon SNCC was in virtual rebellion against "de Lawd"—their name for King—and officially withdrew from his projected Montgomery trek, although members could still participate as individuals.

Harmony between King and SNCC was not the only casualty of Tuesday's demonstration. That night James Reeb, a Unitarian minister from Boston, and several other whites dined at a black café. Afterward, on their way to SCLC headquarters, four men emerged from the shadows and fell upon them with clubs, one smashing Reeb in the head. Reeb collapsed in a coma, and an ambulance sped him to a hospital.

In Selma, Reeb's beating touched off fresh waves of protest marches—one led by six smiling nuns from St. Louis. When Mayor Smitherman banned all demonstrations and Wilson Baker tied a rope across Sylvan Street, civil rights workers dubbed it the "Berlin wall" and started a round-the-clock, sit-down prayer vigil in front of Brown Chapel. Two days later, in a chill rain, an unshaven, red-eyed Baker brought them the news that Reverend Reeb had died.

Reeb's murder whipped up a storm of public indignation. Telephone calls and telegrams blazed into Washington with demands that federal troops be sent to Selma. President Johnson said that he was "concerned, perturbed, and frustrated," then came to a momentous decision: he announced that he intended to appear before Congress the following Monday night, March 15, and personally submit a strict new voting rights bill. The President even asked King to be his special guest in the Senate gallery.

But King was in Selma that Monday, conducting a memorial service for Reeb at the courthouse. That night he and his assistants settled down to watch Johnson's congressional appearance on television, the first time a President had personally given a special message on domestic legislation in nineteen years. "It is wrong—deadly wrong—to deny any of your fellow Americans the right to vote," Johnson said in his slow Texas drawl, and he reviewed all the obstacles to black voting in the South. His bill proposed to abolish these impediments through federal overseers who would supervise registration in segregated counties—exactly what King had been demanding. With Congress interrupting him repeatedly with applause, Johnson pointed out that "at times history and fate meet at a single time in a single place to shape a turning point in man's unending search for freedom. So it was at Lexington and Concord. So it was a century ago at Appomattox. So it was last week in Selma, Alabama." But "even if we pass this bill, the battle will not be over. What happened in Selma is part of a far larger movement . . . the effort of blacks to secure for themselves the full blessings of American life." In closing he spoke out of his south Texas past and his own brush with poverty and racism as a young schoolteacher. "Their cause must be our cause too. Because it's not just blacks, but really it's all of us who must overcome the crippling legacy of bigotry and injustice." He added slowly and deliberately, "And we *shall* overcome!"

Congress exploded in a standing ovation, the second of the night, indicating that the passage of Johnson's bill was certain. As television cameras swept the hall, King wept. "President Johnson," he said later, "made one of the most eloquent, unequivocal, and passionate pleas for human rights ever made by the President of the United States."

Nine days later, in Montgomery, Judge Frank Johnson handed the movement still another victory. After almost a week of hearings, during which contempt charges against King were dropped, Johnson ordered Alabama officials not to interfere with the Selma-to-Montgomery march. The plan Johnson endorsed, one worked out with military precision by civil rights leaders, called for the pilgrimage to commence on March 21 and culminate in Montgomery four days later. Only three hundred select people were to cover the entire distance, with a giant rally at the Alabama capitol to climax the journey. "The extent of the right to assemble, demonstrate, and march should be commensurate with the wrongs that are being protested and petitioned against," Judge Johnson ruled. "In this case, the wrongs are enormous."

King and his followers were ecstatic, but Wallace was furious. He telegraphed President Johnson that Alabama could not protect the marchers because it would cost too much. Scolding Wallace for refusing to maintain law and order in his state ("I thought you felt strongly about this"), the President federalized 1,863 Alabama National Guardsmen and dispatched a large contingent of military police, U.S. marshals, and other federal officials to Selma.

And so on Sunday, March 21, some thirty-two hundred marchers left the sunlit chinaberry trees around Brown Chapel and set off for Montgomery. In the lead were King and Abernathy, flanked by Ralph Bunche of the United Nations, also a Nobel Prize winner, and Rabbi Abraham Heschel of the Jewish Theological Seminary of America, with his flowing white beard and wind-tossed hair. Behind them came maids and movie stars, housewives and clergymen, nuns and barefoot college students, civil rights workers and couples pushing baby carriages. In downtown Selma, Clark's deputies directed traffic, and the sheriff himself, still wearing his NEVER button, stood scarcely noticed on a street corner. As two state trooper cars escorted the marchers across the bridge, a record-store loudspeaker blared "Bye Bye Blackbird."

The procession headed out Highway 80 now, helicopters clattering overhead and armed troops standing at intervals along the route. Several hundred whites lined the roadside, too, and a car with "Cheap ammo here" and "Open season on niggers" painted on the sides, cruised by in the opposite lane. Confederate flags bristled among the bystanders, some of whom gestured obscenely and held up signs that read, "Nigger lover," "Martin Luther Kink," and "Nigger King go home!" A woman in her early thirties screeched, "You all got your birth-control pills? You all got your birth-control pills?" On the whole, though, the spectators looked on in silence as King and his fellow blacks, United States flags floating overhead, trampled forever the old stereotype of the obsequious Southern black.

At the first encampment, some seven miles out, most people headed back to Selma by car and bus. King and the rest bedded down for the night in well-guarded hospital tents, the men in one and the women in another. "Most of us were too tired to talk," recalled Harris Wofford, a friend of King and a former adviser to John F. Kennedy. But a group of Dallas County students sang on: "Many good men have lived and died,/So we could be marching side by side."

The next morning, wrote a *New York Times* reporter, "the encampment resembled a cross between a *Grapes of Wrath* migrant labor camp and the Continental Army bivouac at Valley Forge," as the marchers, bundled in blankets, huddled around their fires downing coffee and oatmeal. At eight they stepped off under a cloudless sky.

As they tramped through the rolling countryside, carloads of federal lawmen guarded their flanks, and a convoy of army vehicles, utility trucks, and ambulances followed in their wake. Far ahead Army patrols checked out every bridge and searched the fields and forests along the highway. Presently, a sputtering little plane circled over the marchers and showered them with racist leaflets. They were signed by White Citizens Action, Inc., which claimed the leaflets had been dropped by the "Confederate Air Force."

At the Lowndes County line, where the highway narrowed to two lanes, the column trimmed down to the three hundred chosen to march the distance. They called themselves the Alabama Freedom Marchers, most of them local blacks who were veterans of the movement, the rest assorted clerics and civil rights people from across the land. There was Sister Mary Leoline of Kansas City, a gentle, bespectacled nun whom roadside whites taunted mercilessly, suggesting what she really wanted from the black man. There was one-legged James Letherer of Michigan, who hobbled along on crutches and complained that his real handicap was that

"I cannot do more to help these people vote." There was eighty-two-year-old Cager Lee, grandfather of Jimmie Lee Jackson, who could march only a few miles a day, but would always come back the next, saying, "Just got to tramp some more." There was seventeen-year-old Joe Boone, a black man who had been arrested seven times in the Selma demonstrations. "My mother and father never thought this day would come," he said. "But it's here and I want to do my part." There was loquacious Andrew Young, King's gifted young executive director, who acted as field general of the march, running up and down the line tending the sick and the sunburned. And above all there was King himself, clad in a green cap and a blue shirt, strolling with his wife, Coretta, at the front of his potluck army.

They were deep inside Lowndes County now, a remote region of dense forests and snake-filled swamps. Winding past trees festooned with Spanish moss, the column came to a dusty little black community called Trickem Crossroads. Walking next to King, Andrew Young pointed at an old church and called back to the others: "Look at that church with the shingles off the roof and the broken windows! Look at that! That's why we're marching!" Across from it was a dilapidated black school propped up on red bricks, a three-room shanty with asphalt shingles covering the holes in its sides. A group of old people and children were standing under the oak trees in front of the school, squinting at King in the sunlight. When he halted the procession, an old woman ran from under the trees, kissed him breathlessly, and ran back crying, "I done kissed him! I done kissed him!" "Who?" another asked. "The Martin Luther King!" she exclaimed. "I done kissed the Martin Luther King!"

On the third day out King left Alabama and flew off for an important speaking engagement in Cleveland; he would rejoin the marchers outside Montgomery. It rained most of the day, sometimes so hard that water spattered high off the pavement. The marchers tolled seventeen endless miles through desolate, rain-swept country, some dropping out in tears from exhaustion and blistered feet. When they staggered into a muddy campsite that evening, incredible news awaited them from Montgomery. The Alabama legislature had charged by a unanimous vote that the marchers were conducting wild interracial sex orgies at their camps. "All these segregationists can think of is fornication," said one black marcher, "and that's why there are so many shades of Negroes." Said another, "Those white folks must think we're supermen, to be able to march all day in that weather, eat a little pork and beans, make whoopee all night, and then get up the next morning and march all day again."

On Wednesday, as the weary marchers neared the outskirts of Montgomery, the Kings, Abernathys, and hundreds of others joined them for a triumphal entry into the Alabama capital. "We have a new song to sing tomorrow," King told them. "We *have* overcome." James Letherer hobbled in the lead now, his underarms rubbed raw by his crutches and his face etched with pain. Flanking him were two flag bearers—one black and one white—and a young black man from New York who played "Yankee Doodle" on a fife. As the marchers swept past a service station, a crew-cut white man leaped from his car, raised his fist, and started to shout something, only to stand speechless as the procession of clapping, singing people seemed to go on forever.

And so they were in Montgomery at last. On Thursday the largest civil rights demonstration in Southern history made a climactic march through the city, first capital and "cradle" of the old Confederacy. Protected by eight hundred federal troops, twenty-five thousand people passed the Jefferson Davis Hotel, with a huge Rebel flag draped across its front, and Confederate Square, where blacks had been auctioned in slavery days. There were the three hundred Freedom Marchers in front, now clad in orange vests to set them apart. There were hundreds of blacks from the Montgomery area, one crying as she walked beside Harris Wofford, "This is the day! This is the day!" There was a plump, bespectacled white woman who carried a basket in one arm and a sign in the other: "Here is one native Selman for freedom and justice." There were celebrities such as Joan Baez and Harry Belafonte, the eminent American historians John Hope Franklin and C. Vann Woodward. Like a conquering army, they surged up Dexter Avenue to the capitol building, with Confederate and Alabama flags snapping over its dome. It was up Dexter Avenue that Jefferson Davis's first inaugural parade had moved, and it was in the portico of the capitol that Davis had taken his oath of office as President of the slave-based Confederacy. Now, more than a century later, Alabama blacks—most of them descendants of slaves—stood massed at the same statehouse, singing "We Have Overcome" with state troopers and the statue of Davis himself looking on.

Wallace refused to come out of the capitol and receive their petition. He peered out the blinds of his office, chuckling when an aide cracked, "An inauguration crowd may look like that in a few years if the voting rights bill passes." But a moment later Wallace said to nobody in particular, "That's quite a crowd out there."

Outside King mounted the flatbed of a trailer, television cameras focusing in on his round, intense face. "They told us we wouldn't get here," he cried over the loudspeaker. "And there were those who said that we would get here only over their dead bodies, but all the world today knows that we are here and that we are standing before the forces of power in the state of Alabama saying, 'We ain't gonna let nobody turn us around.'" For ten years now, he said, those forces had tried to nurture and defend evil, "but evil is choking to death in the dusty roads and streets of this state. So I stand before you today with the conviction that segregation is on its deathbed, and the only thing uncertain about it is how costly the segregationists and Wallace will make the funeral."

Not since his "I Have a Dream" speech at the Lincoln Memorial had an audience been so transfixed by his words rolling out over the loudspeaker in rhythmic, hypnotic cadences. "Let us march on to the realization of the American dream," he cried. "Let us march on the ballot boxes, march on poverty, march on segregated schools and segregated housing, march on until racism is annihilated and America can live at peace with its conscience. That will be a day not of the white man, not of the black man. That will be the day of man as man. How long will it take? I come to say to you this afternoon, however difficult the moment, however frustrating the hour, it will not be long, because truth pressed to earth will rise again. How long? Not long, because no lie can live forever. How long? Not long, because you will reap what you sow. How long? Not long, because the arm of the moral universe is long but it bends toward justice." Then King launched into "The Battle Hymn of the Republic," crying out, "Our God is marching on! Glory, glory hallelujah! Glory, glory hallelujah! Glory, glory hallelujah!"

In August, Congress enacted the voting rights bill, and Johnson signed it into law in the same room in which Lincoln had endorsed the first confiscation act, which seized all slaves employed in the Confederate war effort. And for those who had participated, the movement of 1965 became the central event in their lives. They were surprised at themselves, proud of the strength they had displayed in confronting the state of Alabama, happy indeed, as one of the marchers put it, to be "a new Negro in a new South—a Negro who is no longer afraid."

During the summer of 1977 I visited Selma and interviewed some of the people who had been involved in the movement. Among them was Mrs. Richie Jean Jackson, an articulate, animated black teacher whose home had often served as King's Selma headquarters. On a brilliant June afternoon she took me to all the sites of the movement, to the marble courthouse, Sylvan Street, and Brown Chapel, wheeling her Gran Torino through Selma with uninhibited gusto. The city's police force and city council were both racially mixed now, she told me, the schools and public accommodations all integrated. She related how Wilson Baker had defeated

Clark in a bitter election for sheriff in 1966, how Baker was dead now and Clark was gone (nobody knew where), and how she and her white team teacher could tease and talk to each other without worrying about a color barrier. "I would rather live here now than anywhere else," she said. "Though we still need a few more funerals."

Later that same day I called on Marie Foster, Mrs. Jackson's sister-in-law. As we sipped coffee in her neat, well-furnished home, she recounted those days in vivid detail, squinting her eyes and wrinkling her nose when she stressed a point. On the third day of the great march to Montgomery, she recalled, she became so tired that she could hardly lift her feet. "Andy Young saw how tired I was and walked a ways with me. 'Come on, Mrs. Foster,' he said. 'I'm gonna put you in one of the escort cars.' But I shook my head and kept on somehow, and Andy Young just smiled and shook his head and went on down the line. In camp that night I rubbed alcohol on my feet—they were all swollen and sore—and I prayed. I asked God to please help me, please give me the strength to go on tomorrow." She paused. "Well, He must've been working on me, because the next morning I was refreshed and ready. It was a wonderful experience—the march into Montgomery. We all felt so close to each other. I'll never forget it." She brought out a box and showed me a pair of shoes. Across the top of the box she had written: "Shoes that carried me through 50 mile trek from Selma to Montgomery, Ala. 1965. We walked for freedom, that we might have the right to vote."

MY SEARCH FOR LYNDON JOHNSON

Robert Dallek

Thirty years after his presidency ended, Lyndon Johnson remains one of America's most controversial presidents. With the GOP-lead Congress of the 1990s determined to end all vestiges of Johnson's Great Society, renewed attention is being given to those programs and the president who drove their creation. Often vilified for his foreign policy, crude personal behavior and overpowering manner, LBJ is the subject of this article which shows this most American of presidents in a balanced light. Robert Dalleck, author of Lone Star Rising: Lyndon Johnson and His Times, 1908–1960, *presents Lyndon Johnson for what he was: a complex character. Maybe more than any other American leader, Johnson embodied all of the elements of a character in a Dostoyevsky novel or a subject worthy of a Shakespearean tragedy.*

Writing a biography is an act of self-discovery. As James Atlas, *New York Times Magazine* editor, said in a recent article, "Choosing a Life," "the biographer's subject enact[s] the main themes of the biographer's own life." Atlas quoted Leon Edel, who spent twenty years writing a five-volume life of Henry James: "Biographers are invariably drawn to the writing of a biography out of some deep personal motive."

What possible connections could my life have to Lyndon Johnson's? A Jew, a New Yorker, an academic, I am light-years removed from the Texas power broker whose sixteen-hour workdays were studies in political wheeling and dealing. Although Johnson believed that if he had not become a politician he would have been a teacher, his fascination with power and action, as opposed to the world of books and contemplation, belies his conviction. Lyndon Johnson would have been a very unhappy academic. And however much I enjoy people—one point of connection to LBJ—I would have been equally unhappy in the fierce give-and-take I associate with political life.

Yet a lifelong fascination with people, politics, and power drew me previously to write about Franklin Roosevelt and Ronald Reagan. And Johnson in some curious way was a combination of the two: the master politician and showman, the consummate actor playing a role, using his powers of persuasion to convince an audience—Congress, the press, the public—of the need for political programs he believed essential to the national well-being.

But there was more drawing me to this rough-and-tumble Texan. He reminded me of my father: overbearing, in need of constant attention, tyrannical, crude, abusive. I had seen it all before. And as a research associate at the Southern California Psychoanalytic Institute for four years, I had studied it.

But if Johnson was so familiar a figure, why spend years of my life writing about him? Because what ultimately made this man so interesting to me was my conviction that he had become a caricature of himself, that behind the surface qualities was someone more interesting and important—a complicated man who would tell us a great deal about twentieth-century America. The appearance of Robert Caro's first volume about LBJ, in 1982, with its acerbic tone and overdrawn conclusions, deepened my conviction that the picture of Johnson as a narcissistic ogre was too reductionist, too one-sided, too ahistorical to do justice to the man and his times. And subsequent evidence in the last nine years has added to my belief that we badly need something more than what we have on LBJ.

In the course of my research I heard, read, and saw numerous assertions of Johnson's crudeness, grandiosity, and unlikability. Consider, for example, Edward Sorel's drawing of LBJ in the December 1988 *Atlantic*. Dressed in a blue Napoleonic uniform with gold epaulets, a red sash, medals, and a saber at his side, Johnson sits at a dressing table, smiling at himself in a mirror that reflects not only his image but that of two black cherubs holding a halo above his head. Large ears, a jutting chin, and a long, pointed nose accent Johnson's prominent head. A photograph of an avuncular FDR and a gold pocket watch are on the dressing table. It is a portrait of a totally self-absorbed character intent on his Image in history.

"Why do the people like Bobby Kennedy more than they like me?" Johnson asked former Secretary of State Dean Acheson. "Because, Mr. President," Acheson replied, "you're not a very likable person." The hatred of Johnson, someone told the historian William E. Leuchtenburg, springs from the fact that "Johnson took something that was great and important . . . and . . . made it small. It's as though he defecated in the Oval Office." What people are angry about "is the *vulgarization of* the presidency." Johnson, Leuchtenburg concluded, "debased the office he had sworn to uphold."

Twenty years after he left the White House, the dislike of Johnson had not abated. A November 1988 Louis Harris poll on presidential performance from Franklin Roosevelt to Ronald Reagan consistently ranked Johnson near or at the bottom of eleven categories. Asked which of these Presidents made people feel proudest of being an American, most inspired confidence in the White House, and could be trusted most in a crisis, respondents consistently put LBJ last alongside Gerald Ford and behind Richard Nixon. Whom will history view as the best among these Presidents? Only 1 percent chose Johnson. The President best able to get things done? Just 3 percent said Johnson, 1 percent more than said Jimmy Carter and 2 percent more than said Ford. And the President setting the highest moral standards? JFK, Reagan, and Carter, in that order, led the list. Johnson stood alone in last place, chosen by only 1 percent of the sample. Even Richard Nixon fared better with 2 percent of the vote.

Johnson's unsavory reputation is well deserved. He was a master fixer who never met an election he couldn't manipulate. In 1937, when he made his first run for a congressional seat, he broke all the campaign finance laws, and his managers apparently gave Elliott Roosevelt, FDR's son, a five-thousand-dollar bribe for a telegram implying FDR's support of LBJ. Someone in the Agriculture Department allowed Johnson campaigners to distribute parity checks to farmers, further identifying LBJ with FDR and a popular New Deal program in Texas's Tenth Congressional District. In 1941 Secretary of the Interior Harold Ickes helped suppress an FBI investigation of LBJ's fund raising in the 1940 congressional campaigns. In 1944 FDR settled an Internal Revenue Service investigation of Brown & Root, a Texas construction firm that put hundreds of thousands of dollars into Johnson's 1941

Senate campaign. The uninhibited   pursuit of the inquiry could have sent Johnson's clos-est supporters to prison and ruined his career. In 1946 Tommy Corcoran, an FDR fixer and later a Washington attorney, helped Johnson secretly obtain the military records of his opponent in hopes of finding something they could use against him in the primary cam-paign. In 1948 Corcoran and Attorney General Tom Clark, whom Johnson had helped win his appointment by Truman, apparently lobbied Associate Justice Hugo Black to reject Coke Stevenson's plea that Johnson's tainted victory over him in the Democratic senatorial primary was grounds for keeping LBJ off the November ballot. In his 1954 primary cam-paign Johnson received help from the Federal Bureau of Investigation against a hopelessly outclassed opponent who commanded less than 30 percent of the vote. When John Kennedy won the nomination in 1960, Johnson aggressively sought the Vice Presidency, something he denied to his dying day but which now is confirmed by abundant evidence. John Connally says that LBJ asked him to arrange a draft at the 1968 Democratic conven-tion despite his March 31 announcement that he wouldn't run again.

The Federal Communications Commission offers yet another example of Johnson's be-hind-the-scenes manipulation. There is telling evidence in the recollections of Arthur Ste-hling, a Fredericksburg, Texas, attorney and a friend of Johnson, in FBI wiretaps of Tommy Corcoran, and in the pattern of FCC actions that despite his insistent denials, Johnson ef-fectively manipulated the FCC into favorable decisions affecting his considerable broadcasting properties.

Did Johnson commit all this skulduggery out of some flaw in his character? It's clear that his consuming ambition propelled him into unholy actions. But that's only part of the story. Johnson also took his cue from other successful politicians who broke the rules to get ahead. Indeed, in LBJ's view, almost all politicians he admired and loathed-FDR, Truman, Eisenhower, Nixon, Sam Rayburn, Richard Russell, Harold Ickes, Tommy Corcoran, Tom Clark, Hugo Black, Herbert Brownell, Maury Maverick, Alvin Wirtz, the Kennedys, Wil-bert Lee ("Pappy") O'Daniel, Coke Stevenson, and many others he served with in the House and Senate—had cut political corners—and worse—to win their ends. In Johnson's mind he was no more than a representative political figure who operated within the "real" rules of the game.

He saw the Kennedys as a particularly good case in point. Johnson was initially contemp-tuous of Jack Kennedy's ambition to be President. Behind his back Johnson called him "sonny boy," sneered at his meager accomplishments in the House and Senate, and puzzled over his rise to prominence as a candidate. "It was the goddamnedest thing," Johnson later told Doris Kearns; "here was a whippersnapper, malaria-ridden and yellah, sickly, sickly. He never said a word of importance in the Senate and he never did a thing. But somehow . . . he managed to create the image of himself as a shining intellectual, a youthful leader who would change the face of the country. Now, I will admit that he had a good sense of humor and that he looked awfully good on the goddamn television screen and through it all was a pretty decent fellow, but his growing hold on the American people was simply a mystery to me."

But Johnson admired the boldness, calculation, and even ruthlessness with which the Kennedys went after the nomination. In the fall of 1955 Joe Kennedy sent Tommy Corco-ran to ask Johnson to announce his candidacy for President. Corcoran was also to say that if LBJ would privately promise to take Jack as his running mate in 1956, Joe would arrange fi-nancing for the campaign. Johnson understood that the Kennedys wanted to use him as a stalking-horse for Jack's White House ambitions. Joe Kennedy made it clear to Corcoran that the ultimate aim was to make Jack Kennedy President. From the Kennedy perspective a losing Johnson campaign against Ike, with Jack as Lyndon's running mate, was a fine way to launch Kennedy's campaign for the presidential nomination in 1960. Joe believed that Lyndon would lose to Ike, but not by the landslide that seemed the likely outcome of another Adlai Stevenson campaign, and a lopsided Eisenhower victory over a Stevenson-Kennedy ticket could be blamed partly on Jack's Catholicism and might damage his political standing. Believing it premature to reveal his intentions, understanding that the Kennedys wanted to use him for their purposes, and seeing little need for their help in any event, Johnson turned them down.

When Charles de Gaulle came to the United States for Kennedy's funeral in 1963, he said, in effect: This man Kennedy was America's mask, but this man Johnson is the country's real face. De Gaulle's observation has much to recommend it; Johnson is an excellent vehicle for studying American politics since the 1930s.

He is also a wonderful starting point for understanding the transformation and integration of the South into the mainstream of American economic and political life. Johnson was more concerned about larger national issues than people have generally appreciated. It is accepted wisdom that Johnson deserves credit for advancing civil rights and the cause of economic and social justice during his Presidency. But few have understood that Johnson was a man of considerable vision who from his earliest days in government supported programs that could have a redefining influence on the country in general and the South in particular. The psychiatrist Robert Coles had it right when he wrote in 1976 that Johnson was "a restless, extravagantly self-centered, brutishly expansive, manipulative, teasing and sly man, but he was also genuinely passionately interested in making life easier and more honorable for millions of terribly hard-pressed working class men and women. His almost manic vitality was purposefully, intelligently, compassionately used. He could turn mean and sour, but . . . he had a lot more than himself and his place in history on his mind."

Desegregation is a fine example. Johnson was a Southerner who could talk comfortably to other Southerners in the vernacular. "Sam, why don't you-all let this nigger bill pass?" he asked Sam Rayburn during the congressional debate on the 1957 civil rights bill. Even as late as 1965, when, as President, he appointed the first black associate justice to the United States Supreme Court, he privately used the same pejorative term to describe his appointee. When a young Texas attorney joining his staff suggested a fine but obscure black federal judge for the position, Johnson said, "Son, when I appoint a nigger to the Court, I want everyone to know he's a nigger." The attorney never heard him speak about blacks that way again and believed that Johnson was playing a part and trying to create a kind of rapport between two "good old Southern boys" at their first meeting.

This posturing aside, Johnson, according to the White House aide Harry McPherson, was "your typical Southern liberal who would have done a lot more in the field of civil rights early in his career had it been possible; but the very naked reality was that if you did take a position . . . It was almost certain that you would be defeated . . . by a bigot. . . . But Johnson was one of those men early on who disbelieved in the Southern racial system and who thought that the salvation for the South lay through economic progress for everybody."

Johnson had given expression to this view in the 1930s, when he had served as the Texas director of the National Youth Administration. His efforts to help black youngsters—28 percent of the young people in the state—were similar to those he made for whites, though most of them were made behind the scenes. In fact, the impact of the NYA college-aid program Johnson put in place was proportionately much greater on blacks than on whites: Whereas 24.2 percent of all eligible black college students received help, only 12 to 14 percent of whites did. The plight of black youngsters moved LBJ to special efforts in their behalf. When white colleges got donations of equipment that freed some of their NYA funds,

Johnson would pass the savings along to blacks. In an era of strict segregation he would occasionally spend a night at a black college to see how the NYA programs were working. More than thirty years later "a venerable and distinguished Negro leader" told Doris Kearns how "we began to get word up here that there was one NYA director who wasn't like the others. He was looking after Negroes and poor folks and most NYA people weren't doing that."

After Johnson became a congressman in 1937, he kept on making special efforts to help blacks. When he learned that black farmers in his district were not getting the same small loans given to white farmers for seed and equipment, he raised "unshirted hell" with the Farm Security Administration, and applications from blacks began to be approved. Milo Perkins, a top official in the FSA, recalled that Johnson "was the first man in Congress from the South ever to go to bat for the Negro farmer." Johnson also worked quietly to ensure that blacks were included within the provisions of the Agricultural Adjustment Act of 1938 and to bar school lunch grants to any state with separate school systems for blacks that did not make an equitable distribution of school lunch funds. Likewise, in 1937 and 1938, after Roosevelt signed the Wagner-Steagall Act creating the United States Housing Authority and making available five hundred million dollars in loans for low-cost housing, Johnson arranged for Austin to be one of the first three cities in the country to receive a loan. Johnson persuaded city leaders "to stand up for the Negroes and the Mexicans" and designate 100 of the 186 housing units built under the program for them.

By the 1950s Johnson was more convinced than ever that, in McPherson's words, "the race question . . . obsessed the South and diverted it from attending to its economic and educational problems. . . ." Doris Kearns reached a similar conclusion about Johnson's view of how segregation hurt the South. He told her that by 1957 Congress had to act. Inaction would injure the Senate's prestige, erode black support for the Democratic party, and "brand him forever as sectional and therefore unpresidential." Moreover, he believed that Southern opposition to civil rights legislation made it impossible for the region "to act on its most fundamental problem—economic growth." Johnson was convinced that a major determinant of Southern prospects "would be the willingness of Southern leadership to accept the inevitability of some progress on civil rights and get on with the business of the future, or its continued insistence on conjuring the ghost of Thaddeus Stevens." And Johnson felt there was a compelling moral argument for racial equality. Clark Clifford, who got to know Johnson well in the 1950s, believes that his sincerity could be in doubt on many things but not on racial equality. LBJ looked at blacks and Hispanics, "looked at their lives, and saw they really did not have a chance. They did not have a decent chance for good health, for decent housing, for jobs; they were always skating right on the edge, struggling to keep body and soul together. I think he must have said to himself, 'Someday, I would love to help those people. My God, I would love to give them a chance!'"

Johnson, as this brief glimpse at him suggests, was, in the journalist Russell Baker's words, "a human puzzle so complicated nobody could ever understand it. . . . He was a character out of a Russian novel, one of those human complications that filled the imagination of Dostoyevsky, a storm of warring human instincts: sinner and saint, buffoon and statesman, cynic and sentimentalist, a man torn between hungers for immortality and self-destruction." Another journalist, Sidney Blumenthal, says Johnson was more complex than any Manichaean picture of him can convey. He was not a case of good and evil living side by side but of "an unlovable man desperate to be loved, whose cynicism and idealism were mysteriously inseparable, all of a piece." Blumenthal quotes Robert Penn Warren's observation in *All the*

King's Men: "A man's virtue may be the defect of his desire, as his crime may be a function of his virtue." Lyndon Johnson was a study in ambiguity.

Someone once told me that you write a book in order to forget a subject. But how do you forget someone as brilliant, foresightful, funny, devious, nasty, and unwise as LBJ? Not easily. Besides I'm writing a second volume on the most interesting part of his life—the Presidency. And in an era when leadership sometimes seems more a matter of risk-free public relations—putting the right spin on things—than a genuine commitment to ideas and programs openly aimed at transforming the national life, Johnson reminds us that large designs and a bold reach can make a difference. Dare I confess I hear him thundering from the heavens about curing world poverty and promoting a great universe? Get on with that second volume, he says. If I don't, he's got a fine ghost writer to suggest.

VIETNAM: THE WAR THAT WON'T GO AWAY

George Herring

For the generation known as the baby boomers there is no event more defining of their time and their generation than the war in Vietnam. It was a struggle that would divide the members of that generation at the time it occurred and would continue to follow some of them, even the first baby boomer president, for decades after. The Vietnam War, America's first television war, would impact society, culture, politics and diplomacy like few other events in the nation's history. In this interview, historian George Herring discusses the effects of this war on America's domestic as well as diplomatic policies and the lessons that can be learned from that war for the future.

Q. *Please explain how American involvement in Vietnam grew naturally out of the post World War II policy of containment of communism.*

A. The containment policy I think is the key to understanding when and how we got involved in Vietnam. Before 1941, our interest in that area of the world had been very slight, but once we were committed after 1947 to a policy of global containment [of communism], then Vietnam suddenly becomes very important to us because the insurgency against the French at that time is led by people who happened to be communist and this gives a revolution in a remote part of the world a connection with communism and is the explanation really why a whole series of commitments were made between 1950 and 1965 that eventually led to a full-scale war.

Q. *Did the Bay of Pigs fiasco and the failure to keep communism out of Cuba encourage President Kennedy to think he had to hang tough in Vietnam? What effects did the Cuban missile crisis have on refocusing the United States to engage in limited wars as opposed to superpower confrontation?*

A. There are a number of important linkages, I think, between Cuba and Vietnam in the Kennedy years in particular. Kennedy's embarrassment at the Bay of Pigs in the spring of 1961 along with other events—the agreement to neutralize Laos, the building of the Berlin wall, a rather devastating encounter with Khrushchev at Vienna in June—all of these things lead Kennedy to feel by the later part of 1961 that he is not being as firm with communism as he'd said during the election campaign that he would [be]. So when a crisis develops in

Vietnam in the fall of 1961, I think there's a feeling that we must take a strong stand. So there is a linkage with Cuba. The fact that the United States had stood down the Soviet Union rather skillfully during the Cuban missile crisis gave the policy makers of the Kennedy administration—people who were later advising Lyndon Johnson—a sense of confidence that if they'd face down the Soviet Union, surely they could manage a crisis with a country much smaller, that being Vietnam. And so, I think there's a certain element of confidence in their skills of crisis management that encouraged them to escalate the war in Vietnam with the hope that they can succeed there.

Q. *What were the other rationales beyond containment for pursuing the Vietnam war? Specifical-ly, why did we aid the French in Vietnam? We didn't support Ho Chi Minh. Was it our usu-al policy to support colonialism in the sense of aiding the French? Was that something out of the ordinary or in keeping with our tradition?*

A. Our support for France in the period immediately after World War II in Vietnam was a very complex problem for policymakers at the time. They did not feel good about sup-porting colonialism. We were the first anticolonial nation in a sense. We have a long tra-dition of anti-colonialism, and they were embarrassed by supporting French colonialism and felt awkward about it. On the other hand, because France was so important to the United States and Europe in the early days of the containment policy, policymakers felt that if they did not support France in Indo-China, France could not support the United States in Europe, and at least until 1950 Europe was considered a great deal more impor-tant than Indo-China. The other thing was that Ho Chi Minh, of course, was an avowed communist and this made support for France somewhat easier to justify and ra-tionalize. In other parts of the world, in Indonesia for example, where the nationalists were non-communists, [where] in fact, [they] even suppressed a communist rebellion, the United States leaned toward the nationalists rather than the Dutch. But in the case [of Vietnam], where the nationalist movement is communist and where we're commit-ted to containing communism, I think it's much easier to accept something that we don't like, that being supporting colonialism.

[The July 1954 Geneva Conference provided for elections two years later to unify all of Vietnam under one government.]

Q. *Why did the United States support South Vietnam's decision not to participate in the 1956 elections in Vietnam? Was this hypocritical not to support elections? Was it typical of the U.S. when potential communists were involved? And what were the consequences of that decision?*

A. The issue of elections in Vietnam in 1956 is another example, I think, where the United States found itself in a position of going against principles that it had stood for through-out much of its history. In this particular case, the feeling was that if elections were held at that point in time, then very likely Ho Chi Minh, who had been the leader of the na-tionalist movement in Vietnam, would have won. Eisenhower himself at one point said that Ho Chi Minh might get as much as 80% of the vote in a national election. The ra-tionalization that was given was that any election held in Vietnam could not be a genu-inely free election because the communists would have [manipulated] that election at least in the northern part of Vietnam. But quite clearly, the basic reason was a fear that Ho and the north would have won.

Q. *Do you see that as a key turning point in terms of consequences?*

A. I think that the failure to hold elections in 1956 is very definitely a turning point. This eliminated probably the last chance to resolve the Vietnam situation without military conflict. And of course, once the elections are not held, within a very short time the insurgency begins in the south, certainly it's begun by 1957, and within a short time after that, the north has committed itself squarely to supporting the insurgency in the south and you're on the verge [of] what becomes called the second Indo-China war.

Q. *Why did the U.S. involvement in Vietnam escalate with Kennedy first, and then especially after that between the years 1964–68? What factors shaped public perceptions of the war during those years?*

A. The war in Vietnam escalates of course dramatically between 1961 and 1965. I think the reason very simply is that the perception in Washington [is] that South Vietnam is crumbling [in the] face of the insurgency and later the outside pressure from North Vietnam, and that if something isn't done South Vietnam will be lost. It will fall to communism. This in the eyes of U.S. policymakers would have serious international consequences and it might have serious domestic political consequences in the United States. So as each step fails to bring results then the tendency is to go to the next step, until ultimately you have 500,000 U.S. troops in Vietnam by 1967–68.

Q. *Was the public perception during those years that we would win the war?*

A. I think the public perception when the major commitment is made in July 1965, is generally cautious optimism. I think we go into the war with the feeling that we are the United States, we're in a very small country in a remote part of the world, but surely we have the power and the capacity to succeed in what we are trying to do out there at a cost that will be acceptable. This confidence or optimism begins to weaken rather dramatically in the spring/summer of 1967 and then quite sharply after Tet in 1968. And I think it's the growing feeling in the United States that we can't achieve what we've set out to do at a cost that seems to us acceptable that's the basis eventually for the significant public opposition or disillusionment with the war.

Q. *How did the Tet offensive, although not a military disaster for the United States, begin to turn American public opinion against the war?*

A. The Tet offensive in early 1968 is generally recognized as one of the most significant turning points of the Vietnam war. I think it's particularly important in terms of American attitudes. In the latter part of 1967, to counter what it perceived as growing public skepticism, the Johnson administration had launched a systematic, far ranging campaign to try to convince the American people that the United States was in fact winning the war. This had worked and public support began to rise in December 1967, and then came Tet, literally like a bolt out of the blue in early 1968. And what it seemed to be saying was that no, we're not winning, if in the face of all we have done, the North Vietnamese and Vietcong can still mount an offensive of the scope where they hit literally every city and town in South Vietnam. Where they strike right into the very heart of American power in Saigon, even getting inside the U.S. embassy compound. I think this has a devastating effect. And it persuades Americans that, if in fact we are going to win this war, it's going to last a great deal longer and cost a great deal more than what we had anticipated. And I think people began to wonder whether it's worth what by this time it seems it will cost.

Q. *How and why did the war divide American families? What was the generational conflict spawned by the war?*

A. The war is of course one of the most divisive events in recent American history. I think many scholars feel that it is as divisive as anything going back to the American Civil War about a hundred years earlier. Probably the reason it is divisive is that the threat to American interests or to American security is not readily apparent. It's a war that's far from home, in a seemingly insignificant part of the world. There had been no Pearl Harbor, nothing to dramatize the threat to the United States. It's a war fought for an abstract principle, containment, and it isn't always easy to convince people that this is essential. It also takes place at a time when Americans are questioning everything—the civil rights revolution, the rebellion of American youth. Nothing is sacred anymore by this time and so Vietnam is just one issue in a whole range of issues that Americans are divided about at a time when nothing is sure anymore, when everything is up to be questioned.

Q. *How did the war affect the soldiers who served in Vietnam?*

A. Vietnam is a very difficult war for American G.I.s to fight for a lot of different reasons, and I would add that the longer the war goes on, the more difficult it becomes to fight. In the first years, 1965 and '66, certainly America sent fine troops there, they fought very well, [and] were generally successful in the engagements they were in. The problem was that this didn't seem to produce larger results. What are we fighting for? It was not a war where you advanced from one spot to the next and took territory, it was a peoples' war. Americans found it very difficult to understand the Vietnamese. They did not find the South Vietnamese terribly friendly. In many cases South Vietnamese seemed hostile to them. They had a difficult time telling friend from enemy. Who's on our side, who isn't on our side? Among the Vietnamese it was not always easy to tell. And of course the really devastating period in terms of the morale of the G.I.s is after Tet when it's very apparent that what we're doing there is conducting a holding operation. And then when President Nixon begins troop withdrawals, it's obvious that there's going to be no effort to win this war. Americans are still out there dying in significant numbers, just so that we can escape with some degree of face. And I think the period of '68 and '70 is the period when you really have the most severe drug problems, the most severe racial problems, the most severe morale problems, fragging, the actual killing of officers, all because there seems to be no purpose anymore.

Q. *How did the cost of the war affect domestic policy and programs?*

A. Vietnam has many costs and many consequences and clearly one is in terms of domestic programs. It was Johnson's hope when he committed the United States to war in July 1965, that he could have both guns and butter. That's to say he could fight a war successfully and maintain the domestic society programs, which were his true love, his real commitment. But the longer the war drags on the more money it absorbs, the more divisive it becomes at home, the more the Great Society programs are its victims, in a very real sense. And so ultimately, Johnson has to abandon programs, or funds for programs are reduced. The attention of the nation turns to the war, something very much he had hoped to avoid but something which clearly has happened by 1967.

Q. *Why did President Johnson pursue the war so long even after it appeared that a clear cut victory wasn't possible? Was Nixon's policy much different than Johnson's? What alternatives did Nixon have?*

A. One of the most difficult questions to answer in terms of the Johnson administration, is why Lyndon Johnson persisted in the war after it was becoming increasingly clear that the policies weren't working. Why didn't he change policies at least? It's not an easy question to answer. Johnson was a stubborn man. He was a man who I think was very much committed to success, who could not tolerate the thought of failure. For those reasons he was very reluctant to back off of something he was so deeply committed to. The other thing, and getting at a much simpler level, is that nobody could show him a way out. Nobody could chart a path for him that would get the United States out of Vietnam without costs that he thought were intolerable in terms of prestige. President Nixon's decisions are very intriguing in 1969. If ever there might have been a chance to liquidate a lost venture, Nixon had not been connected with this before. He could have come in and said that the Democrats really made a mess of things and I'm going to try to liquidate this, as in fact Eisenhower had done in Korea. I think the delusive thing with Nixon is that he somehow thought he could pull off what Johnson had not been able to pull off, because maybe he was cleverer than Johnson, or maybe he was prepared to use means that Johnson had not used, namely, trying to get out of Vietnam through opening up contacts with the Soviet Union that might lead to peace in Vietnam. Also, I think he thought he could get out of Vietnam successfully, that is to say, maintaining an independent noncommunist Vietnam and getting the United States out, too. Eisenhower had gotten out of Korea by threatening to use nuclear weapons, and thus intimidating the North [Koreans] into accepting the American position. It could not work of course [in Vietnam] and Nixon paid a huge price to get the United States out four years later.

Q. *What were the effects of the war protest movement on President Nixon and on the public support for the war? Also, could you comment on the impact of the media in shaping the public perception of the war?*

A. The issue of the role of the media in Vietnam is still I think one of the most controversial and hotly debated issues deriving from that war. There is a perception that the reporting of the war by the media, particularly by television, had a major impact in turning [the] American public against the war. I don't really buy that. Careful studies of media coverage suggest first that at least up until 1967 media coverage of the war was generally positive or at least neutral. More often than not it reflected the position of the government. Media coverage does not become critical until '67 and particularly after Tet in '68 by which time public opinion had already started to shift. So I would argue in terms of the media that the media reflects as much as influences public attitudes toward Vietnam. The anti-war movement, in terms of its impact on [the] public and leaders, there again, there's a lot of mythology that we are still living with. It is not at all clear to me as many argue that the anti-war movement turned the American public against the war. One could even argue the reverse, I think, up to 1968. Polls show very clearly that the solid majority of Americans are very much opposed to the anti-war movement, don't approve of what it stands for, don't approve of its methods and one could even argue in a perverse sort of way that the anti-war movement up to a point may increase support for the war. What the anti-war movement does is to continually raise questions. To question the authority of government, to raise questions about a war that by 1967 and '68 Americans for other reasons are raising questions about themselves. And so, this plus creating division in the country, both leaders and the public get very weary of the division. And so it's in this indirect way, I believe, that the anti-war movement had its greatest impact, not in the more direct way of changing the minds of leaders or turning the public against the war. There is [a] very clear linkage between Nixon's demise in Watergate and Vietnam. It is Nixon's efforts to contain domestic protest to the war that lead him eventually to take extreme measures, the plumbers group [the nickname for a secret group of White House operatives under Nixon whose mission was to plug embarrassing "leaks" about the Vietnam war], all those things that eventually get him in trouble and are exposed in the Watergate revelation.

Q. *How did the outcome of the Vietnam war affect American willingness to get involved in subsequent or future armed conflicts abroad? Did the relatively easy operations in Grenada, Panama, and the Persian gulf overcome the Vietnam syndrome, and would you explain that term.*

A. There is no doubt that Vietnam had a tremendous impact on American attitudes toward foreign policy and intervention in particular. The outcome of the war, the embarrassment of it, the frustration of it, the cost of it, with no apparent gains, all of these contribute to what is often called the Vietnam syndrome, which is a reluctance in the aftermath of Vietnam to take on commitments that resemble Vietnam, which is to say interventions and interactions in the third world. I think quite clearly, you see [this] in Central America in the 1980s, where without memories of Vietnam, the United States might possibly have intervened more directly than it did in El Salvador, or possibly in Nicaragua. In the aftermath of the Persian Gulf war of 1991, President Bush commented that we've kicked the Vietnam syndrome once and for all. I am not at all sure that this has been the case or that this will be the case. Certainly the Persian Gulf war restored a certain confidence in the American military and a confidence in America's ability to control events internationally. But this war did not last very long. I think that wars that last longer and have negative results may have a great deal more long-term impact than a shorter war that does not have much cost attached to it. So, I would say we'll have to really wait and see to determine whether the demise of the Vietnam syndrome has been exaggerated or not.

Q. *With the hindsight of some time now since the Vietnam war ended, what are the lessons of Vietnam for the American people? What are the domestic prerequisites for pursuing a successful war? What did the war teach us about the limits of American responsibilities and power in the world?*

A. I think we have to be very careful about drawing precise lessons from any historical event and applying them to another contemporary situation. The first thing we have to keep in mind is that each situation is unique. It has its unique circumstances, its unique historical context. And if you extract [rigid] specific lessons from one event and apply them to another, you are as likely to mislead yourself as you are to find guidance. So, I'm in general skeptical of those lessons. I do think Vietnam indicates if nothing else that there are certain events in this world which are beyond our control. It suggests also that any foreign policy or intervention in particular must be solidly grounded in domestic support, if it can be carried out over a long period of time. I think it suggests in a broad way that you had best know the situation you are intervening in well before you [do] intervene. You also need to know your enemy, I think that's very crucial. We underestimated the North Vietnamese and the National Liberation Front [South Vietnamese opposed to the American-backed government there] and I think we should know who we are getting involved with, and who we are fighting.

Q. *Would you elaborate on the financial effects of the war? Is there a direct link between some of the economic problems experienced in the 1970s, maybe even later, and the way Vietnam was financed or not financed?*

A. Vietnam is one of a whole series of things that happened in the '60s that helped to bring on the economic crises of the '70s that persist on into the '80s. Usually the key thing that is cited here is Johnson's refusal to raise taxes in 1965 to pay for the war. His effort to have both guns and butter is one of the factors that is very, very important in fueling the inflationary pressures that get very much out of control in the 1970s. So yes, there is no doubt that it has important economic consequences.

VI

I AM NOT A CROOK!
CORRUPTION IN PRESIDENTIAL POLITICS

Kenneth G. Alfers

Recent polls and studies indicate that many Americans have become deeply cynical about and disengaged from the political process. In presidential elections, it is cause for celebration if over fifty percent of the eligible voters show up at the polls. In local and state elections, the statistics are even worse. The prevailing sentiment is that "They are all crooks," or "It doesn't matter which party wins," or, only a bit more charitably, "If they go into office honest, they won't stay that way." The Watergate scandals, government deception during the Vietnam War, Reagan-era corruption, and recent questions about the Clinton White House have bred this climate of a distrustful citizenry.

While corruption has certainly been present in recent American history (and not just on the federal level, it is well to remember), a careful look at the historical record shows it to be a sporadic phenomenon. Moreover, our present age has no monopoly on public servants who betray the trust placed in them. As Kenneth G. Alfers shows in this revealing essay, the Grant administration immediately after the Civil War harbored some of the most alarming corruption. It wasn't until a half century later, in the wake of World War I, that massive malfeasance again "permeated" the Executive branch, in this case in the presidency of Warren G. Harding. Then, for another 50 years, the presidency remained relatively scandal-free until the widespread and pernicious affairs of the Nixon years known as Watergate. Unfortunately, the next major outbreak of "sleaze" came much sooner, in the Reagan era of the 1980s. Of the four Presidents noted here, Nixon was certainly the most guilty, for his deep personal involvement in the crimes and cover-ups of his administration. Grant, Harding and Reagan may have been less involved but guilty instead of naivete, misplaced trust, and looking the other way.

While the great majority of office-holders are honorable men and women struggling to do a difficult job, these periodic outcroppings of corruption should serve as a reminder to all Americans that effective democracy is not a machine that runs of itself, that citizen involvement and oversight are absolutely necessary, and that, in Alfers' words, "the price of liberty is still eternal vigilance."

One of the most severe tests the U.S. political system can experience is the removal of the President for reasons of corruption. What makes political corruption so abhorrent is the fact that politicians are supposed to be representative of a particular district, state, or the nation as a whole. Unfortunately, the crooked politician may be more representative than it is sometimes realized. In "non-political" affairs there is often pressure to get ahead by any means necessary. Therefore, it might follow naturally that some politicians, who on the whole are usually little better or little worse than the rest of society, engage in illegal conduct. Even though they may be given the authority to act in the public interest, some of them may not rise above the drive for selfish, personal gain.

When political corruption reaches all the way to the President of the United States, the whole country justifiably takes an interest. The President is the one politician on whom all the voters can decide, and, therefore, all citizens feel that they have a stake in how the President conducts himself. As Head of State, the President does represent the United States at national and international functions. Thus, if a President engages in, or allows his administration to engage in, corrupt activities, the nation feels a sense of betrayal.

Three times within the last century the American presidency and, therefore, the American people, have been shaken by the exposure of widespread political corruption in the executive branch. First during the era of Reconstruction after the Civil War, later in the aftermath of the first World War, and more recently as the country emerged from the Vietnam War, the American people have had their faith in their national leaders severely tested. The nation weathered each storm without collapsing, but the damage has been great nevertheless. As historian Jarol B. Manheim has said, the nation emerged

> with its confidence shaken, its trust disabused, and its cynicism predominant. Indeed, in each instance the greatest cost of scandal has been, not the dollars lost through corrupt practices or the disservice to the national interest resulting from improper policies, but rather the decline in political interest and . . . support among the American population. The greatest cost of political corruption, in other words, has been to the political system itself. (Jarol B. Manheim, *Deja Vu: American Political Problems in Historical Perspective*, p. 96. For an analysis of the three presidential scandals discussed in this essay, read Chapter 4 of Manheim's book.)

By taking a closer look at the scandals attached to Presidents Grant, Harding, and Nixon, we can more fully understand how corruption ruined each man's presidency. We can attempt to understand the forces which led to their betrayal of public trust. We can examine what forces, both inside and outside the political system, exposed scandals to public scrutiny and brought about rectification. Finally, perhaps a fuller understanding of past corruption can lessen the chance that it will be allowed to reach such proportions in the future.

The Grant Administration

Ulysses S. Grant is often considered one of America's worst presidents, primarily because of the widespread political corruption which existed during his presidency.

Ironically enough, the scandal most often associated with the Grant era was not of his making. However, the uncovering of the so-called Credit Mobilier Scandal took place during his tenure and, therefore, was associated in the public mind with all the other misdeeds.

The Credit Mobilier was a railroad construction company established by the directors of the Union Pacific Railroad. The Union Pacific was interested in building a transcontinental railroad, especially since 1864 when the government offered a grant of 20 million acres of land and a loan of $55 million to encourage railroad construction. In effect, when the directors of the Union Pacific created the Credit Mobilier, there existed two corporations, separate but with identical ownership. Once they had this dual mechanism in place, the fraud commenced.

The Union Pacific proceeded to award construction contracts at inflated rates to the Credit Mobilier, which, of course, was owned by the very people who were letting the contracts. For example, a man named Oakes Ames, a shovel manufacturer and holder of Credit Mobilier stock, received a contract to build 667 miles of railroad for $42,000 a mile. This included a stretch of 238 miles *that had already been built*—at a cost of $27,000 per mile! The two companies kept a fantastic system of duplicate books, and between December 1867 to December 1868 the Credit Mobilier netted an estimated $40 to $50 million and paid a dividend of 595 percent.

Since these financial shenanigans involved government funds, it behooved the swindlers to keep the government out of its affairs. They accomplished this in two ways. First, they simply bribed the government commissioners whose jobs it was to oversee the construction of the railroad. Second, they distributed Credit Mobilier stock to members of Congress. They were aided in the latter pursuit by the above-mentioned Oakes Ames, who doubled as a member of the House of Representatives and sat on the Pacific Railroad Committee in the House. Ames put the matter quite succinctly in a letter later made public. "We want more friends in this Congress. There is no difficulty in getting men to look after their own property."

The scandal finally broke in 1872 when a suit was filed against the Credit Mobilier for delivery of stock which the plaintiff claimed to have purchased. Documents in the suit were leaked to the press, and the resulting outcry led to a congressional investigation. The disclosures in the investigation tainted several members of Congress and the Vice President. Two congressmen, Oakes Ames and James Brooks, who sat on the U. P. Board of Directors, were censured. Vice President Schuyler Colfax was shown to have cashed-in twenty shares of Credit Mobilier stock, and he escaped impeachment proceedings by the fact that his term had almost expired anyway. But in the end the House white-washed the whole affair when the investigative report said that dishonest practices had been committed but that no one was guilty of them. A later governmental suit aimed at recovering some of the money was thrown out when the courts ruled that the government had no claim against the Credit Mobilier, since the Union Pacific, not the government, had let contracts to that company. Not surprisingly, the directors of the Union Pacific did not seek to recover funds from the directors of the Credit Mobilier!

President Grant was clearly not involved in the Credit Mobilier Scandal, but it became associated with him in two ways. First, Grant proclaimed total and badly misplaced confidence in Vice President Colfax's innocence. Second, the exposure of the Credit Mobilier Scandal coincided with disclosures of wrong-doing within the executive branch.

As Jarol Manheim has stated, "the President's own judgment was more clearly at issue in the second great scandal of the era, the Gold Conspiracy." Briefly stated, this scheme involved the attempt by two crafty businessmen of questionable ethics, Jay Gould and Jim Fisk, Jr., to corner the gold market by manipulating the government's policy regarding the price of gold. Gold was used as a medium of exchange for foreign and some domestic transactions, so there was a demand for the commodity which was in relatively short supply. The government attempted to regulate the price of gold and stabilize the economy by selling off some of its gold every month. Gould and Fisk sought to stop government sales after they had bought gold at a low figure. When scarcity drove the price up, they would sell!

To accomplish their objective, Gould and Fisk worked through an elderly real estate operator named Abel Corbin, who also happened to be President Grant's brother-in-law. Corbin introduced Gould and Fisk to the President, who was impressed by wealth and those who had it. Gould convinced the President that the economy would benefit from higher gold prices, which would result from reduced government sales. Grant went along with this reasoning and ordered the Secretary of Treasury to halt government sales. Grant then went on vacation, aboard a special train provided by Gould.

The conspirators now began to buy gold furiously, and soon they held contracts on roughly twice the available supply. The price of gold rose sharply. Grant, finally realizing what was happening, ordered the Treasury to sell $4 million in gold on September 24, 1869, a day that became known as "Black Friday." The price of gold fell drastically, leaving Fisk and a number of innocent businessmen facing bankruptcy. Gould had sold out before the crash when Corbin told him of Grant's decision to order the government sale. The public saw Grant as a slow-witted associate in an obvious scheme against the public interest. Their confidence in his judgment was considerably lessened.

Grant's naivete was further illustrated by the Whiskey Ring Scandal, which involved his personal secretary, Orville E. Babcock. The Whiskey Ring consisted of a sizable group of distillers, shippers, and government inspectors who conspired to deprive the government of tax revenues on whiskey produced in several large cities. When Babcock was implicated to the tune of $25,000 cash, plus diamonds, rare liquors, and other amenities, Grant went to extreme lengths to protect him. At Babcock's request, Grant tried to get him a trial before a friendly military tribunal. Failing at that, Grant issued an order that essentially denied the use of plea bargaining and trades of immunity for those aiding the government's case against Babcock. When the trial began, Grant filed a deposition assuring the jury of Babcock's integrity. The deposition, along with apparently perjured testimony of defense witnesses, led to Babcock's acquittal. Afterward, Grant dismissed from the government those who had played a leading role in prosecuting Babcock, including Treasury Secretary Benjamin H. Bristow.

As one historian phrased it, the Grant presidency was "The Era of Good Stealings." Further examples include the Treasury Scandal of 1873, in which James Sanborn made $213,500 by collecting delinquent taxes. Grant's Secretary of War, W. W. Belknap, augmented his $8,000 annual salary by selling appointments of War Department positions, most notably those as traders on Indian posts, for as much as $20,000 apiece. Belknap resigned but was impeached by the House of Representatives anyway. He escaped conviction in the Senate only because most of those voting "not guilty" thought it improper to impeach someone who had already resigned.

Still other examples of political corruption under Grant can be cited. One instance involved presidential appointees to direct the customhouses in New York and New Orleans— the latter position being filled by one of Grant's brothers-in-law—who used their positions for personal and political gain. Another scandal involved the wife of George Williams, Grant's third Attorney General, who, apparently with her husband's advice and consent, accepted a bribe of some $30,000 to halt a suit in which her husband was involved. Grant's Secretary of Interior, Columbus Delano, resigned after being implicated in a scheme involving fraudulent land warrants for veterans. Finally, George M. Robeson, Secretary of the Navy, used his influence to help a Philadelphia grain dealer, as well as his own income.

The list of misdeeds could go on, but the point has been amply illustrated. The Grant Era was one of the most corrupt in U.S. history, although Grant himself was not dishonest. Rather, his weaknesses were in his inability to judge character and in his blind loyalty to unworthy appointees. He made possible and naively defended the indiscretions of others. That, more than anything else, earned for Grant his lowly position in American political history. Unfortunately, he would be joined by others.

The Harding Administration

It was another fifty years before political corruption permeated the executive branch as it did under Grant. That does *not* mean that political corruption did not exist. In fact, in the late nineteenth and early twentieth centuries it became almost an accepted fact that big industrialists kept politicians on retainer. John D. Rockefeller was said to have had the best state legislators and U.S. Senators that money could buy. However, the Presidents from Hayes through Wilson, although many of them were hardly more than adequate in performing their jobs, were not remembered for political corruption. It was not until Warren Gamaliel Harding became President in 1921 that the Chief Executive was again surrounded by scandal.

It was once said that Harding's only qualification for President was that he looked like one. A kind and friendly man, Harding had risen to the position of U.S. Senator prior to his presidential nomination. He had played along with the Ohio political machine, also known as the Ohio Gang, and was the available man when the Republicans sought to capitalize on the post-World War I disillusionment with Democrats. Harding, like Grant, was to be "more guilty of poor judgment and misplaced loyalties than of any personal corruption. Still, in a president of the United States such characteristics can be fatal, and in Harding's case were quite literally so" (Manheim, p. 109).

Before considering the infamous Teapot Dome Scandal, let us take note of several other examples of political corruption during Harding's presidency. One scandal involved Charles R. Forbes, who headed the Veteran's Bureau. Forbes was an amiable fellow who could play poker, the type of man that Harding liked. He proceeded to use his position for personal gain and to help his friends and relatives. He made appointments—one of the appointees was his brother-in-law—to government jobs which hardly demanded any work. In fact, one employee picked up an annual salary of $4,800 for two hours of work each *year*. Forbes also connived with private business firms to swindle the government out of money appropriated for building veterans' hospitals. Furthermore, he conspired to dispose of "surplus" hospital goods at a considerable loss to the government and considerable gain to himself. When Forbes' misdeeds were exposed, Harding, like Grant in earlier times, stuck by his appointee. Finally, Forbes resigned, and after a Senate investigation and nine week trial, he was sentenced to two years in jail and a $10,000 fine.

Another Harding appointee, Thomas W. Miller, was caught with his hand in the till. Miller was the Alien Property Custodian, whose job it was to oversee the settlement of claims on alien property seized during World War I. In one celebrated case, Miller ended up splitting some $441,000 with another Harding crony, Jess Smith, after approving a fraudulent transfer of $7 million worth of alien property. When the case was exposed, Miller was sentenced to eighteen months in prison, Attorney General Harry Daugherty refused to testify on grounds he might incriminate himself, and Jess Smith committed suicide. Smith had apparently decided that his career of dispensing government positions, immunity from government prosecutions, and access to government files could last no longer. Daugherty's Justice Department, popularly known as the "Department of Easy Virtue," was under constant suspicion for illegal acts ranging from the illegal sale of pardons and liquor permits to the operation of an espionage network which shadowed Congressmen in search of blackmail material. Harding's successor, Calvin Coolidge, requested Daugherty's resignation, something the loyal Harding would not do. Daugherty later stood trial twice on corruption charges, but the juries failed to convict him both times.

Another cabinet member was not so fortunate. Albert Fall, Harding's Secretary of Interior, became the first cabinet member to be sentenced to jail for engaging in illegal activities while holding public office. Fall's conviction resulted from his involvement in the Teapot Dome Scandal. Teapot Dome referred to a rock formation which set atop Naval Oil Reserve Number Three in Wyoming. The Teapot Dome Reserve and two others in California had been established prior to World War I as a safeguard for the preservation of oil possibly needed for military operations. When Fall took over the Interior Department he persuaded Harding to order the transfer of the oil reserves from the Navy Department to the Interior. Harding later wrote a letter to the Senate declaring that he not only approved the transfer but also all "subsequent acts" in the matter. Had he not died, such an admission may have brought about impeachment proceedings against Harding, for the "subsequent acts" of Albert Fall led to his imprisonment.

What Fall did was to lease to private oilmen E. L. Doheny and Harry Sinclair the rights to develop the naval oil reserves, with the government to receive a portion of the oil. He also improved his own finances in the process, receiving a $100,000 "loan" from Doheny and a payment of $68,000 from Sinclair. (Testimony on the Sinclair money received a humorous twist when Sinclair's secretary testified that he had been talking about "six or eight cows" not "sixty-eight thous." It seems that secretaries have to contrive some fabulous stories to cover misdeeds, *a la* Rosemary Woods with the Nixon tapes). When suspicions arose about the oil transfer and about Fall's new-found wealth, a congressional investigation was launched by Montana Senator Thomas J. Walsh. Similar to the Watergate Hearings fifty years later, other congressional business ground to a halt while the scandal was exposed.

The congressional hearings led to the appointment by President Coolidge of two special prosecutors and a lengthy series of trials which began in late 1926. By March, 1930, the trials were over, but the results were less than clear. The leases on the Teapot Dome and the other naval reserves were invalidated because they resulted from fraud, corruption, collusion, and conspiracy. But Fall and Doheny were acquitted on charges of conspiracy as were Fall and Sinclair in a second trial. However, Sinclair did serve brief sentences for contempt of Congress and contempt of court, and Fall was convicted of receiving a bribe from Doheny and was sentenced to a year in jail and a $100,000 fine. On the other hand, Doheny was acquitted of bribing Fall! The verdicts caused Senator George W. Norris to remark that it is "very difficult, if not impossible, to convict one hundred million dollars." Similarly, a historian has remarked that the decisions undermined faith in the courts and gave currency to the saying that "in America everyone is assumed guilty until proven rich."

Harding, who had also been the object of whispers that he maintained a mistress at the White House, was spared the full revelations of the scandals. His suspicions had been aroused, however, and he was heard to have grumbled about the disloyalty of his "god-damned friends." While returning from a speaking tour on the West Coast, he died of pneumonia and thrombosis on August 2, 1923. At the time, he was mourned sorrowfully and emotionally by a country unaware of the corruption yet to be disclosed. His reputation was subsequently tarnished, although like Grant, his personal honesty was not the issue. Rather, like his predecessor of fifty years earlier, his weakness in judgment and guidance submitted the country to its worst display of political corruption since Grant had left office.

Fortunately for the Republicans, Calvin Coolidge was President when most of the revelations about the Harding scandals became public. Coolidge had the image of a Puritan ascetic, and no one questioned his integrity. Years later, FDR was accused of abusing his powers of patronage, Truman was criticized for tolerating influence peddling, Eisenhower was said to be too protective of aide Sherman Adams, and some referred to LBJ as "Landslide" Lyndon for his suspicious victory in a 1948 Senate race. "But fifty years passed before another major scandal . . . the most centralized and most pernicious of all, shook the nation to its very foundations and forced the de facto impeachment of a president of the United States. That scandal was Watergate, and the president was Richard Milhous Nixon" (Manheim, p. 119).

The Nixon Administration

The name Watergate originally referred to a posh apartment and office complex in Washington, D.C., which housed the headquarters of the Democratic National Committee. On June 17, 1972, five men were arrested for breaking into those headquarters, and from that day on Watergate became the name for the most scandalous of all presidential corruptions. The burglars had in their possession cameras, electronic bugging devices, several crisp new $100 bills in sequential order, and notebooks which included the names of E. Howard Hunt and G. Gordon Liddy, the latter a counsel to the Committee to Re-elect the President (CREEP). Questions were thus raised about the connection between the Nixon White House, whose press secretary, Ron Ziegler, termed the affair "a third-rate burglary," and the burglars. By the time those questions were answered several years later, some sixty-three people were charged with crimes associated with the Nixon presidency, fifty-four of them were convicted or pleaded guilty, and the President himself resigned in disgrace.

Obviously, the break-in itself did not seem to merit such an extensive list of guilty parties. Had matters been handled openly at the time the break-in occurred, the fallout would not have been so great. However, the White House decided to cover up any connection between the President and the burglary. Elements of the cover-up included payment of "hush-money," frequent lies by the President and his spokesmen (the White House referred to these as "misstatements" or as "inoperative" remarks), misuse of the Justice Department, and manipulation of the Central Intelligence Agency.

Very few of the details of the cover-up were revealed before Richard Nixon had defeated George McGovern in the 1972 presidential election. During the summer following that election a Senate committee, chaired by Senator Sam Ervin of North Carolina, began investigating campaign practices. Television viewers took more than a casual interest as John W. Dean, former counsel to President Nixon, traced an elaborate White House plot to cover up the Watergate Affair, a cover-up that was denied by two top White House aides, H. R. Haldeman and John Ehrlichman. With Dean standing virtually alone, the committee needed corroboration. It got that and more when a White House assistant, Alexander P. Butterfield, revealed that a taping system in the President's office had probably recorded Dean's conversations, and all others, held in that office. The Senate Committee and Special Prosecutor Archibald Cox, who had been named earlier by Nixon to handle Watergate-related prosecutions, went after a whole series of relevant tapes. Nixon refused to turn them over on the grounds of executive privilege. A lengthy political and legal battle was now joined, with the first turning point occurring on Saturday, October 20, 1973, when President Nixon fired Cox and accepted the resignations of Attorney General Elliot Richardson and Deputy Attorney General William Ruckelshaus, who had both refused Nixon's order to dismiss Cox. Known as the "Saturday Night Massacre," this event caused a massive public outcry of indignation aimed at the President. It was becoming more obvious to the public that Nixon, indeed, must have something to hide (See Manheim, pp. 121–122).

Numerous revelations throughout the Watergate investigation added to Nixon's problems. At the end of 1972 it was revealed that even though Nixon had become a millionaire while in office, he had paid less than $ 1,000 in income taxes in 1970 and 1971. Meanwhile, when the White House agreed to release tapes subpoenaed by the special prosecutor, it announced that two critical tapes were missing and one had an eighteen and one-half minute gap where a presidential discussion of Watergate should have been. In March, 1974, seven presidential aides and election officials were indicted for their roles in the coverup, and seven for involvement in a break-in at the office of the psychiatrist for Daniel Ellsberg, who had been implicated in releasing sensitive Pentagon documents to the press. On April 29, 1974, Nixon went before a national television audience to announce that he was releasing more than a thousand pages of edited transcripts of presidential conversations. Contrary to his hopes, the transcripts only deepened public outcry, for they revealed the tone of the White House conversations as being "cynical, amoral, vindictive, self-serving, and conspiratorial." (Thomas A. Bailey and David M. Kennedy, *The American Pageant*, Sixth Edition, p. 914) In July the Supreme Court ordered Nixon to release the tapes themselves, and the discrepancies with the transcripts became obvious.

Finally, the House Judiciary Committee voted impeachment of the President of the United States. The Committee approved three articles of impeachment: the first charged the President with obstruction of justice; the second charged Nixon with abuse of the power of his office; the third accused him of conduct "subversive of constitutional government" by ignoring lawful subpoenas for tapes and other written documents. Most observers thought at least the first article would be approved by the full House of Representatives and, therefore, necessitate a trial in the Senate.

The House vote and the Senate trial never happened. On August 5, 1974, Nixon released three subpoenaed tapes of conversations he had with aides soon after the Watergate break-in. The "smoking gun" that skeptics had wanted had been found, for the tapes left no doubt that Nixon had been deeply involved in the cover-up all along. What congressional support he had left now collapsed, and on August 8, 1974, Nixon told a national television audience that he was resigning the following day. Had he not resigned he likely would have become the first U.S. President to have been impeached by the House and removed from office after conviction in the Senate. (Incidentally, resignation also allowed Nixon to receive his full retirement benefits.)

Nixon's closest associates, former Attorney General John Mitchell and presidential advisers H. R. Haldeman and John Ehrlichman, were convicted of Watergate-related crimes and sentenced to prison. John Dean, White House counsel and star witness in the Watergate investigation, pleaded guilty to charges of participating in the cover-up and served four months in jail. Charles Colson, a political adviser and reputed "hatchet man" in the White House, served six months in jail for obstruction of justice. Jeb Stuart Magruder, a high official on Nixon's campaign staff, was jailed for seven months for obstruction of justice. G. Gordon Liddy, who presented the burglary plans to Mitchell, spent more than four years in jail. E. Howard Hunt, who recruited the burglars, served thirty-two months.

The Watergate break-in, the cover-up, the resignation of Richard Nixon, and the imprisonment of his aides did not constitute the whole story of the Nixon scandals. Ten months before Nixon resigned, his Vice-President, Spiro Agnew, stepped down from his position. Agnew had come under investigation from a Baltimore grand jury investigating charges of kickbacks and tax fraud in Maryland. When evidence of his guilt seemed overwhelming, Agnew pleaded no contest to a charge of income tax evasion and resigned. Nixon, under terms of the Twenty-fifth Amendment, appointed Gerald R. Ford as Vice-President, who then became President following Nixon's resignation. A few weeks after Nixon's departure, Ford pardoned the former President for any misdeeds he may have committed while President.

There were other scandals in the Nixon years as well. Richard G. Kleindienst, Mitchell's successor as Attorney General, pleaded guilty to a charge of obstructing prosecution of an antitrust suit against International Telephone and Telegraph (ITT). There were a number of charges related to illegal campaign contributions, which led to guilty pleas from former Nixon attorney Herbert Kalmbach and former Treasury Secretary Maurice Stans, who was director of fund-raising activities for CREEP. Still other illegalities involved the so-called "dirty tricks" of the 1972 campaign and the actions of the White House "plumbers."

The list of guilty parties in the Nixon scandals could go on, but it is clear that political corruption reached new depths under Nixon. The pervasiveness of wrongdoing outstripped even that of the Grant and Harding eras. Like his predecessors in corruption, Nixon had encouraged a political atmosphere which led to disregard of the law. Unlike his predecessors, Nixon was personally involved in direct abuse of presidential power.

There are some other interesting similarities in a retrospective glance at the three periods of corruption. Each occurred during a Republican administration. In each instance, the reflexive response of the President was to deny scandal and to cover it up and protect associates. Congressional hearings and special legal procedures outside the executive-controlled Justice Department were significant in bringing the corruption into the open. This supports the importance of the system of checks and balances within the constitutional framework. The press also played an important role in each case, most notably in the Nixon scandals. The dogged reporting of Carl Bernstein and Bob Woodward of the Washington *Post* will be long-remembered as an example of the press's role in exposing wrongdoing in public office.

Three additional considerations deserve comment. First, all three crises in the presidency followed extended periods of national turmoil and each followed costly wars. Secondly, each scandalous administration followed a period in which the powers of the presidency were expanded. The development of this "imperial presidency" contributed to Richard Nixon's view that the President of the United States was above the law. Grant and Harding were not seeking personal power, but their trusting nature allowed subordinates to take advantage of the presidency for financial gain. Nixon's offense was greater than the two earlier Presidents in this sense, for he sought to acquire and maintain illegal political power as well as financial gain. Finally, each period of corruption resulted in a breakdown of trust between the American people and their government. The losses here cannot be measured, but they are nevertheless real and extremely significant.

There is some scandal in almost every presidential administration and in almost every session of Congress, but the massive scale of corruption during the Grant, Harding, and Nixon eras reached shocking proportions. It seems that there is a regular pattern of a fifty-year interval between such extensive political abuses. Perhaps by keeping in mind the forces which brought about the scandals, by keeping a vigilant watch on the activities of political leaders, and by making sure that their own sense of proper conduct serves as a model for politicians, the American people can prevent such abuses of political power from happening again.

Epilogue: The Reagan Administration

Unfortunately, it did not take fifty years for serious and widespread scandal to mar the record of another president. Those who elected Ronald Reagan in 1980 believed that he stood for family values, religious ethics, and a strict construction of the law. By the time Reagan left the presidency in 1989, well more than 100 senior administration officials had come under investigation for improper conduct. Some resigned under fire, were dismissed, had their nominations withdrawn or rejected, pleaded guilty to crimes, and/or were convicted of serious offenses. Among the most prominent administration officials tainted by corruption were Michael Deaver, the president's aide and confidant, Attorney General Edwin Meese, and, of course, Oliver North, a former national security aide. At the end, the president himself escaped responsibility only because he seemed so "detached" and confused that it was hard to believe that he could have orchestrated much of this wrongdoing. Indeed, what had gone wrong?

Part of the explanation lies with the philosophical absolutes which Ronald Reagan and those around him brought to the presidency. At home, the government was a hindrance to un-regulated pursuit of personal and/or corporate gain. Restrictions, otherwise known as laws, were often considered "technical, trivial, even avoidable." (See Mark Green and Peter H. Stone's article in The *Dallas Morning News*, July 12, 1987, p. 35A). Too many Reagan appointees could not make the transition from the private sector to the public service. The scandals emanating from the Department of Housing and Urban Development (HUD) under Reagan illustrate the point. It was here that administration officials and private developers schemed to defraud the taxpayers of hundreds of millions of dollars. Meanwhile, housing for the poor, which they were supposed to be rehabilitating, languished. Some pundit coined the term "the sleaze factor" to refer to the administration's failure "to comprehend ethics and outright scandals."

Abroad, the Soviet Union was simply "the evil empire," so anything done to stop the spread of this pernicious influence, even selling weapons to terrorists, was deemed morally per-missible! While the Pentagon went on a spending spree accompanied by examples of gross ex-cess and corruption, high-level Reagan administration officials engaged in one of the most contemptible scandals in the nation's history, the Iran-contra affair. Simply put, investigations revealed that Oliver North of the National Security Council, William Casey of the Central In-telligence Agency, and others secretly sold weapons to Iran, a nation branded as terrorist by the United States. They apparently believed that Iran could use its influence to help free hostages held at that time by terrorist groups in Lebanon. Despite President Reagan's pledge never to pay ransom for hostages, that appeared to be what was happening. Furthermore, the profits from the sales of the weapons was to be diverted, illegally, to aid the contras, the name given to those who were fighting against a left-wing government in Nicaragua.

The Iran-contra affair raised questions about constitutional rule and the competence of President Reagan. The threat to the Constitution involved more than the duplicity of selling weapons to terrorists. Oliver North and the others involved apparently believed that they had the right to circumvent congressional legislation. Furthermore, when the story of this unseem-ly affair began to be exposed in late 1986, the major operatives had already begun a coverup operation that proved to be similar to the Watergate affair of the Nixon era. The public's reac-tion to North was especially interesting, for a man who admitted to lies and illegal acts became a national hero to some. He played the media for all it was worth, and he wrapped himself in the flag. Or, as one commentator aptly put it, he tried to destroy the Constitution and hid be-hind the flag. What was President Reagan's role in all of this? Had he deliberately lied to the American people about an arms-for-hostages deal? Or was he totally unaware of what was go-ing on in the White House? Either answer was appalling and alarming.

What should we have learned from the Iran-contra affair and the other scandals of the Re-agan administration? First, we must demand that any president must know and be accountable for the actions of administration officials. Presidential styles may vary, but the president is re-sponsible for faithfully executing the laws of the nation. Secondly, we must demand that the president's staff obey the law. The United States cannot tolerate non-elected officials (nor any-one else) taking the law into their own hands—this endangers the very foundation of our con-stitutional system of government. Thirdly, we must accept the idea that Congress has a legitimate role to play in foreign policy. It was not without thought that the framers of the Con-stitution gave Congress the sole power to declare war as well as the powers of appropriating funds and congressional oversight of executive operations. The system of checks and balances can help avoid excesses in foreign as well as domestic affairs. Lastly, the American people must be alert to abuses of power, for the price of liberty is still eternal vigilance.

VII

REVOLUTION IN INDIAN COUNTRY

Fergus M. Bordewich

In few areas of American life have myths and misconceptions been more potent and polarized than in Indian-white relations. Many Indians, past and present, have seen the white majority as out to rape the landscape and brutalize and ultimately destroy the sacred ways of Indian life. Whites, for their part, have tended to view the Indians as wallowing in poverty, disease, and backwardness that they could overcome if they would only adopt the "modern" ways of the larger society within which they stubbornly remain as a ghettoized fragment.

In the course of four years of research and travel for his book Killing the White Man's Indian (1996), Fergus M. Bordewich discovered a more complex reality. After centuries of treatment as second-class tenants, Indian tribes are now aggressively claiming a new sovereignty over their own affairs in the areas of government and economics. Yet many Indian leaders realize that the Indian will never fully control his own affairs in total isolation. As in the past, there will be "calculated compromises, mutual accommodation, and deliberately chosen risks . . . in order to survive . . . Self-determination gives Indian tribes the ability to manage the speed and style of integration but not the power to stop it, at least for long." Bordewich quotes Mexican writer Carlos Fuentes: "People and their cultures perish in isolation, but they are born or reborn in contact with other men and women . . . of another culture, another creed, another race." As in all areas of American racial and ethnic interaction, Indian-white relations will continue to be a mixture of push-pull, adjustment, and accommodation on both sides.

Micki's Cafe is, in its modest way, a bulwark against the encroachment of modern history and a symbol, amid the declining fortunes of prairie America, of the kind of gritty (and perhaps foolhardy) determination that in more self-confident times used to be called the frontier spirit. To Micki Hutchinson, the problem in the winter of 1991 seemed as plain as the grid of streets that white homesteaders had optimistically laid out in 1910, on the naked South Dakota prairie, to create the town of Isabel in the middle of what they were told was no longer the reservation of the Cheyenne River Sioux Tribe. It was not difficult for Hutchinson to decide what to do when the leaders of the tribal government ordered her to purchase a $250 tribal liquor license: She ignored them.

"They have no right to tell me what to do. I'm not Indian!" Hutchinson told me a year and a half later. She and other white business people had by then challenged the tribe's right to tax them in both tribal court and federal district court and had lost. The marks of prolonged tension showed on her tanned, angular, wary face. "If this were Indian land, it would make sense. But we're a non-Indian town. This is all homestead land, and the tribe was paid for it. I can't vote in tribal elections or on anything else that happens on the reservation. What they're talking about is taxation without representation."

When I visited, everyone in Isabel still remembered the screech of the warning siren that someone had set off on the morning of March 27, 1991, when the tribal police reached the edge of town, as if their arrival were some kind of natural disaster, like a tornado or fire. The convoy of gold-painted prowl cars rolled in from the prairie and then, when they came abreast of the café, swung sideways across the road. Thirty-eight tribal policemen surrounded the yellow brick building. The tribe's police chief, Marvin LeCompte, told Hutchinson that she was in contempt of tribal court. Officers ordered the morning breakfast crowd away from their fried eggs and coffee. Then they went back into the pine-paneled bar and confiscated Hutchinson's stock of beer and liquor—"contraband," as LeCompte described it—and drove off with it to the tribal government's offices at Eagle Butte.

A few days before I met Hutchinson, I had interviewed Gregg J. Bourland, the youthful chairman of the Cheyenne River Sioux Tribe. Bourland is widely reckoned to be one of the most effective tribal chairmen in the region and, with a degree in business from the state college in Spearfish, also one of the best educated. "Let them talk about taxation without representation," Bourland told me dismissively. "We're not a state. We're a separate nation, and the only way you can be represented in it is to be a member of the tribe. And they can't do that. They're not Indians. These folks are trespassers. They are within reservation boundaries, and they will follow reservation law. They've now had one hundred years with no tribal authority over them out here. Well, that's over."

More than Micki Hutchinson or than any of the other angry whites in their declining prairie hamlets, it was Bourland who understood that what was at stake was much more than small-town politics. The tax, the ostentatious convoy, and the lawsuit were part of a much larger political drama that was unfolding across the inland archipelago of reservations that make up modern Indian Country. They symbolized the reshaping of the American West, indeed of the United States itself. By the 1990s, almost unnoticed by the American public or media, a generation of legislation and court actions had profoundly remade Indian Country, canonizing ideas about tribal autonomy that would have shocked the lawmakers who a century before had seen the destruction of the reservations as the salvation of the American Indian. If Bourland was right, Micki Hutchinson and the white residents of Isabel were living in a sovereign tribal state. They were tolerated guests with an uncertain future.

Until the 1870s, reservations were established throughout the Dakota Territory and other parts of the West with the promise that they would be reserved in perpetuity for the Indians' exclusive use. Those promises were broken almost everywhere when reservations were opened to homesteading at the end of the century, usually with only perfunctory consultation with the tribes or none at all. As I listened to Gregg Bourland, it was easy to sympathize with the tribe's striving for some kind of control over forces that were felt to have invaded their land and undermined their culture. Bourland justified the tax as a means both to raise revenue for the tribe and to control alcohol consumption on a reservation where more than 60 percent of the adults were unemployed and 53 percent were active alcoholics.

But promises that had been made a century ago to the ancestors of settlers like Micki Hutchinson were now being broken too. From the 1880s until the 1930s, the cornerstone of federal Indian policy had been the popular program known as allotment, the systematic breaking up of most of the nation's reservations into private holdings. In its day allotment seemed the perfect panacea to resolve at a single stroke the perennial problems of white settlers' insatiable desire for new land and Indians' growing dependency on the federal government. Sen. Henry L. Dawes, the idealistic architect of the Allotment Act of 1881, which set the pattern for a generation of similar legislation, ringingly proclaimed that as a result of allotment, the Indian "shall be one of us, contributing his share to all that goes to make up the strength and glory of citizenship in the United States."

The means of the Indian's salvation was to be the family farm, which most people of the time had been taught to regard as the ultimate repository of American individualism and the democratic spirit. Each Indian allottee would receive 160 acres of land and eventual United States citizenship, along with money for seed, tools, and livestock. The "excess," or leftover, land would be offered for sale to white settlers, who would be free to form their own municipal governments. The promise of the allotment policy was twofold: that the nation would integrate Indians into white society and that non-Indian settlers would never be subject to tribal regimes.

At the time, the Commissioner of Indian Affairs dismissed notions of separate Indian nationality as mere sentimentality: "It is perfectly clear to my mind that the treaties never contemplated the un-American and absurd idea of a separate nationality in our midst, with power as they may choose to organize a government of their own." To maintain such a view, the commissioner added, was to acknowledge a foreign sovereignty upon American soil, "a theory utterly repugnant to the spirit and genius of our laws, and wholly unwarranted by the Constitution of the United States."

As I left Isabel, I wondered who really was the victim here and who the victimizer. Behind that nagging question lurked still more difficult ones that occupied me for many months, from one end of the United States to the other, in the course of researching what was to become *Killing the White Man's Indian*, an investigation into the political and cultural transformation of modern Indian Country. Are Native Americans so fundamentally different from other Americans that they occupy a special category to which conventional American values and laws should not apply? Or are they simply one more American group, whose special pleading is further evidence that the United States has become a balkanized tangle of ghettos and ethnic enclaves? Do we discriminate against Indians by failing to blend them more effectively into the national mainstream? Or is the very notion of "mainstreaming" Indians so inherently racist that it should not even be contemplated as a component of national policy? Are Indian reservations and the way of life they preserve a precious national resource that must be maintained without the taint of contact with white America? Or is tribal self-determination creating a new form of segregation that merely freezes decayed tribal cultures like ghettoized versions of Colonial Williamsburg? Who, ultimately, are Indians in the 1990s? What are they to other Americans, and the others to them?

Killing the White Man's Indian represented a return to familiar country. As a youth in the 1950s and early 1960s, I often accompanied my mother, who was the executive director of the Association on American Indian Affairs, in her travels around reservations, part of her tireless effort to prod the federal government into improving tribal economies, education, health care, and law and order. Vivid experiences were plentiful: participating in a night long peyote rite in a teepee on the Montana prairie; a journey by pirogue deep into the Louisiana bayous to meet with a forgotten band of Houmas who wanted Washington to take notice of their existence; walking the Little Bighorn Battlefield with an aged Cheyenne who, as a small boy, had witnessed the annihilation of Custer's command. Poverty shaded almost every experience. Staying with friends often meant wind fingering its way through gaps in the walls, a cheese and bologna sandwich for dinner, sleeping three or four in a bed with broken springs. It seemed there was always someone talking about an uncle who, drunk, had frozen to death on a lonely road or about a cousin already pregnant at sixteen. More generally those years left me with a sense of the tremendous diversity of the lives and communities that lay submerged within the catchall label of "Indians" and a recognition that Native Americans were not mere vestiges of a mythic past but modern men and women struggling to solve twentieth-century problems.

In the course of four years' research on my book, I visited reservations from upstate New York to southern California and from Mississippi to Washington State, meeting with tribal leaders, ranchers, farmers, educators, and hundreds of ordinary men and women, both Indian and white. In Michigan I sailed Lake Superior with waterborne Chippewa police, searching for poachers on tribal fisheries in the lake. In Oregon I hiked the Cascades with professional foresters from the Warm Springs Tribe, which with its several hydroelectric dams and thriving timber industry is one of Indian Country's great success stories. I sweated with a group of recovering Navajo alcoholics in a traditional sweat lodge in the New Mexico desert. I also spent many a night in dust-blown reservation towns where, as an old South Dakota song puts it, "There's nothing much to do except walk up and down." In a few places, as a result of childhood connections, I was welcomed as a friend. More frequently I met with suspicion rooted in the widespread belief that curiosity like mine was just a form of exploitation and that whites are incapable of writing about Indians with objectivity and honesty.

My original intention had been to use the lives of several men and women whom I had known in the 1950s as a microcosm and through them to chart the changes that had been wrought in Indian Country during the intervening years. But I soon realized that such a focus would be far too narrow, for it had become clear to me that a virtual revolution was under way that was challenging the worn-out theology of Indians as losers and victims and was transforming tribes into powers to be reckoned with for years to come. It encompassed virtually every aspect of Indian life, from the revival of moribund tribal cultures and traditional religions to the development of aggressive tribal governments determined to remake the relationship between tribes and the United States. The ferment was not unalloyed, however. Alongside inspired idealism, I also found ethnic chauvinism, a crippling instinct to mistake isolation for independence, and a habit of interpreting present-day reality through the warping lens of the past.

In the 1970s, in a reversal of long-standing policies based on the conviction that Indians must be either persuaded or compelled to integrate themselves into mainstream America, the United States enshrined the concept of tribal sovereignty at the center of its policy toward the nation's more than three hundred tribes. In the watershed words of Richard Nixon, federal policy would henceforth be guided "by Indian acts and Indian decisions" and would be designed to "assure the Indian that he can assume control of his own life without being separated from the tribal group."

In 1975 the Indian Self-Determination and Education Assistance Act amplified this principle, calling for a "transition from Federal domination of programs for and services to Indians to effective and meaningful participation by the Indian people." This has been reflected in a national commitment to the strengthening of tribal governments and to more comprehensive tribal authority over reservation lands. More ambiguously, it has also led to the increasing development of a new sphere of political power that rivals, or at least claims to rival, that of the states and the national government and for which there is no foundation in the Constitution. In the mid-1990s I found tribal officials invoking "sovereign right" in debates over everything from highway maintenance and fishing quotas to law and order, toxic-waste disposal, and the transfer of federal services to tribal administrations, not to mention the rapid proliferation of tribally run gambling operations. Reflecting the sentiments of many tribal leaders, Tim Giago, the publisher of Indian Country Today, the most widely read Indian newspaper in the United States, likened state legislation that affects Indians to "letting France make laws that also become law in Italy."

To people like Micki Hutchinson, it often seemed that Indians were playing an entirely new game, and that no one but the Indians understood the rules. In Connecticut, and elsewhere, tribes were exploiting a principle of sovereignty unknown to the average American in order to build casinos that sucked colossal sums of money from neighboring regions. New Mexicans found that they were equally helpless in the face of the Mescalero Apaches' determination to establish a nuclear-waste facility on their reservation outside Alamogordo. In Wisconsin and in Washington State, recurrent violence had accompanied the judicially mandated enlargement of Indian fishing rights in accordance with nineteenth-century treaties. In Nevada farmers found themselves on the brink of failure as the Paiutes of Pyramid Lake gained political leverage over the watershed of the Truckee River.

In some states Indian demands for the return of sacred lands posed significant threats to local economies, including, most prominently, the Black Hills region of South Dakota. Nor was science exempt. Tribal claims on ancestral bones and artifacts were depleting many of the most valuable anthropological collections in the country.

Strangely enough, these conflicts-widespread, often bitter, and with profound ramifications for American institutions-seemed to be happening beyond the ken of most Americans, for whom Indians largely remain a people of myth and fantasy. Like no other inhabitants of the United States, Indians have nourished our imagination, weaving in us a complex skein of guilt, envy, and contempt; yet when we imagine we see "the Indian," we often see little more than the distorted reflection of our own fears, fancies, and unhappy longings. This was vividly brought home to me on a visit to the reservation of the two-hundred-member Campo Band of Mission Indians, in the arid hills an hour's drive east of San Diego. This reservation landscape is a profoundly discouraging one. It offers nothing to comfort the eye, produces nothing of value, and provides almost nothing to sustain life as it is enjoyed by most Americans today. The single resource that the Campos possess is wasteland. In 1987 the band learned that the city of San Diego had named the reservation as one of several potential dump sites for the city's refuse.

"We just need this one little thing to get us started," the band's chairman, Ralph Goff, told me as we walked through the redshank and yucca and ocher sand where the first trenches had been cut for the new landfill. "With it we can create our own destiny." Goff, a formidably built man with little formal education, grew up in the 1940s, when the only work available was as a cowhand or day laborer for whites. When there was no work, people went hungry. "You just had to wait until there was some more food." In the 1960s most of the unskilled jobs disappeared, and nearly every Campo family went on welfare. "We needed it, but it really wrecked us as people. It created idleness. People didn't have to do anything in order to get money."

If the Campos have their way, by the end of the decade daily freight trains will be carrying loads of municipal waste to a three-hundred-acre site on a hilltop at the southern end of the reservation. For the privilege of leasing the band's land, a waste-management firm will pay the Campos between two and five million dollars a year. Goff argued that the dump would put an end to the band's dependence on federal largess. It would create jobs for every adult Campo who is willing to work, provide long-term investment capital for the band, supply money for full college scholarships for every school-age member of the band, and finance new homes for the families that now live in substandard housing. The dump would, in short, give the Campos financial independence for the first time in their modern history.

The landfill would be one of the most technically advanced in the United States; to regulate it, the Campos enacted an environmental code more stringent than the State of California's. Nevertheless, the dump generated fierce opposition in towns near the reservation, where thousands of non-Indians live. Geologists hired by the dump's opponents have suggested, but not proved, that seepage from the dump might contaminate the water supply of ranches beyond the reservation boundary. Environmentalists accused the band of irresponsibility toward the earth and charged that the Campos had been targeted in an "assault" on reservations by "renegade" waste-dumping companies. A bill was even introduced in the California legislature that would have made it a crime to deliver waste to the Campo landfill. Goff shrugged away the protests. "It's a sovereignty issue. It's our land, and we'll do what we want to with it."

"How can you say that the economic development of two hundred people is more important than the health and welfare of all the people in the surrounding area?" an angry and frustrated rancher, whose land lay just off the reservation, asked me. "It's hard making a living here. The fissures will carry that stuff right through here. We'll have all that stuff in our water and blowing down on us off the hills. If our water is spoiled, then everything's spoiled."

There were predictable elements to her rage: the instinctive resistance of most Americans to any kind of waste dump anywhere near their homes and the distress of many white Americans when they realize the implications of tribal sovereignty for the first time and find themselves subject to the will of a government in which they have no say. But there was something more, a sort of moral perplexity at Indians' having failed to behave according to expectation, an imputation that they were guilty of self-interest. Revealingly, I thought, on the wall of the rancher's trailer there was a poster decorated with Indian motifs. Entitled "Chief Seattle Speaks," it began, in words that are becoming as familiar to American schoolchildren as those of the Gettysburg Address once were: "How can you buy or sell the sky, the warmth of the land?" Here, in sight of the dump, the so-called testament of Chief Seattle was a reproach to the Campos, an argument rooted in what the rancher presumably believed to be Indians' profoundest values. "Before all this I had this ideal about Indian people and all they've been through," she told me. "I used to think they had this special feeling about the land."

More than any other single document, Seattle's twelve-hundred-word "testament" lends support to the increasingly common belief that to "real" Indians any disruption or commercialization of the earth's natural order is a kind of sacrilege and that the most moral, the most truly "Indian" relationship with the land is a kind of poetic passivity. Having been translated into dozens of languages and widely reproduced in school texts, the "testament" has attained a prophetic stature among environmentalists: In 1993 Greenpeace used it as the introduction to a scarifying report on toxic dumping, calling it "the most beautiful and profound statement on the environment ever made." Unfortunately, like much literature that purports to reveal the real nature of the Indians, the "testament" is basically a fiction. Seattle was indeed a historical figure, a slave-owning chief of the Duwamishes who sold land to the United States in the mid-1850s and welcomed the protection of the federal government against his local enemies. However, the "testament," as it is known to most Americans, was created from notes allegedly made thirty years after the fact by a white doctor who claimed to have been present when Seattle spoke, and which then were extravagantly embroidered by a well-meaning Texas scriptwriter by the name of Ted Perry as narration for a 1972 film on the environment, produced by the Southern Baptist Radio and Television Commission. How is it, I wondered, that Americans have so readily embraced such a spurious text, not only as a sacred screed of the ecology movement but also as a central document of "traditional" Native American culture?

Increasingly it became clear to me that to be able to describe the realities of modern Indian life and politics, I would have to strip away the myths that whites have spun around Native Americans ever since Columbus arbitrarily divided the peoples he encountered into noble Arawaks and savage Caribs, conflating European fantasies with presumed native reality and initiating a tradition that would eventually include Montesquieu, Locke, Hobbes, and Rousseau, as well as a vivid popular literature stretching from *The Last of the Mohicans* to *Dances*

With Wolves. Untamable savage, child of nature, steward of the earth, the white man's ultimate victim: each age has imagined its own mythic version of what the historian Robert F. Berkhofer, Jr., termed the "white man's Indian."

Typically the Denver *Post* could declare, not long ago, in an editorial attacking the University of Arizona for a plan to build an observatory atop an allegedly sacred mountain: "At stake is the very survival of American Indian cultures. If these sacred places are destroyed, then the rituals unique to those places no longer will be performed and many tribes simply may cease to exist as distinct peoples." Such logic implies both that only Native Americans who profess to live like pre-Columbians are true Indians and that Indians are essentially hopeless and helpless and on the brink of extinction. Apparently it never occurred to the paper's editorialist that the religion of the great majority of Indians is not in fact some mystical form of traditionalism but a thriving Christianity.

In keeping with our essentially mythic approach to the history of Indians and whites, Americans were generally taught until a generation or so ago to view their national story as a soaring arc of unbroken successes, in which the defeat of the Indians reflected the inevitable and indeed spiritual triumph of civilization over barbarism. More recently, but not so differently, numerous revisionist works like Kirkpatrick Sale's *The Conquest of Paradise: Christopher Columbus and the Columbian Legacy* and Richard Drinnon's *Facing West: The Metaphysics of Indian-Hating and Empire Building* have tended to portray the settlement of North America as a prolonged story of unredeemed tragedy and failure, in which the destruction of the Indians stands as proof of a fundamental ruthlessness at the heart of American civilization. Such beliefs have steadily percolated into the wider culture—to be embodied in New Age Westerns like *Dances With Wolves* and popular books like the best-selling *Indian Givers: How the Indians of the Americas Transformed the World*, which purports to show how practically every aspect of modern life from potatoes to democracy derives from the generosity of American Indians—and into the consciences of journalists, clergy, and others who shape public opinion.

On the whole the complex and intricate relationship between whites and Indians has been presented as one of irreconcilable conflict between conqueror and victim, corruption and innocence, Euro-American "materialism" and native "spirituality." The real story, of course, is an often contradictory one, disfigured by periods of harsh discrimination and occasional acts of genocide but also marked by considerable Indian pragmatism and adaptability as well as by the persistent, if sometimes shortsighted, idealism of whites determined to protect Indians from annihilation and find some place for them in mainstream America.

For instance, in contradiction of the notion that Indians were innocent of even the most elementary business sense, it was clear during negotiations over the Black Hills in the 1870s that Sioux leaders had a perfectly good grasp of finance and that indeed they were determined to drive the best bargain they could. "The Black Hills are the house of Gold for our Indians," Chief Little Bear said at the time. "If a man owns anything, of course he wants to make something out of it to get rich on." Another chief, Spotted Tail, added: "I want to live on the interest of my money. The amount must be so large as to support us." Similarly, in contrast with the popular belief that the United States government was committed to a policy of exterminating the Indian (no such policy ever existed, in fact), Senator Dawes publicly described the history of Indians in the United States as one "of spoliation, of wars, and of humiliation," and he firmly stated that the Indian should be treated "as an individual, and not as an insoluble substance that the civilization of this country has been unable, hitherto, to digest."

Indeed, the impulse behind the allotment of tribal lands and the national commitment to Indians was dramatically (and, with the benefit of hindsight, poignantly) acted out in a rite of citizenship that after 1887 was staged at Timber Lake, in the heart of the Cheyenne River

Sioux country, and at many other places in the freshly allotted lands of other tribes. In the presence of representatives of the federal government, new allottees stood resplendent in the feathers and buckskins of a bygone age. One by one, each man stepped out of a teepee and shot an arrow to symbolize the life he was leaving behind. He then put his hands on a plow and accepted a purse that indicated that he was to save what he earned. Finally, holding the American flag, the Indian repeated these words: "Forasmuch as the President has said that I am worthy to be a citizen of the United States, I now promise this flag that I will give my hands, my head, and my heart to the doing of all that will make me a true American citizen." It was the culminating, transformative moment of which Senator Dawes had dreamed.

It is true enough, however, that, as so often in Indian history, reality failed to live up to good intentions. Unscrupulous speculators soon infested the allotted reservations, offering worthless securities and credit in return for land. Within a few years it was found that of those who had received patents to their land at Cheyenne River, 95 percent had sold or mortgaged their properties. When the Allotment Act was passed in 1881, there were 155 million acres of Indian land in the United States. By the time allotment was finally brought to a halt in 1934, Indian Country had shrunk by nearly 70 percent to 48 million acres, and two-thirds of Indians either were completely landless or did not have enough land left to make a living from it. In the mid-1990s Indian Country as a whole is still a daunting and impoverished landscape whose inhabitants are twice as likely as other Americans to be murdered or commit suicide, three times as likely to die in an automobile accident, and five times as likely to die from cirrhosis of the liver. On some reservations unemployment surpasses 80 percent, and 50 percent of young Indians drop out of high school, despite progressively increased access to education.

Is the tribal-sovereignty movement a panacea for otherwise intractable social problems? In the cultural sphere, at least, its importance cannot be underestimated. "Our people live in a limbo culture that is not quite Indian and not quite white either," said Dennis Hastings, surrounded by books, gazing out toward the Iowa plains through the window of the sky blue trailer where he lives in a cow pasture. Hastings, a burly former Marine and the tribal historian of the Omaha Nation, which is in northeastern Nebraska, has almost single-handedly led an effort to recover tribal history as a foundation for community renewal that is probably unmatched by any other small tribe in the United States. "It's like living in a house without a foundation. You can't go back to the old buffalo days, stop speaking English and just use our own language, and ignore whites and everything in white culture. If we did that, we'd become stuck in history, become dinosaurs."

Teasing small grants and the help of volunteer scholars from institutions around the country, Hastings has initiated an oral-history project to collect memories of fading tribal traditions. "We go into each family, get an anthropologist to record everything right from how you wake up in the morning," he said. Hundreds of historic photographs of early reservation life have been collected and deposited with the State Historical Society, in Lincoln. A friendly scholar from the University of Indiana recovered a trove of forgotten Omaha songs recorded in the 1920s on wax cylinders. Another at the University of New Mexico undertook a collective genealogy that would trace the lineage of more than five thousand Omahas back to the eighteenth century. Hastings explained, "Until now everything was oral. Some people knew the names of their ancestors, and some knew nothing at all. There was a loss of connection with the past. Now people can come back and find out who their ancestors were." In sharp contrast with the combative chauvinism of some tribes, the Omahas invited scientists from the University of Nebraska and the Smithsonian Institution to examine repatriated skeletons to see what they could discover about the lives of their ancestors. In 1989, astonishing perhaps even themselves, tribal leaders brought home Waxthe'xe, the True Omaha, the sacred cottonwood pole that is the living embodiment of the Omaha people, which had lain for a hundred years in Harvard's Peabody Museum; at the July powwow that year, weeping hundreds bent to touch it as if it were the true cross or the ark of the covenant.

"We want the benefits of modern society," Hastings told me in his nasal Midwestern drawl. "But America is still dangerous for us. The question is then, How do we take the science that America used against us and make it work for us? The answer is, we try to build on the past. It's like a puzzle. First you see where the culture broke and fragmented. Then you try to build on it where people have been practicing it all along. Then people start to think in a healthy way about what they were in the past. If you can get each person to be proud of himself, little by little, you can get the whole tribe to become proud. We're going to dream big and be consistent with that dream."

In its broadest sense the tribal sovereignty movement is demonstrating that the more than three hundred Indian tribes in the lower forty-eight states (more than five hundred if you count Alaskan native groups) are distinct communities, each with its unique history, traditions, and political environment, for whom a single one-size-fits-all federal policy will no longer suffice. Greater autonomy will surely enable well-governed and economically self-sufficient tribes-mostly those located near big cities and those with valuable natural resources-to manage their own development in imaginative ways. For many others, however, far from airports and interstate highways, populated by ill-trained workers and governed, in some cases, by politicians who do not abide by the most basic democratic rules, the future is much less assured.

There is nothing abstract about such concerns in Timber Lake, South Dakota, which lies a short drive east from Isabel across the rolling plains of the Cheyenne River Sioux Reservation. Like Isabel, Timber Lake has been battered by the general decline of a region that is hemorrhaging jobs and people. Timber Lake is one of the relatively lucky places, kept alive by the presence of the Dewey County offices, the rural electric co-op, the central school, and a cheese factory. Even so, one hundred of the six hundred people who lived there a decade ago have moved away to places with better prospects and more hope. Isabel's population has dropped by half, to three hundred. Trail City has shrunk from three hundred and fifty to thirty, Firesteel to a single general store, and Landeau has disappeared completely. Entire towns have lost their doctors, banks, and schools. From a certain angle of vision, Sioux demands for the restoration of the reservation to its original nineteenth-century limits are simply an anticlimax.

The people of Timber Lake-the mechanics, the teachers, the co-op clerks, the men who work at the grain elevator, the retired farmers-are the human fruit of allotment, the flesh-and-blood culmination of the cultural blending that Senator Dawes envisioned. "Everyone here has relatives who are Indian," said Steve Aberle, a local attorney whose Russian-German father married into the Ducheneaux, a prominent clan of Cheyenne River Sioux. Aberle, who is thirty-five, is one-eighth Sioux; he is a voting member of the tribe and served for two and a half years as chairman of the tribal police commission. Nevertheless he shares the uneasiness of non-Indians who feel themselves slipping toward a kind of second-class citizenship within the reservation's boundaries. "It would be better to be in a situation where everybody works together and deals with people as people, but it's hard to do that when people know they pay taxes but are excluded from benefits and services," Aberle told me. "When my grandparents came from Russia, the United States government told them that they would be full citizens if they moved out here. Now I see people being told that they can't even take part in a government that wants to regulate them. Something is inherently wrong when you can't be a citizen where you live because of your race. It just doesn't fit with the traditional notion of being a U.S. citizen. At some point there has to be a collision between the notion of tribal sovereignty and the notion of being United States citizens. Anytime you have a group not represented in the political process they will be discriminated against. There's going to be more and more friction. It's going to hurt these communities. People start looking for jobs elsewhere."

The Sioux were the victims of nineteenth-century social engineering that decimated their reservation. But the descendants of the adventurous emigrants who settled the land are also the victims of an unexpected historical prank, the trick of the disappearing and now magically reappearing reservation. Reasonably enough, the rhetoric of tribal sovereignty asks for tribes a degree of self-government that is taken for granted by other Americans. However, the achievement of a sovereignty that drives away taxpayers, consumers, and enterprise may be at best but a Pyrrhic victory over withered communities that beg for cooperation and innovation to survive at all.

With little debate outside the parochial circles of Indian affairs, a generation of policy-making has jettisoned the long-standing American ideal of racial unity as a positive good and replaced it with a doctrine that, seen from a more critical angle, seems disturbingly like an idealized form of segregation, a fact apparently invisible to a nation that has become accustomed to looking at Indians only through the twin lenses of romance and guilt and in an era that has made a secular religion of passionate ethnicity. Much of the thinking that underlies tribal sovereignty seems to presuppose that cultural purity can and ought to be preserved, as if Indian bloodlines, economies, and histories were not already inextricably enmeshed with those of white, Hispanic, and black Americans.

Such concerns will be further exacerbated in the years to come as Indian identity grows increasingly ambiguous. Virtually all Indians are moving along a continuum of biological fusion with other American populations. "A point will be reached . . . when it will no longer make sense to define American Indians in generic terms [but] only as tribal members or as people of Indian ancestry or ethnicity," writes Russell Thornton, a Cherokee anthropologist and demographer at the University of Southern California, in *American Indian Holocaust and Survival*, a study of fluctuations in native populations. Statistically, according to Thornton, Indians are marrying outside their ethnic group at a faster rate than any other Americans. More than 50 percent of Indians are already married to non-Indians, and Congress has estimated that by the year 2080 less than 8 percent of Native Americans will have one-half or more Indian blood.

How much ethnic blending can occur before Indians finally cease to be Indians? The question is sure to loom ever larger for coming generations, as the United States increasingly finds itself in "government-to-government" relationships with tribes that are becoming less "Indian" by the decade. Within two or three generations the nation will possess hundreds of "tribes" that may consist of the great-great-grandchildren of Indians but whose native heritage consists mainly of autonomous governments and special privileges that are denied to other Americans.

Insofar as there is a political solution to the Indian future, I have come to believe that it lies in the rejection of policies that lead to segregation and in acknowledgment of the fact that the racially and ethnically variegated peoples whom we call "Indian" share not only common blood but also a common history and a common future with other Americans. The past generation has seen the development of a national consensus on a number of aspects of the nation's history that were long obscured by racism or shame; there is, for instance, little dispute today among Americans of any ethnic background over the meaning of slavery or of the internment of Japanese-Americans during World War II. There is as yet no such consensus, however, with respect to the shared history of Indians and whites, who both still tend to see the past as a collision of irreconcilable opposites and competing martyrdoms.

That history was not only one of wars, removals, and death but also one of calculated compromises, mutual accommodation, and deliberately chosen risks, a story of Indian communities and individuals continually remaking themselves in order to survive. To see change as failure, as some kind of cultural corruption, is to condemn Indians to solitary confinement in a prison of myth that whites invented for them in the first place. Self-determination gives Indian tribes the ability to manage the speed and style of integration but not the power to stop it, at least for long. Integration may well mean the eventual diminishing of conventional notions of "tribal identity," but it must also bring many new individual opportunities, along with membership in the larger human community. "People and their cultures perish in isolation, but they are born or reborn in contact with other men and women, with man and woman of another culture, another creed, another race," the Mexican novelist Carlos Fuentes has written. Tribes will survive, if anything, as stronger entities than they have been for many generations. The question is whether they will attempt to survive as isolated islands or as vital communities that recognize a commonality of interest and destiny with other Americans.

VIII

CAN WE STILL AFFORD TO BE A NATION OF IMMIGRANTS?

David Kennedy

Concerns about immigration seem to be about as old as the American nation itself. Each generation of Americans wonders if the United States has lost its capacity to absorb new waves of humanity, or if the newcomers will somehow change for the worse the character and destiny of the country. Historian David Kennedy of Stanford University has noted how in the nineteenth and early twentieth centuries the American economy grew at such a pace that it could provide employment for waves of immigrants hitting the American shores without economically hurting those already here.

Recently Americans have expressed new fears about both the non-European origins of the new arrivals—Is traditional American culture being shattered beyond repair?—and the economic impact of the numbers of immigrants entering the workforce. In this thoughtful 1990 address, Kennedy gives some reassurances about the need for immigrant labor to sustain desired growth rates of the American economy. As for the growing Hispanic presence in the Southwest, he concludes that we may indeed be "in the presence of something for which we as a country have very little historical precedent."

Now, let me turn to the present moment and ask what light if any, this little historical rehearsal can shed on the present situation. The biggest apparent novelty—apparent, I want to stress—about present day immigration is its source. Present day immigrants do not come from the old mother continent of Europe, but from what we broadly call the third world or less developed countries. Nine countries today account for about 60 percent of immigration to the United States. If we listed in rank order all the countries that contribute immigrants to the United States today, by the time we got to country number nine, we would have accounted for well over half of all immigration. I will read you that list of nine countries in rank order starting from the one that contributes the most migrants to the ninth. They are Mexico, China, Hong Kong, Taiwan, the Philippines, Vietnam, Korea, India, and Laos. I haven't named a European country yet. Those nine non-European countries contribute the great majority of migrants to this country today, both legal and illegal. Now, those nine countries, none of them European, constitute a new, novel source of immigration only if we define them culturally or geographically. If in fact, we ask ourselves, what made migration happen in the nineteenth century, we find that this is not a very new set of sources of immigration at all because all the countries I've

named are undergoing historical transformations that are virtually identical with what was going on in nineteenth century Europe. They're experiencing very rapid population growth and
they are experiencing their own relatively early phases of industrial revolution. The so-called
newly-industrializing countries like Korea and Taiwan you'll notice are prominent on this list.

Now, let us take Mexico as the case in point. Recognizing [that] other countries contribute
to this immigrant stream as well, let me just emphasize Mexico as the most conspicuous example. Mexico has tripled its population since 1950. It's passing through a period of amazingly
large population growth. In the year 1950, Mexico, Central America, South America, all of Latin America and the United States had approximately the same population—about 150 million
people in the United States, about 150 million people in all of Latin America. It will take, we
estimate, to the year 2020 for the United States population to double from its 1950 base. So,
we think we'll have about 300 million people in this country 30 years from now, the year 2020.
In 2020 it is estimated that in Latin America there will be nearly one billion people, [more than]
three times the population in this country, whereas in 1950 we started out at about the same
numerical base. So, Latin America's population is growing at a factor of about six times over this
seventy year period, 1950 to 2020, while the population of the United States is doubling. I
mention that simply by way of making a point that this pressure for immigration on the United
States from Latin America is not going to go away in all of our lifetimes.

As in nineteenth century Europe, this population explosion in Latin America and in
Mexico has had its primary impact not on the United States, but in the cities of Mexico itself, to the extent that Mexico City is now the world's largest city with something in the
neighborhood of 20 million people. It's estimated that about 100 persons per day are mi-
grating into Mexico City from the Mexican countryside. So, what we see coming across the
border into the United States as a vast stream of some legal and some illegal Mexican immigrants is in fact a kind of spillover effect from the urbanization and industrialization of
Mexico. So we're seeing here something that is virtually identical with what was going on in
nineteenth century Europe: enormous population expansion and reconcentration of population from countryside to city, with some incidental spillover into international migration,
in this case, into the United States.

Now what if we turn to this side of the border and ask ourselves about our capacity in the
present day to absorb immigrants? This is where the question that I started with, "Can we still
afford to be a nation of immigrants?" begins to come into sharper focus. Now, you will remember that I offered to you three kinds of structural explanations why I think we succeeded
in accommodating those 35 million Europeans a century ago. I mentioned their relatively
small numbers in the American population, the variety of the immigrant stream that they
composed, and economic growth. Now, what if we tried to apply those considerations to the
present day and ask ourselves, do we still have the capacity to absorb newcomers at the rate at
which our forebears at the early part of this century did? Well, if we look at the relative numbers of immigrants in the United States today, here I think there is grounds for considerable
confidence that as a society, we still have a lot of absorptive capacity, because even if you make
a fairly generous estimate of how many illegal immigrants are in the country, an estimate in
the eight to ten million range, we still come up with a percentage of foreign born persons of
about seven or eight percent. That's about half the proportion of foreign born persons in the
census of 1910 which was, in round numbers, about fifteen percent. So here, it seems to me,
there are grounds for considerable confidence that we still have a lot of absorptive capacity left
as a society, since the relative number of foreign born persons in American society today is
about half what it was 70, 80 years ago.

Now, if we take the second of those factors that I mentioned in historical context, the variety and pluralism of the immigrant stream a century ago, here I think we enter into a new zone altogether. Here is where, potentially at least, we are in the presence of something for which we as a country have very little historical precedent. I'm referring here primarily to Hispanic migration and even more particularly to Mexican immigration to the United States. Unlike that nineteenth century stream of European immigrants, the present day stream of immigrants to the United States is very heavily composed of immigration from a single, culturally unified, linguistically homogeneous source, which is Mexico. And what's more, that immigrant stream from Mexico is concentrated in a relatively closely defined geographical region which essentially stretches from Texas to California. The population of New Mexico, according to the inter-census population report estimates of 1988, is almost 40 percent Hispanic, Texas is a little better than 25 percent, Arizona about 20 percent, Colorado 12 percent, California 24 percent. More than half of all Hispanics in the United States live in California and Texas. We estimate that by the year 2000, there will be no cultural majority in California. Its population will be about 40 percent Hispanic, 40 percent what we very elastically call "Anglo," roughly 10 percent black, 10 percent Asian. Now, this concentration of a large immigrant group, Hispanic immigrants in this case, Mexican immigrants to be more particular, this critical mass concentrated in a given region is something for which we have very little historical precedent as a society, and I offer it to you as a possibility, not a prediction, but a possibility, that we could see evolve in the southwest corner of North America, something that would in the long run resemble what exists in the northeastern corner of this continent in the province of Quebec. That is, a large linguistically and culturally different group that would have available to it the real possibility of preserving its cultural heritage over a much longer period of time than any other comparable immigrant group in American history. And it would have a great degree of economic viability as well as cultural viability, and you might eventually see the demand arise for a kind of autonomous or semiautonomous Hispanic state somewhere in the American southwest. I think that is a distinct possibility in this country over the next century or so, and some of you no doubt have heard the term applied to this of the "reconquista." This is the repossession by Mexican culture of territories that were, after all, wrested from Mexico by force of arms 150 years ago.

Now, finally, let me touch on the economic factor. This is a subject of some complexity. You'll hear the argument made that one of the things that underwrote the relative tranquility of immigration in the last century was economic growth. It allowed this society to avoid questions of redistribution. Recently a lot of economic historians and economists have been turning that question around and instead of asking to what extent did economic growth make immigration possible, they've asked to what extent did immigration fuel economic growth? And in fact at the time when the last piece of immigration legislation, the so-called Simpson-Mazzoli-Rodino bill, was making its way through Congress (also known as the Immigration Reform and Control Act of 1986), there were a number of studies of this sort made, trying to determine what is the relationship between economic health and immigration. Many of those studies focused on southern California for the reason that that is the region that has absorbed more immigrants in the last twenty years than any other comparable region. All of these studies have come up with the same conclusion. One was done by the Council of Economic Advisors, one by the Rand Corporation, and one by the Urban Institute. They all came up with the same conclusion and that was that immigration measurably added to the economic vitality of southern California. So, far from constituting a net drain or depressant on the region's economic vitality, it actually contributed to it. The Urban Institute study concluded as follows, "Large scale [immigration] did not depress and probably increased per capita income in

the region." Now that is a very telling finding because it really tells us that there is a great economic benefit to immigration, that often goes overlooked in many discussions of the cultural
implications of immigration.

Now I'll end by summarizing for you the findings of a Stanford economist, Clark Reynolds, who is the head of a project at Stanford University called the United States/Mexico
project. It's an ongoing research enterprise that brings together Mexican and United States
scholars to study questions of mutual interest to the two countries. Reynolds did a study in
which he projected Mexican and U.S. population growth down to the year 2000, and then
did some projections of Mexican and U.S. economic growth down to the year 2000. He concluded that for Mexico to absorb its population increase into its own labor markets, to find
jobs for its rapidly expanding population, the Mexican economy would need to grow over the
next decade at a compound annual rate of better than seven percent, nearly eight percent in
fact. And he concluded that that was a very unrealistic number. It was really unrealistic for us
to expect that the Mexican economy could sustain a seven-plus percent annual compound
rate of growth, which would be necessary to absorb its new workers into the work force. Then
he turned to the U.S. side and he said that for the United States to grow its economy at a
compound annual rate of three percent between now and the year 2000, a healthy but hardly
robust rate of economic growth, a rate lower than this country experienced in the 1960s, for
example, and fifties, we would need to find about 15 million more workers than we could
find out of domestic sources, unless we wanted to resort to some ancient industrial practices
like child labor. We've transferred in this country all the labor out of agriculture that we can;
less than two percent of the American work force is now in agriculture. We have, in a way of
speaking, invaded the family and drawn women into the work force to about the maximum
extent that we can. So he concluded that we can't find any more workers out of domestic supply. We have a very low birth rate. We need about fifteen million more than we can get.
Where are we going to get them? Mexico is the obvious place. So, he concluded that Mexico
and the United States needed each other to achieve their respective goals of full employment
for their citizens and economic growth rates that would be desirable. So I'll just end by saying
that the proper question for this lecture is not, "Can we still afford to be a nation of immigrants?" but "Can we afford not to be?" Thank you.

CAN WE ALL GET ALONG?

Dale Maharidge

In the previous essay, David Kennedy was optimistic about the economic role of new im-
migrants in present American society, although cautious regarding the growing Hispanic
presence in the Southwest. Here, Pulitzer Prize winner Dale Maharidge, who teaches
journalism at Stanford University, delves more deeply into the experiences of specific fami-
lies in California, both native-born and immigrant, and the growing nativism and anti-
immigrant backlash there. He introduces us to the Dunns, white transplants from Okla-
homa; Martha Escutia, one of a handful of Hispanic-Americans in the California State
Assembly; Donald Northcross, who works with at-risk young black males in Sacramento;
and Vietnam-born Maria Ha, a student at the University of California at Berkeley. Their
stories collectively represent the profound demographic changes that California, and more
broadly the entire United States, is undergoing. As Maharidge says, "Today the continuing
experiment called America is being put to the test of whether it can truly be a harmonious
blend of races and social classes." Moreover, by studying individual case histories of struggle
and perseverance such as these, we learn the folly and danger of categorizing and stigma-
tizing other ethnic groups as "those people."

As we approach the twenty-first century, no challenge presents a more profound test of
our national moral resolve than how we accommodate our immigrants, legal and illegal.
Neither stigmatizing "those people" nor withdrawing into racial or cultural factions will
solve our urgent need to adapt our society to its changing demographics. This is the first in
a series of articles following the lives of four very different California families as they try to
make sense of the American dream.

So long, KTC. His epigraph vanished beneath one quick sweep of my paint roller. In a world
of worsening urban blight, there was something satisfying about wiping out graffiti, which
seemed to cover every sign, wall, curb, truck, and freight train in Huntington Park, this neighborhood in Southeast Los Angeles.

For the past hour, no Anglos had gone by in the rush of cars on Slauson Avenue. I had
the sudden realization that I might be the only white guy for miles around. And I was eras-
ing gang members' *vandalismo*—akin to spitting in their eyes—an unwise act, even when in
the company of local Latino kids taking part in a community anti-graffiti day. When an angry yell erupted from a passing car, it seemed a perfect opportunity to become a drive-by
shooting victim. As the car sped off, I recalled my first visit to Huntington Park a decade

earlier, when it was a lot more white. Now the Census Bureau says it's the most Mexican town in the U.S.; nearly 60 percent of its fifty-six thousand residents were born in Mexico. This changing population recently elected the district's first Latina representative, Martha Escutia, to the state legislature.

In large part because of this kind of immigration influx, California will become the first mainland state in which whites will be less than a majority sometime between 1997 and 2003. By the year 2050, Census estimates show, whites nationwide will be about equal in number to what we now call minority groups.

We can blame or salute J. Hector St. John for our nation being called a "melting pot." During the American Revolution, the Frenchman wrote of the mix of ethnicities found nowhere else on earth: "Here individuals of all nations are melted into a new race of men."

Four American families—named Northcross, Dunn, Escutia, and Ha—could accuse St. John of failing to predict the harsh truth that the melting pot does not work for everyone. The Northcross ancestors were snatched out of Africa and made slaves, and, until segregation ended, were excluded from assimilation. The Dunns left famine in Europe for the 1930s Dust Bowl, later fleeing Oklahoma only to encounter poverty and discrimination in California. Mexican and Chinese immigrants like the Escutias and the Has have long been seen as a disposable resource for picking crops or building railroads.

While success has come to these families, St. John's utopian theory remains largely unproven. The eighteenth-century America that the French writer praised was white and European. Today the continuing experiment called America is being put to the test of whether it can truly be a harmonious blend of races and social classes.

This test is occurring because of immigration, and it's happening in California first because California is a point where West meets East and North meets South. While the influx alarms some conservatives, there's little difference between many new California immigrants and my paternal grandparents, who came from the Ukraine at the turn of the century. They may be a different color but, as in the past, these immigrants bring fresh energy to our nation.

Unfortunately, the plentiful backbreaking jobs in coal mines and factories that were the entree to suburban wealth for my grandparents have disappeared. If recent events are an indication, today's immigrants may face a backlash equal to or worse than the anti-immigrant movements of the 1880s and 1920s—and the bashing could easily extend to minorities rooted here for generations.

Culture is becoming the defining issue of our times. Despite the predictions of optimists that the power of American culture would assimilate the new immigrants as it always has, America is segregating into camps beyond any past class or race differences. This separatism is tearing apart whatever bit of cohesiveness the mythical melting pot gave us, devolving into a free-for-all rainbow of hate pitting Koreans, blacks, Latinos, Hmong, whites, Vietnamese, and other groups against each other. The 1992 Los Angeles riots may have been the warm-up act for some very disagreeable times.

American separatists come in three major forms. The first are the products of what Labor Secretary Robert Reich terms the "secession of the successful." This de facto oligarchy sends its children to private schools, sometimes employs private police, and lives behind literal or symbolic walls. They are often but not always white, often conservative but sometimes liberal. They believe they can shut out the urban nightmare, something like a passenger on the Titanic feeling secure in a locked stateroom.

The second kind of separatist is quite involuntary. They are frozen out of the globalized economy. They are the millions of working, service-sector poor, the jobless factory hands, the homeless.

The third kind of separatist withdraws culturally. While immigrants have historically rushed to assimilate, their modern counterparts often live in isolation. This is happening in tandem with the so-called politically correct movements, the "cult of ethnicity" that, historian Arthur Schlesinger, Jr., argues in *The Disuniting of America,* is fragmenting American society. Vocal ethnic leaders, along with whites weighted with guilt and the best intentions, are disassimilating ethnic groups.

All three kinds of separatism are fraught with problems of Babel-like—or, to be more current, Bosnian—proportions. The cultural and involuntary separatists have formed societies within a society, while the oligarchical separatists have circled the wagons. Kirk Knutsen, a policy analyst for the state of California, sees California (and the U.S.) heading down a Balkan path toward the disconnection of different cultural groups. If a multicultural society is to be successful, Knutsen believes, cultural groups must overlap each other, with the overlap making for a common culture. In this manner, each group can maintain identity, but still be part of the collective culture that we call America.

Cultural fragmentation, however, was given a big boost last summer, when California Governor Pete Wilson proposed federal measures to curb illegal immigration, including banning access to government-sponsored health care and education to illegals, and denying citizenship to their U.S.-born children. Wilson made his announcement just days after the Census Bureau reported that there are four million illegal immigrants in the country, half of them in California. Liberal groups attacked the plan as veiled racism, but the Republican governor, down to just 15 percent approval rating in the polls and facing reelection in 1994, saw his rating jump to 22 percent. Wilson had grabbed an issue that has worked well for politicians at other points in history, when a bad economy has combined with fears of "those people" taking jobs.

For Wilson was really talking to whites. Even though whites in California are a fast-shrinking majority, they enjoy a virtual electoral apartheid. Whites are now less than 55 percent of California's population (down from 67 percent in 1980), Latinos 27 percent, Asians less than 10 percent, blacks 7 percent. But in the 1992 presidential election, 82 percent of the voters were white, 7 percent Latino, 3 percent Asian, and 6 percent black, according to a *Los Angeles Times* survey. Ethnic leaders say the low turnout is due largely to the view in Mexico and most Asian nations that government is corrupt, even dangerous, and something to be shunned. Many Latinos and Asians are culturally separate enough to believe that the same is true here. And, politicians also have not courted their votes.

How the changing demographics and politics play out in California, a nation-state of more than thirty million, will tell a lot about America's future: Florida, Illinois, Texas, and New York are on the same track, with other states not far behind.

This transformation is happening in a global context. According to Paul Kennedy, author of *Preparing for the Twenty-First Century,* the East-West rivalry has perished and been replaced by a North-South division between haves and have-nots. Noting that 95 percent of all population growth between now and the year 2025 will occur in the underdeveloped Southern Hemisphere, Kennedy posits that the "push" factor of overcrowding and poverty will drive many more in the South to emigrate to the U.S. and Europe, "pulled" by opportunity in the relatively empty and wealthy countries.

These migrations to the U.S., combined with the championing of ethnic identity, bring with them a danger of clashing cultures only now being fully realized.

Harvard Professor Samuel P. Huntington has written that cultural, not nation-state, rivalries now dominate world politics. He notes that the world has seven or eight major civilizations: Western, Confucian, Japanese, Islamic, Hindu, Slavic-Orthodox, Latin American, and perhaps African. The "fault lines" where these cultures meet (such as Bosnia) are where post-Cold War conflicts will occur.

At least five of Huntington's major cultures are clattering together in California: the dominant Western, along with Latin American, Confucian, Japanese, and African. The others are present as well, but in relatively small numbers. The L.A. riots were not a "rebellion," as some like to say, nor were they like the 1960s unrest that had clear black-white overtones. They were conflicts between the cultures within our own borders.

I came into this project with some deep-seated liberal notions, and despite some seemingly neoconservative statements, I still have them. I don't think it's incompatible to be progressive and question the cultural separatists. In the current atmosphere of left-right, anti-intellectual polarization, any inquiry is labeled as racism. But cultural separatists can be just as racist as any white rednecks, and sometimes cripple the very people they want to help. According to a recent report, more than one million kids in California schools aren't fluent in English. The multiculturalists, worried about the loss of heritage, have championed bilingual education. But the result of this approach has been that many students are locked into native-tongue programs for years, and then pushed out as adults unable to cope in English. No studies are needed to know that employers won't be in a rush to hire many of these one million kids for any but the most menial jobs—resulting in more poverty, more backlash. The ultimate racism is to not equip people with the skills to succeed.

Similarly, the oligarchical separatists must be held accountable for withdrawing from society. The haves must find some way to help the have-nots—the involuntary separatists—at least if the haves want to reduce their fear of crime and other ills associated with the disenfranchised. It's time that all ideas are placed on the table, as I want to do on these pages over the next few years. My goal in studying California will be to find ways in which this new society can work, how the worst of the hate can be curbed. It's clear we have to reconcile culture and what it means to be an American.

This is a work in progress. Many questions remain to be answered. I'll be talking with liberals, conservatives, and those in the middle as the state goes through its demographic change. In a larger context, I'll be looking at four different communities: polyglot Los Angeles, conservative Orange County, the liberal San Francisco area, and the state's Midwest-like capital, Sacramento. Taken together, these communities are representative of the United States.

Michael Dunn

In 1930, Lillian Counts Dunn left the poverty of Oklahoma with her husband and two young children. The family strapped mattresses and quilts to the roof of an old Chevrolet and headed west. When they made it to California, the Dunns worked the fields, picking oranges. On May 4, 1931, Donald, then seventeen months old, was fed some windfall oranges the farmers gave them. The Dunns didn't know they were frostburned and rotten. The baby fell ill. "We don't treat nonresidents," Lillian was told at the hospital. That meant Mexicans and Okies. On May 10, Donald died of "acute enterocolitis."

The family endured. But when the price for picked cotton fell to sixty cents for a hundred pounds, Lillian went to the Cannery & Agricultural Workers' Industrial Union to join a strike. She had called hogs back in Oklahoma, and the leaders had her use her voice to "clean" fields by calling out to nonstriking workers.

On October 10, 1933, during a strike rally in the San Joaquin Valley town of Pixley, things took an ugly turn: farmers opened fire on several hundred strikers, including Lillian. Two pickers were killed, seven wounded. The violence tipped the strike, and seventy-five cent cotton was won. It was one of the most successful farm strikes in California until Cesar Chavez came along many years later.

But that success wasn't enough. In early 1934, Lillian was forced to seek county relief food. When this was cut back on March 22, 1934, Lillian helped another woman lead a protest. The following day, the *Visalia Times-Delta*, the largest newspaper in the county, carried the headline:

COMMUNISTS LEAD ATTACK ON PIXLEY FOOD DEPOT
Communist Organizers Lillian Monroe and Lillian Dunn Incite
Followers to Violence

The word "Communist" was new to Lillian. She had no idea what it meant. After a long court battle, she was jailed, even though pregnant. When released, she gave birth to a boy and named him Mike, after a sympathetic farmer who'd bailed her out.

Six decades later, Mike Dunn is semiretired, having been a partner in a chain of convenience stores. Mike lives in the two-year-old city of Laguna Hills, in the heart of southern Orange County, the most conservative area in California. Laguna Hills is very white—86 percent, according to an information sheet on the counter at City Hall. But the many who have moved here—often fleeing Los Angeles—aren't necessarily ideologues; they just want a safe community away from gangs.

Mike doesn't feel all that safe, however. He often listens to a police scanner. The night before I first interviewed him more than a year ago, he heard a call about an elderly woman mugged by Mexican nationals at a nearby shopping center. Mike and his mother, Lillian, now eighty-seven, worry about immigration.

Mike echoes Governor Wilson's call to clamp down on illegal immigrants, saying that poverty among Latino immigrants has worsened, leading to more crime. His worry has led him to put his home up for sale; he wants to move into a gated community. "In ten years, I can see what's happened," Mike said. "And in twenty years, it will be unbearable. When my people came from Oklahoma, they settled in; they went to work; they went to school; they didn't go on welfare; they assimilated."

Crime came still closer to Mike not long after we first met. I wanted to meet his brother, Pat, and chatted by phone with Pat's wife, Sandy. She marveled at the success of the family. Ten days later, Sandy vanished. In another week and a half, her mummified body was found in the Mojave Desert.

Pat was convicted of Sandy's murder, largely on the grounds that he stood to inherit more than $2 million from her. He maintains his innocence. Mike believes his brother—at first he blamed Mexicans—and has spent $200,000 on the case, which is now on appeal. Lillian was crushed by what happened, and is now in an Orange County nursing home. The last time I talked with Mike's wife, Katie, she said that Mike's blood pressure was high and the family didn't want to talk to me further. "I've got to think about my grandchildren," she said. The whole family has been consumed by a crime that no walls could stop.

Martha Escutia

South of Orange County at the Mexican frontier, the U.S. Border Patrol makes the conservative estimate that each day 2,700 people enter America illegally. Most are Mexican nationals, coming to what Chicano activists call "Aztlan," the area from Texas to California, lands taken during the Mexican-American War.

On September 13, 1847, at the height of that war, General Winfield Scott's troops stormed the fort at Chapultepec, outside Mexico City. Juan Escutia and five other young cadets, refusing to surrender, wrapped themselves in the Mexican flag and leapt two hundred feet over the cliff that the fort stood upon. They became known as *Los Ninos Heroes* for their martyrdom against American imperialism.

Growing up in Mexico City in the 1930s, Raul Escutia was told he descended from Juan Escutia's kin. He was proud, but he didn't hate the U.S.; in 1946 he moved to Chicago. When Raul became a citizen in the early eighties, his patriotism was fierce, as was his attachment to the Republican party—he voted for both Reagan and Bush.

In 1955 Raul married Martha Sandoval, whose parents came to the U.S. as legal "guest workers" in 1944. In 1957 the couple had their first child, Martha. When the marriage crumbled, Martha Escutia moved in with her mother's parents, Ricardo and Marina Ovilla, who raised her in their East Los Angeles home.

In those days, East L.A. was the center of the awakening Chicano movement. In the summer of 1970, when Martha was twelve, a riot erupted between Chicano activists and police in a park eight blocks away; *Los Angeles Times* journalist Ruben Salazar was killed by sheriff's deputies. At that time, Latinos had no real voice in politics—there was only one in higher office.

Martha was a child of "firsts": first generation born in the U.S., first in her family to graduate from high school, then college, and finally Georgetown Law School. In 1992, she was elected as a Democrat to the California Assembly, becoming the first Latina to represent her newly created district in Southeast Los Angeles; she joined a record eleven Latinos now in the 120-member legislature in Sacramento.

"I always tell myself if it weren't for the generous immigration policy of the United States, I would not be here," Martha said. She is no career politician: she worked for nonprofit agencies such as the National Council of La Raza in Washington, D.C., specializing in immigration issues—a particularly tough job during the Reagan-Bush years. But neither is she like the Chicano activists who view Aztlan as theirs to retake from the American invaders.

"I came from a very conservative family," she said. "My family always told me, 'You're not Chicana, you're not Mexican-American. If you have to identify yourself as something, don't hyphenate yourself; you're either American or you're Mexican, but you can't be both.' So I never related to the so-called Chicano movement."

Martha is something of a Clinton Democrat—she's largely pushing economic issues. Her attitude is that you can't advance the social agenda if people are jobless. But she spent last fall keeping up with the rush of xenophobic developments that followed Governor Wilson's comments on immigration. Both U.S. senators from California, Democrats Barbara Boxer and Dianne Feinstein, subsequently tried to outdo the governor, with Boxer calling for the National Guard to protect the U.S.-Mexico border.

Martha and the Latino caucus responded with a press conference to offer a moderate plan to stem immigration. But it ended in chaos when Cruz Bustamante, a farm-country Fresno Democrat, said, "We could not conduct business without the immigrant." Dumbfounded reporters asked if he supported illegal immigration. "My district requires it," he answered.

Bustamante, speaking for California's $18 billion agribusiness industry, exposed the ugly class edge of the immigration debate: Bustamante's farmers have trouble finding citizens willing to stoop in the rich California fields to pick the food the nation eats, at least at the wages the farmers want to pay. It's the same issue that Lillian Dunn confronted back in 1933.

Democratic lawmakers later introduced a bill proposing asset forfeiture of those who repeatedly employ illegal aliens, in the same way the government now takes assets of drug dealers. The bill, to be argued in 1994, will be the Democrats' weapon against Governor Wilson, hitting below his business-interests belt.

At the end of the legislature's 1993 session, lawmakers voted on their first major anti-immigration bill, which would require proof of citizenship or legal status to obtain a driver's license. Proponents argued that it would deny the undocumented the most common form of identification. But Martha spoke vehemently against the bill, saying it would do nothing to stop immigrants, who come to work, not to drive.

"I think our country is treading on thin ice," she said. "Voting for this bill is going to lead us down a slippery slope to Big Brotherism and race discrimination. In the final analysis only people who look like me and speak like me will be asked to show proof of residency. I cannot help the fact that I have dark hair, dark eyes, and I'm Latina—and that I speak with an accent."

Martha didn't convince her colleagues; the bill passed 51–13.

She fears that the backlash has only begun. "Maybe we're going into a second enlightenment," Martha said. "I hope it's not the Dark Ages. I think we're on the brink right now. It could be something great. Or it could be very, very dark."

Donald Northcross

Nearly four hundred miles north of Los Angeles is Sacramento, spiritually more like Des Moines or Oklahoma City than a California town, a resemblance not lost on the Hollywood filmmakers who come to make movies supposedly set in the Midwest.

While Martha Escutia is trying to make big changes from beneath the capitol dome, Donald Northcross, in the Sacramento suburb of Rancho Cordova, is working for change on a different scale, with a small group of black youths.

Sacramento is a long way from Ashdown, Arkansas, where Don, 34, grew up in the last days of the Old South. Ashdown is just north of Texas and west of Hope, President Clinton's hometown. In 1968, when students were offered the choice of attending either school, Don was one of the first black students to go to the white school. The black school, across the tracks, didn't have a pool; the white school did. Don wanted to learn how to swim, but when integration came, officials cemented over the pool at the white school.

Don's father worked at an Army depot, and also raised truck crops—sweet potatoes, greens—plowing with a mule. The family picked cotton to make extra money. Unlike his father, who didn't make it past third grade, Don went to college at Northeast Louisiana University. He was idealistic in his ideas about fixing things in the black community. After an injury derailed a professional football career, he moved to Sacramento and became a sheriff's deputy.

His first assignment was working in the jail, where he grew angry at what he saw. "All the young black men, healthy, strong men, coming to the jail. I said, 'What a shame. We're not born that way.' " He read a newspaper story reporting that one in three black men is behind bars or on probation or parole, and later discovered that the number-one cause of death for young black men is homicide. Asking himself why, Don figured that many blacks come from broken homes.

"That was the power of the black community when I was a kid. We worked hard, but we took time out for each other. If we had that attitude today, we could get along instead of selling drugs and killing each other."

Don decided to create a community. In 1991 he began the OK Program, which stands for "Our Kids," at Mills Junior High School in Rancho Cordova. The idea was simple—black officers would each mentor several African-American boys. He involved all the African-American boys at school, hoping that in an atmosphere in which learning rather than ignorance was a status symbol, they would excel.

"You can't clean a fish before you catch him," Don said. "You got to catch him, then you clean him. So I don't care if a kid is gang-banging—those are the kids I want."

In each of its first two years, the voluntary program had more than sixty members—almost all the black youths in the school. Teachers report that the program has transformed most of the youths into responsible students. Each Saturday they attend a study hall, followed by basketball. Those who maintain good grades and behavior are rewarded with tickets to major-league sports events. At the end of the year, those who have succeeded are taken to Disneyland.

"We're doing this program because I'm concerned and because I'm a black man and I'm proud to be a black man," Don said. "There are some problems affecting us in this nation. It's my responsibility as a black man to straighten them out." The program at Mills costs about $10,000 per year, not counting his salary. The only thing keeping it from branching out is a lack of funds.

On one level, it seems the OK Program may be feeding into cultural separatism. One day when I was at Mills with Don, a girl asked him why there wasn't a program for girls.

"The Asian kids, the Hispanic kids, the white kids, they ask the same question," Don said. "It's important for them to understand that with limited funds and personnel, you attack the problem where it's the worst. Black males are more qualified to be a role model for young black males than anybody else."

Don's main priority is to extend the program, now in its third year, to girls and Latino students. He thinks of society as a football team. Position coaches train the different members, and in the end, they all come together as a team, which is analogous to Kirk Knutsen's collective culture. "If you train them all together, you get chaos," Don said. "We can have different positions and train for [them] individually. Once every ethnic group does that, we can start to move the ball."

Don works beyond the kids. Last spring, he organized a conference at a local state university to discuss the role of blacks in society. The panelists agreed that blacks have fallen into "victim mode"—that racism has been used as an excuse for not succeeding, though of course many blacks are involuntarily separated from society.

"My message to the students is that there is racism and discrimination, but you have to achieve in spite of it," Don told the audience. "There's not a white man in this country who stands outside my house and says I can't spend time with black kids."

Maria Ha

When the Japanese government challenged the regime of China's Chiang Kai-shek in the late 1930s, events were set in motion that would lead Maria Ha and her family to emigrate to the United States many years later.

During the Chinese-Japanese war in 1939, Maria's grandmother fled China for what was then the safety of Hanoi, Vietnam. A businesswoman and trader, she often stole back across the Chinese border to sell goods. Her son, who would become Maria's father, studied to become a mechanical engineer. He and his Vietnamese wife endured the war with the U.S. Near its end their daughter Maria was born.

When China invaded Vietnam for four weeks in 1979, the ethnic Chinese of Vietnam came under bad times. In 1980 Maria's family made the dangerous boat trip to Hong Kong, where they remained before being accepted as refugees by the U.S. Becoming sick to her stomach on the plane is the only recollection Maria has of the journey.

Her father could not get work of the stature he had had in Vietnam, so he took a job as a mover in San Francisco's Chinatown, where the family lives. But he instilled in his daughter the value of education, and she excelled. First she was accepted to academically exclusive Lowell High School and then to the University of California at Berkeley. Maria started her freshman year this past fall, at an institution at the heart of the multicultural debate.

A few years ago, Berkeley came under fire for a quota system limiting both white and Asian applicants. In one recent year, two thousand straight-A students from both groups were rejected. Whites now seem to be abandoning the school—applications by whites fell by 32 percent between 1986 and 1992. In their voting patterns and choices, whites are defunding public institutions.

Immigrants like Maria are the most harmed by the cutbacks. She worries that she won't be able to get by. Last summer, she worked two jobs, six days a week, to save money for school. "I guess my Dad likes education in the family, he likes us to have opportunity, so I just kind of followed," Maria said of what motivates her to work hard. She studies until 11:00 p.m. most nights, and two days a week she is in classes from morning to evening.

Next term, Maria will take a mandatory course on multicultural education. The issue is still raging on campus: last year, students rallied for a separate Asian-American studies department, battering their way into an administration building.

Not long after that confrontation, I interviewed a member of the Asian-American Student Association who took part. He said, "There's a broad distrust of whites," and informed me that students in his group might not want to talk to a white man.

"Are all whites looked at as being bad?" I asked.

"There were some white students in the takeover," he said. "These are white students who want to do the ethnic thing. They're not being accepted."

The ethnic-studies debate will continue. Maria said she's heard about the factionalism but does not understand why things should be so fragmented. Yet at Lowell High School, which has a policy that restricts Asians and whites each to 40 percent of the student body, Maria found that even though there was little tension, people hung out with their own ethnic group.

"It's like usually Asians hanging around Asians and Caucasians around Caucasians. I don't know why. It just happens that way. I mean, you have more in common with them or something."

UC Berkeley Chancellor Chang-Lin Tien, whose cultural background is similar to Maria's, feels strongly about the power of new immigrants. "This is the future vitality of the society," he said when I told him about Maria and how hard she is working. He points out that immigrant-bashing is not new. "In the nineteenth century, the same statements were made by many political leaders. People forget the fight has gone on and on."

When I began this project more than a year ago, I didn't know what to expect. Now, after dozens of interviews and thousands of notes, I have more questions than when I started.

In the coming year, I hope to find more answers. Does having a shared culture mean we have to be Eurocentric, or is there a different path? I want to better understand why, in Orange County last summer, out of 240 housing projects under construction, 68 are gated communities. I don't yet know that walled culture any better than I know Maria Ha's. But of those I've interviewed so far, I know Maria least of all. Perhaps the Asian student leader was correct when he said it would be impossible for me to understand Confucian culture. But I want to try.

I'll be talking with young men in the OK Program, to determine whether it is separatist or team-building. I also want to explore whether what we call ourselves is in itself separatist. What would it mean if I referred to myself as a "European-Slavic-American?"

It's clear that Governor Wilson is partly right—we cannot sustain unlimited illegal immigration—and I want to study how Martha Escutia deals with xenophobia while at the same time striking a compromise.

Following World War II, writer George Orwell saw the future of much of the world as a totalitarian jackboot stepping on a face forever. That jackboot may now be our own—stepping on the face of the guy who lives down the street. In a post-Cold War world of ethnic divisions, the U.S. must lead by example, for fighter jets are impotent against the strife found in the Balkans or India—or in Los Angeles or New York.